65-

GUARANTEED
INVESTMENT
CONTRACTS
Risk Analysis and
Portfolio Strategies

GUARANTEED INVESTMENT CONTRACTS:
RISK ANALYSIS AND PORTFOLIO STRATEGIES

Second Edition

edited by
Kenneth L. Walker

BUSINESS ONE IRWIN
Homewood, Illinois 60430

© RICHARD D. IRWIN, Inc., 1989 and 1992

For FASB Statements: Copyright by Financial Accounting Standards Board,
401 Merritt 7, P.O. Box 5116, Norwalk, Connecticut 06856-5116, U.S.A.
Reprinted with permission. Copies of the complete document are available
from the FASB.

Sponsoring editor:	Amy Hollands
Project editor:	Paula M. Buschman
Production manager:	Ann Cassady
Designer:	Larry J. Cope
Art coordinator:	Mark Malloy
Compositor:	BookMasters, Inc.
Typeface:	11/13 Century Schoolbook
Printer:	Book Press, Inc.

Library of Congress Cataloging-in-Publication Data

Guaranteed investment contracts : risk analysis and portfolio
  strategies / edited by Kenneth L. Walker. — 2nd ed.
      p.   cm.
    Rev. ed. of: Guaranteed investment contracts / edited by Kenneth
  L. Walker. 2nd ed. 1992.
    ISBN 1-55623-573-9
    1. Guaranteed investment contracts.   I. Walker, Kenneth L.
  II. Walker, Kenneth L. Guaranteed investment contracts.
  HG8079.W35   1992
  332.6—dc20   91–39470

Printed in the United States of America
1 2 3 4 5 6 7 8 9 0 BP 9 8 7 6 5 4 3 2

PREFACE

The first edition of *Guaranteed Investment Contracts: Risk Analysis and Portfolio Strategies* was published in the spring of 1989. In three years, the original publication has become outdated. Changes in required statutory reporting, the issuance of Department of Labor 404(c) regulations, the Financial Accounting Standards Board *book value* review, the entrée of banks with BICs, the introduction of new GIC alternatives, and heightened credit concerns have prompted this second edition.

In the last 25 years, investment professionals have created an efficient marketplace for traditional equity, bond, and short-term cash equivalents. Investment contracts issued by banks and life insurance companies have not been able to achieve these same efficiencies. During this 25-year period, the Employment Retirement Income Security Act, tax legislative changes, and union negotiations have spurred the growth of the pension industry so that today it controls a significant component of the capital markets.

The volatile financial markets of the 1970s and 1980s and shift in focus from defined benefit to defined contribution plans created the demand for a new investment alternative—the stable-value asset. This demand for stability of total returns was met by the life insurance industry with the guaranteed investment contract (GIC). In recent years, banks have entered the marketplace with bank investment contracts (BICs).[1]

The insurance industry has been providing pension investments for many years. As the investment markets have become

---

[1]Throughout this book BICs and GICs will be referred to as *investment contracts*. However, the term *investment contracts* may have certain regulatory meanings and connotations that are not necessarily applied to BICs and GICs.

v

more sophisticated, the industry has kept pace and made many contributions to those markets. Chapter 1, The Metamorphosis, presents the emergence of the life insurance industry as a leader in developing the pension markets.

Investment contracts differ from traditional fixed-income instruments in two ways. They are exempt from registration as a security with the Securities and Exchange Commission. The majority of investment contract products enjoy amortized cost (*book value*) accounting treatment. This accounting basis provides an investment whose principal value remains stable and does not fluctuate with changes in interest rate levels. Chapter 2, What Is a GIC?, more fully describes those issues important to understanding the unique characteristics of the instrument.

Banks are continuing to increase their market presence. Both domestic and international banks are now issuers of investment contracts. Chapter 3, Bank Investment Contracts, provides an introduction to this growing component.

In 1990, the Financial Accounting Standards Board decided to review the issue of accounting for investment contracts. Chapter 4, Accounting Issues, discusses the scope and the long-term implications of the FASB project.

1991 will be remembered as the year of the great credit scare for the banking and life insurance industries. Almost every major periodical provided articles questioning their long-term stability. Several GIC issuers came under control of state regulations. Plan sponsors' awareness of credit heightened—a healthy sign for the industry and thousands of participants in investment contracts. Chapter 5, Quality—Analyzing the Life Insurance Industry, presents the issues relevant to life insurance financial analysis.

Many investment contract buyers do not understand the variables of pricing. The rate goes well beyond the yield of the supporting asset(s) and deductions for expenses. Chapter 6, Pricing the Guaranteed Investment Contract, addresses the many variables involved in arriving at the net yield, including asset/liability mismatch management, capital allocation, reserving, and why wide quote spreads exist in the marketplace.

The way in which insurers manage their internal GIC supporting portfolio is changing. As competitive pressures have grown, managing this supporting portfolio from a credit spread standpoint has forced many insurers to utilize lower quality investments in an effort to pick up yield. Chapter 7, Emerging Asset/Liability Management Strategies, discusses how many insurers are moving to an analytical spread-management approach from a credit spread-management approach in managing the supporting assets.

Understanding the interest crediting methodology utilized by banks and insurers is often confusing. Many different crediting methods are used, producing different results. Chapter 8, Interest Crediting, presents the most frequent methods used.

The GIC is a contract between two parties where a direct relationship exists between the buyer and issuer. Many consider its terms similar to private placement instruments. Negotiations can be complex and should be well planned and presented. In recent years, event risks, including group layoffs, corporate divestitures, and early retirement programs, have become a major concern among buyers and issuers alike. Chapter 9, Contractual Underwriting, presents issues that are important to the negotiation process.

GIC pooled funds have grown in popularity in recent years. It is estimated that there are in excess of 200 pooled funds available to the investor. Chapter 10, Pooled Stable-Value Funds, discusses the growth of this important funding medium.

Many question the future of the marketplace. Will demand outstrip supply? Will the instrument maintain its popularity? What new products are on the horizon? Chapter 11, Managing the Stable-Value Portfolio, provides insight into the management of portfolios that specialize in the use of investment contracts.[2]

In Chapter 12, Fiduciary Considerations for Investment Contracts, a discussion ensues over the fiduciary implications for plan sponsors to consider when choosing investment contracts. Attention to diversification, contract selection, and other factors are presented.

---

[2]The investment markets have typically referred to investment portfolios which use BICs and GICs as GIC, or guaranteed, portfolios. More and more industry experts are changing from this terminology to refer to such portfolios as *stable-value* portfolios. This term is used throughout this book.

Chapter 13, Performance Measurement of Stable-Value Portfolios, explains how to quantify GIC investment performance. For years, plan sponsors, consultants, and managers have sought a methodology for measuring the returns generated in the portfolio. The concept of absolute and relative GIC performance is introduced.

As the insurance industry seeks ways to expand its investment horizons and boundaries, the nonqualified marketplace will prove to be an expanding market opportunity. Chapter 14, The Nonqualified Marketplace, presents both the legal considerations and the opportunities that are available to the issuer and the institutional buyer.

Alternatives to traditional investment contracts are quickly emerging. The first-time buyer is often surprised when reviewing these alternatives as to the differences in contractual terms. Chapter 15, Structured GIC-Like Arrangements: Some Due Diligence Issues, addresses the issues relevant to understanding the terms of the alternative.

It has been estimated that there is over $200 million committed to investment contracts. Investment contracts have gained the respect of the investment community because they have become one of the most popular investment options of employee-directed retirement programs. I hope your reading of *Guaranteed Investment Contracts: Risk Analysis and Portfolio Strategies,* Second Edition, will help in better understanding this popular investment instrument.

Kenneth L. Walker

EDITOR'S NOTE

As this book is being released, the GIC industry is experiencing significant change. Revisions to the first edition, which began in March of 1991, were outdated by the time the book was ready for printing. What has changed is the proliferation of new GIC alternatives from banks, insurers, and investment advisers. Most of the alternatives serve to "credit enhance" the portfolio; others provide yield or return enhancement opportunities.

There is a growing interest on the part of many plan sponsors to diversify away from the general account of the insurance company. These sponsors want a greater degree of control over the assets backing the guarantee. Insurers have responded with separate account structures which can provide for the joint development of criteria governing the selection of the securities between the insurer and the sponsor. Banks have responded with separate account products with similar characteristics. Bank and insurer products are often referred to as "wrapped" products. Investment advisers have developed investment strategies which replicate expected performance patterns of a GIC.

Buyers of these alternatives should be cognizant of the following issues:

1. If the objective is "book value" treatment, does the alternative qualify for book value accounting?
2. Are the assets free from all issuer claims?
3. Who accepts default and prepayment risk of the underlying securities?
4. Does the wrap provider have any control to alter the structure of the supporting portfolio prior to the contract's maturity?

Coincident with the introduction of a new generation of stable-value alternatives[3] is the development of appropriate alternative investment strategies for the supporting portfolio. The buyer now has the opportunity to choose along a risk spectrum from a buy and hold, which most closely resembles the fixed-rate BIC/GIC, to a more active systematic strategy (e.g., active management via indexation, immunization, targeted duration, and other "controlled volatility" investment strategies).

These new alternatives are in response to the changing mood of the marketplace. The desire on the part of many plan sponsors is to move away from the *implicit guarantee* to stable value. Many are renaming their GIC Fund the Interest Income Fund, The Stable-Value Fund, or The Fixed-Income Fund.

Other sponsors are entertaining the idea of introducing a degree of market risk with investments in U.S. treasuries, U.S. agencies, mortgage-backed securities, asset-backed securities,

---

[3]The Editor has chosen to use the term "structured investment contracts" in lieu of the market adopted terminology of "synthetic GICs".

and high-quality corporate bonds. The focus becomes one of *controlled volatility* of returns, where minimal changes in investment returns occur from one reporting period to the next.

Where are these changes leading? The traditional GIC portfolio of bullet and window contracts we have all become accustomed to is changing. Many plan sponsors over time will probably modify their investment objectives and communicate to participants a change in investment philosophy. Dependence on the insurance industry as the sole provider of the contract rate will be diminished, yet will remain an important component of the portfolio.

Over the course of the next several years, plan sponsors will be faced with the dilemma of deciding whether to maintain their focus on yield, or seek higher returns through a focus on return.

The marketplace has witnessed 10 years of declining interest rates. With the exception of periods of the inverted yield curve, this decline has produced a positive lag effect for investors (in money market and GIC funds) as rates declined below the portfolio's blended yield. Should rates begin to trend upward, the positive lag effect could be replaced with a negative one.

As illustrated on Exhibit 1, the plan sponsor may be faced with one of several alternative strategies. The GIC has produced a high yield with little or no perceived real risks over time. Going forward, the decision could encompass a trade-off of risk for return. Stable value will be able to be maintained, but possibly at lower returns; albeit with lower risks. Those plan sponsors wishing to pick up extra return must be willing to accept added risks.

What are the alternatives facing the plan sponsor?

• **Stable-value strategy:** Investment media include traditional GICs/BICs, structured GICs/BICs, and money market securities.

• **Controlled volatility strategy:** Investment media include traditional GICs/BICs, structured GICs/BICs, money market instruments, and marketable fixed-income securities.

• **Conventional fixed-income strategy:** Investment media include money market instruments and marketable fixed-income securities.

EXHIBIT 1

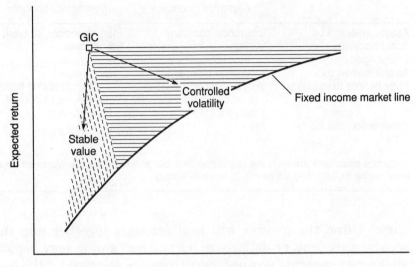

A Note on Emerging Structured Investment Contracts

The creation of structured investment contracts is the next natural step in the evolution of the "GIC" market. The history of every securities market is characterized by increasing efficiency, better liquidity, and improved risk management opportunities (e.g., credit and interest rate risks) at each step in its evolution. The GIC market is no exception.

The objective of a structured investment contract is to diversify the credit exposure of the plan away from the unsecured general account or deposit obligation of the issuer. As Exhibit 2 illustrates, this is accomplished in several different ways. In separate account products offered by insurance companies, separate accounts holding bonds, mortgages, and other fixed-income instruments are established. The investing plan has a beneficial interest in the securities in the separate account. Assets in such accounts appear to be protected by state laws against credit claims on the insurance com-

EXHIBIT 2

	Insurance Company Separate Accounts	Bank Synthetic Products
Assets selected by	Insurance company	Plan, manager, or bank
Assets actively managed?	Usually	Sometimes
Assets owned by	Insurance company	Plan
Fully benefit responsive?	Yes; benefit liquidations may affect future returns	Yes; future returns fixed regardless of benefit liquidations*
Asset credit risk borne by	Plan	Plan

*Assumes structured contracts are negotiated on a buy-and-hold strategy. Managed structured contracts issued by banks may operate differently.

pany.[4] Often the insurer will pool accounts together into the separate account, or dollar size permitting, a plan may negotiate its own separate account. Securities are selected for the separate account by the insurance company within investment guidelines approved by the plan and the insurance company managing those assets. Some will allow the plan sponsor's external manager to select and/or manage the investments. The insurance company provides a "wrap" which serves to amortize realized capital gains and losses in the portfolio and "guarantee" that if an investing plan has a need for liquidity, it can liquidate amounts needed to pay participants at book value.

Structured investment contracts offered by banks are similar. The plan sponsor or the plan's manager selects a portfolio of assets that are purchased and owned by the plan. The bank provides a "wrap" that gives the plan the right to liquidate the securities and receive book value from the bank in the event of a need for liquidity.

In summary, the industry is rapidly maturing and becoming more efficient. Plan sponsors have more opportunities than ever before to provide a safe haven for its participants.

K.L.W.

---

[4]The buyer is cautioned to perform independent research to determine the rights of the plan in the event of issuer insolvency.

ABOUT THE EDITOR

Kenneth L. Walker first published *Guaranteed Investment Contracts: Risk Analysis and Portfolio Strategies* in the spring of 1989. In addition, he has contributed to the *Fixed Income Handbook*, Third Edition, published by Business One Irwin.

Mr. Walker is president of T. Rowe Price Guaranteed Asset Advisers, Inc., of Glen Allen, Virginia. He is recognized as one of the original innovators in the field of professional GIC portfolio management. He and his associates have developed a number of unique GIC portfolio management techniques that have been integrated into investment strategies of many large private and public retirement programs.

He has published in *Barron's, Pensions & Investment Age, Pension World,* and the *International Employee Benefit Foundation Journal*. Mr. Walker is often quoted in *Business Week, Institutional Investor, Fortune,* and *The Wall Street Journal*. He currently serves on the advisory board of *Pension World,* and the Executive Committee of the Board of the GIC Association.

CONTRIBUTING AUTHORS

SAMUEL F. BEARDSLEY

Sam Beardsley is a Vice President of T. Rowe Price Stable Asset Management, Inc., and a controller of the Private Label Investment Products Group, which includes mutual funds, partnerships, pooled GIC Funds, and collective investment trusts. He also functions as tax manager for the T. Rowe Price Mutual Funds. Mr. Beardsley joined the firm in 1982 following five years with Price Waterhouse. In addition to being a Certified Public Accountant, Sam earned an M.B.A. at Loyola College, Baltimore, and received a B.A. from Towson State University, Baltimore. He is a member of the American Institute of Certified Public Accountants, the Maryland Association of Certified Public Accountants, and the Tax Committee of the Investment Company Institute.

FREDERIC (RICK) W. CORWIN, JR.

Rick is responsible for actuarial research, pricing, underwriting policy and product development in connection with GICs and single premium annuity contracts for qualified retirement plans of John Hancock Financial Services. Rick has been working for the Group Pension department since 1983. Prior to that time, he worked for five years in a rotational program and eight years in Group Life and Accident and Health.

Rick received a B.S. degree in mathematics from Williams College, Williamstown, Mass., and an M.S. degree in actuarial science from Northeastern University, Boston. He is a Fellow of the Society of Actuaries and a member of the American Academy of Actuaries.

HUGH FORCIER

Hugh Forcier is a partner in the law firm of Faegre & Benson, a 250-lawyer firm with offices in Minneapolis, Denver, Des Moines, Washington, D.C., London, and Frankfurt.

Mr. Forcier has been with the firm for 22 years. He serves as the Group Practice Head of its Employee Benefits practice group—a group of 14 lawyers who specialize in employee benefits.

CYNTHIA C. GRAVATT

Cynthia Gravatt formerly served as Issuer Liaison for T. Rowe Price Stable Asset Management, Inc. Prior to joining the firm in 1990, she underwrote GICs for The Life Insurance Company of Virginia. Ms. Gravatt earned a B.A. from Virginia Polytechnic Institute and State University. She also earned a paralegal certificate from the Institute for Paralegal Training in Philadelphia.

MICHAEL L. HOOVER

Michael L. Hoover is Vice President and a founding Principal of T. Rowe Price Stable Asset Management, Inc. Mike is Senior Portfolio Manager at T. Rowe Price, with management responsibility for the investment and trading staffs. Mike earned a B.S. from the McIntire School of Commerce at the University of Virginia and an M.B.A. from Virginia Commonwealth University.

KELLI HUSTAD HUELER

Kelli Hustad Hueler is the founder and President of the Minneapolis-based Hueler Companies. K. H. Hueler Inc. provides GIC consulting services to institutional clients nationwide. Hueler Analytics has developed the GIC Pooled Fund Comparative Universe, which currently monitors 30 pooled funds with combined assets of over $6 billion. Hueler LOGIC is a data base software system designed to provide plan sponsors with comparative data on corporate GIC portfolios as a means of producing meaningful portfolio evaluation and performance review.

Prior to establishing these companies, Ms. Hueler was a registered representative for Kidder Peabody, where her responsibilities focused on the GIC market and the development of product evaluation methods. Through 1983, Ms. Hueler was a registered representative for IDS Life.

DAVID L. RENZ, FSA, CFA

David L. Renz is Vice President and Director of Alternative Markets for the Prudential Asset Management Company. He is a Fellow of the Society of Actuaries and a Chartered Financial Consultant.

ALLAN G. RICHMOND, F.S.A.

Allan Richmond is a Vice President and Principal of T. Rowe Price Stable Asset Management, Inc., and a senior credit analyst, specializing in insurance company research. In addition, he serves as Chairman of the Credit Policy Committee for T. Rowe Price Guaranteed Asset Advisers, Inc. Prior to joining the firm in 1990, he was employed for 16 years with Sun-America Corporation as vice president and valuation actuary for its three life insurance subsidiaries and also served as a member of the board of directors for each subsidiary company. Allan earned a B.S. from the Wharton School of the University of Pennsylvania, an M.S. in actuarial science from Northeastern University, Boston, and an M.B.A. from Stanford University.

MARTIN H. RUBY

Marty Ruby joined ICH Capital Management Group in May 1990 to develop an integrated asset/liability spread management business focused on accumulation products. Marty was named President of the Group in the fall of 1990. ICH Capital Management Group has responsibility for managing the accumulation product lines of ICH as well as providing investment management services for the other ICH insurance companies. Also in the fall of 1990, Marty was named President of Constitution Life, the insurance company through which ICH runs its accumulation business.

Prior to joining ICH, Marty was with Capital Holding Corporation for nine years. His previous position at Capital Holding was Managing Director—President, Capital Initiatives Corporation, the subsidiary through which Capital Holding manages its accumulation business. He developed the industry's first floating-rate guaranteed investment contract (GIC) in 1982 and used this as a base to build a wide array of diversified GIC and retail annuity product lines. Marty is a frequent speaker on asset/liability management topics at various industry meetings. He is a Fellow of the Society of Actuaries and holds a B.S. degree from Purdue University and an M.B.A. from Bellarmine College, Louisville, Kentucky.

DAVID J. SALVIN

Dave Salvin has headed the BIC issuance group at Bankers Trust Company since 1987. During this time, Bankers has become one of the premier issuers of BICs and BIC derivatives. Previously, he held positions with Aetna Life & Casualty and with Certus Financial Corporation in GIC credit analysis and new-product development.

Mr. Salvin holds a B.S. degree (operations research) from the Wharton School, University of Pennsylvania, and an M.B.A. (finance) from the University of Connecticut. He is a CFA and CEBS and has spoken and written on several aspects of GIC investing.

WILLIAM H. SMITH

William H. Smith is the Manager of Savings Plans' Fixed-Income Funds in the Du Pont Company Finance Department.

For the past several years he has worked on investing approximately $800 million annually in GICs and alternative investments on behalf of two savings plans' fixed-income funds with assets totaling more than $5 billion. Prior to this assignment he oversaw the externally managed pension assets for two of the company's subsidiaries.

Smith holds a B.S. in Economics from Gannon College and an MBA from the University of Toledo.

JAMES C. TEMPLEMAN II

Mr. Templeman is an Assistant Vice President and portfolio manager for T. Rowe Price Stable Asset Management, Inc. Prior to joining the firm in 1989, Mr. Templeman was a GIC specialist for William M. Mercer, Inc. Mr. Templeman received a B.A. in mathematics from the University of Virginia.

DAVID M. WALKER

David M. Walker is a Partner and National Director of Arthur Andersen's Compensation and Benefits practice based in Washington, D.C. Prior to joining Arthur Andersen, Mr. Walker held a variety of positions in the federal government with the Department of Labor and the Pension Benefit Guaranty Corporation. Among other things, Mr. Walker served as Assistant Secretary of Labor for Pension and Welfare Benefit Programs. He serves as one of two public trustees for the Social Security and Medicare Trust Funds, as a member of the Secretary of Labor's ERISA Advisory Council and as Chairman of the Association of Private Pension and Welfare Plans' Investment and Accounting Issues Committee.

DAVID C. VEENEMAN

David Veeneman founded Veeneman Associates in 1991 to develop an investment consulting and communications business focused on employee savings plans and other defined contribution plans.

Prior to founding Veeneman Associates, Mr. Veeneman was a Principal with William M. Mercer Asset Planning, Inc. While with Mercer, he practiced in the Louisville, Kentucky, and Stamford, Connecticut, offices of the firm. In addition, Mr. Veeneman was a founding Principal of Fiduciary Capital Management, Inc., an investment management firm located in Woodbury, Connecticut.

Mr. Veeneman has advised clients on all aspects of defined contribution plan investing. He specialized in insurance company and bank issues, including GICs, synthetic and derivative products, and plan termination annuities. Mr. Veeneman developed Mercer's national on-line rate desk and its carrier quality-analysis system.

Mr. Veeneman is a regular speaker at national conferences for defined contribution plan sponsors and the insurance industry. He has written for national publications on guaranteed investments and investment communications.

CONTENTS

INTRODUCTION

A PLAN SPONSOR'S PERSPECTIVE

William H. Smith

Manager, Savings Plans' Fixed Income Funds
E. I. du Pont de Nemours and Company

The guaranteed investment contract was first offered as an investment for retirement and savings funds in the early 1970s. For the next 20 years GICs enjoyed spectacular growth. GICs outstanding today total approximately $200 billion and are issued at the rate of about $40 billion annually.

The reasons for this success are clear. No other investment has traditionally provided the combination of stable and attractive return and safety of principal. Principal is protected against default by the guarantee and creditworthiness of the issuer. Book value accounting shields the investor from the market fluctuations caused by volatile interest rates.

The result has been a win–win situation for all involved—savings plans' participants and a whole new industry, comprising issuers, GIC managers, brokers, consultants, publications, lawyers, accountants, credit analysts, and others. Even small and medium-sized businesses throughout the country have benefited from a new and effective source of financing from insurance companies that function as the conduit for GIC funds.

Beginning in 1990, things began to change. Two major events occurred that convulsed the GIC industry and threatened the very existence of the GIC as an investment concept. The book value accounting treatment for GICs came under attack. The Financial Accounting Standards Board (FASB)

1

undertook a project to determine if these investments should be marked to market (i.e., similar to a bond). Market valuation would place principal at risk and make returns unpredictable, thus greatly reducing or eliminating the attractiveness of the instrument.

Numerous reports in the financial press, local newspapers, and on television suggested that the savings and loan (S&L) industry had self-destructed; the banking industry was on the brink of collapse; and the life insurance industry, and its ability to issue and support GICs, probably was not far behind. Attempts by insurance companies and others to convince the public that the insurance industry was different, and more secure, enjoyed limited success. In the spring of 1991 Executive Life Insurance failed, due to excessive investments in junk bonds. This event was soon followed by the seizure by state insurance regulators of several more insurance companies suffering from realized and potential losses in commercial mortgages and from loss of confidence among policyholders. Credit issues had become the most serious threat to the stability of the GIC market.

In response to credit concerns some plan sponsors terminated the GIC-fund option in their employee savings plan. However, most stayed the course but with a new focus, directed to quality enhancement. Many are pursuing new GIC derivative products or alternative GIC-like investments that provide diversification and enhance credit while maintaining book value accounting. These products are growing rapidly and are expected to soon become a major portion of the overall GIC market.

The developments leading to improved security will restore confidence in the safety of these investments but the process will require considerable effort, including improved communications to plan participants, and time. GICs will survive the credit storm and likely will remain the investment of choice among employees and retirees.

Some investment professionals argue that plan participants allocate too much of their savings to the GIC fund—about two thirds, on average. They argue that more of participants' savings should be directed to equity funds to achieve higher returns over the long term. As one representative of a major consulting firm said, "Just because they [GIC funds] are popular doesn't mean they are good."

In the Du Pont Company savings plan, which sponsors one of the largest GIC funds in existence, the GIC fund accounts for 80 percent of the total savings plan assets and approximately 69 percent of monthly contributions. Discussions with employees and retirees indicate the combination of safety of principal and attractive return is more highly valued than the potentially higher long-term return provided by equities with their attendant risk and volatility.

It is presumptuous to conclude that employees should allocate less (or more) of their savings to GIC funds, since tolerance for risk and both short- and long-term investment objectives vary, even among younger employees. Given quality information on investment alternatives and comparative performance data, employees will probably more often than not make the investment choice(s) best suited to their circumstances.

In my opinion, GICs, and their second and third derivatives, will continue to be highly valued by millions of savings plans participants, resulting in a continuation of double-digit growth of funds comprising these investments.

This book is written by leading experts in the field and is the only complete reference text on GICs and similar investments. It is a valuable resource for all who need to understand, or simply want to know more about, this truly unique investment.

CHAPTER 1

THE METAMORPHOSIS

Kenneth L. Walker

The insurance industry deserves the majority of the credit for creating the pension marketplace. Since before the turn of the century, insurance companies have been underwriting retirement coverage and profit-sharing incentive programs for the American work force.

The industry has pioneered many product innovations. From the original concept of the individual annuity contract to the guaranteed investment contract (GIC), the industry has contributed immensely both to the growth of the investment management field and to the American economy. Today the insurance industry continues to be a pioneer in the investment markets, managing portfolios of international investments, practicing dynamic portfolio hedging, and providing other innovative investment strategies.

The industry's early growth, though slow at first, was propelled by the use of statistical analysis in developing mortality trends (and thus more competitive and more cost-efficient pricing) and by the change in social attitudes. The desire for a continuing income flow upon retirement, coupled with the fear of increasing life spans, helped to promote the growth of a profitable industry.

The industry has enjoyed a reputation of conservatism. Assets supporting insurance reserves have relatively long durations and are managed with the goal of generating long-term income streams and preserving principal. This conservative nature has created a degree of comfort and stability for the buyers of its products.

Conservatism has forced the industry to pay a price. The unexpectedly high interest rates of the late 1970s and early 1980s illustrated a structural weakness of the life industry. Bound by regulation and tradition, most insurers had very long-term asset portfolios. While the insurers were able to gain from higher reinvestable income, they incurred enormous unrealized (and sometimes realized) capital losses on a part of their portfolios. If asset holdings had been reported at market value, many insurers would have been declared insolvent.

The years of volatile interest rates that began in the early 1970s and the ensuing unstable fixed-income returns led many investors to desire shorter-term investments that provided more stable returns. This need fostered the growth of the GIC marketplace. With the emphasis on shorter-term investment products, the industry was forced to revamp its investment practices, requiring a shift away from long-term to shorter-term investments.[1] This change initiated a host of problems requiring added attention: better asset/liability structuring, thinner yield spreads, and insufficient availability of high-quality investments to support the underlying guarantee.

THE EARLY YEARS: LEVEL PREMIUM/SINGLE PREMIUM DEFERRED ANNUITIES

The first form of retirement coverage was provided with the nonparticipating deferred annuity contract, an arrangement in which guaranteed retirement benefits were provided by the issuing insurance company. Both single and level premium annuity contracts were offered.

Under the level premium concept, an annuity contract was purchased for each covered participant. As the participant's wage base increased, the annuity base was increased with a corresponding increase in the annual premium to compensate for

---

[1]Thomas P. O'Connor, New York Life Insurance Company, remarks made at the First Annual GIC Symposium, New York, April 21, 1987.

the added future liability. Under the single premium concept, known as *unit credit funding*, an annuity certificate was issued each year to reflect the increasing future retirement benefit. The purchase price for each of these contracts was equal to the present value of the projected lifetime annuity to begin upon retirement.

The annuity benefit, once purchased, was fully guaranteed by the insurer; and neither the plan sponsor nor the trustee had any further liability with regard to annuity benefits.

There were two principal disadvantages of deferred annuities:

1. Since benefit payments were guaranteed for delivery many years in the future, the insurance companies favored themselves by using liberal assumptions regarding expected improvements in future life expectancy and conservative assumptions regarding future long-term rates of investment return. These combined to produce a high cost to the buyer for each dollar of guaranteed annuity.

2. Insurance company sales acquisition expenses were recouped at the front end (i.e., charged when the deposits were made and the annuities purchased). Accordingly, when the majority of employees terminated employment prior to obtaining a vested interest in the plan, the cash surrender value of the deferred annuity that was returned to the trust fund was often minimal—frequently less than the actual premiums paid.[2]

As pension coverage grew, the inefficiencies and disadvantages associated with individual policies required the development of a more cost-efficient investment contract. An improvement occurred when the group annuity contract entered the marketplace. Lower costs resulted for the purchaser, due to economies of scale in pooling administration, underwriting, and distribution as well as to mortality tables established on group

---

[2]"Is an Experience-Rated Investment Contract Ever a Viable Alternative to a GIC?" by D. J. Smith and P. A. Lupo was reprinted with permission from the December 1987 issue of *Employee Benefits Journal*, published by the International Foundation of Employee Benefits Plans, Brookfield, WI. Statements or opinions expressed in this article are those of the author, and do not necessarily represent the views or positions of the International Foundation, its officers, directors, or staff.

experience within the particular industries (or, for larger employers, within each employer's covered group).

THE DEPOSIT ADMINISTRATION CONTRACT

During the mid-1950s, social pressures began to require greater coverage for the American work force. The costs were considered high, however, due in large part to the inefficiencies of the investment products being provided by the life industry and the lack of actuarial experience in assessing the true risks and costs.

The Deposit Administration (DA) contract revolutionized the pension industry, creating enormous growth for the insurance industry. Although today we recognize the many inefficiencies of the DA contract, it did provide major improvements over the individual annuity policy. All funds were pooled on an unallocated basis within the general account of the insurer until such time as the participant retired. At retirement, funds were withdrawn to purchase an individual annuity policy for the participant, withdrawing the fully funded pension liability from the plan.

Unique to the DA was the accounting methodology. Two sets of books were maintained by the insurer: the contractual fund and the experience fund. The contractual fund represented the contractual interest and expense obligations of the insurer. The experience fund represented the actual investment and expense experience of the insurer's general account. Usually only the contractual fund was reported and seen by the contractholder.

Expenses incurred were generally higher for the experience fund than obligated under the contractual fund, because for it the insurer often established low initial expense schedules to make the credited net rate appear higher. The insurer exercised tremendous discretion in the crediting of any excess interest in the form of dividends. Great latitude existed in the setting of reserve levels for anticipated mortality experience. Common to most insurers was the limited information distributed. Items such as mortality, interest, expenses, and other contingency reserves were never fully disclosed. The insurer controlled the new money rate (the rate paid on subsequent deposits), which generally changed annually, and the floor guarantees under the contractual fund usually decreased over a period of time (see Table 1–1).

THE IMMEDIATE PARTICIPATION GUARANTEE

The 1960s saw the establishment of the pension marketplace as a recognized industry. Not only did the insurance companies confirm their dominant position within the industry, but for the first time the banking industry began its thrust toward capturing a share of the market. The insurance companies continued their passive guaranteed minimum rate of return concept, while the banks began offering diversified forms of more active management via equity, fixed income, and balanced portfolios. Competition ensued to see who would emerge with the greater market share.

To meet this challenge, the minimum-return concept was revised to provide a more competitive investment medium. The DA contract was vastly improved with the introduction of the immediate participation guarantee (IPG). The IPG was based on the DA concept (i.e., the general account usually providing a minimum floor rate with an upside, participating feature). It differed in accounting practices and in the retirement payout basis. In essence, the IPG provided what its name implied: an immediate participation in the earnings, expenses, and

TABLE 1–1
The Typical Deposit Administration Contract

	Experience Fund	Contractual Fund
Interest	Credited according to the investment experience of the issuer	Credited under a floor guarantee formula, usually under a declining rate basis over a period of years
Expenses	Debited as incurred	Debited under the contractual formula

mortality. The dual recordkeeping (contractual and experience) was eliminated. Retirement benefits were paid in a different fashion. In lieu of the purchase of the annuity upon retirement, the participants' accrued balance remained in the general account, with monthly withdrawals made for retirement benefits. As such, the plan got the benefit of the funds remaining in the plan. Lower expenses and hence better investment returns were realized due to greater efficiencies.

Most IPG investment contracts issued by insurance companies contained options that permitted amounts to be withdrawn (usually at book value) for the purchase of annuities, for the direct payment of benefits, or for employee-directed investment changes. The policyholder fully participated immediately in the actual investment return achieved by the insurance company's general account portfolio. To accurately reflect the annual investment performance of the assets, insurers used the *investment year method* (IYM) or *new money system,* enabling them to track, on a year-by-year basis, the rates of return earned on each year's balance.

Insurance companies use one of two principal methods for investment year (IYM) accounting: the declining-index method or the fixed-index method. Under the declining-index method, the original cell of funds is adjusted downward to reflect any reinvestment of the original assets. The IYM rate credited to the remaining portion of the original cell remains stable until all of the original assets mature. Under the fixed-index method, the original cell of funds deposited is kept constant and the rate credited is adjusted for reinvestment of funds.

Assuming contributions were made to an IPG contract during a three-year period in the amounts indicated in Exhibit 1–1, the interest credited under the declining-index method on the contract for the last year will be a blended rate of 10.27 percent. To understand fully how an "experience-rated" insurance contract's performance is measured, it is helpful to review an example of a "new money triangle," as shown in Exhibit 1–2.

Exhibit 1–2 demonstrates that not only is the new money rate in Year 5 (9.6 percent in the illustration) an important factor, but equally important is the rate of interest subsequently credited on a particular year's deposit. Deposits made in Year 1 earned 13.1 percent in that year. In subsequent years, however,

EXHIBIT 1–1

Year of Deposit	Amount of Deposit		Rate Credited in 1986 on Each Year's Deposit	1986 Interest Credited
Year 1	$500,000	×	10.5%	$52,500
Year 2	100,000	×	10.1%	10,100
Year 3	150,000	×	9.6%	14,400
Total	$750,000		10.27%	$77,000

these same deposits earned 12.9 percent, 12.6 percent, and 12.8 percent. To review the history of rates being credited on a particular year's deposit, the chart should be read horizontally. To review the matrix of rates being credited in any particular year, the chart is read vertically.

IPG contracts are negotiated to provide specified minimum interest guarantees on all deposits made during the first three to five contract years. IPG contracts are designed to serve as ongoing arrangements available for the funding of all or most of the future plan contributions. The investment return credited each year is based upon the investment income actually generated by the insurance company general account.

Just as positive interest credits to the contract can arise, negative interest can also arise. Negative credits of interest occur when there is a net cash outflow under the contract in any year(s) when current interest rates are higher than existing cell rates. A negative cash flow can significantly impact the overall rate of return.

EXHIBIT 1–2
New Money Triangle

					Year of Deposit
				9.6%	Year 5
			10.3%	10.1%	Year 4
		10.7%	10.8%	10.5%	Year 3
	12.1%	12.0%	11.6%	11.7%	Year 2
13.1%	12.9%	12.6%	12.6%	12.8%	Year 1
Year 1	Year 2	Year 3	Year 4	Year 5	

EXHIBIT 1–3

Year 3	$100,000	×	12.0%	=	$12,000
Year 2	100,000	×	10.0%	=	10,000
Year 1	500,000	×	9.0%	=	45,000
Total	$700,000		9.6%		$67,000

Assume that a deposit of $500,000 was made in Year 1 and is earning 9.0 percent, and that $100,000 was deposited in each of Years 2 and 3. These later deposits earn 10.0 percent and 12.0 percent, respectively. At the end of Year 3, the fund was earning an average or blended rate of 9.6 percent as illustrated in Exhibit 1–3.

Assume a deposit of $100,000 was made in Year 4, but $400,000 was withdrawn to make single sum or other benefit payments. The net deposit for Year 4 was −$300,000 ($100,000 less $400,000). The new money investment rate for Year 4 was assumed to be 13.0 percent as illustrated in Exhibit 1–4.

As a result of the withdrawal of $400,000 in Year 4, the effective interest rate declined from 9.6 percent to 7.0 percent. From these illustrations a unique conclusion is drawn. IPG contracts function well where there is a positive cash flow. If negative cash flow occurs, it can work against the plan.[3]

As the buyers of guaranteed products became more sophisticated, the demand for less complex investments arose. Buyers began demanding investments that provided greater flexibility in portfolio construction.

EXHIBIT 1–4

Year 4	$(300,000)	×	13.0%	=	$(39,000)
Year 3	100,000	×	12.0%	=	12,000
Year 2	100,000	×	10.0%	=	10,000
Year 1	500,000	×	9.0%	=	45,000
Total	$ 400,000		7.0%		$ 28,000

---

[3]Smith and Lupo, "Is an Experience-Rated Investment Contract Ever a Viable Alternative to a GIC?"

THE GUARANTEED INVESTMENT CONTRACT

During the mid-1970s aggressive competition from banks and mutual funds along with the stellar performance of the equity markets forced the insurance industry to revise its investment products. The explosive growth of defined contribution plans and the beginnings of volatile interest rates forced further changes.

The insurance industry responded with the guaranteed investment contract (GIC). It provided the major features of the guaranteed return and book value (or par value) accounting but lacked the negative features of the older generation open-ended contracts. The perpetual relationship as experienced with the DA and IPG contracts disappeared. The GIC had a known maturity date. It had neither a minimum floor rate nor participating earnings. The rate was established on the purchase date and remained constant for the contract period. Its features were akin to certificates of deposit issued by banks and savings and loan associations.

As the product matured and as more insurers entered the market, the GIC became a generic term. Today there are many different types of GICs, all of which will be discussed in Chapter 2, What Is a GIC? and Chapter 11, Managing the Stable-Value Portfolio.

TODAY'S ENVIRONMENT

The most significant legislative impact to affect the pension marketplace occurred in 1974 when Congress passed the Employee Retirement Income Security Act (ERISA). Not only did ERISA provide added protection to the American work force via increased coverage protection, vesting, and annuity options; it provided evidence that Congress recognized the importance of retirement benefits and the need to supplement the social security system. This legislation in turn led to major overhauls in the tax system and ultimately the introduction of the 401(k) plan.

Without the introduction of the 401(k) plan, the GIC probably would never have grown to its current stature. Without the GIC, the insurance industry probably could not have maintained its position in the pension marketplace. The attractiveness of the GIC has allowed the industry to maintain its distribution system via the agency and regional office network. The GIC has provided cross-selling opportunities of other products, primarily plan administration and separate account management, and other investment management services.

The insurance industry has regained the momentum of the 1950s and 1960s. Many mutual companies are evaluating demutualization and the benefits that can be derived from access to the equity capital markets. Many of the major insurers either have expanded or are expanding their investment horizons by acquiring independent investment advisers. They are becoming smarter investors of their asset-to-liability structure. Insurers are better controlling expenses, both overhead and underwriting. Because of recent tax overhaul legislation and the impact on insurance company taxability, many companies are putting more emphasis on effectively managing their tax liabilities. And many are learning how to transfer part of the investment risks to others, primarily to the policyholders.

The attention to insurance company credit quality from the investment marketplace is a sign of a healthy and maturing market. For too many years, GICs and other insurance products were all priced similarly. The buyer bought at random at the highest rate, with little or no attention to creditworthiness. In contrast, the same buyer approached bank CDs, municipal bonds, corporate debt, and other financial products differently from GICs when investment policies restricted the purchase process.[4]

The insurance industry is rapidly changing and expanding. The most significant change is the role the industry is playing in other traditional fixed-income financial markets. The industry is quickly realizing that the concept of the GIC can be used in many areas outside of the qualified pension and profit-sharing markets. GIC derivative products are emerging.

---

[4]O'Connor, First Annual GIC Symposium.

The Secondary Market

Officially, according to the banking and insurance industry regulatory authorities, investment contracts are not traded. They have been assigned, where the original contractholder transfers or assigns ownership to a third party.

Investment contracts are written under the assumption that the contracts will not change hands. Most contracts have built-in inflexibility in the form of language restricting or prohibiting assignment to another party without prior insurer approval. Why? Some issuers contend that a formalized secondary market might jeopardize the exemptive provisions provided by the Securities and Exchange Commission, although the SEC has not endorsed this view. Like the SEC, most state insurance regulators have no formal position on the transfer of GICs. Where the issue has been disputed, some plans have successfully appealed to the courts for ruling on their rights to transfer these substantial assets in attempts to maximize liquidation value over arbitrary *market* values.

What can a contractholder do with an investment contract it no longer wants? Many contracts normally allow termination prior to maturity, in either a lump-sum payout or a periodic-installment payout. Either method can be used, but neither may offer the best opportunity. In the lump-sum method of contract termination, the lesser of book or market value is usually distributed. Those contracts with rates lower than current rates will experience a market discount penalty. If a contractual rate is higher than current rates at the time of distribution, no premium is usually provided; only book value is returned. The appreciation remains with the issuer.

The installment method provides payout over a period of years. An earnings rate is paid on the declining balance and may be either declared in advance or based on an experience rate formula. Most installment formulas imply that the book value is being returned. In many formulas a hidden market penalty is imposed via a lower rate credited to the declining balance.

The alternative to normal contract termination provisions incorporates the assignment (or secondary transaction) of the contract to another buyer either directly between the buyer and seller, or through a broker intermediary. In lieu of contract reregistration, often only cash flows are assigned, with the original contractholder retaining title to the contract while promising to pay a series of future income streams to the buyer.

The steps for direct contract assignment are simple:

1. The contractholder asks permission of the issuer to allow assignment.[5]
2. Assuming permission is granted, the contractholder elects the installment payout option of contract termination.
3. A purchase is arranged and the payment(s) are assigned to the buyer. Coincident with the assignment, the buyer delivers to the original contractholder a lump-sum payment equal to the present value of the future cash flows, discounted at current market yields.

As illustrated in Table 1–2, assignment frequently offers advantages over contractual termination, particularly when higher yielding contracts are terminated in a lower rate environment. The seller seeks to minimize the market value penalty or the reduced installment earnings rate. The buyer is normally obtaining an investment yielding a premium to equivalent maturity and quality investments. Hence each has gained over the prevailing market yields and market value discounts provided in the contract.

EXEMPTIVE PROVISIONS

Section 3(a)(8) of the Securities Act of 1933 exempted insurance, endowment, and annuity contracts from the registration and prospectus delivery requirements. Section 3(a)(8) was based on the assumption that insurance products were not considered

---

[5]Note: While secondary transactions can occur between the buyer and seller without notification to the issuer, it is recommended that issuer approval be obtained prior to entering into the transaction.

TABLE 1-2
Contract Liquidation Values under Four Interest Rate Environments

Contract Terms:

Deposit account	$10,000,000
Net effective rate	14.63%
Effective date	5/15/84
Maturity date	5/15/93
Maturity value	$34,173,120
Contract type	Compound

Liquidation Date	Treasury Yield	BBB Yield	Contractual Book Value	Contractual Market Value	Secondary Market Value	Incremental Value of Sale
5/15/85	10.80%	13.25%	$11,463,000	$12,629,290	$13,150,842	$1,687,842
5/15/86	9.50%	10.35%	13,140,037	17,150,559	17,845,203	4,705,166
5/15/87	8.71%	10.46%	15,062,424	18,812,842	19,087,295	4,024,871
5/15/88	8.53%	11.03%	17,266,057	20,252,700	21,301,473	4,035,416

This nonbenefit-responsive bullet contract provides for a "cash out" value of the lesser of book or "market," where market is derived by discounting contractual cash flow by the BBB long corporate bond yield at the liquidation date. In this example the contract yield exceeds the current market yields. For contracts using the above contractual market valuation methodology, secondary market sales also usually exceed contractual market values.

Courtesy of Morgan Stanley & Company, Mark M. Kimak (Principal).

securities. The Investment Company Act of 1940 and the Investment Advisors Act of 1940 historically also excluded traditional insurance contracts from the normal regulatory provisions.

With the introduction of the variable annuity in the 1950s, the exemptive issues were tested for the first time. In 1956, the Securities and Exchange Commission sued Variable Annuity Life Insurance Company (VALIC), alleging that the variable annuity was not an "annuity contract" within the meaning of Section 3(a)(8). The SEC's position was that the contract was a security required to be registered under the 1933 Act.

In a decision that has become the focal point for virtually all analyses of the status of insurance products under the federal securities laws, the Supreme Court ruled that VALIC's variable annuity was a security. The court determined that the "concept of insurance involves some investment risk taken on the part of the insurance company and guarantees that at least some fraction of the benefits will be payable in fixed amounts." The extent of investment risk required to be assumed to qualify under the Section 3(a)(8) exemption was not specified.

The VALIC suit was followed by the *SEC* v. *United Benefit Life Insurance Company*. This suit attempted to define the degree of investment risk that an insurance company had to assume in order to rely on the Section 3(a)(8) exclusion. Neither suit had any direct impact on fixed-annuity contracts.

In 1970 Congress amended the Securities Act to add an exemption in Section 3(a)(2) from registration for separate account products sold to certain tax-qualified and governmental plans. Fixed contracts were thought to be covered by the exclusion in 3(a)(8). However, with the introduction of more competitive investment vehicles (primarily GIC contracts) in the mid-to-late 1970s, the status of certain fixed-rate contracts was for the first time brought into question.

In March of 1977, the SEC issued the landmark no-action letter, stating "life insurance companies may offer and sell guaranteed investment contracts to tax-qualified corporate pension and profit-sharing plans without compliance with the registration provisions of the Securities Act."

In 1978, after reviewing public comments on the status of GICs, the SEC proposed Rule 154, seeking to provide guidance on which GICs were not annuities within the meaning of Section 3(a)(8). Under the then-proposed Rule 154, the exclusion was not to apply if contracts were deemed marketed "primarily as an investment." The insurance industry opposed the proposal, believing it would subject many traditional contracts to registration.

Reacting to the negative reception of proposed Rule 154, the SEC tried an alternative approach. In 1979, in Release 33-6051, it adopted a "General Statement of Policy Regarding Exemptive Provisions Relating to Annuity and Investment Contracts." This statement pronounced that in order for a contract to fall within Section 3(a)(8), the insurer had to assume (1) a meaningful mortality risk, and (2) significant investment risk with a corresponding lack of assumption of a significant investment risk by the purchaser. Much discussion in the industry ensued about the impact of the statement of policy on the development of various products, particularly as it focused on the marketing aspects of these new products.

On October 21, 1980, Section 3(a)(2) was expanded to exempt from registration fixed as well as variable contracts sold to certain tax-qualified and governmental plans. Therefore, fixed contracts which do not qualify for the exclusion in 3(a)(8) may qualify for the exemption in 3(a)(2) if sales are limited to plans covered by 3(a)(2). This exemption from registration is less valuable than a 3(a)(8) exclusion since the anti-fraud provisions of the Securities Act still apply to sales of the 3(a)(2) contracts.

In May of 1986, the SEC adopted Rule 151 (see Appendix 2), representing its latest attempt to clarify the status of certain annuity and life insurance products under the Securities Act. Rule 151 creates a safe harbor for fixed-annuity contracts under the 1933 Securities Act.

In Rule 151, the SEC abandoned the general policy and guidelines approach issued in the statement of policy. Rule 151 specifically provides a safe harbor if

1. The contract is issued by an issuer subject to the supervision of the state insurance commissioner, bank commissioner, or any agency or officer performing like functions.

2. The contract includes certain guarantees of principal and interest sufficient for the insurer to be deemed to assume the reinvestment risk.

3. The contract is not marketed primarily as an investment.

Item (2) further sets forth three conditions that must be met: (1) the value of the contract must not vary according to the investment experience of a separate account; (2) the insurer; (a) guarantees the principal amounts and interest credits, and (b) credits a specified rate of interest; and (3) the insurer guarantees that the rate of any interest to be credited in excess of the stated rate will not be modified more frequently than once per year.[6]

Clearly, the industry has fought long and hard to avoid the securities registration issue. Any violation of these rules could lead to further action, with the worst case scenario being loss of the registration exemption.

---

[6]Parts of this section appear in abbreviated form from P. J. Mason and S. B. Boehm, "SEC's New Annuity Rule: A Perilous Safe Harbor," *Legal Times* (June 30, 1986). Reprinted with permission of *Legal Times*. Copyright © *Legal Times*.

CHAPTER 2

WHAT IS A GIC?

Kenneth L. Walker

The term *guaranteed return* has enabled the life insurance industry to develop a major asset class with characteristics unique unto itself and unmatched by any competing asset class. The buyer of an investment contract obtains an investment that provides a nonfluctuating principal value as interest rates rise and fall. With this emergence, the implied guaranteed return has produced two of the most misunderstood words in the investment markets.

The term *GIC* generally is defined as a Guaranteed Investment Contract. It sometimes is also referred to as a Guaranteed Income Contract, Guaranteed Interest Contract, or Guaranteed Insurance Contract. Whatever term is used, the instrument implies the same meaning—an absolute, fail-safe guarantee of principal and a predetermined rate of interest to be credited over the investment's life.

The stability of returns is provided through the contract's valuation basis. Unlike stocks and bonds, which are always reported at market value, GICs have traditionally been reported for financial reporting purposes at *book value*.[1]

The term *guarantee* implies that the insurer is providing a "fail-safe" guarantee of the return of principal. In actuality, the guarantee applies to the interest rate (or formula) and expense

---

[1]Book value is defined as "fully accrued cost value minus any deductions." As addressed in Chapter 4, reporting for investment contracts and the many alternatives emerging will be subject to greater scrutiny and reporting requirements.

schedule. Though the issuer may imply the protection of principal, that guarantee is only as good as the issuer's claims-paying ability.

It has often been argued that the issuer's payback ability is equivalent to a corporate debenture. Although it is not legally accurate, an analogy can be drawn between the two instruments. A debt holder enjoys a lien position as a general creditor as dictated in the corporate indenture. A corporate debt issue's payback ability is supported by the issuer's earnings power, and may be collateralized by specific assets.

A GIC owner becomes a policyholder of the insurer. In most states, policyholders enjoy a senior lien over the general creditors of the insurer. In an insurance company bankruptcy, the policyholder generally ranks ahead of the general creditors.[2] The actual settlement depends on the assets available from the state's guaranty fund, which may or may not exist and may or may not extend protection to GIC policyholders; plus the amounts that can be assessed against unrelated parties, including other parties that are proven to be involved in any wrongdoing.[3]

Different interpretations of the term *guarantee* exist. The issuer is guaranteeing a predetermined rate of interest and return of principal upon contract maturity. The buyer is assuming that the insurer is guaranteeing as if the insurer enjoyed some level of supreme or divine status. As previously noted, the guarantee is only as good as the general credit and claims-paying ability of the insurance company.

---

[2]In the case of the Executive Life of California conservatorship situation, the California Department of Insurance ruled that participants covered under GICs issued by Executive Life of California would be treated as policyholders.

[3]The guaranty fund is designed to provide financial protection to policyholders of life insurance companies in the event of carrier insolvency or impairment. Where a guaranty fund has been established, most states provide that should insolvency or impairment occur, all life carriers licensed in the state where policyholders (life, health, annuity, and supplemental contracts) are located would be requested to pay an assessment for amounts needed to cover outstanding liabilities of the policyholders, subject to maximum aggregate liability limits. The fund is maintained on an as-needed basis; it is not a reserve funded periodically. (In Chapter 5, more discussion on guaranty funds is provided.)

THE GENERAL ACCOUNT, SEPARATE ACCOUNT, AND SUBSIDIARIES

Insurance companies provide pooled investment products in two ways: through the general account and through separate accounts. GICs and annuities are predominantly issued through the general account, become liabilities of the issuing company, and enjoy the full backing of the issuer. Sometimes GICs are issued through a separate account. The question then becomes whether equivalent payback protection is provided for GICs issued through the separate account. Generally, when GICs are issued through a separate account, the backing of the general account is afforded to the policyholders.

The general account is the portfolio of unpledged assets of the insurance company. These assets meet the general obligations of the insurer without any priority on those obligations and with no separate identification of assets for any particular policy. Investments are made primarily in bonds, common and preferred stocks, mortgage loans, real estate, cash policy loans, and other investments as outlined in Exhibit 2–1. This distribution is shown in Exhibit 2–2 for a sample GIC issuer, Prudential Life Insurance Company of America.

The separate account is an account established by the insurer to hold the assets of a determinable group of investors. Equity funds, bond funds, real estate funds, and money market funds are typically issued through a separate account. When GICs are issued through the separate account, it is usually done to allow the insurer the ability to better account for the amount of GICs outstanding, including (1) the allocation of supporting assets from the investment department, (2) the management of the asset/liability structure of the guaranteed instruments from other product lines, and (3) better allocation of associated expenses. The use of the GIC separate account becomes one of management and bookkeeping convenience.

In recent years a number of insurance companies have created pension subsidiaries. Many have done so from the segmentation and issuance of pension investment products and/or for tax-related reasons. In this parent/subsidiary relationship, the financial strength of the subsidiary may not be as strong as that

EXHIBIT 2–1
Asset Statement (partial)

---

1.   Bonds
2.   Stocks:
    2.1 Preferred stocks
    2.2 Common stocks
3.   Mortgage loans on real estate
4.   Real estate:
    4.1 Properties occupied by the company
    4.2 Properties acquired in satisfaction of debt
    4.3 Investment real estate
5.   Policy loans
6.   Premium notes
7.   Collateral loans
8.1   Cash on hand and on deposit
8.2   Short-term investments
9.   Other invested assets
10.   Aggregate write-ins for invested assets
10A. Subtotal, cash and invested assets (Items 1 to 10)
11.   Reinsurance ceded:
    11.1 Amounts recoverable from reinsurers
    11.2 Commissions and expense allowances due
    11.3 Experience rating and other refunds due
12.   Electronic data processing equipment
13.   Federal income tax recoverable
14.   Life insurance premiums and annuity considerations deferred and
    uncollected
15.   Accident and health premiums due and unpaid
16.   Investment income due and accrued
17.   Net adjustment in assets and liabilities due to foreign exchange rates
18.   Receivable from parent, subsidiaries, and affiliates
19.   Amounts receivable relating to uninsured accident and health plans
21.   Aggregate write-ins for other than invested assets
22.   Total assets, excluding separate account business (Items 10A to 21)
23.   From separate account statement
24.   Totals (Items 22 and 23)

---

of the parent. The subsidiary may be undercapitalized, with the parent maintaining minimum statutorily required capital and surplus. Many subsidiaries' incomes are derived from single product lines, something that no analyst likes to see. Pyramiding of surplus can result from one dollar of true surplus in the subsidiary company being shown in each and every parent company in the pyramid of companies forming the corporate struc-

EXHIBIT 2-2
The Prudential Life Insurance Company of America Distributions
(December 31, 1990)

			Asset Distribution			
Bonds	Stocks	Mortgages	Real Estate	Policy Loans	Cash	Other
54.6%	6.8%	25.3%	2.7%	5.4%	1.4%	3.8%

	Bond Maturity Distribution			
1 Year or Less	1–5 Years	5–10 Years	10–20 Years	Over 20 Years
9.3%	29.4%	29.5%	17.0%	14.8%

ture. Evaluation of the reinsurance activities can compound the problem since the parent can provide surplus relief through a letter of credit.

In buying from the pension subsidiary, the purchaser must assess the level of protection provided by the parent company, particularly if it is evident that the subsidiary's quality is inferior to that of its parent. Most companies provide some degree of general endorsement. However, vast differences exist with regard to the relative degrees of protection and guarantees from the parent.

Maximum protection is afforded the subsidiary's GICs through a general endorsement by the parent life company. There is an important distinction between endorsement by a *life* company and an endorsement by a *holding* company. Many life insurers have established holding company structures. In many of these structures, the holding company is little more than a shell. The holding company's assets may be primarily invested in its subsidiaries, and hence it provides little, if any, real protection. Insurance regulations at each respective state level dictate the amount that a parent or holding company can withdraw in the form of annual dividends from the subsidiary. Most states allow the parent to withdraw the greater of (a) 10 percent of the previous year-end total surplus or (*b*) the previous year's total statutory earnings. Any amount in excess of these limits requires prior approval by the insurance department in the issuer's state of domicile.

General endorsements differ in levels of protection. Some provide coverage where the parent is legally obligated to cover 100 percent of the subsidiary's liabilities. Others provide guarantees of maintenance of minimum surplus levels in the subsidiary, thus guaranteeing that the subsidiary will never be allowed to become bankrupt, but not guaranteeing 100 percent payback should the subsidiary incur financial difficulties.

In addition, protection differs among carriers due to their legal structuring. The buyer is cautioned to know both the insurer and the contract being issued to ensure a thorough understanding of risks. Legal structuring does not in itself determine quality. Those with the most complicated structuring could be the best in quality. Conversely, those with the simplest structure could be the weakest. Structuring determines the degree of risk, the pecking order of payment, and eventually the amount of payment should carrier insolvency or impairment occur.

WHO ARE THE BUYERS?

Attention in this book is directed primarily to the 401(a) qualified market: pension, profit-sharing, and savings plans. In Chapter 14, the nonqualified marketplace is presented. The remainder of this chapter is directed toward the use of investment contracts in qualified retirement plans.

Who are the buyers of investment contracts?[4] At the plan sponsor level, investment contracts are purchased by those who desire to provide a conduit for a perceived relative risk-free investment, whose returns do not fluctuate. When the participant is given the right to select among several investment options, the stable-value option is often the most popular choice, as evidenced in Exhibit 2–3. Approximately 50 percent of all 401(k)

---

[4]Hereinafter, *investment contracts* refer to both BICs and GICs.

EXHIBIT 2–3
Projected Dollar-Weighted Asset Mix of All Defined Contribution Plans (Q8)

Type of Investment	Total Companies	Over $500 Million	$201–500 Million	$50–200 Million	Under $50 Million
Common Stocks					
Active	12.7%	12.2%	12.7%	15.6%	16.5%
Company stock	24.2%	26.5%	18.1%	12.4%	31.0%
Passive	5.3%	5.9%	3.6%	4.3%	2.2%
Total domestic stocks	42.2%	44.6%	34.3%	32.3%	49.7%
International Stocks					
Active	0.8%	0.9%	0.8%	0.3%	0.5%
Passive	0.3%	0.2%	0.5%	0.3%	0.3%
Total international stocks	1.1%	1.1%	1.3%	0.6%	0.8%
Bonds					
Active	7.7%	8.1%	6.2%	6.4%	7.9%
Immunized or dedicated	0.4%	0.4%	0.7%	0.3%	0.3%
Other passive	0.9%	0.7%	1.3%	1.5%	1.3%
Total bonds	9.0%	9.2%	8.2%	8.1%	9.5%
Other					
Guaranteed Investment Contracts	**38.2%**	**36.6%**	**43.6%**	**40.6%**	**28.0%**
Equity real estate	0.6%	0.6%	0.9%	0.6%	0.8%
Cash and short-term securities	7.1%	5.5%	9.0%	9.5%	8.3%
Other	1.8%	1.5%	2.5%	2.2%	2.9%

Source: Greenwich Associates: *Strengthening Relationships, Improving Performance,* 1992.

assets surveyed are committed to this option. The largest 25 carriers alone have in excess of $100 billion of GICs outstanding as illustrated in Exhibit 2–4. Banks have an estimated $10 billion of BICs outstanding. Exhibit 2–5 provides further insight into BIC/GIC popularity.

Defined benefit plans have not had interest in investment contracts since yields fell below double digits. In addition, their usage was primarily yield-spread driven. Many who bought in the late 1970s and early 1980s dropped out of the market for new purchases when yields declined to single digits. Over inter-

EXHIBIT 2–4
Twenty-Five Largest U.S. GIC Writers by Total GIC Liabilities (December 31, 1990)

Firm	$ millions
Prudential	$ 21,808
Metropolitan Life	17,161
Aetna Life	12,585
John Hancock	9,648
Equitable	8,726
Travelers	8,444
New York Life	8,440
Provident National	6,640
Massachusetts Mutual	4,805
Continental Assurance	4,498
Principal Mutual	4,078
Hartford Life	3,442
Executive Life	3,067
Allstate Life	3,045
Pacific Mutual	2,919
MONY	2,856
Commonwealth Life	2,725
State Mutual	2,535
Connecticut Mutual	2,226
Peoples Security	1,887
Northwestern National	1,780
Sun Life of Canada (U.S.)	1,631
Lincoln National	1,588
New England Mutual	1,446
Home Life	1,433
Total	$139,433

Source: 1990 statutory statements. Canadian insurers not shown due to differences in statutory reporting.

EXHIBIT 2-5
Available Investment Options by Company Size and Plan Asset Size

	Base	Company Stock	Actively Managed Common Stock Fund	Common Stock Index Fund	Money Market Fund	Inter-mediate Bond Fund	Long-Term Bond Fund	Balanced Fund	GIC	BIC	Real Estate Fund	Intern'l Equity Fund	Other
Fortune Rank													
001–100	(37)	89%	49%	70%	43%	19%	11%	24%	86%	30%	0%	5%	5%
101–200	(43)	63%	49%	47%	44%	44%	5%	21%	77%	16%	0%	5%	5%
201–300	(32)	72%	59%	31%	44%	13%	3%	28%	88%	22%	3%	3%	3%
301–400	(20)	50%	75%	20%	60%	40%	0%	40%	70%	10%	0%	5%	0%
401–500	(23)	43%	57%	22%	48%	22%	9%	43%	74%	0%	0%	9%	0%
Industry Rank													
Total industrials	(155)	66%	55%	42%	46%	28%	6%	29%	80%	17%	1%	5%	3%
Total utilities	(78)	76%	62%	35%	37%	28%	9%	28%	64%	8%	1%	5%	6%
Very large utilities	(45)	80%	60%	44%	38%	38%	9%	27%	64%	11%	2%	9%	7%
Large utilities	(27)	70%	59%	26%	33%	19%	7%	30%	56%	4%	0%	0%	7%
Retail	(51)	29%	61%	25%	31%	22%	2%	31%	73%	6%	2%	12%	0%
Transportation	(14)	50%	71%	14%	36%	57%	14%	29%	71%	7%	0%	7%	0%
Diversified services	(29)	62%	69%	38%	38%	31%	10%	34%	69%	14%	3%	10%	0%

29

EXHIBIT 2–5 (concluded)

Plan Assets

	Base	Company Stock	Actively Managed Common Stock Fund	Common Stock Index Fund	Money Market Fund	Intermediate Bond Fund	Long-Term Bond Fund	Balanced Fund	GIC	BIC	Real Estate Fund	Intern'l Equity Fund	Other
Over $1 billion	(78)	81%	49%	63%	37%	37%	9%	28%	85%	23%	0%	8%	5%
$501–1000 million	(54)	56%	65%	43%	46%	31%	7%	31%	74%	20%	2%	7%	4%
$351–500 million	(30)	63%	53%	47%	37%	17%	10%	37%	73%	13%	0%	3%	0%
$251–350 million	(26)	58%	54%	8%	46%	35%	4%	38%	62%	12%	0%	12%	4%
$201–250 million	(35)	40%	71%	37%	54%	26%	6%	34%	74%	6%	3%	6%	6%
$151–200 million	(32)	50%	50%	31%	41%	28%	6%	22%	72%	9%	0%	6%	9%
$101–150 million	(59)	49%	73%	29%	47%	22%	10%	24%	68%	5%	0%	9%	3%
$76–100 million	(50)	28%	68%	18%	48%	22%	6%	30%	70%	6%	0%	3%	4%
$51–75 million	(61)	38%	70%	21%	41%	30%	10%	41%	61%	8%	0%	6%	7%
$41–50 million	(21)	29%	62%	24%	48%	14%	0%	38%	81%	0%	5%	7%	5%
$31–40 million	(26)	31%	81%	12%	46%	19%	27%	38%	85%	0%	15%	0%	8%
$20–30 million	(19)	37%	68%	0%	47%	11%	16%	37%	47%	0%	15%	15%	5%
Under $20 million	(6)	33%	83%	33%	67%	33%	33%	33%	67%	0%	0%	11%	0%
Total companies	(497)	49%	64%	32%	44%	27%	9%	32%	72%	10%	1%	7%	5%

Source: Greenwich Associates, *Strengthening Relationships, Improving Performance*, 1992.

TABLE 2-1
GIC Yield Spreads (Three-Year Maturity)

Year	High Rate	Low Rate	High Spread	Low Spread
1982	16.25%	11.17%	1.86	0.71
1983	12.14%	10.57%	1.78	0.39
1984	13.56%	10.75%	0.82	0.06
1985	11.46%	8.57%	0.64	0.18
1986	8.84%	7.14%	1.02	0.27
1987	9.52%	6.99%	0.68	−0.13
1988	9.63%	8.61%	1.11	−0.43
1989	10.09%	9.61%	0.93	0.37
1990	9.77%	9.27%	0.91	0.35
1991	7.90%	5.58%	0.61	0.28

Source: Yield spreads reflect spreads over equivalent maturity U.S. Treasury issues unadjusted for semiannual versus annualized yields. GIC rate data obtained from The Laughlin Group and T. Rowe Price GIC Index.

vals of a complete market rate cycle, the yield premium pro-vided by the equivalent "private placement" GIC has varied, as illustrated in Table 2–1 and Table 2–2.

In the early 1980s, guaranteed yields approximated the returns expected from the traditional equity and bond markets. If one were to ask their equity managers what the annualized total returns were projected to be over the next three to five years, most managers would have responded: the 14–16 percent range.

TABLE 2-2
GIC Yield Spreads (1982–1991)

Maturity (years)	High	Low	Average
1	2.40%	−0.65%	0.31%
2	2.24%	−0.53%	0.37%
3	1.86%	−0.13%	0.55%
4	2.25%	−0.02%	0.68%
5	2.28%	0.06%	0.79%
7	2.48%	0.05%	0.75%
10	2.77%	−0.17%	0.79%

Source: Yield spreads reflect spreads over equivalent maturity U.S. Treasury issues unadjusted for semiannual versus annualized yields. GIC rate data obtained from The Laughlin Group and T. Rowe Price GIC Index.

Total returns of 12–14 percent were typically projected for bond portfolios. It is no wonder that when a guaranteed annualized compounded return of 14 percent could be negotiated for a five-year period, many pension plans bought investment contracts.

Those pension funds that have always used investment contracts as a part of the investment portfolio have done so for a number of reasons. First, they may have wanted to protect an overfunded status for actuarial purposes. Second, some plan sponsors like to maintain downside protection for a percentage of the portfolio. Third, there has been a shift in focus among many plan sponsors toward a more passive form of management through the use of immunization, portfolio dedication, indexing, and investment contracts.

Defined contribution profit-sharing and money-purchase plans have historically utilized investment contracts for different reasons. Defined contribution plan usage is primarily driven by the principal guarantee and participant-directed book value withdrawal features. The buyers in these plans incorporate investment contracts as a method of smoothing the volatility of returns from one year to the next. Since most defined contribution plans provide at least annual statements of account balances to the participants, the last thing a plan sponsor wants is to answer questions about negative returns. Hence, using investment contracts as a complementary hedging strategy to other asset classes in the portfolio provides downside principal protection.

The use of investment contracts in 401(k) plans could be the sole subject of an entire chapter. With the explosive growth of the 401(k) marketplace in the early 1980s, the asset allocation process was rewritten. When the plan sponsor had the opportunity to shift the burden of asset allocation to the participant via employee-directed plans, the sponsor was only too happy to do so. All the employer had to do was provide investment choices covering a spectrum of risk–return trade-offs with distinct characteristics: an equity fund; and a bond, money market, or stable-value fund. While bond funds are yield-oriented, they also provide fluctuating returns, as illustrated in Table 2–3. Money market funds provide principal protection but lower yields in comparison to GIC funds, as illustrated in Table 2–4

TABLE 2–3
GIC Returns Compared to Bond Returns

Year	Lehman Brothers Intermediate Government/Corporate Index			GIC Average Rates (Four-Year Maturity)		
	Total Return	Yield	Average Maturity	High	Low	Average
1982	26.11%	12.03%	3.7–3.9	16.53%	11.52%	14.31%
1983	8.60%	10.93%	3.8–3.9	12.37%	10.83%	11.69%
1984	14.37%	11.33%	3.8–3.9	13.87%	11.09%	12.56%
1985	18.00%	10.64%	3.9–4.1	11.80%	8.84%	10.40%
1986	13.13%	9.29%	4.0–4.2	9.11%	7.39%	8.03%
1987	3.66%	8.70%	4.1–4.2	9.87%	7.35%	8.34%
1988	6.67%	9.39%	4.2–4.3	9.02%	8.16%	8.59%
1989	12.77%	8.25%	4.2–4.3	9.17%	8.61%	8.89%
1990	9.16%	7.94%	4.2–4.3	9.13%	8.59%	8.86%
1991	14.62%	5.77%	4.2–4.3	8.24%	6.05%	7.61%

Source: GIC rate data obtained from The Laughlin Group and the T. Rowe Price GIC Index. Bond data obtained from "Bond Market Report"—Lehman Brothers.

TABLE 2–4
GIC Rates Compared to Money Market Rates

Year	GIC Average Rates (Two-Year Maturity)			Money Market Yields	Spread Average
	High	Low	Average		
1982	16.40%	10.67%	14.00%	12.23%	1.77
1983	11.86%	9.25%	10.85%	8.58%	2.27
1984	13.23%	10.26%	11.94%	10.04%	1.90
1985	11.02%	8.01%	9.58%	7.71%	1.87
1986	8.43%	6.10%	7.30%	6.26%	1.04
1987	9.17%	6.58%	7.55%	6.12%	1.43
1988	8.62%	7.28%	7.95%	7.10%	0.85
1989	8.97%	8.29%	8.63%	8.90%	−0.27
1990	8.69%	8.11%	8.40%	7.90%	0.50
1991	7.51%	5.04%	6.76%	5.71%	1.11

Source: GIC rate data obtained from The Laughlin Group and the T. Rowe Price GIC Index. Money market yields obtained from IBC/Donoghue's Money Market Fund Averages/All Taxable.

(except in an inverted yield curve environment, which generally occurs in 5 percent or less of an interest rate cycle). With the higher yields, principal protection, and liquidity provided by the stable-value fund, most chose to combine the equity and stable-value options.

Although interest rates have declined from their recent historical highs, the popularity of the stable-value option has not changed. Defined contribution plans, particularly 401(k) employee-choice plans, are maintaining their commitment based primarily on the conservative nature of the typical investor and the positive inflation-adjusted returns provided.

TYPES OF GIC INSTRUMENTS

Many alternative investment contracts exist. The insurance and banking industry has done an excellent job of creating flexible funding instruments.[5] As a result, investment contracts are increasingly being used as substitutes for other fixed-rate instruments. In addition, the user has become more creative in structuring stable-value portfolios to suit better specific fund needs.

Bullet Contracts

A *bullet contract* is the most popular investment contract used because of its simple terms: a lump-sum deposit, a pre-set rate of interest, and a lump-sum payment at maturity. Interest either can be reinvested at the contract rate or can be paid periodically to the contractholder. Bullet contracts can be negotiated on a benefit-responsive basis to provide for the plan's liquidity needs.

---

[5]In Chapter 11, Managing the Stable-Value Portfolio, a more detailed discussion is presented on contract characteristics and how they are typically integrated into the fund's investment strategy.

Window Contract

A *window* accepts recurring deposits, usually from 3 to 12 months, followed by a holding period of one to four years. A rate is committed at contract negotiation for the additional deposits during the window period and continues to be credited throughout the holding period. Windows are utilized primarily for annual cash flows in 401(k) plans because they allow the plan sponsor to communicate a definite rate to the plan participants.

Indexed/Floating-Rate Contracts

Indexed, or floating-rate, contracts provide a rate that changes periodically and is tied to a preestablished market benchmark, usually an established corporate or Treasury bond index. Some provide yields comparable to the short end of the yield curve; some to the longer end. They may be open-ended with predefined "advance notice" contract termination language or they may have a predefined maturity date.

Participating Contracts—Open-Ended

Often referred to as immediate participation guarantee contracts (IPGs) or experience-rated contracts, open-ended participating contracts can provide competitive returns, particularly in declining interest rate environments. As discussed in the previous chapter, these forerunners of the GIC were considered outdated by the early 1980s.

Participating Contracts—Preestablished Maturity

The newer generation of participating contracts has characteristics similar to the older generation contracts except that they typically provide a predetermined maturity date. They may be issued through either the insurer's general account or separate account. The rate is initially set at the point of negotiation and reset periodically (typically annually, based on the prior period's investment experience).

Synthetic/Derivative Investment Contracts

The latest alternative to emerge is the contract that is designed to mimic the traditional investment contract. They are offered primarily by banks and investment firms to compete directly with GICs issued by life insurance companies. Investment advisers, too, are introducing products to compete directly with banking and insurance products. They are often marketed as credit enhancement alternatives and/or rate enhancement alternatives.

CHAPTER 3

BANK INVESTMENT CONTRACTS

David J. Salvin
Vice President, Liability Management
Bankers Trust Company

Bank Investment Contracts (BICs) are a growing component of the stable-value marketplace. BICs are issued by domestic and foreign banks[1] and are designed to offer many of the same features found in traditional GICs.

The term *Bank Investment Contract* has no legal or regulatory meaning; to most people it refers to a form of deposit agreement. The actual legal form of the BIC differs from institution to institution. Banks typically issue BICs either in time deposit or money market deposit account form. The Board of Governors of the Federal Reserve, the primary regulatory body of the banking industry, provides definitions of each form of deposit account in Regulation D.

Most BICs are issued as fixed-rate instruments (although the market demand is growing for floating-rate BICs). They are usually issued as benefit-responsive instruments. They are nonnegotiable. They may contain a window provision, and will probably have an early-withdrawal provision that allows withdrawals to be made before maturity for reasons other than benefit payments after the imposition of a market value

---

[1]Foreign banks typically issue BICs through a New York branch, in U.S. dollars.

adjustment. Each of these salient features of BICs is typically shared by GICs.

If the benefit-responsiveness and window provisions are removed, what remains is a fixed-rate, nonnegotiable instrument that contains some form of early-withdrawal penalty. This instrument is known as a time deposit or nonnegotiable certificate of deposit. It is not inaccurate to call these agreements "BICs," and discussions of different names already have been published in banking texts. When considering nonbenefit responsive BICs, it's also very important to consider if and how they might be accounted for differently from benefit-responsive BICs (see Chapter 4, Accounting Issues).

DIFFERENCES BETWEEN BICS AND GICS

While BICs are considered to be similar to GICs, there are significant differences. These include the industry of the issuer, contract terms and conditions, credit-related differences, plan language and government reporting, and pricing.

ISSUER INDUSTRY

Industry diversification helps explain the relative success BICs have experienced in recent years. Prior to the introduction of BICs, a plan wishing to offer a stable-value option could choose between a fund investing in GICs or a money market fund. Plan sponsors chose GICs because the usually upward-sloping yield curve favored GICs over money market funds.[2] Once the decision to offer GICs was made, the plan was virtually locked in to buying them for every dollar directed to the option. As such, the sponsor was obligated to rely solely on the credit risk of the life insurance industry. Industry diversification was not available.

---

[2]Note: The author uses the comparison of money market funds to GICs for two reasons. First, money market funds are usually valued at a constant or "book value." Second, money market funds provide the same level of benefit-responsive liquidity at the participant level.

With the advent of BICs, industry diversification became possible. For many plans, the ability to diversify industry risk and to increase individual issuer diversification was an attractive and prudent aspect. Many BIC purchases in the late 1980s were driven by this consideration.

But diversification for its own sake is no panacea. At the same time that BICs were becoming popular, a number of large banks saw their credit ratings decline.[3] Many banks were experiencing downgrades and negative press while insurance companies, temporarily at least, remained immune, coupled with the fact that most buyers were more familiar with the intricacies of the insurance industry than with the intricacies of banks. The bank downgrades and poor press went a long way in negating the positive effects of industry diversification that BICs offered.

Contract Terms and Conditions

Contract terms are another point of departure of BICs and GICs. Banks have shown more flexibility in drafting their investment contracts than have insurance companies. BIC agreements must comply with all applicable federal and state regulations but are not reviewed by regulators prior to their issuance. Guaranteed investment contracts must be approved by the insurance regulators in those states in which they are licensed.

GIC agreements typically include annuity purchase language. The rates guaranteed on these annuities are almost without exception unattractive and are rarely used. The existence of these annuity purchase rates, it is argued, is one of the reasons that a GIC is an insurance annuity contract rather than a debt equivalent instrument. BIC agreements do not contain annuity language.

In a BIC agreement, the reader will find provisions related to the depository regulations as required by state and federal

---

[3]Insurance companies were not to experience significant downgrades until approximately two years later, 1990.

regulatory bodies. Most of these provisions have little impact on the operation of the contract. The reader may also find that the language of the BIC agreement is more precise or "legalistic," with primary focus on the issues of contractual governance, not on insurance protection.

Credit-Related Differences

The issue attracting the most attention in the BIC/GIC debate is the question of third-party insurance coverage. BICs offered by domestic banks that are members of the Federal Deposit Insurance Corporation (FDIC) carry the required insurance; certain GICs may carry coverage to varying degrees by state insurance guaranty funds. FDIC coverage is generally considered to apply, under certain conditions, to each beneficial owner (the plan participant) as if he or she were the actual depositor; that is, the coverage "passes through" to each beneficial owner. U.S. branches of foreign banks in most cases are not required to be members of the FDIC and rarely elect to be. Domestic banks that are owned by foreign banks are usually FDIC members.

An FDIC member bank pays assessments to the FDIC, based on the bank's total amount of domestic deposits. (The assessment rate has almost tripled in the short time that banks have been offering BICs.) The high level of FDIC premium is a drawback for issuers and buyers because the amount of the premium is a direct reduction in the rate that can be offered by member banks.

The value of the coverage is open to debate. The majority of the BIC market share has been captured each year by Aaa- and Aa-rated banks; these banks clearly do not need to rely on third-party credit enhancement. Even though lower-rated banks usually pay a higher rate of interest, buyers clearly have not shown a great willingness to supplant a bank's own creditworthiness with that of the FDIC. As such, the higher-rated domestic banks begin with a rate handicap. The fact that these banks captured approximately 10 percent of total new GIC placements in recent years indicates that buyers perceive limited value in the FDIC coverage.[4]

Care must be taken when comparing the relevant asset size between banks and insurance companies. Many buyers make size an important credit consideration in their purchasing decision. The relevant statistic for comparison when looking at issuer size should be the amount of assets standing behind the borrowing obligation. This simple approach has many problems, primarily that it overlooks a consideration of the amount of other liabilities also supported by the same assets. These buyers, on the other hand, correctly identify a bank's reported "total assets" as the amount, less any pledged assets, supporting an unsecured obligation such as a BIC. Applying a similar rule for insurance companies, the correct statistic then would be general account assets, not total assets. Separate account assets, if indeed these assets are not available to meet general account obligations, should not be included in an asset comparison relative to a general account obligation.

Most of the major BIC issuers are larger than the competing middle-tier insurance companies. Larger doesn't necessarily mean better (especially in terms of creditworthiness) but there is an important conclusion concerning diversification of liability sources implicit in this analysis. GIC liabilities make up a considerably larger percentage of all "general account" liabilities for insurance companies than they do for banks. While part of this dichotomy is explained by the fact that insurance companies have been in this business longer, this significant divergence does not have clear ramifications from a liquidity and credit quality standpoint.

Plan Language and Government Reporting

There are just two considerations relative to plan language and government reporting. Older plans whose language has not been brought up-to-date may not permit investment in instru-

---

[4]At this writing, Congress is considering a major banking reform bill. Several versions call for major adjustments in the operation or elimination of the "pass-through" coverage.

ments other than GICs. To allow BIC purchases, a plan amendment may be necessary.

Because Schedule A of Form 5500 (the Department of Labor's required annual report) is applicable only to insurance contracts, BICs are not reported on Schedule A and BIC issuers do not send Schedule A information to investors.

Pricing

Pricing is probably the most important point of departure of BICs from GICs. BIC pricing is *liability* driven, while GIC pricing is typically *asset* driven. Banks view the BIC business primarily as a means of borrowing money and will offer to pay a rate on BICs no greater than the rate the bank is currently paying on other forms of liabilities. Insurance companies view GIC issuance as a spread lending business and base their rates on what they are earning on the assets in which they invest. A buyer with an understanding of the various bank liability markets and of the markets for the assets making up an insurance company's portfolio will have additional insight into the dynamics of spreads between GICs and BICs. The pricing basis is different and rates offered by the two groups differ over time. Similarly, to the extent that different insurance companies invest in different assets and to the extent that different banks have different liability structures, pricing will vary from institution to institution.

THE BIC PROCESS

History of the BIC

The beginning of the BIC market can be traced to early 1987. Several major domestic banks began eyeing the market closely and began active issuance programs. Bankers Trust and Citibank were the earliest entrants. Together, all banks likely borrowed about $250 million in the BIC market in 1987 and about $2 billion in 1988. During 1988, new banks joined the list of "active" BIC issuers, with as many as 25 banks being identified on

Moody's list of credit ratings as active BIC issuers. By 1989, aided by a favorable (i.e., inverted) yield curve and relatively higher-cost alternative liabilities, banks borrowed in excess of $5 billion in the BIC/GIC market.

Subtle changes have occurred in the BIC and GIC markets since 1987. J. P. Morgan entered the business in 1988 and began issuing from its Delaware bank. Soon thereafter, Citicorp was issuing from its Nevada and South Dakota affiliates and Bankers Trust shifted all issuance to Bankers Trust (Delaware). These affiliates had the greatest funding needs in their respective organizations. Not coincidentally, these are also the organizations with the most restricted access to third-party liquidity. Citibank (New York), for example, with its extensive New York City branch network, is able to raise a large amount of deposits relatively quickly and inexpensively. But Citibank South Dakota, on the other hand, is responsible for funding a large and growing book of credit card assets and has little access to liquidity outside of its own corporate parent. BIC deposits are an especially attractive source of funds to these subsidiary relationships.

The number of potential BIC issuers was expanded greatly when Merrill Lynch introduced the concept of the *BIC arrangement* to the market in 1989. Boasting a large network of bank customers and lacking a highly rated bank of its own, Merrill offered to arrange BIC deposits on behalf of client banks, and to protect these banks from the interest rate risk arising from window deposits and benefit-responsive withdrawals. Merrill structured an interest rate swap to help these banks better match their assets and liabilities. Other firms, including Chemical Bank, soon offered similar services. But changes in foreign banks' credit ratings and a rather predictable approach to pricing allowed insurance companies to regain the upper hand.

BIC Pricing

BIC rates, unlike GIC rates, are based on the issuing institution's alternative cost of funds. A bank enters the BIC business primarily for the purpose of raising funds at a competitive cost. There are secondary motivations, including increasing liquidity and the desire to round out a range of services. Most of the variability in BIC pricing can be explained by looking at the yield curve of a bank's own cost of funds. This is different from the approach taken by insurance companies and results in significant opportunities being available at different points on the yield curve.

Most assets of money center banks carry a floating rate of interest. The most common bank assets are loans, interbank assets, trading account assets, and investment securities. Many of these assets carry a floating rate. But BICs typically carry a fixed rate. To avoid risk resulting from an asset/liability mismatch, banks often transform a fixed-rate BIC liability into a floating-rate liability through the use of an interest rate swap. The BIC issuer contracts to pay another firm (the swap "counterparty") a floating interest rate on a "notional" amount of principal (the amount of the BIC deposit). In exchange, the BIC issuer receives from the counterparty a stream of payments at a fixed interest rate on the notional amount. The fixed interest payment received from the floating-rate payor matches the deposit liabilities on the BIC and the net result for the BIC issuer is a floating-rate liability.

The basic rate that a bank pays on a BIC is a function of its floating-rate cost of funds and the so-called "swap spread" or the spread over Treasuries that a counterparty is willing to pay on the fixed side of a swap transaction. From this basic rate a risk margin, representing compensation for the cash flow risk due to benefit-responsiveness or a window feature, is deducted. The pricing process is simple, yet is different enough from the process used by insurance companies to provide increased yield opportunities.

Underwriting

When banks first entered the market, a curious warning was broadcast; the banks do not know what they are doing—they have neither the underwriting experience nor actuarial staff. By comparison, any insurance company that has written a significant amount of GIC business is likely to have mispriced on occasion. It is not a result of not knowing what one is doing;

rather, it is the expected result of rational risk taking. Every firm competing in this market faces a trade-off between risk control and volume of business. It is a direct trade-off; to grow, a firm must either increase the rate it is willing to pay (a certain money-loser from one perspective) or underwrite cases with an increased amount of risk.

This line of reasoning comes to a curious conclusion. Rates offered by insurance companies or banks are inelastic. They are set at or below the maximum rate (determined by reference to alternative funding sources for banks or asset yields for insurance companies) and then pushed up to the maximum levels by competitive forces in the marketplace. That would seem to leave risk taking as the only distinguishing characteristic. Unfortunately for plan participants, years of oligopoly-type control of the GIC market by a small number of major GIC issuers has resulted in the "natural selection" or evolution of only those plans whose risk is deemed acceptable by most of the issuers. Competitive advantage, therefore, arises only through cost control and effective asset selection for an insurance company. For most banks, already operating with a very low cost structure, asset selection is not a variable in the equation and alternative funding cost is a given.

BIC FEATURES

FDIC

No other single topic has generated as much controversy as the implied FDIC protection afforded BICs. The insurance industry, acting through the American Council of Life Insurance (ACLI) has put forward two arguments against pass-through insurance coverage. First is the public policy argument. The ACLI argues that the risks assumed by the FDIC as a result of insuring each BIC deposit are not appropriate for the FDIC, considering its current financial state. Second is the competitive argument: pass-through coverage gives banks an unfair competitive advantage.

Banks have two counterarguments. Their public policy argument is that pass-through coverage has been an important aspect of the FDIC for a long time and that, without this coverage, the FDIC would be less effective in realizing its goal of protecting the individual investor. The banks' competition argument is that investors do not favor banks that offer the coverage over other banks and insurance companies. The result, banks say, is that they are at a disadvantage to the extent of the amount of FDIC premiums on BIC deposits.

The marginal risks assumed by banks by running their BIC programs are not insignificant, but are not of the magnitude that could cause a bank to fail. A review of the breakdown of GIC/BIC liabilities as a percentage of total liabilities reflects that many insurance companies, as evidenced by the management of their own balance sheets, feel that a large amount of GIC liabilities can be undertaken without undue risk to the institution. The rating agencies apparently agree.

The question becomes how much of an advantage do banks have over insurers. Deposits are often attracted to banking institutions whose credit ratings are considerably lower than those of most GIC-issuing insurance companies. Some smaller banks have received an "AAA-L" rating from Standard & Poor's Corporation for their BIC product.[5]

Accounting

FASB 35 is the primary accounting directive for defined benefit pension plans. It has also been extended in its application to defined contribution plans. FASB 35 requires "fair value" accounting for all pension assets, except "contracts with insurance companies," which may be carried at contract value.[6]

Because BICs are not subject to FASB 35, most BIC issuers and buyers have had to look to the terms of the instrument to

---

[5]An AAA-L rating is an AAA equivalent "limited" to the extent of any FDIC insurance protection.

[6]See Chapter 4, Accounting Issues, for standards of the FASB (Federal Accounting Standards Board).

determine proper accounting. For benefit-responsive BICs, most purchasers are taking the position that contract-value accounting is appropriate, basing the defense on participant-initiated withdrawals occurring at contract value.

The argument for nonbenefit-responsive BICs is less straightforward. A nonbenefit-responsive BIC or GIC has no such contract-value liquidation provision. Guidance concerning accounting for nonbenefit-responsive BICs comes from two sources. A nonbenefit-responsive BIC is basically the same instrument as a nonbenefit-responsive GIC and many buyers account for them in the same way. On the other hand, the nonbenefit-responsive BIC is usually the same as or very similar to a nonnegotiable time deposit or certificate of deposit, where there is accounting guidance available for these instruments. The problem is that the guidance is different. This is one of the reasons that the FASB (Financial Accounting Standards Board) took up the question of how to account for both types of instruments in 1990. Curiously, the Emerging Issues Task Force, a "subcommittee" of the Board, failed to resolve the issue when it examined the question in 1988–90.

THE FUTURE

With the continuing heightened credit concerns, the predictable annual 15 percent growth rate for investment contracts appears to be in jeopardy. Participants and many plan sponsors are concerned about the perceived credit deterioration of the financial services sector. To offset these fears and instill a greater degree of confidence, the banking and insurance industries are responding with new and innovative products that not only address the immediate credit concerns, but also facilitate the introduction of professional management techniques and application of modern portfolio theory.

These innovations are referred to as *synthetic* or *derivative* products. The objective is simple: to recreate all or some of the attractive aspects of a GIC while reducing or eliminating the negative aspects.

Bank offerings in the derivative arena are emerging as *synthetics* while insurance company offerings are best described as *participating*.[7] The term *synthetic* is used because the bank products aim to synthesize or recreate the economics of a GIC. A participating product, on the other hand, seeks to share with the contractholder participation in some of the risks that are typically borne solely by the insurance company.

As the names imply, there are significant differences between these two types of products. Participating products offer the investing plan the ability to take advantage of active management of a pool of underlying assets typically held in a separate account.[8] The plan receives the rate of return on the pool, adjusted for any investment gains or losses. The plan thus participates in its own cash flow risk and investment management performance risk. Although the plan does not hold legal title to the securities in the pool, it does bear the credit risk since losses due to default and credit deterioration are passed through to the plan.

In synthesizing a BIC the credit rating of the bank is replaced with that of other borrowers. These borrowers may be the government, its agencies, corporations, or pools representing an ownership interest in a group of assets. A synthetic replicates the important economic aspects of a BIC but at the same time changes or enhances the overall creditworthiness of the package via the identifiable high-quality supporting asset composition.

There are two generic ways in which this can be accomplished. The credit enhancement can be done on a collateralized basis. This technique has been used widely for investment of the proceeds of municipal bond issues. The issuer accepts a sum of money and issues a standard BIC in exchange. Additionally, the issuer posts collateral (usually Treasuries or agencies) which

---

[7]See Chapter 11, Managing the Stable-Value Portfolio.

[8]Insurers issuing participating contracts use both general account and separate account structures. It is generally accepted that a separate account product provides greater protection to the contractholder, assuming the legal structure of the account prohibits access by the insurer in the case of insurer default.

become available to the lender if the borrower defaults under the terms of the BIC agreement.

The second way to accomplish the synthesis is through the use of a benefit-responsive "put." The exact legal form of this type of product varies from firm to firm, but the underlying concept is standard. A BIC contains two distinct components: an investment aspect and a benefit-responsive aspect. The investment aspect is handled by direct ownership of fixed-income securities. Benefit responsiveness is provided by a bank through a redemption feature (the "put") that allows the plan to liquidate the fixed-income investment at book value any time liquidity is needed for benefit purposes. The bank in essence guarantees through the "put" that any investment losses that would result from the liquidation of securities for benefit purposes will be replaced by the bank.

Both methods offer new and exciting opportunities for plan sponsors and intermediaries to improve the performance of the GIC funds. The second method in particular offers important, unique ways of addressing some of the credit and liquidity problems inherent to the marketplace.

SUMMARY

The "guaranteed" market of tomorrow will bear little resemblance to today's market. Strong competitive supply-side forces of the industry, coupled with shifting patterns of demand, will bring additional changes to the two industries.

Participation by banks in the traditional fixed-rate BIC market will continue to be sporadic—a function of a bank's cash needs for loan demand. Synthetic BICs, being tied less to these cash needs, will be a more consistent alternative. Many banks not currently issuing BICs will discover this relatively cheap source of funds and become BIC issuers. This is good for the stable-value marketplace. More players represent more capacity, which is indicative of a healthier market.

The future of the BIC business is dynamic and is being changed by those firms that are developing stable-value alternatives. A review of the evolution of the BIC shows unmistakable parallels with the histories of many other asset classes. Increased liquidity, greater disintermediation, and a need for greater control over credit quality continues to fuel the fire of demand for these alternatives.

CHAPTER 4

ACCOUNTING ISSUES

Samuel F. Beardsley

Vice President
T. Rowe Price Stable Asset Management, Inc.

One of the primary advantages that make GICs attractive to plan sponsors and participants is constant asset value. The marketplace has traditionally recorded these instruments in pension plan financial statements at purchase cost plus accrued interest; also known as *book value* or *contract value*. This accounting treatment has been challenged in recent years, leading to an accounting controversy of significant concern within the industry.

BACKGROUND

The rulemaking body for the accounting profession is the Financial Accounting Standards Board (FASB). The failure of a pension plan's financial statements to comply with FASB guidelines can result in a "qualified" report by the plan's independent accountants that could result in disqualification of the plan.

In 1980, the FASB issued Statement of Financial Accounting Standards No. 35 (*FAS 35*), *Accounting and Reporting by Defined Benefit Pension Plans,* which set forth the accounting standards for defined benefit pension plans. *FAS 35* required that contracts with insurance companies be presented "in the same manner as that contained in the annual report

filed . . . pursuant to ERISA."[1] ERISA requirements permit contract value accounting for unallocated funds held with an insurance carrier.[2] Pension plan accountants interpreted this
language to permit contract value accounting for GICs and similar instruments in all plans. This differed from the *FAS 35* general requirement that plan assets be carried at fair value[3] and
became known as the "exemption for GICs."

The FASB, however, confirmed its position that plan assets
be carried at fair value in *FAS 87*. This statement, which
applies only to defined benefit plans, requires that "other contracts with insurance companies . . . be accounted for as investments and measured at fair value." For some contracts, however,
"the best available evidence of fair value may be contract
value."[4] *FAS 97* stated that "investment contracts issued by an
insurance enterprise . . . do not incorporate significant insurance risk . . . and shall not be accounted for as insurance
contracts."[5] *FAS 106*, which discusses the valuation of plan assets to determine unfunded postretirement benefits, requires
fair value accounting for contracts with insurance companies
that do not "unconditionally undertake a legal obligation to provide specified benefits to specified individuals." It recognizes
that "for some contracts, the best available estimate of fair
value may be contract value."[6]

On December 31, 1990, FASB issued a Proposed Statement
of Accounting Standards, *Disclosure about Market Value of
Financial Instruments* ("Exposure Draft"). This statement requires the disclosure of the market value of financial instruments.[7] It includes investment contracts;[8] however, if
investment contract reporting is in compliance with *FAS 35*, it

---

[1]*FAS 35*, paragraphs 12 and 123.
[2]*Form 5500*, Instruction to line 34c (*xii*) and Schedule A, line 6.
[3]*FAS 35*, paragraph 11.
[4]*FAS 87*, paragraph 62.
[5]*FAS 97*, paragraph 15.
[6]*FAS 106*, paragraph 71.
[7]*FASB*, Exposure Draft, paragraph 10.
[8]*FASB*, Exposure Draft, paragraph 52.

is in compliance with the exposure draft.[9] It is not clear how these statements interact. Conceivably, investment contracts exempted from the market value provisions of *FAS 35* could still be subject to these requirements.

A second accounting regulatory body involved in maintaining accounting standards is the American Institute of Certified Public Accountants (AICPA).The AICPA issued in 1983 the Audit and Accounting guide, *Audits of Employee Benefit Plans* (Audit Guide), which expanded the *FAS 35* treatment of GICs to defined contribution plans. Certified public accountants who audit defined contribution or defined benefit plans must comply with these guidelines in issuing a report on financial statements.

ERISA guidelines require "current value"[10] but permit contract value treatment of unallocated insurance contracts. The Internal Revenue Service requires that fair market value be used by defined contribution plans in the periodic investment valuation required for qualification under 401(c).[11] The Office of the Controller of the Currency (OCC), which regulates bank common trust fund investment in GICs, issued an interpretation[12] requiring the use of fair value for fund valuation purposes and stated they would not automatically accept the conclusion that fair value equals contract value.

In the late 1980s, pension plans began to invest heavily in BICs and other noninsurance company investment contracts. FASB was asked to determine whether the exemption for GICs under *FAS 35* also applied to BICs. FASB's Emerging Issues Task Force met on the subject in January 1989 but failed to reach a conclusion. However, it raised serious concerns about the current accounting treatment for GICs.

In April 1990, the FASB added a project to its agenda to reach a final conclusion on the proper accounting treatment for

---

[9]FASB, Exposure Draft, paragraph 17.

[10]ERISA, Section 103 (b) (3) (A).

[11]IRS, Revenue Ruling, 80–155.

[12]OCC, Trust Interpretation No. 211, March 10, 1989.

investment contracts of all types.[13] The FASB position is expected to establish accounting treatment for a GIC or similar contract, based on the terms of the contract and the type of plan in which the contract is held. A portfolio strategy that invests in GICs must consider these factors if contract value accounting treatment is desired.

CONTRACT VALUE ACCOUNTING

Contract value accounting records the GIC at initial purchase cost plus accrued (credited) interest. For example, a 7 percent compound interest, five-year, bullet contract would be carried at the values shown in Exhibit 4–1 for each year of its life.

EXHIBIT 4–1

	Purchase Cost	Accrued Interest	Contract Value
Initial purchase	$1,000,000	$ 0	$1,000,000
End of Year 1	1,000,000	70,000	1,070,000
End of Year 2	1,000,000	144,900	1,144,900
End of Year 3	1,000,000	225,043	1,225,043
End of Year 4	1,000,000	310,796	1,310,796
End of Year 5	1,000,000	402,552	1,402,552

From FASB discussions a tentative list of conditions for contract value accounting has been established:

• The contract must be a negotiated agreement that provides for a guaranteed return on principal, invested over a specified time period.[14]

---

[13]It should be noted that as of this writing the FASB has not formed its final conclusion on the appropriate accounting treatment for BICs, GICs, synthetics, and derivative alternatives. The guidance in this chapter is based on the published positions as of June 30, 1991, comments made by FASB members at public meetings, and analyses by industry experts.

[14]FASB, Emerging Issues Task Force: Issue Summary No. 89–1, page 1, January 12, 1989.

• The investment contract should provide for limited transferability. If contracts are freely transferable, actual or estimated quotes to acquire the contracts in an arm's length transaction will be the more appropriate value.

• The investment contract should be benefit responsive. Benefit responsiveness is an agreement that permits withdrawals or partial liquidations at contract value for all benefits allowed by the plan. The plan may provide that employer-directed liquidations such as plan terminations be made at market or a penalty value and still be considered benefit responsive.

Of these terms, benefit responsiveness is the most critical to ensuring contract value treatment. Benefit responsiveness clearly distinguishes the investment contract from other short-term instruments such as nonnegotiable certificates of deposit. In addition, it ensures that contract value is used to pay benefits, making reporting any other value in financial statements misleading.

Contract value does not ignore credit concerns. If a loss of principal or interest is anticipated due to a decrease in credit-worthiness of the underlying issuer, a GIC must be revalued to reflect the loss.[15]

MARKET VALUE ACCOUNTING

Market value accounting requires that the GICs be revalued at each scheduled reporting date. If the 7 percent, compound interest, five-year bullet contract mentioned in our previous illustration were valued using a bid-yield method, it would have a changing value depending on the level of interest rates, as shown in Exhibit 4–2.

While there is no prescribed method to determine the fair value of a security, *FAS 35* provides the following guidelines:

> The fair value of an investment is the amount that the plan could reasonably expect to receive for it in a current sale between

---

[15]*FAS 5*, Accounting for Contingencies, paragraph 8.

EXHIBIT 4-2

End of Year	Principal	Accrued Interest	Total	Current Market Yield	Fair Value
1	$1,000,000	$ 70,000	$1,070,000	7%	$1,070,000
2	1,000,000	144,900	1,144,900	6%	1,177,610
3	1,000,000	225,043	1,225,043	6%	1,248,266
4	1,000,000	310,796	1,310,796	8%	1,298,659
5	1,000,000	402,552	1,402,552	8%	1,402,552

a willing buyer and a willing seller, that is, other than in a forced or liquidation sale.

Fair value shall be measured by the market price if there is an active market for the investment. If there is not an active market for an investment but there is such a market for similar investments, selling prices in that market may be helpful in estimating fair value. If a market price is not available, a forecast of expected cash flows may aid in estimating fair value, provided the expected cash flows are discounted at a rate commensurate with the risk involved.[16]

This is the required method for the valuation of assets in defined benefit plans. Its primary focus, however, is marketable securities and it provides little guidance for investment contracts. Other sources of guidance are other FASB pronouncements, the Securities and Exchange Commission, the AICPA Audit Guide, and the OCC. A list of the factors used to determine fair value is set forth in Table 4-1.

Although the regulatory bodies adequately state the factors affecting market value, they provide little guidance on how to quantify the impact of an economic event. Thus the determination of fair value is a highly subjective process.

SUMMARY

As this book goes to press, this chapter remains incomplete. FASB has yet to reach definitive conclusions on the issue of contract value and has requested that the American Institute of

---

[16]*FAS 35*, paragraph 11.

TABLE 4–1
Factors to Consider in Establishing Fair Value

Factor	Source
1. Current sales price	1
2. Market price if active market	1
3. Market price of similar investments if no market	1
4. Forecast of cash flows or yield to maturity	1
5. Cash surrender or conversion value (insurance contracts)	2
6. Contract value (insurance contracts)	2
7. Changes in economic conditions	3
8. Financial condition of the issuer	3,6
9. Nature and duration of restrictions on disposition	3,4
10. Liquidity-ability to meet redemption payments	3,4
11. Financial models (option or matrix pricing models)	5

1. *FAS 35*, Par. 11.
   Audit Guide, Par. 3.12.
   FAS 87, Par. 49.
   FAS 106, Par. 65.
   SEC, Accounting Series Release 118.
   FASB, Exposure Draft, Par. 5., 11., and 28.
2. *FAS 87*, Par. 62.; FASB 106, Par. 71.
3. Audit Guide, Par. 2.8.
4. OCC, Trust Interpretation 211.
5. FASB,Exposure Draft, Par. 11.
6. FASB, Exposure Draft, Par. 28.

Certified Public Accountants (AICPA) become involved in the "book value" question.

This issue has provided one of the greatest challenges to the BIC/GIC marketplace. Loss of contract value would change the investment perspective of millions of plan participants. It would impact the capital markets, possibly destroying a $200 billion marketplace. Banks and insurers would have to look for product alternatives to replace the income stream generated from this income source.

It has been proven that plan participants do not like volatility or to lose money with their retirement assets. This explains the popularity of the guaranteed marketplace. Hopefully, regulators will recognize the importance of continuing this *stable-value* option.

CHAPTER 5

QUALITY—ANALYZING THE LIFE INSURANCE INDUSTRY[1]

Allan G. Richmond, FSA
Vice President and Principal
T. Rowe Price Stable Asset Management, Inc.

As the GIC market has grown and matured, the interest in and understanding of the underlying quality of the insurer(s) has increased. This interest and understanding has been fueled by the attention in recent years given by the trade press and their focus on the acceleration in junk bond defaults and by the writedowns in the commercial real estate portfolios of many insurers. Hence, many GIC investors have learned that the quality of the GIC issuer should be viewed in the same manner as issuer quality is viewed in the purchase of other fixed-income, debt-equivalent issues.

The quality of the GIC carrier is nothing more or less than the likelihood that it will be able to honor its commitments. That ability depends on the contract provisions, the carrier's investment strategy, net worth, the quality and liquidity of the assets, and the profitability of its various lines of business.

In the past, buyers relied on carrier size as the primary test for quality. Strength and size were viewed as being synonymous. Size, however, only implies substantial staying power to "weather the storm," if one believes in the "deep pockets" theory.

---

[1] Parts of this chapter were originally contributed in the first edition by Peter Chapman, FSA.

The Society of Actuaries identifies four major risks for insurance companies. These risks include asset default risks (C1 risks), pricing inadequacy and mortality risks (C2 risks), interest rate risks for both reinvestment and disintermediation (C3 risks), and management risks (C4 risks). The quality of the carrier research is determined by the basis on which the review of these risks is conducted. Professional analysts agree that in addition to performing the standard financial ratio analysis, the structure of the organization needs to be evaluated, all inherent risks identified and evaluated, and the lines of business reviewed independently.

Before exploring the intricate aspects of insurance company credit research, an understanding of the general issues is essential. In the absence of such understanding, one can easily become confused because the insurance industry operates under a much different accounting and regulatory environment than the traditional corporate entity.

GENERAL ISSUES

Accounting

The insurance departments of all states require uniform reporting under the prescribed statutory accounting basis. An annual calendar year report (or convention statement) is required to be filed in all states where the carrier is licensed. See Exhibit 5–1 on pages 106–8 for an outline of the statutory statement.

Statutory accounting differs significantly from generally accepted accounting principles (GAAP) and produces an entirely different picture of the financial status of the company. GAAP accounting attempts to match revenues with expenses. Statutory accounting is based on a liquidation model of accounting, measuring the ability of the insurance company to pay future claims, with its primary goal being to help regulators monitor the solvency of the carrier and to identify early signs of difficulty. Considerable emphasis is placed on the adequacy of surplus. The following examples illustrate the significant differences between statutory and GAAP reporting.

• Under statutory accounting, acquisition costs (underwriting, policy issue and agent's commission expenses) must be expensed in the year in which the policy is issued. GAAP recognizes these expenses as capital costs and requires them to be amortized in accordance with the financial standards issued by the Financial Accounting Standards Board in December 1987, "Accounting and Reporting by Insurance Enterprises for Certain Long-Duration Contracts and for Realized Gains and Losses from the Sale of Investments" (FASB 97). Specifically, for universal life and other interest-sensitive life insurance policies, acquisition costs are amortized over the lives of the policies in relation to the present value of estimated gross profits from surrender charges and investment, mortality, and expense margins. For traditional life, health, and annuity policies, acquisition costs are amortized over the premium-paying period of the related policies, using assumptions consistent with those used in computing policy reserves. A company that writes an enormous amount of business in any one year will show reduced or negative earnings for that year on its statutory statement regardless of how profitable that business may prove to be in the long run.

• Statutory accounting produces a distortion of the true net worth of the insurer. The assets of the company do not reflect the true market value. Bonds and preferred stocks, for example, are reported at amortized costs. Should the company ever be forced to liquidate all or a part of these assets, the liquidation value could be much different from the value of the security carried by the company on its books.

Other differences between statutory accounting and GAAP include the following:

1. Certain assets and investments recognized under GAAP are not admitted under statutory accounting practices. Principal among these are certain loans and receivables, investments not authorized by statute or in excess of statutory limitations, and furniture and equipment.

2. Income tax effects due to differences between tax and book accounting are not, in all cases, recognized under statutory accounting. With one notable exception resulting from the Omnibus Budget Reconciliation Act of 1990 (OBRA), which became law on November 5, 1990, accounting for income taxes generally is on an incurred basis. That exception requires insurance companies to amortize policy acquisition expenses on a straight-line basis over a 120-month period. The amount of amortizable acquisition expenses is to be based on a specified percentage of premiums and will vary by category of insurance contract.

3. The carrying value of investments in subsidiaries is limited, as prescribed by the National Association of Insurance Commissioners.

4. The methods of accounting for certain aspects of reinsurance under GAAP may vary from statutory accounting.

5. Under statutory accounting, life insurance companies are required to establish a Mandatory Securities Valuation Reserve (MSVR), which is maintained to cushion the company against fluctuations in the value of its bonds, preferred stocks, and common stocks. Beginning with the December 31, 1992 statutory statement, the MSVR will be replaced with an asset valuation reserve (AVR) and an interest maintenance reserve (IMR). In addition to the asset categories already covered by the MSVR, the AVR will require a reserve for mortgage loans and real estate. This change to the MSVR will be phased in over a three- to five-year period.

The IMR is a reserve for realized capital gains and losses taken after January 1, 1992. These capital gains or losses are due to interest rate changes as opposed to credit quality changes. Such capital gains or losses—which currently flow directly into statutory income and, in turn, are added to capital and surplus—will become part of the IMR and will be amortized into statutory income over the remaining lifetime of the security sold. Gains and losses from credit quality changes, on the other hand, will continue to be recognized immediately into statutory income.

Regulation

An understanding of regulation is important. Insurance companies abide by regulations at the state level. A carrier must be licensed in each state where it does business. Most states either pattern exactly or follow closely the requirements of the New York Insurance Department, considered to be the strongest of all state regulatory departments.

Some insurance companies voluntarily elect not to become licensed in New York. Their reasons may vary and should not be confused with a lack of quality. Many are not willing to meet the reserving requirements imposed or to limit commissions and other agency-related expenses. Many do not wish to carry the burden of the extra administrative or regulatory requirements.

New York is unique in at least four major regulatory initiatives. Section 213 of the insurance code sets limitations on commissions and other field compensation. Section 81 imposes limitations on the types of assets that can be held in the general account. Regulation 102 prohibits certain types of reinsurance transactions. Regulation 126 requires a demonstration of matching of assets and liabilities for all annuity products, including GIC contracts, and interest-sensitive single premium life products.

In addition to the regulation at the state level, there is the National Association of Insurance Commissioners (NAIC), an association of the 50 insurance commissioners throughout the United States. Long considered the unofficial watchdog of the industry, this group attempts to promote harmony within the industry. It has no regulatory status and acts only as an advisory body. It recommends model laws and regulatory issues important in maintaining consistency between the thousands of licensed insurance companies. For example, New York Regulations 102 and 126 have served as the model for NAIC legislation, which will likely be approved by all the states within the next year or two.

The Insurance Regulatory Information System (IRIS) developed by the NAIC assists the state insurance departments in regulating the insurance companies licensed within each respective state. IRIS's main function is to monitor these companies through the statistical and analytical review based on the input from the annual statutory statement. It seeks to identify those companies that may be headed for financial difficulties. This is done by first ranking the companies by the number of ratios which do not fall within the prescribed benchmark range. The companies with the most ratios outside the prescribed ranges are then individually reviewed for potential problems.

Although life insurance companies are currently regulated at the state level, there is increasing concern in Congress that the NAIC and the various state regulators are either unable or unwilling to properly regulate insurer solvency. Therefore, the United States General Accounting Office (GAO) is investigating whether a future solvency regulatory system should be established on a national level.

In response to the concern about federal supervision, the industry is in the process of developing "risk-based capital" regulations. The purpose of the regulations is to impose capital requirements on life insurance companies based on the risks on both the asset and liability sides of the balance sheet. Hence, reserve factors will take into account the credit and price risks of the various asset classes as well as the underwriting and interest rate risks of the various types of liabilities.

The intent of this regulation is to allow regulators to determine capital adequacy and to better monitor solvency, rather than as a means to rank companies. The risk-based capital formulas for life insurance companies are currently being reviewed by the industry. It is expected that the regulations will be finalized during 1992 and will become effective in 1993.

A final layer of protection for policyholders is the state guaranty funds that indemnify losses incurred by policyholders of insolvent companies. In reality, a state insurance department will usually first attempt to arrange for another insurer to assume the business of the troubled company. If that does not work, the state insurance department will assess insurers in the state to pay off the obligations of the insolvent company.

However, the state guaranty system is not uniform. The District of Columbia has no guaranty association coverage, and another 15 states that have coverage specifically exclude GICs. Moreover, states have different limits on the level of coverage, and some states only provide coverage for residents of the state. Table 5–1 here summarizes the status of each state's GIC protection at the end of 1990.[2]

---

[2]The table data is believed to be correct. However, research was based in significant part on secondary sources. Counsel of an attorney familiar with guaranty association matters should be sought in specific cases.

TABLE 5–1
Fifty-State Survey of Guaranty Association Protection

Category 1—States Specifically Covering GICs

Alaska	Illinois	New Jersey	Ohio
Arkansas	Iowa	New York	Texas
Connecticut	Michigan	North Carolina	Utah
Delaware	Mississippi	North Dakota	Washington
Georgia			

Category 2—States Specifically Excluding GICs

California	Kansas	Missouri	South Dakota
Colorado	Kentucky	Nevada	Tennessee
Hawaii	Louisiana	Oklahoma	Virginia
Idaho	Massachusetts	Oregon	

Category 3—States Not Having Guaranty Association Coverage

District of Columbia

Category 4—States Where Statute is Not Specific

—4A: States Where Lower Court Judicial Decision Extends Coverage to GICs

Indiana
Minnesota

—4B: No State Judicial Decision

Alabama	Montana	Pennsylvania	Vermont
Arizona	Nebraska	Puerto Rico	West Virginia
Florida	New Hampshire	Rhode Island	Wisconsin
Maine	New Mexico	South Carolina	Wyoming
Maryland			

INSURANCE COMPANY CREDIT RESEARCH

The insurance industry has traditionally been slow to change. The stoic nature of the life insurance industry, the general conservative investment posture taken by most insurers, and the inability of the mutual companies (the majority of GIC issuers) to follow aggressive corporate structuring due to limited availability of new capital, have historically forced the industry along a road of slow movement. However, the recent trends, which find insurance companies focusing on investment-type products and competing with other types of financial institutions for savings dollars, have substantially quickened the pace of change. Investment philosophies have become more aggressive, product profit margins have narrowed, and mutual companies have begun to contemplate demutualization as a means to raise public capital.

In light of these changes, credit research should be directed toward the insurance company's investment strategy, the size and composition of the company's net worth, the quality and liquidity of the company's assets, and the company's earnings potential. Each of these areas is discussed in the following sections.

Investment Strategy

In the earlier years of GICs, investment strategies of the insurance companies were simple, calling for the accumulation of long-term, interest-bearing assets—all intended to be held to maturity. Liquidity was not a concern. Hence the industry became a major player in the private placement and commercial mortgage markets. Investment performance was measured by current yield, since market valuations, active trading, and asset/liability mismatches were unheard of and not a concern during a stable interest rate environment. "Buy and hold" was the strategy considered a sound investment approach at the time.[3] Then things changed. Interest rates became more volatile.

If a carrier were to pursue a risk-free strategy, the carrier would fund each GIC with a noncallable government bond scheduled to mature on the same date as the GIC. While this zero-risk strategy would earn a 100 percent quality rating, it would attract business only from the totally risk-averse purchaser. In the GIC marketplace, the emphasis is on guaranteed yield with the environment being intensely competitive.

To attract GIC revenues, the carrier must offer a competitive yield. This is accomplished by pursuing a credit or an

---

[3]Moody's Investors Service, "Moody's Industry Outlook—Life Insurance," August 1988.

investment risk, or mismatching the cash flow timing of the asset and the liability, or both.

Buying non–Treasury instruments introduces a risk of default. Suppose, for example, that a bond issued by the XYZ Corporation is deemed to have a 1 percent risk of default. Suppose further that a default would reduce its book value by 50 percent. The expected default loss is 50 basis points, an expected loss that must be recovered from the insurer's general assets.

The intensity of the competition makes it almost certain that many insurers are backing a portion of their GIC obligations with instruments at or below the minimum investment-grade quality. High-yield, or "junk" bonds, have become extremely controversial, especially in light of the deterioration in value of many such issues during 1990 and 1991 and the depletion of statutory surplus resulting from the writedowns of these securities. At issue is the probability of default and the post-default value of the instrument. Does the risk premium in the yield compensate adequately for the expected loss of value?

Now that lower-quality bonds have been publicly traded for a reasonable period of time, more sophisticated and timely information is available on these high-yield bonds. For example, *The Wall Street Journal,* beginning in January 1991, has provided daily statistics on the "junk" bond market using figures compiled by Salomon Brothers, Inc. In addition, Salomon Brothers has a PC-based service that provides daily price quotes on approximately 400 of the most actively traded high-yield bonds, and monthly quotes on approximately 1,000 high-yield bonds.

In addition to quality risks, the appraisal of investment strategy must also include timing risks. A switch from noncallable to callable bonds can increase both the yield and the likelihood of a call, or redemption, during a period of declining interest rates. The risk is inadequacy of the call premium, which is often unable to compensate for the lower yield on the reinvested proceeds.

The deliberate mismatch goes beyond callability. This is a strategy for increasing the credited yield and the profit margin by attempting to anticipate changes in interest rates between the date of issue and the date of maturity of the GIC.

If the carrier expects interest rates to decline over the next five years, it can fund a five-year GIC with a seven-year bond. At the GIC's maturity, the bond can be sold at a price dictated by current yield rates, and the carrier's yield will be supplemented by the realized capital gains. On the other hand, if the insurer expects rates to increase, it may purchase a three-year bond and reinvest the proceeds at a higher-yield rate for the remaining two years. If the insurer's forecast of future interest rates proves wrong, the impact on the company will depend on any hedge instruments it may have acquired to modify its losses, or more importantly, its overall net worth and the quality and liquidity of its general account assets.

A final note about GIC investment strategy: It is desirable for the insurer to avoid introducing reinvestment-yield increases into its pricing calculations. For that reason, zero coupon bonds and bullet mortgages (single-sum payment at maturity, including principal and interest) are popular funding vehicles for GICs.

If GIC deposits exceed the availability of such instruments, a technique called "stripping" is generally used to reduce the reinvestment risk. Stripping consists of buying a bond with regularly scheduled coupon payments and selling these coupons internally (for a consideration determined by the current investment yield) to the unit within the same insurer that is responsible for making monthly payments to retirees and other annuitants. Stripping, in effect, converts a regular instrument into a zero coupon bond.

If stripping does not solve the problem, the carrier must decide how much the guaranteed interest rate has to be reduced to reflect reinvestment risk. Table 5–2 indicates that while the net yield can absorb considerable declines in the reinvestment rate, extreme reductions are a significant risk.

Insufficient allowance for declining reinvestment yields can leave the GIC contractholder dependent on the general resources of the insurer.

Up to now we have assumed implicitly that all GICs will be held to maturity. It is not always possible or desirable to do so. The pension or 401(k) plan for which the GIC is an invested asset may be terminated or curtailed. The assets may have to be

TABLE 5–2
Annual Coupon Purchased at Par

Coupon Rate	Reinvestment for Coupons	Maturity Period Effective Annual Yield Rate		
		3 Years	5 Years	7 Years
8%	4%	7.71%	7.47%	7.25%
8%	6%	7.86%	7.73%	7.61%
12%	4%	11.19%	10.53%	9.99%
12%	8%	11.59%	11.25%	10.96%
12%	10%	11.79%	11.62%	11.47%

redeployed for business reasons. Or, if the company has a subsidiary which has been sold, the assets may be transferred to the 401(k) plan of the acquiring company. Alternatively, rising interest rates and future cash flow requirements may make it advisable to cashout the GIC before it matures.

In general, most GICs provide for a market value adjustment upon premature surrender (see appendix on page 109). The terms of the contract define the process of determining the market value of the underlying assets. A few carriers reserve the right to refuse all GIC cashouts prior to maturity. Since such an action could adversely affect the carrier's future marketing efforts, it is presumed that this extreme prohibition will be restricted to the type of large-scale disintermediation that is likely to occur during a sudden, sharp spike in interest rates.

Not all assets backing GICs can be sold. Private placement bonds and bullet mortgages have limited secondary markets, or none at all. The insurer's ability to meet substantial premature cashout demands may, consequently, depend on its ability to absorb liquidation losses and on the liquidity and quality of its non-GIC assets.

Net Worth

The net worth of an insurance company is the amount by which its assets exceed its liabilities. The amount of assets depends on the method of valuation, that is, market value, amortized value, cost, etc. The amount of liabilities also depends on the method of valuation, that is, are the reserves backing the insurance policies based on the net level method, the Commissioners Reserve Valuation Method (CRVM), or some combination thereof? Hence, net worth clearly is a matter of judgment.

Regulatory financial reporting limits the range of net worth (called "statutory net worth") by prescribing the basis of valuation of invested assets (bonds at amortized cost, preferred stocks at cost, common stocks at market, mortgages at amortized cost, and real estate at cost less accumulated depreciation) and a minimum basis of valuation for reserves. Because statutory accounting is generally more conservative than generally accepted accounting principles (GAAP), statutory net worth is usually lower than the net worth reported to stockholders. For mutual life insurance companies, only statutory net worth is reported (see Exhibit 5–2 for the capital and surplus levels for major U.S. GIC issuers as of December 31, 1990).

When one assesses the insurer's financial resources, statutory net worth—despite its shortcomings—is the most appropriate measure to determine the insurer's protection against adverse fluctuations in the company's assets, in its mortality and morbidity experience, in its investment yield experience, and in its ability to expand, either through acquisitions or through writing new business. The insurer's continuing solvency depends on its ability to satisfy its state of domicile so that it meets its minimum statutory surplus requirements. The higher a company's surplus in relation to its liabilities, the stronger the company. A high ratio of statutory surplus to statutory liabilities means that the company is more likely to have resources to overcome adverse financial results due to:

- Improper pricing (i.e., inadequate profit margins due to understating the level of future mortality/morbidity and expenses and/or overstating the level of future interest rate spreads).
- Asset default or deterioration in value.
- Changes in either the level of interest rates or the shape of the yield curve.

"Surplus strain" from issuing new business can add extra burdens to the carrier and hence impact net worth and earn-

EXHIBIT 5–2
**U.S.* GIC Issuers (Capital and Surplus Position, December 31, 1990,
Excluding the Mandatory Securities Valuation Reserve)**

	Amount (MMs)		Amount (MMs)
Aetna Life	$1,760	New England Mutual Life	551
Allstate Life	800	New York Life	2,405
Commonwealth Life	243	Northwestern National Life	290
Connecticut General	1,067	Ohio National Life	125
Connecticut Mutual	465	Pacific Mutual Life	309
Constitution Life	102	Pan-American Life	105
Continental Assurance Company	846	Penn Mutual Life	195
Equitable Life	1,124	People Security Life	189
Executive Life	474	Principal Mutual Life	1,143
General American Life	232	Protective Life	155
Hartford Life	321	Provident Mutual Life	173
Home Life	171	Provident National (Pension	
John Alden Life	131	Subsidiary of Provident Life	
John Hancock Life	1,417	and Accident)	198
Life of Georgia	188	Prudential Life	5,393
Life of Virginia	314	Reliance Standard Life	115
Lincoln National	907	Safeco Life	191
Massachusetts Mutual Life	1,192	Security Life of Denver	220
Metropolitan Life	4,306	State Mutual Life	216
Minnesota Mutual Life	196	Sun Life of America	300
Mutual Benefit Life	439	Transamerica Occidental Life	440
Mutual of New York	581	Travelers Life	2,010
National Home Life	363	Union Labor Life	63
Nationwide Life	391	United of Omaha	299

*Canadian carriers not shown due to difference in reporting formats. Major Canadian GIC issuers include Canada Life, Confederation Life, Crown Life, Great-West Life, Manufacturer's Life, and Sun Life of Canada. The above list is believed to be representative of the GIC marketplace and may exclude some carriers who have been recent entrants, or who are currently not active in issuing GICs.

ings. On life insurance policies, because of the large first-year commissions and other acquisition costs, such as issue and underwriting, insurers usually pay out $1.25 to $2.00 for every $1.00 of first-year premium received. On annuity contracts, including GICs, when interest rates are credited in excess of the NAIC annually determined valuation interest rates, the excess necessary for providing the additional required reserve is funded from surplus, thus producing the "strain."

A company's net worth normally comprises (1) a limited amount of Common Capital stock, which was used to capitalize the organization when it was formed, (2) unassigned surplus, which is the surplus produced from the insurance and investment operations of the company and reflects the profitability of the company's lines of business, and (3) gross paid in and contributed surplus, which are basically contributions from a parent company to augment the unassigned surplus.

There are no restrictions or conditions associated with *unassigned surplus*. However, *gross paid in and contributed surplus* may be in the form of surplus notes or surplus debentures that may have annual/periodic interest payback requirements or that may have a schedule that requires repayment of principal and interest over a specified period of time. Since the interest and, especially, principal repayments would have an impact on the growth of surplus, it is important to understand the components of net worth before making a final assessment about the absolute level.

QUALITY AND LIQUIDITY OF ASSETS

The tendency to seek higher interest rates through lower quality assets could lead to significant losses under certain economic scenarios. The danger to solvency depends on the proportion of high-yield instruments, their quality (there are substantial gradations of quality even among so-called "junk" bonds), the level of interest rates, and the rate of growth of the national economy. While the degree of risk is not always predictable, the quality of an insurer is clearly linked to the combination of its net worth and the quality of its assets. A company with a high net-worth-to-liabilities ratio is in a better position to hold a lower-quality asset portfolio than an otherwise comparable company with a lower ratio.

It is easier to rate the quality of an insurer's assets than it is to rate their liquidity. The latter is important when interest rates have increased and cash flow has turned negative. Specifically, interest rates significantly above current crediting levels can lead to increased surrender demands that, in turn, may require sales of assets. If the insurer is required to sell assets that are far from their maturity dates, substantial capital losses can result. If the situation is sufficiently severe, the insurer's continued survival can be endangered.

Excessive liquidity can be equally dangerous when interest rates are falling. As assets mature, it may not be possible to reinvest the proceeds at a rate that will allow the insurer to honor its guarantees without incurring a loss. This further supports the need for proper asset/liability management.

Appropriate but not excessive degrees of liquidity are necessary for all of the insurer's assets, not just those backing the GICs. A considerable investment in private placement bonds or large, uninsured mortgages can cause severe liquidity strains. The need to sell assets can exacerbate the strains on net worth resulting from debt instruments issued by financially troubled entities.

Evaluating the quality and liquidity of an insurer's assets has become an increasingly complex task. New asset classes, or variations of existing ones, seem to crop up with regularity. For example, the last few years have seen collateralized mortgage obligations (CMOs), bank loan participations (BLPs), and asset-backed securities (ABSs) become part of many insurers' asset portfolios. Just as with any asset group, the degree of creditworthiness of these securities varies considerably between issuers and demands the same degree of credit scrutiny as the more traditional investment classes.

In addition, just because an insurer's liquidity is high or low does not necessarily mean that it is good or bad; that is, an insurer's liquidity must be viewed in relation to its liabilities. If a company has a substantial amount of GICs or single-premium deferred annuities or medical expense business, which have relatively large cash demands for withdrawals, a higher-than-average degree of liquidity would be appropriate. If, on the other hand, a company has a substantial amount of life insurance or terminal funded annuities or structured settlements on its books, where current cash demands are less and/or more predictable, a lower-than-average degree of liquidity would be called for. Again, an asset/liability model would be the appropriate tool to use to determine whether or not there is a mismatch that would cause problems for the company under certain interest rate scenarios.

Exhibits and schedules supporting the insurer's annual statement, filed annually with the regulatory authorities, provide substantial detail. Quality of bonds and preferred stocks can be measured on a relative scale by the strength of the statutory ratings determined by the Standard Valuation Office of the NAIC.

Mortgages, however, can be evaluated only by the absence of defaults. A distribution of mortgages by state is available as well as a listing of mortgages with interest past due more than three months, mortgages in process of foreclosure, and mortgages transferred to real estate as properties acquired in satisfaction of indebtedness. The information by state is helpful, since often mortgage/real estate problems are limited to certain states or regions of the United States. The delinquency information is useful for comparing insurers' experience on a relative basis with one another and to compare a company's results with industry averages.

Earnings

The standard methodology of any research analyst is to focus on the earnings potential of the company. Earnings projections and return on assets or equity calculations are based on the perceived long-term track record of management. A GIC contractholder is associated with the company for a relatively short period of time—two to five years on average. Thus, an argument can be made that in assessing GIC protection in the short term, primary attention should be given to the balance sheet (i.e., the general account—and separate account if those are the assets supporting the GIC—and the protection afforded through the assets that comprise the general account).

Annuity contractholders are in a somewhat different position. Association with the carrier is generally for a longer period of time. Thus, both the balance sheet items and income statement items are important—balance sheet foremost and income statement secondary.

The best way to understand the earnings potential of an insurance company is to first look at the environment in which the insurer's lines of business are operating and then analyze the profit margins of the products which make up the line. Life insurance companies are primarily in three lines (discussed below): individual life insurance, group life and health, and individual and group annuity and asset accumulation.

Individual Life Insurance

The key issues affecting this line are:[4]

• Investment requirements to support product development and distribution systems will continue to rise, placing margin pressure on less-efficient carriers.

• In the small-business/professional market, breadth of product portfolio is required to attract and retain a tried distribution force. Moreover, this market remains highly dependent on various tax advantages, which continue to be at risk.

• Mortality risk in the term insurance market continues to be a concern, primarily as a long-term profitability issue rather than as a solvency/viability concern.

• Cost control and persistency are becoming increasingly important elements of success as new business volume is sluggish.

The major products within the line are traditional whole life insurance, term insurance, fixed- and flexible-premium universal life insurance, and variable life and variable universal life insurance.

Older blocks of traditional whole life insurance tend to be the most profitable because acquisition costs have been expensed many years before, and the systems used to administer the business are in place, with little additional investment in systems development required. In addition, the policies are being credited with fixed interest rates in the 3 percent to 4 percent range, and the mortality assumptions used to price the product many years before are usually conservative. This means that the company should earn substantial investment margins

---

[4]Moody's Investors Service, "Life Insurance Industry Outlook," July 1990.

on the product, and the death claims incurred should be below those projected when the product was developed.

Term insurance tends to be a more volatile product. Profitability is usually correlated with the company's mortality experience. Since a majority of this business was issued in the 1980s, when companies were aggressively competing for sales, mortality margins were often low, and insurers hoped that large volumes of new issues would enable them to reach their profit goals. In addition, because term insurance premiums are significantly lower than whole life premiums, this business has an above-average exposure to claims from the disease AIDS. Life insurance companies today have more stringent underwriting requirements for new policies, but still face a large exposure from in-force business written in the mid-1980s and prior.

Fixed- and flexible-premium universal life insurance and variable life and variable universal life insurance have, for the most part, been only marginally profitable. These products are more complex to market and to administer—they require expensive investment in support systems to administer the business efficiently. Moreover, since a portion of the excess investment earnings are credited to policyholders, there is additional pressure on profit margins. Only the companies that have a large block of business in force, usually more than 100,000 policies, over which to spread the substantial amount of fixed administrative and systems costs, will be consistently profitable. In many instances, the profits from the older, traditional business subsidize this block until it has reached "critical mass."

Because of the wide variability in both the original pricing assumptions used by insurance companies and the companies' current mortality, lapse, investment, and expense experience, there is no simple answer as to the rate of return being earned on specific products. From industry statistics, we do know that the after-tax return on premiums for individual life insurance was above 10 percent in the 1970s and has gradually decreased to about 6 percent in the late 1980s. An educated guess would be that the traditional block of life insurance products sold in the 1970s and prior has an after-tax return in the range of 10 percent to 15 percent; the more current traditional and term products have a return in the range of 2 percent to 5 percent; while the more contemporary universal life and variable life insurance products are in the range of -2 percent to 2 percent, largely due to the unrealistically low per-policy expenses used in the pricing assumptions compared to the large overhead required to support this business.

Group Life and Health

The key issues in this line are:[5]

• Although this segment is currently enjoying a cyclical recovery, there is nothing to suggest that the next downturn will not be difficult for companies with fundamentally weak positions (inadequate scale) in this segment.

• Managed care operations of large carriers continue to show losses and have not yet demonstrated effectiveness in cost control.

• Several large providers have attempted to consolidate their positions over the past few years. Continued consolidation in the group market is likely.

• This sector of the insurance industry faces significant political and regulatory risks if it cannot find productive solutions to society's health care problems, such as the uninsured population and the absolute level of health insurance premiums for small business.

• Business continues to drift to managed care; this situation limits the upside profit potential from indemnity business, and it gives a competitive advantage to the leading managed-care companies.

The major products in this line are conventional group coverages, administrative services only (ASO) business, and minimum-premium plans.

Conventional group coverages used to be limited primarily to indemnity coverages, such as major medical and hospital and surgical expense plans. Now, however, the range of health insur-

---

[5]Moody's Investors Service, "Life Insurance Industry Outlook," July 1990.

ance options has broadened considerably and includes managed health care delivery systems, comprising health maintenance organizations (HMOs) and preferred provider networks (PPOs).

The purpose of managed health care is to give the insurer greater control over selection of doctors and medical care facilities, thereby having some influence on the cost of delivery of health care services. Unfortunately, the investment required to establish HMOs and PPOs on a regional, let alone a national, basis has been larger than expected, and the anticipated cost-containment benefits have not occurred. Hence, managed health care has turned out to be riskier than the traditional indemnity plans because of the significant investment in products and services and because such companies are competing on price while they are trying to achieve competitive-scale advantages.

Only the large insurers with a presence on a national basis and some middle-sized insurers that have established local-provider market share will be the long-term survivors. Other companies will stop writing new business and/or sell their block of business to a company that has achieved critical mass or needs the block to achieve critical mass.

Because of the volatility and low profit margins in most conventional group business, insurance companies have begun to offer alternative products such as administrative services only (ASO) products and minimum-premium plans, which either have no medical expense risk or eliminate the risk of first-dollar coverage. The ASO option allows companies that already have a back-office operation to provide claims and administrative services for indemnity plans that are self-insured by the employer. Minimum-premium plans, on the other hand, provide coverage to employers but only when claims exceed a previously agreed-upon limit, such as 125 percent of premiums. Up to those limits, the employer is self-insuring the business and is responsible for reimbursing the employee once any deductibles have been satisfied.

The bottom line is that it is extremely difficult to make money in group life and health coverage. While group life insurance does tend to be consistently profitable due to large mortality margins, the health side is typically characterized by up cycles and down cycles, each lasting two to three years, during which profits emerge in the up cycle and then are more than off-set by rising medical costs/inflation. This results in losses during the down cycle, often substantial in size, which last until the rate increases requested by the insurance companies are able to bring premiums back to an adequate level to cover claims and expenses. Then profits emerge again, and a new cycle begins.

Again, because of the wide variability in products, pricing assumptions, and company experience, there is no easy answer as to the profitability of specific products. However, industry statistics indicate that the after-tax return on premiums were 4 percent to 5 percent in the early-to-mid-1980s but have trended down to zero percent to 1 percent by the late 1980s. With the industry now in an up cycle, the better-managed companies are hoping to achieve a 2 percent after-tax return. Even this may be difficult if medical claims inflation continues to significantly exceed the consumer price index, physicians continue to practice defensive medicine by ordering additional tests, and federal limits on Medicare and on reimbursements cause providers of medical services to increase charges to insured patients.

Individual and Group Annuity and Asset Accumulation

The key issues in this line are:[6]

• GIC market will remain highly competitive; competition may not always be rational because of the presence of non-insurance competitors.

• Benefit-responsive and window GICs may contain hidden options that will cause future financial difficulties for underwriters.

• Competition will remain keen in the structured settlements market. We expect that financial strength will be a competitive advantage, as the market becomes more sensitive to this issue.

---

[6]Moody's Investors Service, "Life Insurance Industry Outlook," July 1990.

• The single-premium deferred annuity market will increasingly be led by specialist carriers that have invested in processing capacity and use nontraditional investment and distribution methods.

The major products in this line are GICs, single-premium deferred annuities (SPDAs), structured settlement annuities, pension buyout contracts, and investment/asset management products.

Although the predominant types of GICs currently being written are still the fixed-rate bullet and window contracts, new variations are becoming more prevalent. Specifically, there are indexed contracts: long- , intermediate- , and short-term. These float, based on a long-term industrial bond index, intermediate-term treasury index, or CD- or other money market–type index, respectively. These contracts are attractive to plan sponsors because plan participants are always getting a current interest rate, which is especially important in rising interest rate environments.

There are also separate account-type products that minimize direct exposure to the credit of the life insurance company by investing plan assets in a pool of securities—U.S. Treasury or agency securities, securities collateralized by U.S. Treasury or agency securities, highly rated corporate bonds, and asset-backed securities. Although the insurance company still retains ownership of the assets, the separate account is maintained solely for the benefit of plan participants and is not chargeable with any liabilities arising out of any other business of the company, including its general account. The insurance company will guarantee an initial rate, generally for one year. A minimum annual interest rate (typically in the range of 0 percent to 4 percent) may also be provided for an additional fee. The contract-holder normally bears the risk of default of the securities in the portfolio, but the securities are usually of high quality so that such risk is generally small.

After-tax profits on GICs are typically from 15 to 60 basis points, which is a large range, given the commodity nature of the product. Some of the variations can occur because of (1) asset mismatch, that is, increasing the yield by having asset duration longer than the duration of the GIC liabilities, (2) different expense levels and commission levels to administer and acquire the business, (3) the quality of the portfolio of securities backing the GIC, (4) special features, such as indexing, which allow the company to differentiate its product from the competition and thereby earn larger spreads, and (5) the insurance company's internal profit requirement for the product.

Just like GICs, SPDAs tend to be a commodity product—there is an initial 1-to-5-year interest rate guarantee, with a set of declining surrender penalty charges over a 5- to 8-year period to allow the company to recover its acquisition costs on premature withdrawals. Typically, a limited percentage, usually 10 percent or less, of the fund value of the contract may be withdrawn in any year without a penalty being charged.

Variations have also found their way into SPDAs, as companies have begun to differentiate their products so that they can widen their profit margins. Among the variations are (1) a bailout provision, which allows a policyholder to withdraw the entire value of the policy without a surrender penalty if the interest credited ever goes below a given rate, (2) a market value adjustment (MVA) provision, which increases the surrender penalty when market interest rates rise and thus allows the company to recover any realized losses on sales of assets caused by the withdrawal, and (3) a dual interest rate, allowing a higher rate credited on values that ultimately annuitize and a lower rate credited on values that ultimately surrender.

Margins on SPDAs are typically 50 to 100 basis points after-tax. The reasons for the broad range in spreads are similar to that discussed above with respect to GICs. The margins tend to be higher on SPDAs than GICs to compensate the company for the unknown length that the liability will be on its books, which makes it more difficult to construct an asset portfolio that matches the cash flow requirements of the SPDA.

Structured settlement annuities and pension buyout contracts are often sold by life insurance companies to complement the shorter-duration GICs and SPDAs. A structured settlement is an insurance contract that provides a claimant with a stream of future payments to compensate for an injury, typically a bodily injury. A pension buyout is an insurance contract in which an employer sets aside a lump sum today to provide for a fixed monthly or annual payment to an employee at retirement, thereby transferring the pension liability from the employer to the insurance company.

Whereas GICs and SPDAs have an average duration of less than 10 years, structured settlements and pension buyout annuities have an average duration of approximately 10–30 years. By having all of these products in a company's portfolio, a diversification of liabilities is achieved, which gives the insurance company increased flexibility in the investments that can be purchased to support the entire annuity and accumulation line of business. Hence, the insurance company could deliberately mismatch its short-term liabilities—GICs and SPDAs—to increase its profit margin. Then, it could rebalance its assets and liabilities by selling the longer-term structured settlement annuities and pension buyout contracts and backing them with assets that are slightly shorter in duration, so that the entire portfolio of assets and liabilities would be in balance—or matched.

After-tax profit margins on structured settlements and pension buyout annuities range from 70 to 100 basis points. There is somewhat less variability here because the cash outflows to policyholders are relatively fixed. The major risks are (1) the reinvestment of assets that mature prior to the final payout on the liabilities; that is, some structured settlements can last 50–70 years if the claimant is a child, and (2) the lack of industry data regarding the mortality on impaired lives; that is, the claimants usually have substandard mortality, which makes pricing the product extremely challenging.

Traditionally, life insurance companies have provided experience-rated contracts and separate accounts for their pension products. Recently, however, life insurance companies have begun to acquire or form investment/asset management subsidiaries to focus on stock and bond investment management. These products add stability to the spread income produced from the GICs, SPDAs, etc., since the fees generated do not depend on the interest rate environment but only on the volume of assets under management and the size of the fees. Moreover, since the investment management skills needed to service this line may require little additional expenditures of capital, depending on the expertise of the existing investment staff, the return on investment is usually very good.

On-Site Visits with Management

The statutory and GAAP financial statements of a life insurance company typically show information in summary form only, so that it is difficult to determine the profitability and earnings potential of the products within each line of business. For example, the company's life line of business could show relatively level profits over recent years. However, on further discussion with management and/or analysis of internal data provided by the company, we could find out that the traditional life insurance block written in the 1970s and prior is producing all the profits and the currently selling universal life products are losing money. The additional data shows that the future earnings prospects for the line are dim because the percentage of universal life products in the line is probably increasing while the percentage of the closed block of traditional life business is likely decreasing.

The important thing to note is that sometimes the only way to obtain certain kinds of information is to visit a company, sit down with management, and ask the questions or request the data that is not generally available in the published financial statements. In addition to product profitability information, other questions and/or information might include:

- What is the company's AIDS experience over the past few years, and what underwriting measures have been employed by the company to screen out such potential insureds?
- How do the company's mortality, interest, lapse, and expense assumptions in its major products compare to what is actually being experienced, and what is the current and future impact of any such deviations?
- Are the company's systems adequate to handle the current in-force block or will significant expenditures be re-

quired to administer the more complex universal life and variable annuity–type products?

• How is the company positioning itself to cope with the volatility in the health insurance sector, caused by cost-shifting, rising medical costs, and the increased investment required to compete in the managed-care area?

• Does the company have critical mass in its product lines to allow it to operate the lines on a marginal-cost basis and, if not, what is it doing to get to that point?

• How is the asset/liability matching and/or cash flow testing done, and is there a description of the methodology and an analysis of the results under various different interest rate scenarios available to review?

• What is the company's philosophy on setting renewal credited interest rates on annuity products in a rising interest rate environment? In a falling interest rate environment?

• Does the company plan to buy or sell any blocks of business to create economies of scale or relieve itself of an unprofitable product or line of business?

• Does the company have any off-balance-sheet transactions, such as securitization of assets, sale of future loadings, or financing/leveling of commissions which distort the true level of surplus?

• Has the company entered into any financial reinsurance transactions and, if so, how has surplus and the incidence of earnings been affected?

• What reserving methods are being used by the company for all of its major products?

Games that Can Be Played

Even after obtaining the additional information discussed above, there are a number of ways that insurance companies are able to distort earnings and net worth. Examples include reinsurance, pyramiding, reserve valuation methods, and capital gains.

Insurance companies can acquire a one-time infusion of surplus by entering into reinsurance agreements, referred to as "surplus relief reinsurance agreements." Reinsurance is an agreement by which an insurance company transfers all or part of its risk under an insurance contract to another company. The company that issues the policy is called the *primary insurer, direct writer, or ceding company*; and the company to which the risk is transferred is called the *reinsuring* or *assuming company*. The process of transferring the risk from the ceding company to the reinsurer is known as a *cession.* If an assuming company, in turn, transfers a portion of this risk, the process is called a *retrocession.* A retrocession is customarily made when the amount assumed is beyond the reinsurer's limits of retention. Reinsurance commonly is undertaken in ordinary life insurance, in group insurance, in credit insurance, and in individual health insurance.[7]

Generally, a liability is established on the balance sheet for the excess of any reserve credit over funds withheld. Funds withheld may include letters of credit (LOCs) if the reinsurer is not a licensed reinsurer in the carrier's state of domicile. It is then possible for a parent holding company to issue an LOC to enable its subsidiary to avoid the required additional liability. In addition, carriers have been known to enter into reinsurance agreements with unauthorized reinsurers. This action leads to questions concerning the underlying reinsurers and the underlying quality of the agreement.

In addition, there are some reinsurance agreements entered into where there is very little risk transfer to the reinsurer. The purpose of these transactions is to enable a surplus-poor company to "rent" surplus from a surplus-rich company for a period of years until the surplus-poor company is able to build up its own surplus through future earnings. The surplus-rich company is able to earn anywhere from 1½ percent to 4 percent on its surplus, depending on surplus availability in the industry, which allows the surplus-providing company to generate earnings from an otherwise sterile source of income.

---

[7]National Association of Insurance Commissioners, *Accounting Practices and Procedures Manual.* Reprinted by permission of the National Association of Insurance Commissioners.

Examples of such reinsurance transactions include:

• Ceding the excess interest reserves on annuity products.
• Reinsuring the difference between statutory and tax reserves.
• Obtaining commission and expense allowances in excess of the actual commissions and acquisition expenses that have been incurred.

What is important to note here is that a majority of these surplus-enhancing transactions are temporary in nature; that is, excess interest gradually decreases to zero at the end of the interest guarantee period, statutory and tax reserves eventually equal each other, and the excess allowances are normally amortized over a 5–10 year period. Hence, the surplus relief gradually disappears, which means that if the reinsuring company is unable to achieve surplus growth through operating earnings, it will continue to seek "surplus relief" on an almost annual basis.

Therefore, a credit analyst must try to determine how much of a company's capital is permanent and how much is a result of these reinsurance transactions—in order to get an accurate picture of the quality and size of a company's surplus position.

Carriers have been known to pyramid their surplus structure. Under a pyramid scenario, one dollar of true surplus in the subsidiary is shown in every parent company in the pyramid of companies in the overall corporate structure. Should one subsidiary incur financial problems, these problems could transfer to all other subsidiaries, producing a domino effect.

Pyramiding is also important to understand because it can obscure the true capitalization of every parent company in the pyramid chain. Therefore, where a subsidiary's surplus is included in the surplus of its parent, the capital of the parent is its own capital stock, surplus, and MSVR *plus* the MSVR of its subsidiaries. To include the subsidiaries' capital and surplus would double-count the true amount of surplus which actually exists.

Surplus should also be evaluated on the strength of the company's reserve assumptions. A less-conservative approach to reserve calculations will produce lower reserves and consequently more surplus. Conversely, a more-conservative basis requires greater reserves and thus less net worth.

Statutory reserving standards, which establish a fund for the company's obligations to its policyholders, have been adopted by state legislation and are based on mortality and morbidity statistics and conservative estimates of future investment earnings. These standards further consider the values to which the policyholder is entitled in the event of the termination of the policy (cash or nonforfeiture values). The statutory assumptions for mortality, morbidity, and investment earnings are intentionally determined on a conservative basis reflective of the long-term nature of the liabilities, the desire to stabilize the evaluation process over a period of time, and the omission of separate assumptions for other factors such as lapse or persistency. It is unlikely they will coincide with the company's actual experience.[8]

Statutory reserving standards are usually described in the laws as the "minimum" level of reserves that a company is required to establish as a liability. For life insurance policies, the minimum is obtained from using the Commissioners Reserve Valuation Method (CRVM) of determining reserves, while the maximum is obtained from using the Net Level Premium (NLP) method. The CRVM basis contains an expense allowance to reflect the substantial acquisition expenses which are intended to be recovered from future margins. Hence, the CRVM reserve in the first year only covers the cost of mortality, and the amount of the allowance is incrementally added into the reserve over a period of years. The NLP reserve, on the other hand, does not contain any expense allowance offset in the first year and, therefore, requires a significant first-year reserve. Reserves on an NLP basis are avoided by surplus conscious companies.

Therefore, to the extent that a company has a substantial percentage of its statutory reserves on a CRVM basis, that company would have a greater net worth than a similar company

---

[8]National Association of Insurance Commissioners, *Accounting Practices and Procedures Manual.* Reprinted by permission of the National Association of Insurance Commissioners.

that has used the NLP method. Since all reserve methods grade to the same reserve by the end of a policy's premium-paying period, the CRVM reserve–based company will have a greater strain on its surplus in future years.

As interest rates fell in the mid-1980s, enormous capital gains were realized as high-yielding assets were sold. Unlike other entities that pass the gain directly to the income statement, insurance companies pass the gain directly to the surplus account. Net worth increased at a faster-than-normal rate due to these capital gains being realized. Problems could surface in later years because the proceeds of these gains were reinvested at lower yields, thus squeezing profit margins.

As evidenced by the issuance of Regulations 126 and 130 by the New York Insurance Department, attempts are being made to require more detailed financial reporting. Better reporting will produce better analyses, although, as discussed above, there will always be much critical information that is not available in the published financial statements.

Regulation 126, released by the New York department on December 17, 1986, requires actuarial certification of the methods used to calculate annuity reserves. Specifically, it requires a statement of reserve sufficiency for all annuity contracts, GIC contracts, and funding agreements. It requires this liability to be determined in accordance with commonly accepted actuarial standards, including future cash flow projections under seven alternative interest rate scenarios detailed in the Regulation. Subsequent to the initial release, Regulation 126 has been amended, so that interest-sensitive single-premium life insurance has been added to the required cash flow analysis. Section 95.9 of New York Regulation 126 (Appendix 3 at end of this book) specifies the details that must be included in the actuarial memorandum, which shows the assumptions used as well as the results of the asset/liability study under the interest rate scenarios which are tested.

Effective June 24, 1987, the New York department issued Regulation 130. This regulation deals primarily with the maximum permissible exposure to high-risk debt obligations. It states that no more than 20 percent of admitted assets may be invested in these issues without prior approval. Those companies that exceeded the 20 percent limitation on the date Regulation 130 was issued were not required to dispose of any investments. Since that date, a few other states have come out with their own limitations with respect to high-risk investments, and more states will, no doubt, continue to follow suit. A copy of New York Regulation 130 is provided in Appendix 4.

THE RATING AGENCIES

Important to the analytical process is the review of the ratings assigned by major rating agencies. Currently, four major agencies provide rating services for life insurers: A. M. Best Company, Duff and Phelps, Moody's Investors Service, and Standard & Poor's Corporation.

A. M. Best Company

The objective of Best's Rating System is to evaluate the various factors affecting the overall performance of each insurance company and provide an opinion of each company's relative financial strength and ability to meet its contractual obligations. The procedure includes quantitative and qualitative reviews of the insurer's operations.

Analytical Approach

The quantitative evaluation involves an analysis of each company's financial condition and operating performance, utilizing a series of financial tests that measure performance in three critical areas of profitability, leverage, and liquidity in comparison with industry norms established by the A. M. Best Company. The norms are based on an evaluation of actual performance of the entire life/health industry.

• **Profitability** is essential for an enduring and strong insurer. It is a measure of competence and ability of management to provide services and prices attractive to policyholders in competitive markets, and to compare cost control and efficiency factors with those of its peers. Statutory earnings over the most recent five-year period are reviewed by Best, with special attention to the degree and trend of overall profitability. Net investment income, federal income taxes, expenses, mortality and persistency results, reinsurance, changes in reserving methods, and underwriting experience are all carefully evaluated for the relative effects on profitability.

• **Leverage** increases return on capital but also raises the risk of instability. Accordingly, Best compares the leverage of each insurer with industry norms to evaluate the relative degree of risk. In reviewing the growth of premium writings and insurance exposure on policyholders' surplus, Best considers affiliated investments to evaluate the effect of pyramiding. A leverage analysis also monitors adequacy and equity of policy reserves and differences between statement and market values of assets.

• **Liquidity** analysis considers insurers' short- and long-term commitments for which assets should be maintained in sound, diversified, and relatively liquid investments to meet unexpected needs for cash without the untimely sales of assets.

The Best review also includes a qualitative evaluation of a company's spread of risk, the amount and soundness of a company's reinsurance, the quality and diversification of investments, the adequacy and valuation basis of policy reserves, and the experience of management. Various other factors of importance are also considered, particularly where some condition exists that may affect the ability of a company to meet its contractual obligations. Meetings with insurance company managements are frequently held to discuss these matters.

Rating Assignment Procedure
Assignment of Best's rating and financial-size category is made in the spring of each year shortly after each company has submitted its annual financial statement (due March 1). Official notifications by letter are sent to the chief executive officer of each company. Each company is permitted to discuss its rating before its release via Best's "Rating Monitor," which is distributed with the weekly publication, *Best's Insurance Management Reports.* Rating assignments are also reported in the monthly magazine,

Best's Review, and ultimately in the annual publication, *Best's Insurance Reports.* The assigned rating subsequently is reviewed and is subject to change or watch listing, based on six- and nine-months' quarterly financial reports.

Best's Rating Classifications

Of the 1,341 companies reported on in *Best's Insurance Reports,* 1991 Edition, approximately 57 percent are assigned a Best's rating ranging from A+ (superior) to C− (fair). The remaining 43 percent are classified as "Rating: Not Assigned." The "Not Assigned" category has classifications that identify why a company was not eligible or assigned a Best's rating.

Effective with the assignment of 1992 Best's ratings, the rating structure has been expanded to add finer distinctions among rated companies by the introduction of six new ratings: A++, B++, C++, D, E, and F. In addition, the structure will be simplified by the elimination of the rating categories of NA-7 (Below Minimum Standards) and NA-10 (Under State Supervision). Also, a new category will be added: NA-11 (Rating Suspended). Table 5–3 describes the new rating scale in more detail.[9]

Duff and Phelps

Duff and Phelps first entered the business of issuing claims-paying ability (CPA) ratings on insurance companies in 1986. Presently, Duff and Phelps issues four types of ratings on insurance companies: fixed income (bonds and preferred stock), commercial paper, structured finance, and claims-paying ability ratings.

Duff and Phelps applies the same rating scale to insurance company CPA ratings that it applies to the rating of bonds and preferred stocks. The highest Duff and Phelps rating is a AAA, and the first 10 CPA rating categories (AAA to BBB−) are considered "investment grade." Table 5–4 describes the rating scale in greater detail.

---

[9]Information provided by A. M. Best Company, Oldwick, N.J.

TABLE 5-3
A. M. Best Company Rating Classifications

Rating Classification	Description
A++ and A+ (Superior)	Assigned to companies which, in our opinion, have achieved superior overall performance when compared to the standards established by the A.M. Best Company. A++ and A+ (Superior) companies have a very strong ability to meet their policyholder and other contractual obligations over a long period of time.
A and A− (Excellent)	Assigned to companies which, in our opinion, have achieved excellent overall performance when compared to the standards established by the A.M. Best Company. A and A− (Excellent) companies have a strong ability to meet their policyholder and other contractual obligations over a long period of time.
B++ and B+ (Very Good)	Assigned to companies which, in our opinion, have achieved very good overall performance when compared to the standards established by the A.M. Best Company. B++ and B+ (Very Good) companies have a strong ability to meet their policyholder and other contractual obligations, but their financial strength may be susceptible to unfavorable changes in underwriting or economic conditions.
B and B− (Good)	Assigned to companies which, in our opinion, have achieved good overall performance when compared to the standards established by the A.M. Best Company. B and B− (Good) companies generally have an adequate ability to meet their policyholder and other contractual obligations, but their financial strength is susceptible to unfavorable changes in underwriting or economic conditions.
C++ and C+ (Fair)	Assigned to companies which, in our opinion, have achieved fair overall performance when compared to the standards established by the A.M. Best Company. C++ and C+ (Fair) companies generally have a reasonable ability to meet their policyholder and other contractual obligations, but their financial strength is vulnerable to unfavorable changes in underwriting or economic conditions.
C and C− (Marginal)	Assigned to companies which, in our opinion, have achieved marginal overall performance when compared to the standards established by the A.M. Best Company. C and C− (Marginal) companies have a current ability to meet their policyholder and other contractual obligations, but their financial strength is very vulnerable to unfavorable changes in underwriting or economic conditions.
D (Below Minimum Standards)	Assigned to companies which meet our minimum size and experience requirements, but do not meet the minimum standards established by the A.M. Best Company for a Best's Rating of "C−". **Note:** This rating category was formerly the NA-7 (Below Minimum Standards) Rating Not Assigned classification.
E (Under State Supervision)	Assigned to companies which are placed under any form of supervision, control or restraint by a state insurance regulatory authority such as conservatorship or rehabilitation, but does not include liquidation. May be assigned to a company under a cease and desist order issued by a regulator from a state other than its state of domicile. **Note:** This rating category was formerly the NA-10 (Under State Supervision) Rating Not Assigned classification.

TABLE 5-3 (continued)

Rating Classification	Description
F (In Liquidation)	Assigned to companies which have been placed under an order of liquidation or have voluntarily agreed to liquidate. **Note:** This is a new rating category in 1992 to distinguish between companies under state regulatory supervision and those in the process of liquidation.

A. M. Best Company Ratings "Not Assigned" Classifications

NA-1 Special Data Filing	Assigned primarily to small mutual and stock companies that are exempt from the requirement to file the standard NAIC annual statement. These company reports are based on selected financial information obtained by the A.M. Best Company.
NA-2 Less than Minimum Size	Assigned to companies that file the standard NAIC annual statement but do not meet our minimum size requirement. To assure reasonable financial stability, we require a company to have a minimum policyholders' surplus of $1.5 million. This rating classification is also assigned to a company that is effectively dormant, has no significant premium volume, or has no net insurance business in force. Exceptions are: the company is 100% reinsured by a Best's Rated company; or is a member of a group participating in a business pooling arrangement; and a company writing stable lines of business that has demonstrated a long history of above average performance when compared to Best's Rating standards. Companies assigned the NA-2 Rating classification are eligible for the assignment of Best's Financial Performance Index (FPI).
NA-3 Insufficient Operating Experience	Assigned to a company which meets, or we anticipate will meet, our minimum size requirement, but has not accumulated five consecutive years of representative operating experience. This requirement pertains only to the age of the company's financial performance and does not relate to the actual experience of its management. Our operating experience requirement requires consistency in both the types of coverages written and the relative volume of gross and net premium writings. Additional years of operating experience may be required if a company exhibits substantial growth in new business or change(s) in product mix whereby the development of the company's business or reserves may not be sufficiently mature at the end of five years to permit a satisfactory evaluation. Companies assigned to the NA-3 category are eligible for assignment of Best's Financial Performance Index (FPI).
NA-4 Rating Procedure Inapplicable	Assigned to a company when the nature of its business and/or operations is such that our normal rating procedure does not properly apply. Examples are: companies writing lines of business not common to the property/casualty or life/health fields; companies writing financial guaranty insurance; companies retaining only a small portion of their gross premiums written; companies which have discontinued writing new and renewal business and have a defined plan to run-off existing contractual obligations; companies that discount loss reserves to the extent that the anticipated future investment income represents a significant part of their current policyholders' surplus; and com-

panies not soliciting business in the United States. This rating is also assigned to life/health companies whose sole operation is the acceptance of business written directly by a parent, subsidiary or affiliated insurance company; or those writing predominantly property/casualty insurance under a dual charter.

NA-5 Significant Change

Generally assigned to a previously rated company which experiences a significant change in ownership, management or book of business whereby its operating experience may be interrupted or subject to change; or any other relevant event which has or may affect the general trend of a company's operations. This may include pending mergers, sale to a new owner, substantial growth in premium writings or a significant redirection of marketing emphasis. Depending on the nature of the change, our rating procedure may require a period of one to five years before the company is again eligible for a rating.

NA-6 Reinsured by Unrated Reinsurer

Assigned to a company which has a substantial portion of its book of business reinsured by/or has reinsurance recoverables from non-Best's Rated reinsurers which represent a substantial portion of its policyholders' surplus. Exceptions are non-Best's Rated foreign reinsurers that comply with our reporting requirements and satisfy our financial performance standards.

NA-7 Below Minimum Standards

Discontinued in 1992 and replaced by the Best's Rating of D.

NA-8 Incomplete Financial Information

Assigned to a company that is eligible for a rating, but fails to submit complete financial information for the current five-year period under review. This requirement includes all domestic insurance subsidiaries in which the company's ownership exceeds 50%.

NA-9 Company Request

Assigned to a company that is eligible for a Best's Rating, but requests that the rating not be published. The majority of these companies, such as captives, operate in markets that do not require a rating, but cooperate with our request for financial information in order that a report can be prepared and published on their company. The classification is also assigned to a company that requests its rating not be published because it disagrees with either our rating assignment or our rating fee. In this situation, our policy normally requires a minimum of two years to elapse before the company is again eligible for the assignment of a rating.

NA-10 Under State Supervision

Discontinued in 1992 and replaced by the Best's Rating of either E or F.

NA-11 Rating Suspended

Assigned to a previously rated company which has experienced a sudden and significant event affecting the company's financial position and/or operating performance, of which the impact cannot be evaluated due to a lack of timely or appropriate information.

(concluded)

TABLE 5–4
Duff and Phelps Insurance Company Claims-Paying Ability (CPA) Rating Scale

CPA Rating Scale	Description
AAA	Highest claims-paying ability. Risk factors are negligible.
AA+ AA AA−	Very high claims-paying ability. Protection factors are strong. Risk is modest, but may vary slightly over time due to economic and/or underwriting conditions.
A+ A A−	High claims-paying ability. Protection factors are average and there is an expectation of variability in risk over time due to economic and/or underwriting conditions.
BBB+ BBB BBB−	Below average claims-paying ability. Protection factors are average. However, there is considerable variability in risk over time due to economic and/or underwriting conditions.
BB+ BB BB−	Uncertain claims-paying ability and less than investment-grade quality. However, the company is deemed likely to meet these obligations when due. Protection factors will vary widely with changes in economic and/or underwriting conditions.
B+ B B−	Possessing risk that policyholder and contractholder obligations will not be paid when due. Protection factors will vary widely with changes in economic and/or underwriting conditions, or company fortunes.
CCC+ CCC CCC−	There is substantial risk that policyholder and contractholder will not be paid when due. Company has been or is likely to be placed under state insurance department supervision.

Analytical Approach

The Duff and Phelps rating process is a combination of quantitative and qualitative analysis. The quantitative analysis is based primarily on statutory accounting principles as reflected in the annual statements filed with the state insurance departments, with available generally accepted accounting principles (GAAP) data also utilized. Some of the key quantitative analysis points are:

• Amount of adjusted surplus (includes reported surplus, MSVR, deficiency reserves, and certain voluntary reserves, if any, established by the company).

• Operating leverage (liabilities related to adjusted surplus, and premiums and deposit funds related to adjusted surplus).

• Return-on-assets profitability.

• Return-on-adjusted-surplus profitability.

• Surplus formation (growth in adjusted surplus relative to growth in adjusted liabilities).

• Net investment income yield.

• Expense ratio.

• Investment risk (exposure of adjusted surplus to noninvestment-grade securities, real estate, common stock, and affiliate investments).

• Accident and health combined ratio (loss ratio plus expense ratio).

Each line of an insurance company's business is reviewed separately from the standpoints of both underwriting and profitability. An analysis is also made of the type, duration, and quality of investment assets.

The qualitative analysis phase includes meetings with key management personnel and an evaluation of the following important factors:

• Economic fundamentals of the company's principal insurance lines.

• Company's competitive position.

• Management capability

• Relationship of rated entity to either parent, affiliate, or subsidiary.

• Asset and liability management practices.

The rating process includes the following steps:

• Certain requested material is sent by the insurance company to Duff and Phelps.

• A team from Duff and Phelps visits the insurance company to meet key management personnel.

• A group of selected executives from the insurance company comes to the offices of Duff and Phelps to meet with members of the Duff and Phelps rating committee.

• Duff and Phelps establishes a rating for the insurance company and reviews the rating with the insurance company.

• Ratings that are accepted by insurance companies are published in the national media. (Duff and Phelps does not publish ratings for insurance companies that initiate the rating process with Duff and Phelps unless the insurance company agrees to a publication of the rating.)

Ratings published by Duff and Phelps are reviewed quarterly or in the event of special developments, and they may be upgraded, downgraded, or put on the Duff and Phelps "watch list" (indicating either a potential upgrade or downgrade). A full-scale review of each claims-paying-ability rating is conducted on an annual basis.[10]

Moody's Investors Service

Moody's Investors Service has rated the debt securities of life insurance companies since the mid-1970s. Moody's began rating insurance companies for their ability to meet senior policyholder obligations and claims in the mid-1980s. Moody's rating symbols for insurance "financial strength ratings" are identical to those used to show the rating quality of bonds. These rating gradations provide investors with a simple system to measure the financial strength of an insurance company in meeting its senior policyholder claims.

Table 5–5 shows how Moody's characterizes the degree of financial strength by rating category. Ratings from Aa to B may be modified by use of a 1, 2, or 3 to show relative standing of the insurer within these rating categories. The modifier "1" indicates that the insurance company ranks in the higher end of its generic rating category; the modifier "2" indicates a mid-range

---

[10]Information provided by Duff and Phelps, Inc., Chicago, Ill.

TABLE 5–5
Moody's Financial Strength Rating Scale

Rating Category	Degree of Financial Security
Aaa	Insurance companies rated Aaa offer *exceptional* financial security. While the financial strength of these companies is likely to change, such changes as can be visualized are most unlikely to impair their fundamentally strong position.
Aa1 Aa2 Aa3	Insurance companies rated Aa offer *excellent* financial security. Together with the Aaa group they constitute what are generally known as high-grade companies. They are rated lower than Aaa companies because long-term risks appear somewhat larger.
A1 A2 A3	Insurance companies rated A offer *good* financial security. However, elements may be present which suggest a susceptibility to impairment sometime in the future.
Baa1 Baa2 Baa3	Insurance companies rated Baa offer *adequate* financial security. However, certain protective elements may be lacking or may be characteristically unreliable over any great length of time.
Ba1 Ba2 Ba3	Insurance companies rated Ba offer *questionable* financial security. Often the ability of these companies to meet policyholder obligations may be very moderate and thereby not well safeguarded in the future.
B1 B2 B3	Insurance companies rated B offer *poor* financial security. Assurance of punctual payment of policyholder obligations over any long period of time is small.
Caa	Insurance companies rated Caa offer *very poor* financial security. They may be in default on their policyholder obligations or there may be present elements of danger with respect to punctual payment of policyholder obligations and claims.
Ca	Insurance companies rated Ca offer *extremely poor* financial security. Such companies are often in default on their policyholder obligations or have other marked shortcomings.
C	Insurance companies rated C are the *lowest* rated class of insurance company and can be regarded as having extremely poor prospects of ever offering financial security.

ranking, and the modifier "3" indicates a rank in the lower end of its generic rating category.

Analytical Approach

Moody's financial strength ratings are based on industry analysis, regulatory trends, and an evaluation of an institution's business fundamentals. Industry analysis examines the structure of competition within the company's operating environment and its competitive position within that structure. Analysis of regulatory trends attempts to develop an understanding of potential changes in the regulatory system and tax structure. The analysis of a company's business fundamentals focuses primarily on financial factors, franchise value, management, and organizational structure/ownership. The steps involved in assigning financial strength ratings can be summarized briefly as follows:

- A statistical review of historical financial performance is carried out. This includes an assessment of the company's profitability, liquidity, operating leverage, financial leverage, asset quality, and reserve quality.

- In its evaluation of management, Moody's considers the company's financial track record in such areas as investment risk taking, profitability, and product innovation. Management's strategy, as measured by rapid growth or new business development, also plays an important role in its overall opinion of a company's financial strength. Moody's analysis typically, but not always, involves meeting with issuer management.

- Moody's discusses industry issues and regulatory policy with the National Association of Insurance Commissioners (NAIC) and with state regulators.

- Generally, an assessment is made of all significant noninsurance operations of affiliates of insurance companies, be they parent companies or subsidiaries. Moody's analysts specializing in other industries are frequently called upon to support such assessments.

- A rating recommendation is made by the lead analyst and is presented to the corporate rating committee. Representatives from other areas of Moody's, such as industrial analysts, banking analysts, and utility analysts, may be included in the rating committee. A final decision is made by the rating committee based on the presentation by the lead analyst.

- Moody's ratings are designed to be current and, at any given date, to reflect its best estimate of an issuer's risk characteristics. As such, its ratings are subject to change as and when its opinion concerning an issuer or the environment in which it operates changes. Changes do not need to await a formal review cycle.

In support of the assigned rating, a detailed report is written which is divided into six major sections:

1. Company fundamentals. This section reviews the company's business, organizational structure, and relative standing within the industry. It includes an assessment of the business segments' products, markets, and distribution, and the company's competitive position in those segments. Commentary is also provided on the company's strategic orientation.

2. Earnings trends and profitability. Elements which contribute to earnings and their sustainability are evaluated here. Growth trends, distribution of income, and cost structure are discussed. A review of profitability by segment is given in a rating context. Earnings trends and future prospects for earnings are related to the ability of the company to meet policyholder obligations.

3. Investments. The composition and quality of the company's investment portfolio is discussed in this section. Investment results relative to portfolio risk characteristics are reviewed and evaluated.

4. Asset/liability management and liquidity. How the company manages the relationship of the asset structure to the liability structure is discussed here. Interest sensitivity, liquidity, maturity structure of both sides of the balance sheet, duration and convexity, and the use of off-balance-sheet devices are discussed. This section is also designed to review the company's asset composition as it relates to asset/liability matching and portfolio liquidity.

5. Capitalization. Analysis of the company's capital base in relation to the risk profile of its insurance operations, balance sheet, contingent liabilities, and regulatory requirements is provided in this section.

6. Affiliates. This section provides a profile of the company's significant unconsolidated affiliates and subsidiaries. Where a company uses a downstream subsidiary as a financing conduit, it will be reviewed in this section.

Moody's Investors Service's financial strength ratings are intended to express the degree of financial security in insurance policies issued by a rated insurer. The ratings are opinions, not recommendations to buy a specific insurance policy, and their accuracy is not guaranteed. A rating should be weighed solely as one factor in an investment decision, and the plan sponsor should make its own study and evaluation of any insurer whose policies or contracts it is considering buying.[11]

Standard & Poor's Corporation

A Standard & Poor's insurance claims-paying ability rating is an opinion of an operating insurance company's financial capacity to meet the obligations of its insurance policies in accordance with their terms. This opinion is not specific to any particular insurance policy or contract nor does it address the suitability of a particular policy for a specific purpose or purchaser. Furthermore, the opinion does not take into account deductibles, surrender or cancellation penalties, the timeliness of payment, or the likelihood of the use of a defense such as fraud to deny claims. Claims-paying ability ratings do not refer to an insurer's ability to meet nonpolicy obligations (i.e. debt contracts).

The assignment of ratings to debt issues that are fully or partially supported by insurance policies, contracts, or guarantees is a separate process from the determination of claims-paying ability ratings, and follows procedures consistent with debt rating definitions and practices.

Claims-paying ability ratings are divided into two broad classifications. Rating categories from 'AAA' to 'BBB' are classified as "Secure" claims-paying ability ratings and are used to indicate insurers whose financial capacity to meet policyholder obligations is viewed on balance as sound. Among factors considered in placing insurers within the spectrum of "Secure" rating categories, is the time frame within which policyholder security could be damaged by adverse developments. That time frame grows shorter as ratings move down the "Secure" rating scale.

---

[11]Information provided by Moody's Investor Services, New York, N.Y.

Rating categories from 'BB' to 'D' are classified as "Vulnerable" claims-paying ability ratings and are used to indicate insurers whose financial capacity to meet policyholder obligations is viewed as vulnerable to adverse developments. In fact, the financial capacity of insurers rated 'CC' to 'C' may already be impaired, while insurers rated 'D' are in liquidation.

Ratings from 'AA' to 'CCC' may be modified by the use of a plus or minus sign to show relative standing of the insurer within those rating categories (see Table 5–6).

Analytical Approach

The Standard & Poor's rating methodology profile is used for all insurance rating analysis and is uniform across all types of insurance companies. The profile covers the following areas: management and corporate strategy, business review, operating performance, capitalization, liquidity, and financial flexibility.

• *Strategy Analysis.* Management and corporate strategy analysis includes a review of four key elements:

1. Organizational structure, and how it fits the company's strategy.
2. The quality of strategic thinking as well as the planning process itself.
3. Operational skills, which involve an assessment of a company's ability to execute the chosen strategy.
4. Financial risk tolerance, which relates to the amount of debt in the capital structure and the level of operating leverage.

• *Business Review.* This review identifies the company's fundamental characteristics and its source of competitive advantage or disadvantage. A description of the portfolio of business units and/or product lines, distribution systems, and the degree of business diversification is included. The business review includes analysis of those aspects of the business that affect the absolute level and growth rate of the revenue base. The assessment focuses on the long-term revenue-generating capabilities of the firm. The actual level of profit derived from the revenue base is not considered. The following items are examples of the type of quantitative information used:

TABLE 5–6
Standard & Poor's Claims-Paying Ability Ratings Categories

Broad Classification	Rating Category	Description
Secure Claims-Paying Ability	AAA	Insurers rated AAA offer *superior* financial security on both an absolute and relative basis. They possess the highest safety and have an overwhelming capacity to meet policyholder obligations.
	AA+ AA AA–	Insurers rated AA offer *excellent* financial security, and their capacity to meet policyholder obligations differs only in a small degree from insurers rated AAA.
	A+ A A–	Insurers rated A offer *good* financial security, but their capacity to meet policyholder obligations is somewhat more susceptible to adverse changes in economic or underwriting conditions than more highly rated insurers.
	BBB+ BBB BBB–	Insurers rated BBB offer *adequate* financial security, but their capacity to meet policyholder obligations is considered more vulnerable to adverse economic or underwriting conditions than that of more highly rated insurers.
Vulnerable Claims-Paying Ability	BB+ BB BB–	Insurers rated BB offer financial security that may be adequate but caution is indicated since their capacity to meet policyholder obligations is considered vulnerable to adverse economic or underwriting conditions and may not be adequate for "long-tail" or long-term policies.
	B+ B B–	Insurers rated B are currently able to meet policyholder obligations, but their vulnerability to adverse economic or underwriting conditions is considered high.
	CCC+ CCC CCC–	Insurers rated CCC are vulnerable to adverse economic or underwriting conditions to the extent that their continued capacity to meet policyholder obligations is highly questionable unless a favorable environment prevails.
	CC C	Insurers rated CC or C may not be meeting all policyholder obligations, may be operating under the jurisdiction of insurance regulators and are vulnerable to liquidation.
	D	Insurers rated D have been placed under an order of liquidation.

1. Compound growth rate of revenue during the last 5 years.
2. Distribution of revenue by business unit, geography, product, and distribution channel.
3. Market share for the total firm and major product lines.

• *Operating Performance.* Through an analysis of operating results on a statutory basis for all companies and a GAAP basis for stock companies, S&P determines a company's ability to capitalize on its strategy and company strengths. Operating results are analyzed independently of the firm's operating leverage. Key items discussed include profitability by major line of business, return on assets, expense ratios, lapse ratios, and the combined ratio for Accident and Health business. Other areas reviewed include:

1. Investment performance, including yield, net capital gains, and the portfolio composition and quality.
2. Asset/liability management, including a brief description of the methodology used and the degree of mismatch in the portfolio.
3. Reinsurance, including the extent used and a description of any major treaties.

Finally, the issuance by life insurers of policies with a participating dividend feature introduces an additional complication to measuring operating performance. While a significant part of dividends to policyholders is at the discretion of management, in practice the maintenance of dividend payments is an important marketing feature from the consumer's perspective. Therefore, S&P treats dividends to policyholders as a cost of doing business, and return on assets is measured on the basis of the gain from operations after dividends and taxes.

• *Capitalization.* The analysis of capitalization for insurance companies incorporates financial-leverage usage and fixed-charge coverage concepts as well as the degree of operating leverage. The analysis of financial leverage is uniform for all insurers.

Operating leverage is analyzed in relation to the business lines of an insurer. Various lines require differing degrees of capitalization, and a company's business mix will influence the appropriate level of operating leverage. Additionally, the quality of capital is analyzed. *Quality* is defined as the degree of exposure to equity assets, such as common stocks, including investment in affiliates, real estate equities, and equity investments in partnerships.

• *Liquidity.* All insurance companies have three basic sources of internal liquidity: underwriting cash flow, investment income cash flow, and asset liquidation cash flow. Compared to other financial institutions, life insurers usually have better internal liquidity due to the relatively long duration and predictability of their liabilities.

• *Financial Flexibility.* This last rating methodology topic is broken down into two sections: capital requirements and capital sources. *Capital requirements* refer to factors that may give rise to an exceptionally large need for either long-term capital or short-term liquidity. Almost by definition, these exceptional requirements tend to relate to the company's strategic objectives and often involve acquisition or recapitalization plans. *Capital sources* involve an assessment of the extent to which a company has access to unusually large amounts of short- and long-term capital. Typically these sources consist of demonstrated access to multiple types of capital markets—the long-term public debt market, the commercial paper market, and the Euromarkets. Additionally, a company may hold assets with significant unrealized capital gains that could be sold without affecting the basic enterprise. The ability or demonstrated willingness to raise common equity capital is another important source of financial flexibility. The ability to obtain reinsurance in adequate amounts from a variety of high-quality markets also is a source of strength.[12]

CONCLUSION

The life insurance industry represents a somewhat complicated structuring. Its members are diverse in products, size, and cor-

---

[12]Information provided by Standard & Poor's Corporation, New York, N.Y.

porate make-up. To illustrate the complexities, the following questions lend insight into the problems of performing absolute and relative analytical reviews.

Do you analyze the insurance company differently if you are buying a life insurance policy, a GIC, or a deferred annuity? Do you analyze a company with $1 billion in capital and surplus differently from one with $100 million? Do you analyze a stock company differently from a mutual company? Do you analyze a multiline company differently from a single-line company?

The answer to each question is yes. Hence, one begins to understand quickly the complexities of insurance company credit analysis. The financial statements are only a part of the picture. For a thorough assessment, one must also (1) understand the regulatory issues, (2) have knowledge of the management of the company, (3) recognize the difference between liberal versus conservative reserving practices, (4) comprehend the impact of "surplus relief" and other reinsurance transactions on the company's profitability and net worth position, (5) analyze the profitability of the major products in the company's lines of business, (6) evaluate the asset/liability management methodology used by the company, and (7) understand the company's corporate structure, including parents, subsidiaries, and affiliated entities. The full financial picture will remain incomplete until the research industry, including the respective rating agencies, acknowledges the latitude available in reporting, demands and receives more detailed and timely information from insurance companies for analyzing the long-term profitability of the insurer, and employs valuation actuaries as a part of the research staff.

Under current industry reporting practices, the necessary information is not provided for a thorough analysis. While the regulatory authorities recognize the needs of the buyer, it will be years before regulations require the missing information, although some strides forward, led by the New York Insurance Department and the NAIC, are being made. As many an analyst has said repeatedly, the insurance industry is the hardest to analyze because of the limited information available and because of the specialized knowledge required to understand reserves, reinsurance, and product pricing.

EXHIBIT 5-1

Insurance Company Annual Statutory Statement Outline

Page 1	Name, address, list of chief officers
Page 2–3	Balance sheet
Page 4	Summary of operations for current year and previous year
Page 4A	Sources of cash flow for current year and previous year
Page 5	Gain or loss by line of business (current year)
Page 6	Analysis of increase in reserves (current year)
Page 7	Premiums by line of business (current year)
Page 7A	Dividends and coupons applied, reinsurance commissions and expense allowances, and commissions incurred (current year)
Exhibit 1, Part 1	
Exhibit 1, Part 2	
Exhibit 2	Net investment income (current year)
Page 8	Gross investment income by type of asset (current year)
Exhibit 3	Capital gains and losses by type of asset (current year)
Exhibit 4	General expenses by type of expense (current year)
Page 9	Taxes, licenses, and fees (current year)
Exhibit 5	Dividends to policyholders (current year)
Exhibit 6	Life insurance reserves by line of business (current year)
Exhibit 7	Changes in reserve valuation basis (current year)
Exhibit 8	Accident and health reserves (current year)
Exhibit 8A	Reserves for deposit funds and other contracts without life or disability contingencies (current year)
Pages 10–11	
Page 11	Claims by line of business (current year)
Exhibit 9	Reconciliation of assets with those from prior year end
Exhibit 10	Admitted assets
Pages 12–12A	Analysis of nonadmitted assets
Page 13	Five-year historical data of key financial information
Page 14	Life insurance in force at end of current year traced from in force at beginning of current year
Exhibit 11	Analysis of life insurance issued and in force at the end of current year
Exhibit 12	
Exhibit 13	
Exhibit 14	
Pages 14A–14B	
Page 15	
Page 15A	

EXHIBIT 5–1 (*concluded*)

Page 31	Schedule D, Part 5	Listing of long-term bonds and stocks acquired and sold during current year by major type
Page 31A	Schedule D, Part 6	Questionnaire relating to valuation of shares of subsidiary, controlled, or affiliated companies
Page 31B	Schedule DA, Part 1	Listing of short-term investments owned at end of current year
Page 31C	Schedule DA, Part 2	Verification of short-term investments between years
Page 31D–31I	Schedule DB	Listing of financial options and futures acquired during year, disposed of during year, or owned at end of current year
Page 32	Schedule E	Banks, trust companies, savings and loan and building and loan associations in which a balance was maintained at any time during current year
Page 33	Schedule F	Claims resisted or compromised during current year
Page 34	Schedule G	Payments in excess of $1,000 to any trade association, service organization, statistical, actuarial, or rating bureau during the year
Page 35	Schedule H	Details of gain or loss on accident and health line during current year by major type of business
Page 36	Schedule I	Commissions and collection fees paid in connection with loans or properties
	Schedule J	Legal expenses paid during the year
Page 37	Schedule K	Expenditures in connection with matters before legislative bodies, officers, or departments of government during the year
Pages 38–41	Schedule L	Proceedings of last annual election of directors or trustees
	Schedule M	Dividends paid or illustrated on policies including a description of the dividend formulas used by the company
Page 42	Schedule O	Development of incurred losses on accident and health insurance
Pages 42–43	Schedule S	Information about reinsurance ceded and reinsurance assumed
Page 44	Schedule X	Assets unlisted on any other schedule owned at end of current year
Page 44A	Schedule Y, Part 1	Organizational chart showing relationship of all affiliated insurance companies
Page 44B	Schedule Y, Part 2	Summary of company's transactions during the year with any affiliates
Page 45	Schedule T	Premiums and annuity considerations by state

Many GICs provide a termination clause should the contractholder desire to withdraw the funds entirely from the contract. At many insurance companies, new fixed-income investments have maturities of from 12 to 15 years. The average duration of the portfolio is perhaps six to seven years. The cashout formula, in theory, should produce an amount available for immediate distribution to the contractholder that closely approximates the current market value of a hypothetical bond with a six- or seven-year maturity (1) having a face or par value equal to the book value of the blended rate being earned on the contract, (2) earning interest at a coupon rate equal to the contract, and (3) being discounted at the currently available rate of interest for new investments.

The current market value of a bond with a face or par value of $750,000 maturing in seven years and a coupon rate of 10.27 percent, where the current rate available on new investments is 9.6 percent, is approximately $774,800. Thus the contract should be redeemable at a premium of about 103.3 percent of book value ($774,800/$750,000). Alternatively, if the rate currently available for new investments were 11.0 percent rather than 9.6 percent, then the value of the same contract would be $724,000, or about 96.6 percent of book value.

The factors used to determine the market value of the contract should be independent of the control of the insurance company. For example, in the illustration just used, the book value and the rate of return on the contract are known. More difficult to verify independently is the rate of interest currently available to the insurance company on new investments. Contracts often provide a surrogate for the current rate available on new investments, such as one of the published bond indexes over which the insurance has no control.

Guaranteed investment contracts usually provide that whenever an amount less than book value is produced by the application of the market value adjustment formula, an alternative installment payout at book value may be elected by the contractholder. Payments frequently are made in six installments over five years. Interest paid on the unpaid balance is usually reduced so that the insurance company is able to make up any loss from book value that would have resulted from the application of the market value adjustment formula. In the foregoing example, it could be expected that the rate of interest paid on the declining balance would be between 8.5 percent and 8.75 percent. In effect, the insurance company is lending the contractholder an amount equal to the market value loss at a current interest rate and then amortizing that loan over five years. The amount paid back each year on the loan is reflected in the form of reduced interest credits on the unpaid balance being repaid to the contractholder at book value over the five-year payout period. In the above example, if the market value loss is $26,000 ($750,000 − $724,000), this amount is treated as having been loaned to the contractholder at 11.0 percent interest. The annual rate of repayments to amortize the loan over five years will be about $7,000 per year.

The contract will pay out $750,000 at book value as follows: $125,000 immediately, and $125,000 per year for each of the next five years plus interest calculated on the unpaid balance at 10.27 percent. The theoretical annual payment is $166,000 per year, but when this amount is reduced by the $7,000 loan repayment, the actual payment is reduced to $159,000 per year. This works out to an effective net interest rate of about 8.6 percent net after the repayment of the "loan."

---

[13]"Is an Experience-Rated Investment Contract Ever a Viable Alternative to a GIC?" by D. J. Smith and P. A. Lupo, was reprinted with permission from the December 1987 issue of *Employee Benefits Journal*, published by the International Foundation of Employee Benefit Plans, Brookfield, WI. Statements or opinions expressed in this article are those of the authors and do not necessarily represent the views or positions of the International Foundation, its officers, directors, or staff.

CHAPTER 6

PRICING THE GUARANTEED INVESTMENT CONTRACT[1]

Frederic W. Corwin, Jr., FSA
Second Vice President
John Hancock Mutual Life Insurance Company

INTRODUCTION

The pricing of investment contracts issued by life insurance companies may appear to be without logic. One day, a AAA-rated insurer quotes the highest market rate; another day, the lowest rate. It has often been said that quote spreads among the major issuers represent one of the market's greatest inefficiencies. In this chapter we will attempt to present the reasons for such spreads.

When structuring the quote, the insurance company, in essence, is borrowing money and investing the borrowed funds at a return in excess of the rate on the contract. The return must be more than the guarantee to provide for all expenses and costs of providing the guarantee and return an adequate profit to the insurer. The insurer's *value added* comes from the management of the supporting assets, the underwriting of risks, and the guarantee of return. The ability to provide a *book value* guarantee is an additional value added.

---

[1]Parts of this chapter were originally contributed in the first edition by Klaus Shigley, FSA, John Hancock Life Insurance Company.

The insurer is managing two portfolios simultaneously—
the assets and the liabilities. While the pricing of a contract is
typically done in relation to the return from an individual asset,
the actual management of the portfolio is accomplished by purchasing assets based on the aggregate of contracts which have
been sold. The individual contracts do not depend on specific individual assets; neither do the acquisitions of individual assets
depend on specific individual contract liabilities.

Each insurer has a strategy, usually based on its competitive advantages, which dictates how it determines its pricing,
including determination of the profit charge. The net investment rate is the gross investment yield less deductions for investment expenses, expected rates of default, and any necessary
adjustment for call features on callable investments.

NET INVESTMENT RATE

The net investment rate should reflect the currently available
investment rate for the company. Twenty years ago this rate
could be forecast for a calendar year. Rates were stable and companies typically invested on an advance-commitment basis.
Since 1979 this practice has become impossible as a result of the
volatility in the fixed-income markets. Today, the investment
rates on GICs must be changed frequently—weekly, daily, even
instantly; this requires excellent lines of communication among
the investment, pricing, and sales departments.

In addition to adjusting the investment rate of return,
there must be an understanding as to how much investment capacity there is for acquisitions of supporting investments at the
quoted rate. There is a limit on the available investment capacity which depends on a variety of factors. These include the relationships with the investment community as a means of
access to deals, the expectations of borrowers regarding interest
rate movements, and economic activity.

The investment department must provide a spectrum of
rates across all maturities. This allows for the development of a
yield curve of rates applicable to contracts at any maturity, or
combination of maturities.

It is important that a common basis be used or understood when communicating rates from the investment area to the pricing area. Typically, investment rates are expressed as bond equivalent yields, that is, the yield for semiannual coupons. Since rates on GICs are expressed as annual effective yields, a conversion from one basis to the other is a necessary step.

Another step is developing the investment rates to correspond to the payout structure. Companies issue either bullet contracts with interest compounded and reinvested at the contract rate or simple-interest contracts with interest paid periodically. The latter works well with bond equivalent yields, whereas the former requires the development of spot rates (zero-coupon yields).

The adjustment for options on investments recognizes that not all of the yield from call provisions in bonds and prepayment options in mortgages should be passed on to contractholders. When rates fall, these bonds will be called and the mortgages prepaid, requiring the proceeds to be reinvested at lower rates. Without some deduction for the call option, the issuer will experience a loss on the investment return.

A similar deduction is necessary for the risk of default. Higher yields available from lower investment grades are not recognized in their entirety. Some amount, varying by the investment grade, is typically deducted.

STRATEGIES

Insurance companies are in the liability-management business. Every policy written creates a liability for the issuing carrier. It must manage this liability so as not to jeopardize the company's net worth.

A fundamental objective of the industry is to avoid the unknown risks or events that can undermine the product's pricing structure. In an effort to manage these unknown risks, insurance companies can employ various stringent actuarial and investment disciplines.

Exhibit 6–1 presents a framework for business strategies. Along one axis, the insurer selects from a spectrum of exposure

EXHIBIT 6–1
Matrix of Business Strategies

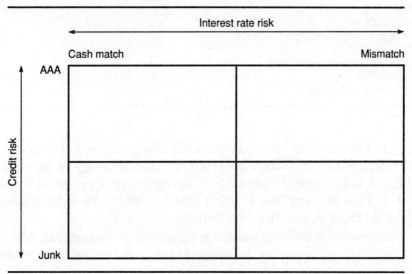

to interest rate risks. Along the other dimension, the insurer selects from a spectrum of exposure to credit risks. Each combination within the matrix represents a different business strategy. For example, the lower right-hand box represents a strategy characterized by an investment policy of large interest rate bets and large credit bets.

INTEREST RATE RISK

It is important to understand how interest rate risks are managed. Exhibit 6–2 lists six methods of managing the interest rate risk. At one extreme, the additional risk can be managed by deliberately mismatching the assets and liabilities. This strategy prevailed for many financial institutions prior to 1980, most notably thrifts and savings banks, but also certain accounts maintained by insurance companies. At the other extreme, interest rate risk can be managed by matching each liability outflow with an asset inflow. This method, referred to as *cash flow matching,* eliminates the interest rate risk.

EXHIBIT 6–2
Managing the Interest Rate Risk

Mismatching
Tactical interest rate bets
Duration matching
Duration/Convexity matching
Horizon matching
Cash flow matching

Between these two extremes, different degrees of exposure to interest rate risk can be selected. One strategy is to make limited bets on the direction of the general level of interest rates. This is a *tactical interest rate bet,* which is to be distinguished from indiscriminate betting.

Duration matching is a more conservative strategy in which exposure to a change in the shape of the yield curve is accepted but protects against exposure to changes in the general level of interest rates.

An even more conservative strategy is to avoid exposure to most of the changes in the shape of the yield curve as well as the general level of rates. This is achieved by matching both duration and convexity, the second order derivative of the pricing function.

Horizon matching combines cash flow matching for a limited period of time with duration matching for the flows beyond the horizon for the cash flow match.

The motive for duration mismatching is to generate higher gross investment rates. An illustrative Treasury yield curve (see Exhibit 6–3) shows that an additional 214 basis points can be obtained if funds are invested in 10-year bonds to cover a three-month liability. The investor can borrow funds for three months at a cost of 5.90 percent and invest them in 10-year instruments at 8.04 percent, ignoring spreads over Treasuries.

It is important to understand both the risks and the implications of mismatching. Exhibit 6–4 illustrates the risk of mismatching. The vertical axis represents price, and the horizontal axis represents interest rates. The three curves demonstrate

EXHIBIT 6–3
Treasury Yield Curve (April 1, 1991)

Maturity	Yield (in percent)	Spread versus 3 Months (percent)
3 months	5.90	——
6 months	6.00	0.10
1 year	6.20	0.30
5 years	7.71	1.81
10 years	8.04	2.14

the sensitivity of prices to interest rate changes for long- and short-maturity assets and an intermediate-term fixed liability.

The price function of the long-term asset has the greatest "slope," or price/unit change in interest rate. The slope of a price function is a measure of its price volatility with respect to interest rates. This measure is more generally called *duration.*

The short-term asset has virtually no price volatility as is indicated by its straight-line price function. Its duration (the slope of its price function) is approximately zero. These price

EXHIBIT 6–4
Asset/Liability Mismatch

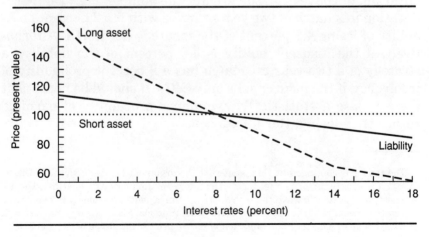

functions are graphical representations of the well-known fact that long-term fixed-income assets have greater price risk (or sensitivity) than short-term fixed-income assets.

This illustration of price functions is useful for two reasons. First, it shows the potential consequences of a mismatch. Consider, for example, the gap between the liability curve and the long-term asset curve when rates rise and there is a duration mismatch (if the slopes of the price functions are not equal). Second, the exhibit illustrates how to use a specific weighted combination of a long- and short-term asset to create a portfolio whose price function matches the slope (or price volatility) of an intermediate-term liability. This portfolio-management technique is called *barbelling*.

The objective in matching the duration of liabilities and assets is to immunize surplus from interest rate changes. If assets and liabilities have the same duration, they have equal price sensitivity. That is, the relationship between the price of the assets and liabilities will not change when interest rates change (and the yield curve shape is unchanged).[2]

Why do we care what strategy an insurer uses to manage the interest risk? If it is believed that interest rates behave randomly, then a strategy other than cash-matching is a gamble. This is illustrated in Exhibit 6–5.

The greater the mismatch (whether in terms of cash flow, duration, or convexity), the greater the gamble. For example, a duration mismatch of two years carries with it a 2 percent probability of losing 4.9 percent of the insurer's net worth. Alternatively, if the insurer's equity is 4.9 percent of the liability, a strategy of a two-year mismatch has a 2 percent probability of insolvency, if the insurer sells only GICs. It should be noted that there is also a statistically symmetric probability of earning, rather than losing, the 4.9 percent.

---

[2]The reader is cautioned at this point that the argument has been simplified here. *Duration* is merely the first-order term in an approximation for price volatility. The approximation is improved when the second-order term is added, commonly referred to as *convexity*, a measure of the curvature of the price function. Matching convexity as well as duration gives a better approximation of future price if the shape of the yield curve changes.

EXHIBIT 6–5
Capital Requirements for Mismatch (in percent)

		Duration Mismatch (in years)			
		.5	1	2	5
	33%	.3	.5	1.1	2.6
Probability	10%	.8	1.5	3.1	7.7
of	5%	1.0	2.0	3.9	9.8
Insolvency	2%	1.2	2.5	4.9	12.3

Assumes: Parallel shifts
Interest rate: 8%
Standard deviation: 15%

The statistical assertions above assume that interest rates behave randomly and that changes in rates have a standard deviation (or *volatility*) of 15 percent.[3] This does not mean that such a bet is inherently unsound. It does mean that the insurer must have sufficient net worth to survive a losing bet. If the insurance company does not have the resources, there is a residual probability of insolvency, and the plan sponsor (or the plan participants) will have to provide the needed funds.

If the insurer wishes to mismatch, then it must be prepared to risk surplus, the magnitude of which depends on the degree of confidence it has in the outcome. In general, it is reasonable to expect that insurers operate in excess of the 98 percent confidence level.

CREDIT RISK

The other dimension of risk is the credit risk. As indicated in Exhibit 6–6, there has been a significant spread over Treasuries for investing in junk bonds. In less than a 12-month period,

---

[3]That is, if interest rates are initially at 8 percent, then 65 percent (i.e., plus or minus one standard deviation from the mean) of interest rate outcomes in the next 12 months will lie between 9.2 percent and 6.8 percent (i.e., 8 percent ± .15 × 8 percent).

EXHIBIT 6–6
High-Yield Bond Spreads

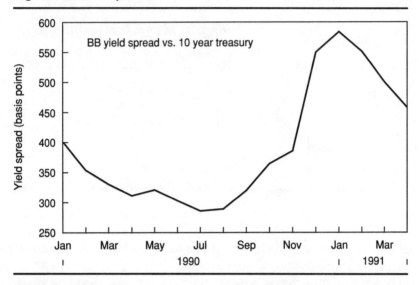

Source: Salomon Brothers.

spreads between junk bonds and Treasuries ranged from about 300 basis points to almost 600 basis points.

The downside to this buying opportunity is the increased probability of default that is indicated in Exhibit 6–7. In 1970 the net default rate for speculative grade bonds exceeded 10 percent, and in 1990 was almost 9 percent. In comparison, during the period from 1970 to 1990, the net annual default rate for investment-grade bonds peaked in 1986 at 0.3 percent.

For the purpose of supporting guarantees with junk bond portfolios, there is not much relevance to the average default of 4.2 percent. Providing for an average default rate is not a *real life, real answers* solution. That would be analogous to the classic illustration of the army that drowned while crossing the stream that was only three feet deep on average! To be viable as a strategy, investing in junk bonds carries with it the obligation not only to provide for an average default rate but also to maintain sufficient capital to survive the disaster scenarios.

It is fair to say that most insurance company managements aim to survive not merely the recession scenarios but also the

EXHIBIT 6–7
Historical Default Rates

Year	Speculative Grade Bonds (in percent)	Investment Grade Bonds (in percent)
1970	10.9	0.1
1971	1.6	0.0
1972	3.7	0.0
1973	1.4	0.2
1974	1.4	0.0
1975	2.3	0.0
1976	1.4	0.0
1977	1.9	0.1
1978	1.8	0.0
1979	0.4	0.0
1980	1.5	0.0
1981	0.7	0.0
1982	3.4	0.2
1983	3.4	0.0
1984	3.5	0.2
1985	4.4	0.0
1986	5.7	0.3
1987	4.0	0.0
1988	3.4	0.0
1989	5.8	0.2
1990	8.8	0.0
Average	4.2	0.1
Standard deviation	2.6	0.1

5-Year Default Rates (in percent)

1970–74	19.0
1975–79	7.8
1980–84	12.5
1985–89	23.3
1986–90	27.7

Source: Moody's Investors Service.

depression scenarios. The data suggests that a portfolio comprised exclusively of junk bonds must be supported by at least an 11 percent capital, or equity, base to survive one disaster year. To assure survival through a longer period of above-average defaults, such as 1986–90, an equity base closer to 30 percent may be necessary.

The quality dimension of credit risk is readily assessed, thanks to the bond rating agencies. There are other aspects of risk, however, which lend themselves less readily to such assessment. For example, geographic and industry diversification of risk are important, too, as is the mix of asset types within a portfolio.

The focus thus far has been on the statistical consequences of aggressive business strategies. Have these potentially disastrous consequences deterred all the players from engaging in these strategies? No.

Within the GIC industry, examples exist of companies at every point on the spectrum of interest rate risks. The insurance industry, long known for its conservative approach to investments, is not generally viewed as taking high degrees of credit risk, with the notable exception of those who invested heavily in junk bonds.

How does the market operate to provide stability and order? There are two fundamental principles which apply. The first principle is that in order to generate similar comfort levels, the capital markets demand greater amounts of capital from those companies engaged in riskier strategies. The second principle is that higher-rated financial institutions will generally hold more equity than lower-rated institutions.

PROFIT MARGINS—PROVIDING FOR A PROPER RETURN ON EQUITY

How does all this explain the issue raised earlier about the large variation in GIC rate guarantees among otherwise similar insurance companies? The answer lies in the determination of the cost of capital and the capital allocation decision.

Exhibit 6–8 shows how the return on equity is calculated for a spread-lending business, such as the management of GICs. The basic idea (which is illustrated in the middle equation) is that with $5 of capital, $100 of someone else's money can be borrowed and invested at a spread of 50 basis points. If the $5 is invested at 9 percent, the total return on the $5 investment is 19

EXHIBIT 6–8
Return on Equity (ROE) Equation

$$\frac{PM \times L + RIE \times E}{E} = ROE \text{ before tax}$$

$$\frac{.5\% \times \$100 + 9\% \times \$5}{\$5} = \frac{\$.95}{\$5} = 19\%$$

$$\frac{(1 - TR)(PM \times L + RIE \times E)}{E} = ROE \text{ after tax}$$

PM	= Profit margin
RIE	= Return on invested equity
L	= Liability
E	= Equity
TR	= Tax rate

percent before taxes. If $1,000 were borrowed with $5 of capital and invested at the 50 basis-point spread, the return on investment would be 109 percent. It is unlikely, however, that a lender would loan $1,000 to support a venture capitalized at $5 unless there were very little risk of failure.

Exhibit 6–9 shows where all this is leading. The table shows the required profit margins for both 10 percent and 15 percent after-tax return on equity (ROE) targets for various capital allocations. To support a 10 percent capital allocation to the business, and to achieve a 15 percent after-tax ROE

EXHIBIT 6–9
Required Profit Margin

		After-Tax ROE	
		10%	15%
	2%	.13%	.28%
Capital	4%	.26%	.56%
Allocation	7%	.45%	.99%
	10%	.64%	1.41%
	15%	.96%	2.11%

Assumes: *RIE* = 9%; *TR* = 35%

objective, the spread between net investment income and the net guarantee requires 141 basis points for profit. It is not difficult to find gross spreads of 141 basis points among GIC quotes, suggesting that some insurers are allocating less capital to the business or requiring a lower return on equity.

How can there be such big differences in GIC guarantees? It was demonstrated earlier that an additional 214 basis points can be obtained for mismatching along the Treasury yield curve and 300 to 600 basis points for investing in junk bonds. The balance of the answer lies in the capital allocation for various risk strategies.

CAPITAL ALLOCATION

How much capital should be allocated to back the GIC? The answer depends on the risks of the strategy employed. For example, a 4 percent capital allocation for a large duration mismatch and a high-risk credit strategy is clearly inappropriate—that is, too low. If 4 percent is the capital allocation that is used to determine the cost of capital, and thus used in setting the price, and the remaining investment spread is passed into the guarantee, the guarantee will be too high. If the correct capital allocation is 10 percent, then the cost of capital is understated by 38 basis points (64 basis points less 26 basis points) for a 10 percent after-tax ROE objective, and 85 basis points (141 basis points less 56 basis points) for a 15 percent after-tax ROE.

For the company choosing to place itself in the lower-right corner of the strategy matrix (Exhibit 6–1), the appropriate level of capital will be extraordinarily high, possibly as much as 20 percent (if, say, 15 percent were required for a 100 percent junk bond portfolio and 5 percent for a two-year duration mismatch). In a 10 percent ROE environment, this requires a profit charge of 128 basis points.

For the conservative strategy of low credit risk and small mismatch, the appropriate level of capital might be 2 percent (1.5 percent, for AAA quality investments, and 0.5 percent for the mismatch). The profit charge is only 13 basis points for this low-risk combination.

Thus, the profit component of pricing can easily differ widely among companies. The exact level of profit depends on the amount of capital that the company allocates to back its GICs. Higher levels of capital are required for taking on credit and interest rate risk, and to obtain high quality ratings. Given the capital allocated to support the product, target returns on capital and actual returns on invested surplus combine to determine the profit margin that should be charged.

There are other risk categories and other uses of capital that are generated on the liability side of the balance sheet. One other use of capital is *surplus strain,* which occurs when the required statutory reserves are greater than the GIC fund balance. Any GIC contract that is issued at a rate higher than the NAIC standard valuation rate for that year will cause surplus strain. The excess of the reserve over the fund balances is a use of surplus. Even though this effect is only for statutory accounting, because the statutory balance sheet is used for public statements of capital, it is appropriate to require a return on surplus strain as well as on risk capital.

BOOK VALUE RISK ON CONTRIBUTIONS AND DEPOSITS

Liability risks generally evolve from the guarantee of book value. The right of participants to change contributions and withdrawals as interest rates fluctuate creates an additional set of risks.

In the early 1980s, many GICs were the ultimate in simplicity. They typically consisted of single-sum deposits that were compounded at the guaranteed rate of interest to maturity. Because of the high levels of interest rates at that time, investment contracts were attractive to defined benefit plans, which did not require interim contract liquidity. As defined contribution plans became popular, especially for 401 (k) plans, two features evolved to accommodate plan design requirements.

First, defined contribution plans receive contributions continuously. Thus, it is desirable to secure contracts that accept all contributions over a fixed period of time, typically a 12-month period.[4] This is the *window* feature.

Second, defined contribution plans allow participants to withdraw their account balances for death, disability, termination of employment, loans, hardship, and to transfer their balances to other investment options available within the plan. This is known as *benefit responsiveness*.

THE CALL OPTION

These two features (i.e., windows and benefit responsiveness) represent options to the plan participants. Under the window option, the issuer guarantees the contract rate of interest to all contributions during the window, regardless of how interest rates have moved. So a participant may, via contributions and transfers from other investment options, direct more money into the investment contract if rates fall and receive the same (but now more attractive) rate of interest. This is a *call* option which the participant holds with respect to contributions.

A somewhat similar option exists with the benefit-responsive feature. Participants have the option not to withdraw benefits and not to transfer out of the investment contract if rates fall. The effect is the same as receiving more in contributions: the insurer has more to invest at lower interest rates.

Exhibit 6–10 illustrates the price function of the call option. As interest rates decline below the guarantee, the option increases in value. The participant may increase deposits into the high-rate contract. As rates decline, the price of the option rises, while the price of the asset, which the insurer must purchase, also rises as shown in Exhibit 6–4. The issuer needs to protect against this situation, either by preventing extra contributions or by assessing a risk charge to reduce the guaranteed rate under the contract.

---

[4]A 12-month period has been the standard for several years, but shorter windows are becoming popular because of the growth in plan size, the desire to reduce window-period risk, and to avoid timing bets.

EXHIBIT 6–10
Liability Call Option

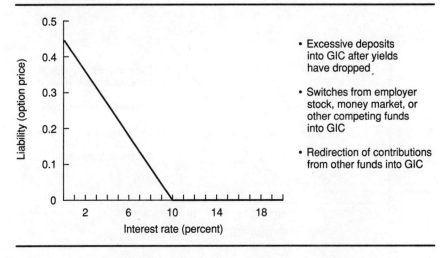

- Excessive deposits into GIC after yields have dropped

- Switches from employer stock, money market, or other competing funds into GIC

- Redirection of contributions from other funds into GIC

THE PUT OPTION

Withdrawals under benefit-responsive contracts and transfers to other investment options represent the exercise of a put option owned by the participants. They can *put* their share of the contract back to the issuer in return for their money at book value. Additionally, the participants can reduce their contributions to the investment contract. If interest rates have risen, this creates a loss to the issuer since asset values fall with rising interest rates.

Exhibit 6–11 illustrates how the value of the put option increases as interest rates rise. In typical GIC applications, the option is owned by the plan participant, who has the right to sell (put) the participation in the GIC back to the insurance company at a fixed price (book value). Exercise of this option can be accomplished by making in-service withdrawals at book value, transfers to money market or other competing funds, and redirection of contributions to other investment options. Again, by comparing to the asset function in Exhibit 6–4, we can see that the value of the liability option increases while the value of the asset decreases.

EXHIBIT 6–11
Liability Put Option

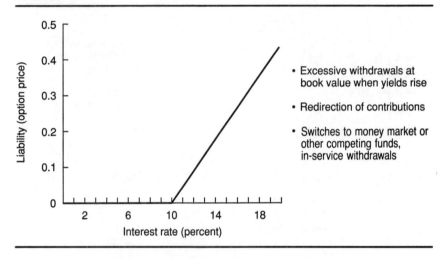

- Excessive withdrawals at book value when yields rise

- Redirection of contributions

- Switches to money market or other competing funds, in-service withdrawals

Both the call and the put options have value to the plan participants. Consequently, these options represent a risk to the insurer regardless of whether interest rates move up or down.

Exhibit 6–12 shows transfers among various investment options made between 1981 and 1984 in the profit-sharing plan of a large bank. All transfers to and from the GIC fund were made at book value. Although most insurance companies no longer issue GICs to plans that permit direct transfers to com-

EXHIBIT 6–12
Breakdown of Flows

	Transfers			
	1981	*1982*	*1983*	*1984*
GIC	(1,674,028)	(187,122)	5,454,985	3,239,474
Stocks and bonds	(313,569)	(1,576,928)	322,235	(2,593,420)
Real estate	(20,239)	139,913	113,577	(61,638)
Money market	2,023,565	1,664,305	(5,248,710)	626,258
Company stock	(15,729)	(40,168)	(642,087)	(1,210,674)

peting money market options, this exhibit clearly illustrates the problems faced by GIC underwriters.

This plan has a money market option as well as a guaranteed interest option. The cash flows evidence the effective utilization of the option granted by the GIC issuer. When yield curves were inverted in 1981, funds were transferred from the GIC fund to the money market option. When interest rates declined in 1983, funds flowed from the money market option to the higher-rate GIC option.

In 1983, the $5 million of transfers from the money market fund to the GIC fund were roughly equal to ongoing contributions directed to the GIC option. In this case the contributions to the GIC fund after interest rates had fallen were double the expected contributions. This exhibit of cash flows is a dramatic example of the more general phenomenon of written options inside GIC contracts.

UNDERWRITING THE WINDOW RISK

The surest method of controlling the window, or deposit, risk is through underwriting techniques to limit the variation in deposits during the window. Restricting contributions to a range, via the use of "floors and caps," eventually gave way to "exact dollar windows." Under the latter technique, the window risk is virtually eliminated.[5] Another technique is to shorten the window period.

The alternative to contractual controls on the window is a risk charge, which reduces the interest rate guarantee. The value of this charge must reflect the expected cost of extra contributions if interest rates decline. This requires determining probable downward interest rate movements and the expected amount of extra contributions at those rates.

---

[5]Practical aspects of underwriting make complete elimination of risk impossible. Excess contributions are typically held temporarily, they may come in faster or slower than expected, and expected maturities may be unavailable to make up deficiencies. A risk charge is necessary for these contingencies.

The cost of the window risk can be calculated through the use of interest rate option models. Such models are designed to mimic expected participant behavior. Unlike mortality, which can be modeled via mortality functions, participant behavior is not reliable for a variety of reasons. In general, participants are expected to require a sufficient premium in yields as an incentive to change their investment strategy. Even then, we can expect that many participants will nevertheless be slow to react, reflecting a group inefficiency.

UNDERWRITING THE POST-WINDOW WITHDRAWAL RISK

Determinants of Option Risk

Most contracts provide that certain actions initiated by the plan sponsor will cause the resultant withdrawals to be paid out at the lesser of book value and the company's approximation to a "market value" reflecting current interest rates.[6] This effectively eliminates the ability of the plan sponsor to exercise the book value option on behalf of the participants. Consequently, in evaluating the option risk only the actions of the participants need to be considered. This is not a simple task, however, since a variety of factors affects the option value as it applies to the participants.

The cost to the GIC issuer is a function of the current interest rate levels and the interest rates in effect at the time of issue. By contrast, the participant should value the option as a function of the *blended rate* for the fund and the interest rates available from alternative investments. As a practical matter, participants do not exercise this option as efficiently as interest rate levels would suggest.

Some of the factors influencing participants' behavior are:

1. *Transfer restrictions.* Plans usually do not allow participants to move funds directly between the GIC fund and

---

[6]Some recent contracts provide for withdrawals, including those from employer-initiated actions, to be paid at book value up to a specified percentage of the fund.

a money market fund. A participant must move money to an equity fund, where the principal is at risk, for up to six months before completing the transfer to the money market fund.

2. *Risk tolerance.* Participants may prefer to keep their investments in as safe an investment as possible, putting a premium on the protection of principal.

3. *Investment horizon.* Many participants use their plan to save for purposes that have a short time horizon, such as purchase of a house or college education.

4. *Sophistication.* A participant's understanding of financial markets and the characteristics of the financial instruments plays a role. Those who do not understand equity or bond funds will likely utilize GIC funds, which are simpler to understand and require less attention. Participant communication materials may influence behavior and should be reviewed.

5. *Withdrawal restrictions.* IRS regulations on 401 (k) plans restrict participant withdrawals to death, disability, retirement, attainment of age 59½, termination of employment, hardship reasons (medical care expenses, education, purchase of principal residence), and plan termination.

6. *Taxes.* Withdrawals of pretax contributions and earnings are subject to a 10 percent excise tax in addition to the ordinary income tax.

7. *Plan blended rate.* Many plans use a "blended rate" approach to credit a portfolio interest rate to participant account balances. When interest rates on new GICs decline, the blended rate declines less rapidly, resulting in a comparatively attractive rate.

The net effect of these factors is to make the participants less sensitive to changes in interest rates. As a result, interest rates need to move significantly before the plan shows a reaction to the new level of rates through changes in the levels of withdrawals or contributions. The effect on the put option for withdrawals is demonstrated graphically in Exhibit 6–13. With

EXHIBIT 6–13
Liability Put Option (Inefficient Exercise)

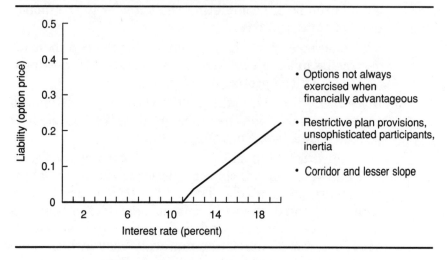

rising interest rates and an inefficient exercise, the option value rises less rapidly than in Exhibit 6–11. We might expect that the differential in rates must be at least 100 basis points to cause a change in behavior.

Even with a significant difference in rates, participants are not expected to exhibit the same sensitivity to interest rate changes as would be calculated in a financial market option. This is characterized as a lesser degree of *sensitivity*.

SUMMARY

Insurance companies are faced with a host of risks. Life and health insurance risks differ from investment contract risks. The latter is more concerned with asset risks, market risks, put and call option risks, and mismatch risks. Prudent management incorporates all risk possibilities into the long-term management strategy of the product as well as the company.

CHAPTER 7

EMERGING ASSET/LIABILITY MANAGEMENT STRATEGIES

Martin H. Ruby, CEO
Analytical Risk Management, Ltd.

INTRODUCTION

When an insurance company issues a GIC it creates a liability on its balance sheet. The funds generated by the GIC deposit are invested in a variety of financial instruments (bonds, mortgages, private placements, etc.) that become assets of the insurer. The ultimate profitability of the GIC product line to the insurance company is determined by the return earned on the assets less the return paid to GIC contractholders and the insurer's expenses. Thus the concept of asset/liability management has gained increased importance as the volume of GICs has expanded over the last several years.

Bank-issued BICs have a similar impact on a bank's balance sheet. Even synthetic structures rely on the underlying asset/liability management concepts to ensure that they are structured soundly. Therefore, even though this chapter focuses on asset/liability management strategies for insurance companies, there is fairly broad application to BICs and synthetic GICs in terms of how they are designed and priced. By understanding these strategies, one can better appreciate the reasons why GICs, BICs, and synthetic GICs have certain design limitations, and how the issuer goes about ensuring that the interest rate and principal guarantees are met.

HISTORICAL BACKGROUND

Historically, insurance companies have not integrated their asset and liability functions to any large degree. Typically, a group pension department would be in charge of marketing, pricing, and administering the contract and an entirely separate investment department would be in charge of investing the funds. Many times a corporate actuarial department provides overall staff support by studying the asset/liability position of a company under various possible interest rate and credit scenarios. However, this is done more to monitor solvency than to actually enhance profitability or reduce risk.

More recently, many issuers have moved to a more integrated approach or have tried to "cross fertilize" functions by having a pricing actuary spend time in the investment department, for example.

The nonintegrated approach has had several significant consequences in terms of product design and investment strategy. These, in turn have driven many insurance companies to certain strategies that became unsustainable when major investment market segments, such as commercial mortgages and junk bonds, deteriorated in the late 1980s and early 1990s.

To understand why, one must go back to the underlying economic basis of investment contracts from the issuing institution's viewpoint. The institutions are in the asset/liability spread management business regardless of how they go about managing their contracts and the underlying investments. Because most institutions have treated asset and liability management as separate functions, they created structures and procedures that could allow each functional area to go about its business. This led to the concept of *duration,* or *maturity matching.* As long as the contract liability being created had a similar cash flow pattern as the asset backing it, the only requirement necessary to produce a positive spread would be that the interest rate on the asset instrument had to be higher than the rate guaranteed to the contractholder.

This requirement is much more onerous than it first appears. On the liability side, there are a number of options available to the contract buyer. Window contracts create uncertainty as to cash coming into the institution. Benefit-responsiveness features create uncertainty as to the timing of outflows. On the asset side, cash flow uncertainties are created by options such as call rights attached to corporate bonds and prepayment rights that exist in many mortgages. This situation is further complicated by the fact that the likelihood of asset or liability cash flow options being exercised varies with changes in interest rate levels.

This uncertainty has led many issuers either (a) to be very restrictive in the options they are willing to grant contractholders and borrowers under commercial mortgages or private placements or (b) to assess substantial risk charges in terms of lower credited rates or higher rates payable on mortgages and private placements.

Regardless of how restrictive the issuers are concerning product and investment provisions, the efficiency of the capital markets does not allow issuers to earn a positive spread if they do not take any risk. To the extent that cash flow risk is eliminated (which is necessary when asset and liability management is unintegrated), there is only one other risk that banks and insurers could take on in order to achieve a positive spread. That risk is credit. Issuers can earn a positive spread even with no cash flow risk if they could take in contract deposits based on the institution's strong credit rating and invest in less creditworthy investments of similar cash flow patterns where the borrower is willing to pay a higher rate.

The history of asset/liability management explains why guaranteed products are designed and priced the way they are, and why such a large portion of GIC deposits have been invested in commercial mortgages, private placements, and more recently, junk bonds. The more that insurance companies treat asset management and liability management independently, the more likely they are to rely on credit as the means to earn a profit and the more likely they are to allow very limited cash flow options to the buyer (or assess large risk charges in order to grant these options).

This also explains the challenges in structuring synthetic GICs. Basically, someone has to bear the risks embedded in any asset/liability structure. To the extent that the buyer is willing to bear these risks, it receives both the benefits, (e.g., in terms of better credit quality or an initially higher credited rate) and the disadvantages (e.g., higher prepayment rates on mortgage-backed securities, which result in a lower return when interest rates drop). There is no free lunch.

During the 1970s and early 1980s the "credit mismatch" strategy of most insurers worked fairly well. Life insurance companies historically had a very large market share of private placements and commercial mortgages. The ability of the insurance industry to custom design the terms of these investment instruments to fit the liability cash flow needs of GICs coupled with their historically high yields (relative to corporate bonds) made commercial mortgages an attractive way to invest GIC deposits. The credit mismatch strategy was extended to junk bonds in the mid-1980s and life insurers became major buyers of these instruments.

However, in the 1980s several forces combined to create problems with the credit mismatch strategy. These problems were generally interrelated and reflected the financial excesses of the times.

In the commercial mortgage market, life insurers were suddenly seeing a lot of competition. Savings and loan associations were rapidly entering the market, driven by deregulation and cheap FSLIC-insured deposits. Generally, this was a new market for the S&Ls and pricing became looser and less disciplined. Adding to the competitive environment was the input of foreign money, which provided even more supply. Unfortunately, the nature of commercial real estate development is such that a supply of money for it tends to create a demand for the money. If institutions were willing to lend money, developers were willing to build regardless of the actual demand for a particular office building or shopping center.

At this point the big GIC-writing life insurers were faced with a real dilemma. They had invested heavily in large commercial mortgage production facilities, both in the home office and the field. These facilities required a continuing amount of deals in order to support their overhead. Thus, many insurers were faced with the situation where the GIC marketing department was witnessing a huge demand for the product from rapidly expanding 401(k) plans, but the investment department was having trouble justifying new commercial mortgage deals based on historically tight loan underwriting criteria. Adding to this problem was the pressure to do mortgage deals because of the need to support and justify overhead.

Because most companies still viewed product management as different from investment management, the result was a weakening in loan quality in order to invest this avalanche of money that the GICs were producing. This also meant that the actual spread the insurer could eventually earn was deteriorating since more of the loans being made would eventually go bad.

As the commercial mortgage market heated up, insurers also began investing in junk bonds. These instruments looked like the perfect way to invest GIC deposits. They generally had similar maturities as GICs and allowed insurers to leverage their credit skills to a new market. The life insurance industry as a whole became a major player in the junk bond market, with a few companies committing major portions of their portfolios to junk.

Another development occurred that was somewhat related to what was happening to life insurers. Several banks entered the GIC market with their version of the product which they called a "Bank Investment Contract" (BIC). Basically, the banks were attracted to this market because it represented a cheap source of funds. These deposits were needed to fund the banks' increased activity in areas such as (you guessed it) commercial real estate lending and, increasingly during the mid-to-late 1980s, senior debt lending to finance LBOs. Often other GIC deposits (many times from the same 401(k) plan) went to insurance companies that bought junior junk bonds of the same LBO deals.

All of these strategies came to a screeching halt in the early 1990s as the United States entered a recession. The junk bond market had already collapsed with the demise of Drexel, Burnham, and the commercial real estate market soon followed, hastened along by the S&L debacle and the generally overbuilt condition of the U.S. real estate market.

These watershed events have caused life insurance companies to completely reevaluate the future of their GIC product line. The industry is going through a substantial change as GIC buyers struggle to insulate plan participants from the severe credit problems of the economy and insurers struggle with deteriorating surplus levels and asset quality.

There are actually a number of different options available to insurers for participating in the retirement plan and accumulation markets of the future. Some insurers are actually exiting the market completely. Many do not feel they have sufficient resources in terms of surplus, people skills, size, or systems to be competitive players in the market. These insurers also feel that they cannot earn an adequate return on their surplus in such a competitive environment. Others have been forced out by credit downgrades of their claims-paying ability and by weak balance sheets.

Another option being pursued by some insurers is to de-emphasize the guaranteed market and instead offer their non-guaranteed, money management skills for a fee. This approach takes pressure off their surplus ratios and allows them to operate in a less credit-sensitive environment. Note that they are abandoning one of their major competitive advantages, which is the ability to guarantee performance.

Plan participants of defined contribution plans have always strongly favored the *guaranteed* option, due to their innate conservative and risk-averse nature. Nothing suggests this will change in the future. Thus, there will continue to be strong demand for guaranteed products. But for insurers who wish to continue competing in this market, a new way of managing the business must be developed. In the following sections the third option available to insurers, the concept of *analytical risk management* (as opposed to *credit risk management*), will be described. Analytical risk refers to the risk related to the volatility of interest rates. It is a highly statistically modeled risk that relies on fairly predictable mathematical relationships to determine changes in the values of assets or liabilities when interest rates change. Analytical risk management will be the principal way that insurers who want to remain in the guaranteed products market will manage their business in the future if they are to stay both competitive and financially strong.

ASSET/LIABILITY MANAGEMENT TOOLS

The following section presents a look at emerging asset/liability management strategies supporting analytical risk management and their impact on risk shifting, investment strategies, and product design. However, it is first necessary to review several of the technical innovations of the last several years that will make these emerging asset/liability strategies work. It cannot be emphasized enough that these innovations are as applicable to BICs and synthetic GICs as they are to insurance-company-issued GICs. Asset/liability risks are not eliminated by merely changing the wrapper of the structure; they are just borne by different entities.

Because this is a section on technical innovations, it must start with the growing role of computer technology and related software advances and how this has changed the way that financial markets are managed.

In addition, it is necessary to review the explosive growth of a wide variety of financial engineering tools such as interest rate caps, futures, and options, as well as the bewildering array of mortgage-backed structures. Many of these financial innovations would not be possible were it not for the technology advances of the 1980s. For example, the increasing complexity of multitranched mortgage-backed securities (MBS) requires powerful software in order to separate the underlying mortgage pool's cash flow into as many as 30 or 40 pieces (tranches) that are aimed at investors with different objectives. Not only are more powerful software and hardware needed to develop these structures, but they are also needed by the buyers of these structures to ensure that they understand what they are buying.

The importance of these technology advances to the GIC/BIC/synthetic GIC marketplace is that they make possible a whole new array of asset/liability strategies that do not depend on credit mismatch strategies but still provide attractive yields relative to what could be earned by simply investing in U.S. Treasury securities (the ultimate no-risk strategy).

Special mention is needed regarding software and data bases. Advances in the computing power of personal computers has enabled their designers and users to do much or all of their work at their desks without fighting for space on big, centralized mainframes. This, in turn, has broadened the types of professionals who can experiment and develop new applications exploiting these advances in technology. Responding to this increased demand, a broad array of sophisticated software has been designed to run on PCs, software that is surprisingly cheap to purchase—running the gamut from actuarially designed asset/liability stochastic models to option-pricing models to MBS software that allows the user to reverse engineer MBS and to understand which tranches are the most attractively priced. No longer can a few major Wall Street firms, banks, and insurance companies dominate certain financial markets because of their superior market knowledge or resources. The playing field is much more level now because everyone has access to the same technology and knowledge resources at very modest costs.

All of these hardware and software advances have allowed a much better and more advanced understanding of the cash flow risks embedded in financial instruments. This has provided developers and issuers of GICs/BICs/synthetic GICs with better tools to create attractive products with little or no credit risk.

There are three risk measures or techniques that the user of GICs should be aware of in this new age of technology-dependent financial instruments and strategies. The first is the concept of *duration. Duration* is defined as the change in the value of a financial instrument (or more properly, a stream of cash flows) when interest rates change by a small increment. For example, a 10-year Treasury bond might have a duration of 7 years. This means that for every 1 percent change in interest rates, the value of the Treasury bond will change by 7 percent.

Duration is an important measurement when an insurance company or bank wants to measure how its financial position changes when interest rates change. By looking at the difference between the duration of its assets and liabilities, it can determine the net financial impact to its balance sheet of a change in interest rates. Fund managers can also use the duration of their stable-value portfolios to measure how much the pension plan is exposed to favorable or unfavorable interest rate changes.

There are some major problems in using duration as an accurate measure of interest rate risk. First, credit-sensitive instruments such as junk bonds and commercial mortgages do not lend themselves to very accurate measurements. The credit component of their underlying value in the marketplace can many times overwhelm any interest rate change. For less-credit-sensitive instruments such as mortgage-backed securities or high-grade callable corporate bonds, there is quite a different problem. Consider a typical GNMA security backed by a pool of residential mortgages. When market interest rates rise, people tend to hold on to their mortgages longer because they have locked up a lower interest rate. When market rates fall, people tend to repay their mortgages more rapidly because they are refinancing or are buying a new home. Therefore, the timing of the cash flow of the GNMA security is impacted by changes in interest rates. But if the cash flow timing is impacted, this means that the duration of the financial instrument must also be changing. This second order measure of interest rate risk is called *convexity* and is defined as the change in the duration of an underlying cash flow for a given change in interest rates.

Why is convexity an important concept for users and managers of GICs and synthetic GICs? The answer is that more and more GICs and synthetic GICs are being supported by asset strategies that contain a large degree of convexity risk. While this risk measure is harder to grasp than credit risk, it nonetheless can be significant if not well managed. Perhaps the easiest way to see this is to consider a synthetic GIC backed by the GNMA security previously described. As rates fall, principal repayments increase, forcing the synthetic GIC to reinvest a larger amount in a lower-interest-rate market, thus lowering the overall return to plan participants. When rates rise, fewer homeowners in the mortgage pool prepay their mortgages, thus preventing the synthetic GIC from reinvesting in a higher-interest-rate market, which results in a lower return than could otherwise be achieved. This is the reason why financial instruments that contain a high degree of convexity risk initially carry a higher yield. The buyers of these instruments demand a risk charge to compensate for increased risk. Of course, if an insurance company uses high-convexity-risk instruments to back its GIC liabilities, it charges for this risk by adjusting the rate it is willing to guarantee.

The last asset/liability management tool that needs discussion is the broad category of stochastic and option-pricing models. These models rely on the multiple random generation of interest rate scenarios and measure the impact on the value of cash flows of an asset and/or liability under each scenario. For example, a typical stochastic model might generate anywhere from 50 to 200 interest rate scenarios. Under each of these scenarios, the value of a particular asset or asset/liability structure is measured. By calculating several statistical measures a risk profile can be developed in the form of a probability distribution. Increasingly, these stochastic models (made possible through the technological advances in computer hardware and software) are used by insurance companies and Wall Street as the most appropriate way to measure and price for duration and convexity risk. This is made necessary by the move to more analytical risk structures and away from credit risk. Indeed, cash flows with a high degree of credit risk do not work well in stochastic models because not enough of their price behavior is related to movement in interest rates. Therefore, reliance on stochastic modeling will become more common as a way to manage asset/liability risk and design new GIC products as insurance companies move away from credit risk and toward analytical risk.

FUTURE GIC PRODUCT MANAGEMENT STRATEGIES

Life insurance companies are totally rethinking how they go about managing their GIC lines of business. This will result in changes in all aspects of GIC product management.

Factors Influencing Asset Liability Management Practices

Internally, there is increasing pressure on line management of insurance companies to earn an adequate return on invested surplus. As a way to ensure that an insurance company's promises (i.e., liabilities) are met, companies are required to maintain certain levels of surplus funds in relationship to their liabilities. This limits the amount of total business a company can write based on the size of its surplus base. In the past, many companies, particularly the large mutuals, had an excess of surplus. This resulted in a less than efficient allocation of this resource and many companies in the past could justify writing GICs at very low profit levels since surplus was not scarce.

This situation has now changed entirely. Because of a variety of reasons, most insurance companies today have less surplus (as a percentage of liabilities) than in the past and surplus is seen as a scarce resource that must be allocated wisely. The impact on GICs is that most companies today are requiring larger spreads to justify using surplus for GICs versus some other corporate use (such as expanding other lines of business). This pressure to earn an adequate return on surplus results in more rational pricing of GICs in the marketplace and ultimately a healthier insurance industry. Of course, by demanding more profitable business, competition in the form of BICs and synthetic GICs is encouraged. Because surplus (or capital) tends to be a scarce resource in all types of financial institutions today, this pressure to emphasize profit over sales or deposit growth will impact the market for many years to come.

Another trend among insurance companies is the need to quantify risks embedded on both sides of the balance sheet. We have examined in previous sections the credit problems caused by the excesses of the 1980s. These credit problems will be with us for years to come, particularly with commercial mortgages. Many observers feel that even good mortgages on insurers' books will eventually go bad as leases supporting the mortgaged properties expire and are renewed at significantly lower rent levels due to the oversupply of properties in most major markets. Junk bonds will also go through many future years of restructuring and defaults, impacted somewhat by the overall health of the economy. The major problem for the insurance industry (and the banking industry, as well) is that these credit risks really cannot be measured. It is very difficult to quantify these risks and therefore judge the overall financial soundness of an institution. This problem of credit risk uncertainty is driving the overall GIC industry to explore new structures that can insulate the buyer from the credit woes of the issuer. It is also driving the emergence of synthetic GICs. However, as was shown, other risks (principally analytical) are substituted instead; these require an understanding and measurement before they are used.

As insurance companies shift to investments containing more analytical risk (and less credit risk) there is growing pressure to build up the resources on the asset management side required to measure and manage these risks. However, analytical risks also exist on the liability side of the balance sheet. These are driven by features such as window contracts (which make inflows uncertain), benefit-responsive provisions (which make outflows uncertain), and specialized products such as floating-rate GICs (which make the interest rate credited uncertain).

Therefore, as companies move toward analytical-risk-management strategies, they will have to start integrating asset and liability management as never before. It will no longer be possible for the liability manager (i.e., the GIC product department) to gather funds through GIC issuance at a given interest rate and duration and hand these funds over to the investment department to invest at the same duration, but at a higher interest rate. The kinds of investment instruments and product features being used today do not lend themselves to a simple and single risk measurement such as duration. Increasingly, GIC issuers will have to view their asset/liability position as an integrated whole and not two semi-independent pieces of the balance sheet.

This also means that there will be a greater reliance on Wall Street and other outside risk management resources to support the development and growth of these new asset/liability management strategies. Internally, there will have to be a rethinking of how the insurance company is organized to compete in the GIC market and what kinds of skills are required by its staff. There will be less emphasis on credit analysis skills and more on analytical and statistical skills. Because the asset and liability functions will become increasingly integrated, investment professionals will need a better understanding of marketing and product development, and marketing professionals and actuaries will need a better understanding of investments. Everyone will need a better understanding of how assets and liabilities fit together.

Another aspect of insurance company issuance of GICs bears mentioning: the emergence of several credit rating organizations which rate the "claims-paying ability" (CPA) of insurance companies. Because of the heightened credit consciousness of the GIC buyer, these credit rating firms have taken on increased importance and influence. Over the last few years each has developed and standardized its own rating criteria and financial ratio analysis. Insurance companies are now required by the marketplace to have CPA ratings from one or more of these firms. This has made insurers gear the management of their business more toward what the rating agencies find acceptable. While this is a healthy development overall for the financial soundness of the industry, it adds yet one more layer of complexity to the management of GICs.

Impact on Investment Strategies and Product Design

If GICs are to continue to provide value to the marketplace, how will they change in order to adapt to this new world of analytical risk management and uncertain credit quality of existing balance sheets? This will be accomplished by changes in two major areas. The first is the types of investments that insurance companies use. The second is the structure and features of the product itself. While the following discussion will focus on the insurance industry viewpoint, it is important to keep in mind that most of these strategies have as much application for BICs and synthetic GICs as conventional GICs.

Consider what makes a GIC so attractive to a pension plan. Typically, GICs are used to fund 401(k) or thrift savings plans where the plan participant chooses how the individual account is to be invested. GICs were developed to accommodate the peculiar needs of these plans. Window features allow the plan to better coordinate cash inflow with credited rates.

Benefit responsiveness allows plans to respond to the withdrawal needs of individual participants without impacting the other participants. Very few financial instruments allow partial liquidation with no market value risk. In fact, money market funds are the only alternative, but historically there has been a substantial yield differential in order to eliminate the benefit-responsiveness risk. The attractiveness of GICs is due to the combination of higher yields than money market instruments and the advantages of benefit responsiveness.

The challenge is to come up with asset/liability designs that meet a set of sometimes conflicting agendas:

- From the buyer's viewpoint, GICs must offer a competitive yield, be flexible enough to handle uncertain cash inflows and outflows, and be viewed as very safe.
- From the issuer's viewpoint, GICs must be adequately priced for all risks being assumed, earn an adequate profit to justify surplus usage, and not require a high degree of credit risk to generate a spread.

On the investment side, insurance companies are increasing their use of analytical risk instruments and strategies so as to provide a competitive rate to GIC customers and meet the profit/risk requirements of the insurance company.

These market forces will drive insurance companies to emphasize analytical-risk type of instruments. Already, there has been a big shift to mortgage-backed securities as a means of getting a higher yield without resorting to credit risk. In the future, GIC users who analyze the credit quality of the issuer will need a very different set of tools since they will be faced with a vastly different type of asset portfolio.

Other types of investments besides mortgage-backed securities can comfortably fit into the analytical risk category. For example, the nondollar fixed-income market is as large as the dollar-denominated one and, generally, of high credit quality. With devices such as currency-forward contracts and options, the currency risk can be hedged. Thus, insurers will increasingly look toward other markets where analytical risk management at times provides better yields.

Finally, there has already been a huge shift to the use of financial engineering tools such as interest rate swaps, floors, caps, futures, and options to modify and manage asset/liability

risk. They are somewhat difficult to understand by simply looking at an insurer's balance sheet. Indeed, certain instruments
are neither assets nor liabilities and are disclosed in footnotes
rather than as part of the balance sheet itself. This puts even
more of a burden on the buyer to understand the risk profile of
the insurer. On the positive side, it allows the insurer to operate
at a much lower risk level. Users of synthetic GICs do not escape
the burden of understanding these financial engineering tools
since they are needed to manage cash flow risks in synthetic
structures as well.

Two Categories of Product Impact

The changes occurring on the product side of GICs is just as rev-
olutionary as the investment side. Product impacts can generally be divided into two categories. The first are those caused by
the credit concerns of the industry. The second, and more positive, are those made possible through the growth in analytical
risk tools, strategies, and instruments.

Dealing with Credit Quality

On the credit impact side, there are two main methods emerging to deal with the weakened credit quality of the industry. The
first is to shift certain risks that had previously been borne by
the issuer back to the buyer. This is done in a variety of ways,
but generally revolve around the creation of a separate account
to segregate the pension plan's assets from the rest of the insurance company. Typically, high-grade corporates or mortgage-
backed securities are used in the separate account to provide
high credit quality. Note that the initial credited rate can be increased when analytical risk instruments are used. The plan
participants bear the prepayment or call risk embedded in the
instruments being used. Normally, the insurance company will
wrap their guarantee around these structures thus enabling
the plan to use book value reporting to plan participants. In
these situations the insurance company is basically "renting"
out the use of its guarantee ability and charging a fee for it.
Most of the noncredit-related risk (i.e., analytical risk) is shifted

to the buyer. This type of structure forces the GIC buyers to give up one of the historical advantages of GICs, which is a definitely defined rate guarantee.

The other main method to improve credit quality is to *credit enhance* the GICs while still providing all the traditional benefits of GICs (guaranteed rate, benefit responsiveness, guarantee of principal, etc.). This can be done in a variety of ways. For example, separate accounts can be structured to serve as "collateral" for the GIC guarantee, but the actual terms of the GIC do not depend on the asset performance of the separate account. There are also a number of bond insurers who can issue an insurance contract that guarantees the performance of the GIC issuer. These third-party guarantors all carry the highest ratings from the major credit rating agencies and thus can "wrap" their high credit rating around the insurance company. Finally, a few insurers that are subsidiaries of large (and, many times, foreign) insurance groups provide a parent guarantee.

Employing Financial Engineering Tools

The other category of product impact involves product designs that are dependent on integrated, analytical-risk-management strategies. These unique instruments are used by GIC portfolio managers to stratify their portfolios. Different parts of the stable-value portfolio need different types of guaranteed instruments. Generally, products providing a floating or indexed rate are of the type needed. These contracts reset their rate periodically, based on an outside index. The asset/liability risk management of these products is more complex since it requires basically a floating-rate asset portfolio. In order to provide a competitive rate, a variety of investment strategies are employed, using the full range of analytical risk instruments and financial engineering tools previously discussed.

The use of financial engineering tools has also allowed the development of "extendable" and "callable" GICs. These GICs allow the buyer or seller to exercise certain options, depending on the future movement of interest rates. For example, an investment contract may provide the buyer the right to extend the maturity of the contract. The buyer would exercise this option if interest rates at the time of the original maturity date were lower. Insurance companies can completely hedge this risk through interest rate swaps or options and pass on the benefits of these financial engineering tools to the buyers.

CONCLUSION

Insurance company management strategies are changing as a result of the credit problems of the U.S. economy as well as of the positive developments in computer technology and the resultant growth in analytical-risk-oriented investments and risk management tools. The challenge for the insurance industry is to continue to provide a desirable array of guaranteed products on a financially sound basis so that the "guaranteed" is realized in a guaranteed investment contract.

CHAPTER 8

INTEREST CREDITING

Michael L. Hoover
Vice President and Principal
T. Rowe Price Stable Asset Management, Inc.

Most fixed-income investments accrue interest using an industry standard algorithm and day count. Interest crediting for GICs, BICs, and other investment contracts does not follow an industry norm, varying among issuers and even among different contract classes of the same issuer.

Investment contracts "guarantee" the manner in which interest is earned by the contract. Interest may be earned at a fixed rate for a specific length of time or may be earned on a floating-rate basis where a spread or ratio to market interest rates is guaranteed. Interest is paid to the contractholder in one of two ways: periodically during the contract's life (simple interest) or at the contract's maturity (compound interest).

THE ANNUAL EFFECTIVE RATE

Investment contracts always state the contractual interest rate as an annual effective rate. A rate of this nature means that nominal interest is compounded within the contract on some periodic basis, usually daily or monthly. As "interest on interest" is earned during the contract year, the contract's annual effective rate is generated.

In order to accurately credit contract interest, an understanding of interest compounding is required. The following examples illustrate a contract that is earning an 8.0 percent annual effective rate with interest compounded daily. The daily interest credit is determined using arithmetic roots, exponents, and factors. The daily interest factor, when annualized, produces a nominal interest rate, and, when compounded, produces an annual effective rate.

The factor for one day's interest, assuming daily compounding, is determined by taking the 365th root of one plus the interest rate (8 percent). The actual interest factor is found by next subtracting one, as the following formula indicates:

$$(1 + .08)^{1/365} - 1 = .000210874$$

By applying this daily rate to the contract balance, the interest for one day is determined:

$$\text{Day 1} \quad \$500,000.00 \times .000210874 = \$105.44$$

The nominal rate of interest can be determined by annualizing, or multiplying by 365, the daily factor of .000210874, as follows:

$$.000210874 \times 365 = .077, \text{ or } 7.7\%$$

The annual effective rate can be confirmed by reversing the formula calculation used to find the factor:

$$(1 + .000210874)^{365} - 1 = .08, \text{ or } 8.0\%$$

At first glance, it may appear that the contract is not delivering the "guaranteed" 8.0 percent. However, the 8.0 percent is an annual effective rate that is achieved by nominal interest compounded daily for an entire year. As such, the interest from Day 1 is "reinvested" in the contract and is eligible to earn interest on Day 2.

$$\text{Day 2} \quad (\$500,000.00 + \$105.44) \times .000210874 = \$105.46$$

The result of compounding is evidenced by the increased interest earned on Day 2. The $.02 increase from Day 1 results from "interest on interest," as confirmed by the following calculation:

$$\$105.44 \times .000210874 = \$.02$$

This calculation, when made for each day in a year, would determine total interest for the year, including "interest on interest." The end result would be a total of $40,000.00, or 8.0 percent of $500,000.00.

Fortunately, the chaining of multiple daily factors is not required to determine interest for several days. Interest for periods greater than one day can be determined by following the algebraic rules for roots and exponents. By raising the 365th root to the 30th power, interest for 30 days is calculated as follows:

$$(1 + .08)^{30/365} - 1 = .006345602$$
$$\$500,000.00 \times .006345602 = \$3,172.80$$

The previous example covered 30 days, thus compounding of daily interest has been realized. Compounding is confirmed by the increase in the annualized nominal rate, as follows:

$$\frac{.006345602}{30} \times 365 = .0772, \text{ or } 7.72\%$$

As compounding occurs over ever-increasing periods during the year, the annualized nominal rate continues to increase, reaching 8.0 percent once twelve months have elapsed.

The difference between compound and nominal interest must be recognized when performing fund valuations. If the 8.0 percent annual effective rate is used in an algorithm designed for a nominal interest rate, accrued interest will be overstated, producing earnings of 8.33 percent if extrapolated for the entire year. The fund's calculation of interest earned on the $500,000 investment would be $1,638.77 more than the interest actually credited by the contract issuer.

Returns reported by stable-value funds are also impacted by the difference between compound and nominal rates. These funds typically own several contracts that, when aggregated, generate composite interest earnings based on each contract's proportion in the fund. Most performance algorithms divide period earnings by the period's beginning balance and annualize the result. Since annualizing is a multiplicative process that does not take into account compounding, this process generates a blended return which is less than the weighted annual effective rates. Annual effective rates can only be realized at the end of a full year if the investment remains in the fund for that year. Plan sponsors who communicate expected returns should be aware that annualized periodic returns will not equal annualized effective rates until the full year has elapsed. Exhibit 8–1 illustrates the annualized nominal returns generated by a monthly valuation of a daily compounding contract.

EXPONENTIAL METHOD

Most issuers utilize the *exponential method* to determine interest credits. This method employs arithmetic roots and factors as shown in the previous discussion on compounding. The primary difference among issuers who use the exponential method is in the frequency of compounding. Compounding can occur on a daily, monthly, or quarterly basis. The basic factors for these respective methods are determined in accordance with the formulas listed below. The formulas shown maintain "1" as part of the factor. When this factor is multiplied by the beginning

EXHIBIT 8–1
Annualized Nominal Returns versus Annual Effective Rate

Number of Days in Month	Beginning Balance	Period Interest	Annualized Monthly Return (in percent)
31	$500,000.00	$ 3,278.91	7.72
28	503,278.91	2,980.08	7.72
31	506,258.99	3,319.96	7.72
30	509,578.95	3,233.59	7.72
31	512,812.54	3,362.94	7.72
30	516,175.48	3,275.45	7.72
31	519,450.93	3,406.47	7.72
31	522,857.39	3,428.81	7.72
30	526,286.20	3,339.61	7.72
31	529,625.81	3,473.19	7.72
30	533,099.00	3,382.84	7.72
31	536,481.85	3,518.15	7.72
Full year	$500,000.00	$40,000.00	8.00%

balance, the result is the ending balance, including interest. Net interest is determined by subtracting the beginning and ending balances.

$$\text{Daily factor: } (1 + .08)^{1/365} = 1.000210874$$
$$\text{Monthly factor: } (1 + .08)^{1/12} = 1.006434030$$
$$\text{Quarterly factor: } (1 + .08)^{1/4} = 1.019426547$$
$$\text{Application of the daily factor:}$$
$$\$500,000.00 \times 1.000210874 = \$500,105.44$$
$$\$500,105.44 - \$500,000.00 = \$105.44, \text{ interest for Day 1.}$$

For contracts which employ daily compounding, multiple days' interest is determined by raising the factor to a power equal to the number of days in the period, as shown below.

For 15 days: $\$500,000.00 \times (1.000210874)^{15} = \$501,583.89$, or
$\$500,000.00 \times (1.08)^{15/365} = \$501,583.89$

For 75 days: $\$500,000.00 \times (1.000210874)^{75} = \$507,969.79$, or
$\$500,000.00 \times (1.08)^{75/365} = \$507,969.79$

If an issuer employs monthly or quarterly compounding, factors for periods shorter than the basic compounding period must be determined. The methods used vary from issuer to issuer. The most frequently observed technique transforms the period factor into a daily factor based on the number of days in the period. For example, the daily factor for a monthly compounding contract for a 28-day month would be determined as follows:

$$((1 + .08)^{1/12})^{1/28} = 1.000229077$$

This factor can now be used as any other daily factor by raising it to the power equal to the number of days in the calculation period. This particular daily factor can be used only in 28-day months for periods of 28 days or less. Months with 30 and 31 days require a different daily factor based on the respective number of days using the same arithmetic technique.

A similar derivation is used for determining a daily factor when quarterly compounding is employed by the issuer:

$$((1 + .08)^{1/4})^{1/92} = 1.000209155$$

This daily factor is appropriate for calendar quarters with 92 days. Quarters with 90 or 91 days would compute a different daily factor based on the number of days. The daily factor must only be used during a quarter with the same number of days as used to determine the factor.

LINEAR METHOD

The *linear method* categorizes the other primary group of interest crediting techniques. Arithmetically, this method is the easiest to compute. However, the linear method has some drawbacks in its application.

Contracts using the linear method calculate the dollar interest credit at the beginning of a designated period, usually the contract year. Since periodic compounding does not occur within the year, interest is straight-lined on a daily or monthly basis. This method essentially credits the contract with the same dollar amount of interest for each day or month of the contract year, depending on which basis is used and assuming no deposits or withdrawals. This method could be called "equal dollar" since the contract will earn the same amount for each of the defined periods.

$$\text{Daily interest credits: } \frac{\$500,000.00 \times .08}{365} = \$109.59 \text{ per day}$$

$$\text{Monthly interest credits: } \frac{\$500,000.00 \times .08}{12}$$

$$= \$3,333.33 \text{ per month}$$

Contracts using the linear method on a monthly basis develop daily interest credits by dividing the monthly interest credit by the number of days in the month. As the following examples show, daily interest will be different for one day during a 28-, 30-, or 31-day month.

$$\text{Daily credit: 28-day month: } \frac{\$3,333.33}{28} = \$119.05 \text{ per day}$$

$$\text{Daily credit: 30-day month: } \frac{\$3,333.33}{30} = \$111.11 \text{ per day}$$

$$\text{Daily credit: 31-day month: } \frac{\$3,333.33}{31} = \$107.53 \text{ per day}$$

If the contract pays out interest annually, the interest crediting schedule for the contract will be the same for each year that the contract is outstanding. If the contract pays interest at maturity, interest is added to the balance at the end of the year and a new interest credit is calculated. This situation is illustrated below on a contract with daily interest credits:

• For Year 1, $500,000.00, the deposit amount, is used to calculate the interest credits.

$$\textit{Year 1} \quad \frac{\$500,000.00 \times .08}{365} = \$109.59 \text{ per day}$$

• For Year 2, Year 1 interest of $40,000.00 is added to the deposit amount, $500,000.00, to determine the basis for interest.

$$\textit{Year 2} \quad \frac{\$540,000.00 \times .08}{365} = \$118.36 \text{ per day}$$

Exhibit 8–2 illustrates linear daily interest crediting and the annualized monthly returns it generates. The methodology produces a declining annualized nominal rate of return throughout the contract year. Year-to-date returns, though, will always equal 8.0 percent.

IMPACT OF CASH FLOWS

Each of the preceding examples has discussed interest credits as they relate to contracts with no cash flow activity during the year. Cash flow in or out of a contract creates the need for extra diligence in determining interest credits and contract values. Contracts based on the exponential method of interest crediting use arithmetic factors to maintain a current fully accrued balance. When a cash flow in or out occurs, this change is impacted against the current fully accrued balance of the contract

EXHIBIT 8–2
Linear Interest Crediting

Beginning Balance	Number of Days in Month		Daily Interest Credit		Period Interest	Ending Balance	Annualized Monthly Return (in percent)
$500,000.00	31	×	109.59	=	$ 3,397.26	$503,397.26	8.00
503,397.26	28	×	109.59	=	3,068.49	506,465.75	7.95
506,465.75	31	×	109.59	=	3,397.26	509,863.01	7.90
509,863.01	30	×	109.59	=	3,287.67	513,150.68	7.85
513,150.68	31	×	109.59	=	3,397.26	516,547.95	7.79
516,547.95	30	×	109.59	=	3,287.67	519,835.62	7.74
519,835.62	31	×	109.59	=	3,397.26	523,232.88	7.69
523,232.88	31	×	109.59	=	3,397.26	526,630.14	7.64
526,630.14	30	×	109.59	=	3,287.67	529,917.81	7.60
529,917.81	31	×	109.59	=	3,397.26	533,315.07	7.55
533,315.07	30	×	109.59	=	3,287.67	536,602.74	7.50
536,602.74	31	×	109.59	=	3,397.26	540,000.00	7.45
$500,000.00	365	×	109.59	=	$40,000.00	$540,000.00	8.00%

to determine a balance net of the transaction. This revised balance is then credited with interest for the number of days up to the next transaction. The next transaction is then included in the cycle, and the crediting process is repeated.

Exhibit 8–3 illustrates the impact of several transactions on an 8 percent contract that uses the exponential method. Interest is determined by multiplying the beginning balance in each case by an arithmetic factor with an exponent equal to the number of days in the crediting period as defined by the length of time between transactions.

EXHIBIT 8–3
Interest Crediting for Transactions-Exponential Method

Beginning Balance	Transaction	Amount Eligible for Interest	Number of Days	Period Interest	Ending Balance
$ 0	$2,000,000	$2,000,000	15	$ 6,336	$2,006,336
2,006,336	(250,000)	1,756,336	10	3,707	1,760,043
1,760,043	100,000	1,860,043	6	2,355	1,862,397
Totals/Month End	$1,850,000		31	$12,397	$1,862,397

Interest accrued at 8 percent net.

Issuers that utilize the linear method of interest crediting can apply interest in several ways. The most commonly observed linear method tracks each transaction independent of other transactions and the balance in the contract. At any point in time, as shown in Exhibit 8–4, the balance in the contract equals the sum of all fully accrued transactions. Interest is credited to each transaction for the number of days between its effective date and the end of the valuation period.

The linear method can be quite awkward if a large number of transactions must be tracked. In essence, the method treats the contract like many separate contracts. At the end of the contract year, all fully accrued pieces are aggregated to determine the contract's beginning balance for the upcoming year.

OTHER CREDITING ISSUES

Most insurance companies and banks use either an exponential or a linear method for crediting interest during a contract year. Additional problems in contract accounting surface as a result of individual company peculiarities.

One common variable in interest crediting concerns the effective date for applying interest to contract transactions. One basis pays interest *beginning on the day the issuer* (or its custodian bank) *receives the deposit through the day before the funds*

EXHIBIT 8–4
Interest Crediting for Transactions—Linear Method

Date of Transaction	Transaction Amount	Valuation as of			
		Day 60	Day 110	Day 210	Day 260
Day 1	$1,500,000	$1,519,726	$1,536,164	$1,569,041	$1,585,479
Day 50	(300,000)	(300,658)	(303,945)	(310,521)	(313,808)
Day 100	500,000	—	501,096	512,055	517,534
Day 200	(200,000)	—	—	(200,438)	(202,630)
Day 250	800,000	—	—	—	801,753
Contract value		$1,219,068	$1,733,315	$1,570,137	$2,388,328

Interest accrued at 8 percent net.

are returned to the contractholder. Another basis credits interest *beginning on the day after the issuer's receipt through the day of withdrawal.*

Accounting for investment contracts can be troublesome during a leap year. Some issuers choose to adjust their interest crediting methodology to account for the extra day during a leap year. Others ignore the extra day.

One final peculiarity concerns the accrual of expenses associated with a contract. Most investment contracts address a gross interest rate and expenses. Some issuers employ one methodology for accruing gross interest and another for accruing expenses within the same contract. A common practice is to accrue interest using the exponential method on a daily basis and to accrue expenses using the linear method on a monthly basis. Exhibit 8–5 illustrates a contract earning gross interest of 8.50 percent with expenses of .50 percent. The result of applying two methodologies is net earnings that do not equate to the net interest rate implied by the contract.

SUMMARY

Accurate interest crediting and contract valuation is the foundation for accurate participant recordkeeping in a GIC portfolio. The process is initiated by the contractholder's thorough understanding of the interest-crediting methodologies and practices used by each and every issuer in the portfolio.

EXHIBIT 8–5
Exponential Interest and Nominal Expenses

Number of Days in Month	Beginning Balance	Period Interest (Actual Days)		Period Expenses (.005/12)		Net Earnings	Ending Balance	Annual Effective Yield (in percent)
31	$500,000.00	$ 3,476.39	−	$ 208.33	=	$ 3,268.05	$503,268.05	7.97
28	503,268.05	3,159.42	−	209.70	=	2,949.73	506,217.78	7.92
31	506,217.78	3,519.62	−	210.92	=	3,308.69	509,526.47	7.97
30	509,526.47	3,427.96	−	212.30	=	3,215.66	512,742.13	7.95
31	512,742.13	3,564.98	−	213.64	=	3,351.34	516,093.46	7.97
30	516,093.46	3,472.14	−	215.04	=	3,257.10	519,350.56	7.95
31	519,350.56	3,610.93	−	216.40	=	3,394.53	522,745.09	7.97
31	522,745.09	3,634.53	−	217.81	=	3,416.72	526,161.81	7.97
30	526,161.81	3,539.88	−	219.23	=	3,320.64	529,482.45	7.95
31	529,482.45	3,681.37	−	220.62	=	3,460.75	532,943.21	7.97
30	532,943.21	3,585.50	−	222.06	=	3,363.44	536,306.65	7.95
31	536,306.65	3,728.82	−	223.46	=	3,505.36	539,812.00	7.97
Year End	$500,000.00	$42,401.52	−	$2,589.52	=	$39,812.00	$539,812.00	7.96%

CHAPTER 9

CONTRACTUAL UNDERWRITING

Cynthia C. Gravatt

The investment contract is a legally binding instrument negotiated between two parties. Its terms make it analogous to a *private placement* instrument. Proper contractual underwriting is critical to the successful administration of the contract and plan.

The GIC document establishes the relationship between the plan and the insurance company. Most contracts set forth the following terms:[1]

• The parties' rights and duties.

• Procedures for administering the parties' relationship.

• Procedures for terminating or extending the parties' relationship.

There is a lack of uniformity among issuers in contractual terms. There is often a lack of contractual uniformity within the same issuer depending on the amount of deposit, frequency of withdrawals, and type of client. Issuers have different

---

[1]Andrew Irving, Esq. of Robinson, Silverman, Pearce, Aronsohn, and Berman. From "Importance of Understanding and Evaluating the GIC Contract Document," speech given at the first Annual GIC Symposium, April 21, 1987, New York.

philosophies regarding the role of the contract. Some contracts are vague in contractual terms, while others are precise in their obligations.

Often, first-time readers of investment contracts are surprised to discover that seemingly simple "details"—the amount, rate, and maturity date—take up to 20 or more pages to explain. There may be difficulty in understanding many definitions that appear to be meaningless, why annuity tables are present, and why there are references to genders.

A typical contract begins with the cover page, followed by a set of definitions that refer to particular items or sections of the contract. The next several sections normally present the method of crediting interest and debiting expenses. If the contract provides for any type of withdrawals prior to contract maturity, a section is included describing the withdrawal basis, including group annuity tables that illustrate annuity purchase rates. The final sections deal with the rights of either party to initiate contract termination, including nonassignability language, and the basis for which the contract is the governing document.

Many issuers go to extremes to ensure that they are not fiduciaries to the plan under the provisions of ERISA. As evidenced by the following excerpt from a GIC contract issued by a major insurance company, the industry goes out of its way to avoid any liability implications:

> In the event (name of insurer) is determined by a court to be a plan fiduciary, it is understood and agreed that (name of insurer) will be completely indemnified by the Contractholder for any and all liability incurred in connection with the performance of this Contract as such liability may be related to its status as fiduciary.

Most contracts, when issued, have been preapproved by the state insurance department in the domiciled state of the contractholder. Issuance to the contractholder can be as short as two weeks and as long as one year, depending on the insurer and state. If the boilerplate document has been preapproved, often a material change to the contract will warrant a new filing. Some issuers prohibit the use of side letters to clarify ambiguous contract language and instead file all amendments or endorsements with the state of issue.

For years the argument that the contract was written by the issuer, for the issuer, to serve only the issuer was well founded. Documents were ironclad, written clearly to protect the issuer's interest. The contractholder had little input as to its terms.

Fortunately, times have changed. Contractual terms have become negotiable. The buyer has more opportunity than ever before to negotiate an investment effectively for the plan.

There are stories of major corporations who bought for their retirement plan a GIC with terms in violation of plan design. One such story concerns the Fortune 100 company whose plan had a money market fund option. The plan sponsor was surprised after notifying the issuer of a withdrawal for participant transfers to the money market option, that the issuer refused to honor the withdrawal request. The contract violated the plan design, and the plan design violated industry-accepted standards of not allowing direct transfers to competing fixed-income options.

Another story concerns the company that neglected to negotiate a benefit-responsive option in its bullet contract. When the cash reserves had been exhausted, the company was angered at the issuer's refusal to pay its pro-rata share of the additional needed liquidity. The fault was not with the issuer; it was with the negotiator of the contract.

The contract review must begin early in the planning process. It must be beyond doubt that all bidders are proposing the same terms. There are three key issues in considering the contract proposal. First, the contract must suit the plan. Second, the administrative procedures must be workable for the plan, the administrative staff, and the trustee. And third, the reinvestment options must be clear and definitive.

Smart buyers follow an action plan.

1. Prepare detailed bid specifications denoting important/ relevant items. These items include cash flow (deposits and withdrawals), list of assets, and interfund transfer history. A detailed description of the plan should also be provided. It should set forth provisions regarding eligibility, covered pay, vesting, transfer rights, benefit payment events, and any other items directly or indirectly affecting cash flow to or from the plan. A copy of the plan and Summary Plan Description should be included in the bid specification package as a final precaution to ensure that the underwriter has all relevant information. The buyer should also clearly articulate the investment strategy and liquidity structure.

2. Obtain from the issuer a letter documenting their willingness to comply with all the terms of the bid specifications. Obtain in writing any specific deviations from the bid specifications.

3. Obtain and review the specimen contract and other required documents.

4. Get written clarification of all ambiguous items.

The buyer should assess all information and decide if the contract suits the bid specification requirements.

1. In making the commitment, specify that the commitment is based on the previously submitted bid specifications.

2. Obtain a commitment letter immediately after the verbal commitment prior to the execution of the application.

3. Obtain a letter of agreement outlining any extracontractual agreements negotiated.

With the complexities of plan design, the investment markets and the many alternatives offered in today's environment, the central issue to the buyer is protection. The buyer must ensure that the correct commitment has been made. Because the investment contract is a legally binding instrument, there is no room for error. Mistakes can be severely penalized.

Contract protection should include the following:

1. Full Guarantee. With few exceptions, most insurance companies issue a guaranteed rate and expense schedule for the full contract term; there is no right to change or adjust (except floating-rate, indexed, or participating contracts) during the contract period.[2]

---

[2]Note: Those who issue one-year renewable rates normally provide a formula that ensures the contractholder a cashout with a present value that provides a yield to maturity equal to the original contract guarantee. (See Exhibit 9–1 at the end of this chapter.)

2. Early Surrender. With the illiquidity provided by the nature of the GIC instrument, the ability to terminate the contract in whole or in part at the contractholder's discretion in a lump sum at fair value (see Illustration 5–1 in Chapter 5 for an example) provides an opportunity to maintain better control over the GIC portfolio. This provision is important when there is:

a. A lowering of the carrier's quality rating to a point where it is felt termination prior to maturity is warranted.

b. A change in plan design or investment objectives.

c. Language in the contract that insulates it from plan amendment and operation changes. Withdrawals attributable to such could then be made at the lesser of book value or market value.

3. Benefit Payments. Benefit payments at book value at the participant level are normally negotiated for defined contribution plans. These payment events are normally made in cash at book value for death, disability, retirement, termination of employment, in-service withdrawals including hardship and attainment of age 59½, loans, and investment crossovers. Annuity purchase options, although rarely utilized, are normally provided for death, disability, retirement, and termination of employment benefits.

4. Contract Liquidity. The buyer incorporating a liquidity feature should consider whether the existing contracts have a liquidity feature that is consistent with the plan liquidity basis. If previous contracts were negotiated on a pro rata basis, new purchases cannot be negotiated on a LIFO basis unless issuers currently in the portfolio have been notified and approve the change. The operation of the Fund must be clearly described. There is a cost for liquidity whether or not the contract will ever be accessed. The contractual terms should agree with the plan design with regard to any alternative investment options, the ability to transfer between alternative-option funds, and the frequency with which transfers can be made.

5. Corporate Event Risk. There is no industry standardization as to how payments are to be made in the event of employer-initiated corporate events. Some issuers provide payments at book value; some at market value. Others provide what is known as a "book value corridor" that allow payments on a prespecified percentage at book value; the remainder is paid at the lesser of book or market value. Some issuers will underwrite a corridor at an extra charge; others will provide a corridor at no extra charge. For those employers who may periodically acquire or dispose of other companies, this protection may be required. For those who do not need to cover extraordinary events, this protection may not be necessary.

Examples of these events include:

a. Group layoff or work force reduction.

b. Sale, merger, or divestiture of operating unit.[3]

c. Early retirement incentive.

d. Plant closing.

e. Bankruptcy.

f. Partial or total plan termination.

The decision regarding the required payment method for corporate event withdrawals should be carefully considered. A plan requiring book value for all such events limits the eligible issuer universe. For those issuers who provide extraordinary event coverage, the rates will reflect the cost of such coverage. The employer should carefully consider if it is a risk they want to manage in the portfolio in lieu of requiring the issuers to manage this risk.

6. Contract Maturity. Specific language should incorporate a lump-sum book value payment of the contract balance at contract maturity.[4] Split payment dates, if the contract matures in installments, should be clearly noted.

7. Grace Period. When window contracts are used, either the contract or a supplemental letter of agreement should incorporate a grace period for deposits—including ongoing deposits

---

[3]If the participant remains in the employ of the acquiring organization, a clone contract may be issued.

[4]For some issuers, a contract's maturity date is merely the date after which the issuer's obligations change. For example, the contract could provide for automatic renewal at a noncompetitive rate.

and lump-sum employer profit-sharing contributions—to be transferred after the deposit period for accrued contributions.

8. Payment Method. The contract should make clear whether payments are made by wire or check and which circumstances govern the payment method. Most issuers have minimum wire amounts. Payment at maturity should be via wire transfer of immediately available funds. Valuable investment earnings can be lost if checks for large amounts are mailed.

9. Registry. The carrier must be licensed in the state of domicile of the contractholder. This is an important detail—particularly when the contractholder is a New York-domiciled master trustee, as some issuers are not licensed in New York.

10. Interest Crediting. Specific language, including the frequency of compounding, should define the basis for the crediting of interest. Interest should be credited on the day of deposit through the day prior to withdrawal or, on the day after deposit through the day of withdrawal.

11. Timing of Withdrawals. The notice period for benefit payments should be compatible with the time frame acceptable to the administrator. Typically a 2- to 10-day turnaround is provided. Some issuers limit withdrawals to two per month. Others have limitations on an annual basis.

12. Contract Cloning. The contract should contain a cloning feature. In the case of a sale, divestiture, or merger of an operating unit, and participants continue in the employ of the successor employer, the contractholder should have the option of transferring the applicable portion of the assets in the original contract to a clone contract. The clone should have the same provisions as the original contract, contain the same net interest guarantee and maturity date, and continue to allow for benefit withdrawals. Some issuers charge a fee and/or have minimum asset requirements for a clone contract.

13. Other Events. Specific reference should be included to address those events that allow the carrier the right to terminate the contract prior to its scheduled maturity. These events may include:

- Plan amendments.
- Changes in administrative practices.

- Distribution of a communication to participants which reflects negatively on the fund.
- Misstatement of facts.
- Plan termination.

SUMMARY

The buyer's obligations to an issuer do not end when the contract is finalized. The buyer must continue to work closely with the issuer if there are plan amendment or operation changes, or if there is a change in the liquidity structure of the portfolio.

Errors can be costly. The buyer must understand the terms of the sale. In the world of GICs there is no "spirit of intent." When all is said and done, it is what the contract says that governs the administrative delivery. It is not what the contract was intended to say.

EXHIBIT 9–1
One-Year Renewable Guarantees

Life insurance companies are required to set aside reserves on a prescribed basis to ensure that adequate provision is made for all guaranteed benefits. Interest rate assumptions for reserve valuation purposes are prescribed by a statutory formula that modifies a 12-month or 36-month moving average based on Moody's index of seasoned corporate bonds. When a contractual guarantee exceeds the prescribed annual reserve rate, the insurer is required to set aside additional reserves to cover the difference between the contractual guarantee and the prescribed rate. The additional reserve is funded from the carrier's surplus, resulting in a "surplus strain."

Issuers can minimize their surplus strain by issuing one-year renewable guarantees. By having the annual opportunity to reset the guaranteed rate, they limit their reserving requirement to the single year. To provide protection to the contractholder, liberal termination provisions may be offered, thus placing the carrier in the position of probably never needing to invoke the change in the guaranteed rate.

The typical contractual provision would become effective if the issuer lowered the contractholder's rate. The contractholder could accept the newer, lower rate, or, upon 30-days notice to the issuer, request a lump-sum payout equal to the higher of the book or market value of the contract, or take delivery of securities whose maturity values equal the maturity value of the original contractual rate. (See the example in Exhibit 9–2.)

EXHIBIT 9–2
Cashout Illustration

Three-year U.S. Treasury rate	7.00%
Current three-year GIC rate	7.50%
Original contract rate	9.00%
Original contract duration	5.0 years
Term to contract maturity	3.0 years
Amount of original deposit	$1.0 million

Value at end of two years at 9%	$1,188,100
Value at end of five years at 9%	1,538,624
Amount of premature payout	1,255,976
Maturity value discounted at 7.5% for three years	1,238,532
Gain to contractholder/loss to carrier	$ 17,444

*Assuming the Contractholder Reinvests the Payout into a Three-Year,
7.5% Contract:*

Maturity value of $1,255,976 reinvested at 7.5%	$1,560,295
Maturity value of original 9% contract	1,538,624
Gain to contractholder in fifth year	$ 21,671
Effective five-year yield	9.31%
Minimum three-year reinvestment rate needed to achieve original, projected maturity value	7.00%

CHAPTER 10

POOLED STABLE-VALUE FUNDS

Kelli Hustad Hueler
President
Hueler Companies

In the early 1980s, the first version of GIC pooled funds appeared. These funds were designed to "pool" together deposits of multiple plans—usually those deemed too small for individual contract placement—in order to gain better yields and diversification. This pooling concept was not new to the investment community, yet represented an important evolutionary step in the GIC marketplace.

Pooled GIC funds are typically established as collective trusts sponsored by trust institutions.[1] They are not established as mutual funds, as they do not meet certain SEC liquidity requirements. There are two major types of pooled GIC funds: closed-end pooled funds and open-end pooled funds. In the earlier years of pooled funds, the earliest funds were primarily closed-end funds. Open-end funds were introduced later; predominantly after 1985.

In the closed-end fund, each participating plan has a specific commitment to a contract(s) in the fund. Originally, one

---

[1]Trust institutions are typically part of a state or national bank. Often, they are set up as free-standing entities to provide personal and/or institutional trust services. Most major mutual fund companies maintain a trust subsidiary to provide collective investment trust.

Banks are licensed as either state or national institutions. State banks are subject to state banking laws (which often follow federal laws). National banks are subject to federal laws, and operate under the requirements of the Office of the Comptroller of the Currency.

investment contract was purchased per fund due to the interpretation of earlier rules issued by the Office of the Comptroller
of the Currency (OCC).[2] Today closed-end funds typically have
only one investment contract at a time open for new cash plan
contributions. These contracts are generally designed to accept
cash flows over a 6- to 12-month period, followed by a predetermined holding period which is commonly between two to four
years. Each contract becomes a cell of the fund that matures
and can either be paid out or reinvested.

The open-ended pooled fund provided greater flexibility.
When new plans invest in the open-end pool, they purchase
shares of the fund that represent small percentages of all assets
held in portfolio. Contracts are purchased continuously, and
every participant shares in the blended return on the entire
portfolio. Because open-end funds have emerged as the more
popular pooled vehicle, this chapter will focus on open-end
pooled funds.

The early funds were basic in nature, using nonbenefit-
responsive contracts that were staggered to create a laddered
portfolio in conjunction with a cash reserve to provide sufficient
liquidity. Defined contribution plans were in their infancy and
complicated transfer provisions did not exist. As such, fund operating policies were not originally designed to meet today's
more complicated needs.

The pooled fund market has experienced substantial
growth in a relatively short period of time. With this growth has
come significant change for not only the general pooled fund
market, but product specific changes as well. In the mid-1980s,
there were only a handful of trust institutions offering pooled
funds, with less than $1 billion in combined assets. In contrast,
today there are at least 60 independent pooled funds and as
many as 30 additional funds that primarily purchase shares of
other pooled funds to form a "fund of funds", with an estimated
$8 billion of combined assets.

---

[2]Prior to changes in the OCC rules in 1987, interpretation of the OCC rules was that
if a pooled trust maintained more than one investment, the trust must be valued at market value. As such, most pooled funds were designed as closed-end, single-contract
funds. Those pooled funds established prior to 1987 as open-end funds were often set up
in states that did not have this "single contract" requirement for contract accounting.

Initially, pooled fund growth came from fairly equitable participation from both defined benefit and defined contribution plans. The primary growth in recent years however, is attributable to small- to medium-sized 401 (k) and profit-sharing plans. These plans definitely became the driving force behind the rapid growth experienced by pooled funds in the latter half of the 1980s. As illustrated in Exhibit 10–1, defined contribution plans make up at least 87 percent of pooled fund assets today.[3]

Throughout the late 80s and early 90s, pooled fund products continued to evolve in order to meet the changing needs and increasingly complex benefit provisions of 401 (k) plans. Growing concerns about fiduciary responsibility, prudent diversification, credit quality, and the cash flow flexibility required to meet enhanced transfer provisions contributed to the growing popularity of pooled funds. In the one-year period ending March

EXHIBIT 10–1
Allocation by Plan Type

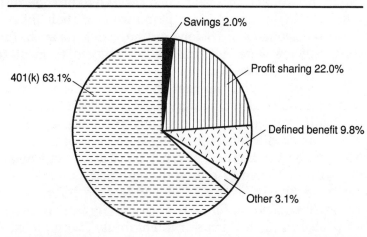

---

[3]Statistics presented in this chapter are compiled from data in the Hueler Analytics Universe that monitors in excess of $7 billion dollars of pooled fund assets or approximately 75 percent of the national pooled fund market.

31, 1991, it is estimated that assets grew by approximately 33.73 percent. The following growth occurred on a quarterly basis over that period:

$$\frac{\text{Increase in}}{\text{assets quarterly}} = \frac{6/30/90}{7.03\%} \quad \frac{9/30/90}{7.33\%} \quad \frac{12/31/90}{7.57\%} \quad \frac{3/31/91}{11.80\%}$$

This growth is attributable to a number of factors; ease of administration, flexibility, competitive returns, and professional investment management. In addition, due to size, staffing, time constraints, or unpredictable cash flow history, some plans have had difficulty obtaining contracts that provide sufficient liquidity and competitive rates of return. As shown in Exhibit 10–2, from late 1984 through first quarter of 1991 monthly pooled fund returns outperformed monthly spot rates for five-year GICs better than 50 percent of the time and monthly spot rates for three-year GICs approximately 70 percent of the time. This is especially noteworthy since during that same period pooled funds generally maintained an average weighted maturity of between 2.5 to 3.5 years.

With the growth in pooled fund assets came increasing product complexity. Selecting a pooled fund can be a frustrating experience, not only because of the great number of funds available but because of the variations in fund operating procedures, investment style, policy restrictions, redemption provisions, credit quality, and fees. If all pooled funds were constructed alike and had only slight differences in operating procedures, it would be feasible to simply distinguish or rank funds by investment track record.[4] As an example, fees alone range from 20 to 80 basis points, depending on the amount of money invested. On deposits of up to $1 million, fund fees range from 25 to 80 basis points, with a median fee of 50 basis points. On deposits of $10 million or greater, fund fees range from 20 to 58 basis points with a median fee of 36 basis points. It is also important to bear

---

[4]See Chapter 13, Performance Measurement of Stable-Value Portfolios, for a more detailed discussion of monitoring investment performance.

EXHIBIT 10–2
Pooled GIC Fund versus Spot GIC Rates

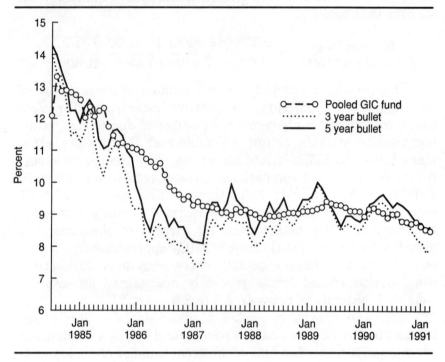

in mind that the lowest fund fees do not necessarily correlate with the highest net fund returns.

Due to the variety of portfolio structures of pooled funds, ranking funds based on a single criteria is a very incomplete analysis. Fund selection based solely on current yield can be misleading. Distinguishing characteristics of pooled funds can be broken down into two main categories:

1. Operating policies and corresponding contract provisions.

2. Investment strategy and policy restrictions.

A fund's operating policies define how contributions and withdrawals can be made, how frequently, on what dates, and what type of withdrawals are allowed or restricted. Often included as part of fund operating policy are restrictions regarding the type and size of plan. Many funds restrict certain types of deposits, limiting themselves only to defined contribution plans. Size limitations as a percent of total assets may be enforced so that one plan does not dominate the fund. A lack of such diversification restrictions by plan type and plan size may cause undue exposure to cash flow volatility resulting from excessive sponsor contributions or withdrawals.

The flexibility of deposits and withdrawal dates differs from fund to fund, which stems directly from the varying fund valuation frequencies. Traditionally, pooled funds were valued on a monthly or bimonthly basis. With the dawn of daily valuation capabilities, many funds are moving to daily valuation frequencies.

Pooled funds also have a wide range of operating procedures relating to withdrawals; from extremely flexible to extremely restrictive. Some pooled funds have very specific rules clearly distinguishing employee- versus employer-directed withdrawals, allowing unrestricted access for bona fide benefit payments but more restrictive provisions for any employer-initiated withdrawals. Others may not have specific restrictions unless a withdrawal request is deemed to infringe on sufficient fund liquidity.

Each fund sponsor will argue that their methodology makes the most sense, and given the right circumstances, they all may be valid. The best litmus test is whether the particular fund's operating provisions and objectives meet the needs of the plan. It is crucial to ensure that the operating policy and fund objectives are consistent with the way this investment has been communicated to plan participants.

A pooled fund's operating policies should be supported with consistent contract underwriting. There is significant debate regarding contract language used by pooled fund managers, specifically as it relates to liquidity for employer-directed withdrawals and benefit payments.

Many pooled funds provide a collapsibility feature for total plan withdrawal. This feature provides the plan sponsor the right to withdraw from the fund, typically with 12 months' notice to the fund sponsor. The contracts in the fund may be tapped if liquidation requests cannot be met by the fund's normal sources of liquidity. Not all insurance companies will underwrite this feature. Others will write only to those funds with a sufficient liquidity cushion.

When a fund's operating policy states that employer-initiated plan withdrawal requests will be honored within 12 months, the investment contracts must carry this 12-month collapsibility rider feature. If not, it is a promise by fund management to honor those withdrawals rather than a promise by the issuers represented in the portfolio.

Similar issues apply to benefit payment provisions. A fund may allow for employee-directed transfers and bona fide benefit payments in their operating policy. This liquidity need is typically underwritten in the investment contracts through a benefit-responsive rider. The distinction is which party is ultimately responsible for the commitment to pay benefits. Is the commitment based on underlying benefit-responsive investment contracts, or the fund manager's ability to provide sufficient liquidity through an established investment strategy? The investor should have a clear understanding of how strategy and contract provisions work together. Exhibit 10–3 provides a breakdown of contract provisions for 23 funds. It is interesting to note that only two of the funds represented provide no liquidity protection through contractual provisions. While 18 of the funds purchase contracts with collapsibility riders for a given percent of the portfolio, 15 of the funds purchase contracts with benefit-responsive provisions for a given percent of the portfolio, and 12 purchase contracts with both features for a given percent of the portfolio.

The investing plan needs to be assured that the pooled fund selected has an acceptable methodology for assuring sufficient liquidity to meet all types of withdrawals allowed under the terms of the governing plan document. After thoroughly reviewing a fund's operating policies and the underlying contract provisions, the next step is to analyze the components of the fund's investment strategy and related policy restrictions, including:

Liquidity management   Diversification

Weighted average maturity   Credit quality

EXHIBIT 10–3
Contract Provisions

Fund	Collapsibility Rider Coverage (percent)	Benefit-Responsive Feature (percent)
1	20%	25%
2	100	100
3	100	100
4	52	0
5	100	100
6	100	100
7	60	0
8	89	0
9	0	0
10	95	5
11	100	100
12	100	16
13	0	0
14	0	100
15	100	0
16	0	100
17	100	100
18	100	100
19	100	100
20	100	100
21	0	100
22	20	0
23	20	0

LIQUIDITY MANAGEMENT

Pooled GIC funds should have an established strategy relating to the fund's liquidity structure. This structure may include targeted cash-reserve levels, the basis for contract withdrawals (e.g., LIFO, pro-rata), the frequency with which withdrawals may be made, and the use of simple-interest contracts as an additional liquidity source.

In addition to stated minimums and/or maximums, funds generally have a reserve target established. This represents a range within which the cash positions of the fund are allowed to fluctuate. Some funds, given a change in market conditions, management's outlook, or the timing of specific investment opportunities will use the full range of their allowable cash position, while others maintain a very stable cash position. To better illustrate the varying cash management strategies employed by pooled fund managers, Exhibit 10–4 shows the range among the funds in minimum cash requirements, the managers' targets, and the actual cash positions for the funds represented. The minimum cash requirement for a fund is always a fixed percent of the portfolio. For those funds represented, the stated minimum ranges from zero percent to 40 percent. Managers state a fund's cash target as either a specific percent or a percent range. Of the funds represented, the smallest target

EXHIBIT 10–4
Allocation to Cash

Fund	Minimum (percent)	Target (percent)	Current (percent)
1	10%	10–20%	15.0%
2	5	5–10	8.1
3	0	5–10	4.4
4	40	40–60	42.8
5	5	10	20.9
6	5	5–10	14.6
7	n/a	5	12.2
8	25	25	24.5
9	15	15–20	58.0
10	5	5–15	10.9
11	5	5–15	10.6
12	5	20–50	7.3
13	20	20	23.0
14	5	10	6.9
15	10	10–20	22.2
16	0	0	3.6
17	10	10	9.6
18	15	20–30	24.6
19	25	25	27.3
20	20	25	24.2
21	0	5	4.6
22	5	25	36.7

range is 5 percent and the greatest is 30 percent. Actual cash positions as of March 31, 1991, ranged from 3.6 percent to 58 percent.

WEIGHTED AVERAGE MATURITY

Investors often analyze a fund's current weighted average maturity. Investors are cautioned on making the fund selection solely on relative maturity comparisons. A fund's weighted average maturity is not static. Any two funds with the same weighted average maturity can have different portfolio maturity structures, which could lead to different performance patterns over time.

The investor should consider the change, or lack thereof, in a fund's weighted average maturity over a specified period of time; a minimum of a 12- to a 24-month period. In addition, the investor should consider the prevailing market conditions over the same period to see if there was a change in strategy.

After gaining a historical perspective of the fund's weighted average maturity, the portfolio's maturity structure should be analyzed on a more frequent basis (e.g., over a two-year period). It should be determined if the fund has specific policy provisions that dictate a minimum percent of the portfolio that must be due in any 12-month period. The table incorporated in Exhibit 10–5 is very useful in assessing a fund's total liquidity, as it shows what percent of the portfolio matures over seven specific time periods. This table allows you to effectively highlight an undue concentration of assets in any one period, which should in turn prompt questions about reinvestment risk. Note that in the last time period alone (over 4 years) there is a significant difference in asset concentrations, ranging from 0 to over 49 percent.

The portfolio structure of a given fund should be analyzed in conjunction with the fund's corresponding cash position, liquidity policy, withdrawal provision, and contract language. This process should provide a more complete picture as to how a fund's weighted average maturity relates to the question of liquidity.

EXHIBIT 10–5
Portfolio Maturity Structure

Fund ID	0–3 Months	3–6 Months	6–12 Months	1–2 Years	2–3 Years	3–4 Years	Over 4 Years
1	13.6%	1.8%	12.7%	24.8%	20.7%	12.2%	14.2%
2	14.3	14.2	18.4	39.1	5.5	8.5	0.0
3	25.5	0.0	14.5	11.5	22.9	17.6	8.1
4	38.7	1.9	11.1	12.0	9.9	15.6	10.7
5	28.8	3.4	21.5	20.2	16.7	5.7	1.5
6	23.4	1.4	12.3	24.5	27.3	6.4	4.7
7	14.0	4.4	17.8	17.0	14.7	13.7	18.5
8	26.2	3.6	8.0	12.0	15.1	19.5	15.6
9	36.9	9.1	12.9	22.0	19.0	0.0	0.0
10	17.7	0.8	6.4	6.8	9.6	12.3	46.5
11	18.0	2.0	12.9	29.7	24.6	2.8	10.1
12	8.1	24.4	6.4	11.4	15.2	10.4	24.0
13	27.4	0.0	16.0	12.1	18.6	15.6	10.3
14	8.4	1.1	8.3	11.1	16.2	27.9	27.0
15	38.2	0.0	8.8	5.6	7.4	19.5	20.5
16	4.4	1.2	14.4	13.8	23.8	18.9	23.4
17	15.9	1.0	3.2	8.8	16.2	27.4	27.5
18	33.9	2.8	17.7	12.1	14.9	12.1	6.6
19	27.5	2.6	6.4	21.9	16.6	12.9	12.1
20	27.8	2.0	0.7	4.7	7.9	7.2	49.6
21	14.8	0.9	17.7	10.8	18.1	17.5	20.3
22	8.9	21.2	14.7	13.4	19.3	11.1	11.4

DIVERSIFICATION

A pooled fund will most often elect a multilevel approach to portfolio diversification by:

Contract type
Instrument type
Issuer

Contract type refers specifically to types of investment alternatives utilized (e.g., fixed- or floating-rate investment contracts). A fund manager's decision to use one type or a combination of both has an impact on future fund performance and can play a significant role in investment strategy. Floating-rate contracts increase a fund's sensitivity to current interest rates, which, in a volatile interest rate environment, can cause a greater variability in returns. These contracts are also used to enhance returns on the short end of a portfolio, as many floating-rate contracts are designed to be shorter-term commitments with more flexible redemption terms than traditional fixed-rate contracts.

A fund's universe of issuers is often limited by either an internal set of credit criteria, or an approved list of issuers as deemed acceptable by an outside fund manager. In addition, most pooled funds limit investment exposure to any one institution by establishing maximum exposure guidelines. As presented in Exhibit 10–6, the maximum exposure guidelines for those funds represented ranges from 10 percent to 100 percent, with 10 percent being the most common. The guidelines encompass total portfolio holdings, including cash or other assets, requiring percent calculations to be based on total assets rather than on the GIC assets alone. It is important to verify this type of exposure restriction against actual portfolio holdings to determine ongoing compliance.

Another limiting factor is inherent in the type of contracts a fund is purchasing (e.g., benefit-responsive riders and/or put rider provisions). As previously mentioned, not all insurance companies will issue contracts with a collapsible put rider provision. A fund that requires all contracts to carry put riders must purchase contracts from only those insurance companies that will issue the put rider provision. Approximately 32 of the 53 insurance companies who issue contracts to pooled funds also issue put rider provisions.

CREDIT QUALITY

It is very difficult for plan sponsors to assess insurance company credit quality, as most do not staff in-house credit analysts. Conversely, many professional money managers have dedicated significant time and resources to developing internal credit analysis procedures and research staff. While some investment

EXHIBIT 10–6
Diversification by Issuer

Fund	Maximum Percent per Carrier	Largest Carrier (percent)	Issuers (Current Portfolio)
1	10%	6.1%	26
2	15	13.8	14
3	20	9.7	13
4	10	6.5	22
5	15	9.9	18
6	15	11.6	20
7	10	8.1	24
8	15	9.2	23
9	10	6.0	7
10	10	13.0	18
11	15	9.5	24
12	10	7.2	23
13	10	5.8	23
14	100	27.1	6
15	10	7.4	13
16	20	20.3	8
17	15	12.5	13
18	10	8.9	12
19	10	7.6	16
20	25	17.6	11
21	10	9.7	11
22	20	8.9	19
23	10	6.8	15

professionals argue that rating agency information is secondary to their own independent credit analysis, it is still useful for sponsors to view the public rating agencies as a reasonable point of reference.

A simple numerical scale can be useful to determine the average weighted credit rating of a pooled fund's portfolio. Exhibit 10–7 illustrates a numerical scale correlating 10 through 1 to the equivalent ratings as provided by Moody's, S&P, and Duff & Phelps. This method helps validate claims made by the fund manager and presents an excellent opportunity for discussion regarding the specifics of their credit analysis methodology.

Universe data concludes that there is no consistent correlation between credit and fund returns. As illustrated in Exhibit

EXHIBIT 10–7
Credit Rating Scale

Moody's		S&P		Duff & Phelps	
Aaa	10	AAA	10	AAA	10
Aa1	9	AA+	9	AA+	9
Aa2	8	AA	8	AA	8
Aa3	7	AA-	7	AA-	7
A1	6	A+	6	A+	6
A2	5	A	5	A	5
A3	4	A-	4	A-	4
Baa1	3	BBB+	3	BBB+	3
Baa2	2	BBB	2	BBB	2
Baa3	1	BBB-	1	BBB-	1

10–8, it is incorrect to assume that a fund with lower returns will naturally have higher overall credit quality. Of the 11 funds represented with returns above the median, 7 are also above the median in terms of credit.

EXHIBIT 10–8
Average Credit versus Performance

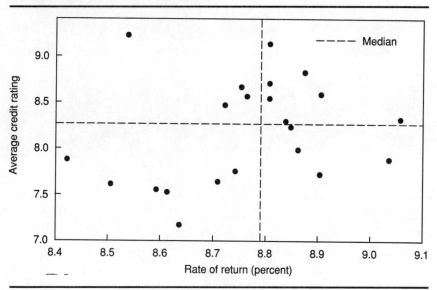

SUMMARY

Continued growth is anticipated for pooled funds, primarily from defined contribution plans. In an effort to fulfill their fiduciary responsibility to their plan participants, plan sponsors are becoming more attuned to the management strategies of the pooled fund in which they are participating.

At the pooled fund sponsor level, strategies are changing. Stable-value investment alternatives are being incorporated into the portfolios. Liquidity strategies are becoming more defined. Specific styles of portfolio management are emerging. Finally, performance patterns are becoming evident.

The decade of the 1990s will present consolidation opportunities as pooled funds merge (primarily a result of the banking industry consolidation). Mega-funds will emerge, forcing the issuer community to develop new attitudes toward the pooling concept, and possibly new products to meet the needs of these larger funds.

CHAPTER 11

MANAGING THE STABLE-VALUE PORTFOLIO

David C. Veeneman, President
Veeneman Associates, Inc.

The 1980s began with the participating insurance contract as the backbone of the *book value* investment industry. As the decade progressed, there was an explosion in the demand for stable-value products with the advent of 401(k) and other employee savings plans. As presented in Chapter 1, The Metamorphosis, coincident with the shift from defined benefit plans to defined contribution plans, there was a shift away from participating products in favor of nonparticipating, fully guaranteed GIC contracts. By the mid-1980s, the participating contract was practically extinct. Over $30 billion was being written annually in new nonparticipating GIC contracts. No-risk or low-risk were the watchwords and the word *guaranteed* had an element of magic associated with it.

As the market began maturing in the early 1990s, the term *guarantee* became suspect due in large part to the credit concerns of the industry, as plan participants and sponsors began asking what stood behind the guarantee. Management philosophies and strategies of plan sponsors that applied to GIC funds began changing. The emphasis changed from *yield* to *quality*. Plan sponsors began looking for ways to enhance overall portfolio quality. GIC portfolio management created a new industry, as plan sponsors looked for external professionals to manage and add value to the stable-value portfolio.

Presented here are the various styles of management for GIC portfolios, and the variety of synthetic, derivative, and participating GIC products (SDPs) available from banks, insurance companies, and other financial institutions to manage stable-value portfolios. The review will focus on the elements of investment risk associated with the management styles and the products available and the appropriateness of each type of product for various management styles and strategies.

Among the questions to be considered are the following:

- Are risk-based products or management styles appropriate for all employee savings plans?
- What risks do SDPs carry that are not found in more traditional, fully guaranteed GIC contracts?
- Can an SDP act as a credit enhancement?
- How can SDPs be integrated into traditional GIC portfolios?
- Can a GIC portfolio be "actively managed"?
- Does active management introduce inappropriate risks into a GIC portfolio?

This chapter will then review traditional GIC portfolio management techniques and the differences between *index* GIC management and *active* GIC management; providing an analytical framework for understanding SDP products and determining their role within any given set of investment objectives.

WHAT ARE SYNTHETIC, DERIVATIVE, AND PARTICIPATING PRODUCTS?

The terms *synthetics* and *derivatives* come to the GIC lexicon from more traditional fixed-income investing. A synthetic financial instrument is an investment that behaves like a different type of investment. For example, the sale of a long-term corporate bond for delivery in three months locks in the value of the bond at the time the deal is struck. From that time until the delivery of the bond three months later, the bond will cease to exhibit its normal characteristics in the hands of the seller.

From the seller's point of view, the bond will act as a cash asset and earn no more than a cash return. Since the price is locked in by the forward commitment, the bond will have the same principal volatility as cash—none at all. The seller has turned a bond into cash for a 90–day period without completing a sale of the asset.

The example above illustrates the creation of a synthetic as a hedge. The synthetic cash was created as a defense against a rise in interest rates and a resulting decline in the price of the bond at the time that it is sold. In many cases, synthetic instruments are created as an aggressive attempt to add value to a fixed-income portfolio by exploiting inefficiencies or mispricings that a fixed-income manager perceives in the marketplace.[1]

A derivative instrument gets its name from the fact that it derives its value from an underlying instrument. Like the synthetic, the derivative endows one investment with the risk and return characteristics of a different investment. But unlike the synthetic, the characteristics of a derivative may be unavailable or too costly.[2] In other words, a synthetic is one type of investment behaving like another known investment. A derivative will often act like a totally new type of investment.

Participating products have no analog in traditional fixed-income investing. The buyer of a bond or other fixed-income investment assumes all investment risk with respect to the instrument purchased, unless the risk is hedged through the use of options, futures, or similar instruments. The buyer of an investment contract, on the other hand, typically assumes only the credit risk of investing with the particular insurance company in question.

With this background, we can define the three categories of SDP products as follows:

A *synthetic* GIC is an instrument offered by an insurance company or other issuer that exhibits the same general risk

---

[1]Robert W. Kopprasch, Cal Johnson, Armand H. Tatevossian, *Strategies for the Asset Manager: Hedging and the Creation of Synthetic Assets* (New York: Salomon Bros., 1985).

[2]*The Handbook of Fixed-Income Securities*, 3rd ed. Frank J. Fabozzi, ed. (Homewood, Ill.: Richard D. Irwin, 1991), p. 669.

and return characteristics as a traditional insurance company investment contract. What distinguishes the synthetic from a traditional investment contract is the fact that it is offered by an issuer other than an insurance company, or it is issued by an insurance company out of a separate account.

A *derivative* GIC is a contract that exhibits characteristics not found in traditional investment contract products. A derivative investment contract may be issued by an insurance company out of its general account, or it may be structured as a synthetic. In either case, a derivative will exhibit certain characteristics not found in traditional, fully guaranteed products. It retains its character as an investment contract only because it qualifies for book value accounting.

A *participating* GIC looks very much like a derivative product. Like that product, the participating investment contract (or "par contract") has risk and return characteristics that depart from the traditional investment contract model. However, the participating investment contract is unique in its use of experience rating, a long-standing insurance industry method of passing through the investment experience of a pool of funds to its constituent contracts. Par contracts could be considered a subset of derivatives; however, the form is prevalent enough in the industry that we will consider it separately.

The benchmark against which all SDPs should be evaluated is the traditional, nonparticipating, fully guaranteed investment contract offered by major insurance companies for the past decade. In order to establish the benchmark, we will briefly review the characteristics of the traditional investment contract and the investment management techniques utilized with respect to investment contracts as an asset class.

STABLE-VALUE PORTFOLIO MANAGEMENT

As GICs became dominant during the 1980s, plan sponsor perceptions and attitudes about them changed. IPGs (immediate participation guarantees) and their predecessors had been considered insurance contracts and treated as such. One carrier typically "insured the plan" and offered all investment options that were made available to participants. A GIC was thought of as nothing more than another insurance policy held by an employee benefit plan.

As the industry developed experience with GICs, a different attitude emerged. GICs were not insurance policies, but considered true fixed-income investment contracts. It was popular to characterize GICs as private placement bonds issued by insurance companies. In fact, GICs do bear some resemblance to intermediate bonds in their fixed interest rates and maturities.

For most plan sponsors, GIC investment strategy was directed toward getting the highest rate available from a creditworthy insurance carrier. Plan sponsors adopted a procedure of preparing specifications and soliciting bids from at least several different insurance companies. Given the fixed maturity of GIC contracts, sponsors and their advisers were faced with the question of how to determine which maturity to buy.

Similarities between GICs and bonds guided early strategies for GIC portfolios. Plan sponsors and their advisers gravitated toward one of two approaches:

> Yield curve optimization: The best GIC was believed to be the one that offered the highest rate at the shortest duration. Adherents of this approach paid close attention to historical versus current spreads between U.S. Treasury notes and GICs and to current versus historical premiums paid for buying longer durations.
>
> Risk optimization: This approach placed priority on the need to minimize reinvestment risk in the portfolio. Followers of this strategy emphasized portfolio structure and the use of dollar cost averaging to minimize the risk of reinvesting an unusually large portion of the portfolio at low interest rates. A risk optimization strategy is usually built around a laddered portfolio, where maturities are staggered in regular amounts to minimize reinvestment risk.

Both strategies implied that GICs are investment assets to be managed as a part of an overall investment portfolio. This development was the first step in the evolution of the GIC from an insurance policy to its own recognized asset class.

Plan sponsors who treated GICs as insurance policies tended to buy them in much the same manner as they bought other corporate or pension insurance policies. They surveyed the market, either on their own or with the assistance of a broker or consultant, to find the best rate in an individual contract. As the asset class approach took over, many plan sponsors began to look at outside firms to assume management of their GIC portfolios. To meet this demand, a number of GIC management firms were formed in the mid-1980s.

Not all plan sponsors moved to outside management of their GIC portfolios. Many continued to manage their portfolios in-house, sometimes with the help of an outside consultant or other adviser. Those plan sponsors that did shift to outside firms did so for several reasons:

• Plan sponsors became concerned about potential fiduciary liability for management of a GIC portfolio.

• Plan sponsors looked for specific resources, such as carrier credit evaluation.

• Plan sponsors looked for a nationally recognized investment manager name to lend credibility to their participants.

• Plan sponsors looked for a manager to add investment value to the portfolio through their management.

• As the number of contracts in larger plans grew (50 or more contracts is not unusual), the need for administrative services grew.

Most plan sponsors who have moved to outside management have done so for a combination of reasons, with one of the reasons usually being the dominant motive for selecting a manager. The combination of factors influences the "style" of management that is most appropriate for a particular GIC portfolio.

STABLE-VALUE PORTFOLIO MANAGEMENT: ATTITUDES TOWARD INVESTMENT RISK

As can be seen from a comparison of yield curve optimization to risk optimization, there are different approaches and strategies with differing implications for a stable-value portfolio. These strategies can be grouped into two major styles of stable-value management: *index management* and *active management*.

Both styles of management are characterized by their approach to portfolio risk. Index management[3] has as its primary goal the minimization of all elements of risk in a stable-value portfolio. Active management involves the assumption of a prudent level of investment risk in the portfolio in order to enhance returns.

Attitudes toward Risk

Some experts contend that any form of active management is inappropriate for a stable-value portfolio. They argue that a stable-value fund is intended to be the "safe fund in a savings plan," the fund where participants can accumulate funds for their retirement with as little risk as possible. Most savings plans provide several different investment options, and those participants with a tolerance for investment risk and an appetite for higher returns can invest in one of the other options. The primary goal of a stable-value fund, these experts say, should be minimization of investment risk.

A countervailing view says that some degrees of investment risk is prudent and appropriate for a stable-value portfolio, even in a savings plan. The proponents of this view point out that savings plan participants typically have 10 to 30 years until retirement. Logically, these participants would be expected to invest in capital market investments such as stocks or bonds. Net of inflation, these investments can earn as much as double the yield of a GIC. Moreover, over a long period of time (10 years or more), there is a high probability that the participants will make, rather than lose, money in these investments.

---

[3]Index management has sometimes been referred to as "passive GIC management." In fact, many managers who follow this style are very aggressive in negotiating contracts with insurance companies and banks. The term *index management* has been adopted because the performance of this type of manager should mirror the performance of the GIC market in general, with no value added or detracted through management.

Most participants avoid capital market investments in favor of stable-value investments. The reason appears to be book value accounting; participants want to avoid unrealized investment losses in their savings plan accounts. Proponents of active management hold that the assumption of a prudent degree of investment risk is appropriate to investment contracts as an asset class because:

- If properly implemented, the strategy will produce yields in excess of an *index-managed* portfolio.
- Book value accounting will prevent portfolio strategy from affecting account balances.
- Participants will accumulate savings over a long enough period of time that the actual investment risk is negligible.
- If a participant terminates employment before retirement (as many do), the book value protections of an investment contract will protect the participant from losses.

A plan fiduciary must assume some posture toward investment risk in a stable-value portfolio. Identifying this posture will help direct the fiduciary toward which style is most appropriate for its portfolio.

ELEMENTS OF RISK IN A STABLE-VALUE PORTFOLIO

Many fiduciaries will find a middle ground between the two positions. For example, few fiduciaries would be willing to compromise the credit quality of a portfolio in search of higher-yielding contracts. Yet many may find other investment risks quite acceptable. If a fiduciary determines that some types of investment risk may be acceptable, the next question becomes, "What types?"

There are four major elements of investment risk in a stable-value portfolio:[4]

---

[4]Note that an insurance company or bank underwriter looks at a different set of risks when pricing an investment contract. These risks, and the underwriting process, are discussed in Chapter 6.

- Credit risk.
- Benefit liquidity risk.
- Maturity reinvestment risk.
- Call or put risk.

Credit Risk. There are two risks included within this category. The first is the risk of an actual default by an issuer, which would result in investment losses to the portfolio. The second is publicity risk, which surfaces as negative comments or stories about issuers in the trade press. Although publicity risk will not directly result in losses to the portfolio, negative publicity about an issuer can reduce participant confidence in the fund and reduce overall satisfaction with the savings plan. As such, it is a very real and very important risk.

Most fiduciaries and stable-value managers take a conservative posture toward credit risk. Few express any willingness to take significant credit risk in search of higher yields, and most invest only with a universe of banks, insurance companies, and other issuers generally recognized to be investment-grade.

Benefit Liquidity Risk. Investment contracts can be structured with a full guarantee to pay their share of all benefits paid from the plan during the life of the contract (the so-called benefit-responsive contract). An issuer assumes a certain amount of investment risk in making that guarantee. As a result, issuers will offer a slightly higher yield for contracts that do not contain the benefit-responsive feature. A stable-value fund can improve its yield by assuming the benefit liquidity risk for itself.

Many plans assumed this risk during the first half of the 1980s. These plans generally held cash in a buffer fund to pay benefits, paid their benefits out of new contributions to the fund, or relied on regular contract maturities to provide benefit liquidity. They ran the risk, however, that if benefits exceeded these sources of liquidity, they would be forced to liquidate one or more investment contracts in the portfolio at a loss.[5]

---

[5]Withdrawal(s) from a GIC contract prior to maturity is subject to a premature liquidation adjustment unless the withdrawal is participant directed and the contract(s) have been negotiated to provide benefit liquidity.

Stable-value funds made increasing use of benefit-responsive contracts during the last half of the 1980s. The shift occurred for several reasons. First, the spread between benefit-responsive and nonbenefit-responsive contracts declined significantly. Issuers reduced their benefit-responsive risk charges for portfolios that developed alternate sources of benefit liquidity. A well-structured fund that could show an ability to fund most liquidity needs through contract maturities, ongoing contributions to the fund, or a buffer fund could pay as little as five basis points or less for a guarantee of benefit responsiveness.

Second, the accounting profession expressed increasing concern about the use of nonbenefit-responsive contracts in a savings plan. The Financial Accounting Standards Board has questioned whether a nonbenefit-responsive GIC should be accorded a different accounting treatment than a corporate bond. (See Chapter 4 for a more detailed discussion.)

Third, some industry experts have found an element of insurance lacking in nonbenefit-responsive contracts. The similarities of such a contract to a corporate bond raise the prospect of regulation by the Securities and Exchange Commission, which currently maintains a hands-off posture toward GICs.[6]

For these reasons, most plan sponsors and outside managers have developed a conservative attitude toward the assumption of benefit liquidity risk. Few portfolios assume such risk in toto. Many portfolios do assume the risk in part, particularly as it relates to a large layoff or plant shutdown. These employer-initiated events expose an issuer to a significant risk of large losses, and many issuers limit their benefit-responsive guarantees to individual, rather than large group, terminations.[7] Most plans that assume these risks do so as a matter of necessity, and not as a strategy for adding value to the fund.

Maturity Reinvestment Risk. This element of stable-value portfolio risk has been the one most often used by managers and

---

[6]See SEC Rule 151, Appendix 2.

[7]Many GIC contracts provide that the benefit-responsive guarantee does not apply to any group termination that exceeds a certain threshold level (such as 20 percent of the contract) or that is large enough to constitute a "partial plan termination" as defined under the Internal Revenue Code.

plan sponsors to add value. Assumption of this risk does not expose the portfolio to potential investment losses, as would the assumption of credit risk or benefit liquidity risk. Maturity reinvestment risk will affect only the yield of the portfolio. This may account for the increased willingness of plan sponsors and managers to assume this risk.

Maturity reinvestment risk can surface in a stable-value portfolio as either *rate lag* or *rate shock*. Rate lag occurs when an unusually large portion of an investment contract is reinvested at low interest rates. For example, suppose that a single contract representing one-third of a portfolio matures and is reinvested at an 8 percent interest rate. Suppose further that the next maturity in the portfolio is 18 months in the future. Finally, assume that interest rates rise to 9 percent after the reinvestment, but the rise is not sustained for the full 18 months. Under this scenario, the savings plan would miss the opportunity to secure a yield 100 basis points higher than the actual contract rate.

Many plan sponsors and outside managers minimize this risk by staggering their contract maturities. The maturities may be staggered so that one contract matures each year (for plans with roughly $5 million or less to reinvest annually), or for larger plans, more frequently. It is not unusual for plans to stagger their maturities monthly or quarterly. This portfolio structure (known as a laddered portfolio) introduces dollar cost averaging, a widely used technique for minimizing reinvestment risk.

The example given above assumes that the savings plan placed a large contract just before a rise in interest rates. Suppose that the fund manager had anticipated the rise in rates and had placed the contract at the higher rate? Many savings plans did exactly that during the first half of the 1980s. Astute fund managers recognized that interest rates were at historically high levels and placed unusually large portions of their portfolio at those higher rates. Nominal interest rates declined to more normal levels in the second half of the decade. However, the portfolios that made large placements before the decline maintained an overall earnings rate well above the lower market rates.

Rate shock set in as the high-rate contracts matured. The most astute managers staggered their maturities so that their portfolio could transition gradually from an abnormally high earnings rate to the lower rates prevailing in the marketplace in the second half of the decade. However, many plans saw large, high-rate contracts mature at a single point in time. As a result, the earnings rate reported to participants dropped dramatically overnight. In some cases, overall fund yields declined from as much as 12 percent to as low as 8 percent as a single large contract matured. In such cases, a plan participant may not remember that the portfolio manager made an astute judgment five years before in locking in an unprecedented yield. Instead, the participant may be left with the perception that the fund manager somehow killed the goose that laid the golden egg. For this reason, many plan sponsors adopted laddered portfolios not only as a defense against their bad decisions, but as a defense against their good ones, as well.

Call or Put Risk. This type of risk is not found in the classic investment contract. Investment contracts typically guarantee the repayment of principal and interest on a fixed maturity date, and neither the issuer nor the contractholder has the right to call or put the contract back to the other prior to maturity. The sole exception to this rule is benefit payments made under benefit-responsive contracts and the contractholder's right to surrender the contract subject to a premature liquidation adjustment.

A class of modified investment contracts, known as extendable contracts, appeared in the mid-1980s and has remained popular. These contracts resemble classic contracts in most respects. However, they typically provide that the issuer will make a renewal offer on the maturity date. If the contractholder accepts the renewal offer, then the contract will be renewed at that rate for a specified period of years. If the contractholder declines the renewal offer, then the contract proceeds will be paid out.

The manner of payout depends on whether the interest rate stated in the renewal offer was higher or lower than the rate of the original contract. If the renewal rate was lower than the original rate (implying a lower rate environment generally), the contract would pay out in a lump sum at book value with all accrued interest. But if the renewal rate was higher than the original contract, the contract would pay out in installments over a period of years specified in the contract.

It is entirely conceivable that a contractholder would decline a renewal offer that was higher than the rate of its original contract. If the original contract was placed in a low-rate environment, a renewal offer could be higher than the original contract rate, yet well below prevailing market rates for similar contracts. In those cases, some contractholders asserted that the contract gave the issuer an opportunity to call the contract on its nominal maturity date[8] if interest rates generally had declined or to extend the contract for an installment payout period if interest rates generally had risen. In short, the issuer had an opportunity to select against the contractholder and in its own favor at the maturity date.

The rates offered for contracts of this type generally exceed rates offered on contracts with a maturity equal to the extended term. For example, an issuer might offer an extendable contract with a four-year nominal maturity and an installment payout over six years if the contractholder declined a renewal offer higher than the original contract rate. The duration of the contract, if extended, would be approximately seven years. In most cases, the rates offered for such contracts were slightly higher than the rates offered for straight seven-year contracts. The premium over seven-year contracts can be viewed as a call premium. It is the contractholder's compensation for the issuer's right to call the contract on its nominal maturity date.

As was noted at the outset of this section, a portfolio manager's attitudes toward these elements of stable-value portfolio risk determine the investment policy of the portfolio and the style of management implemented. We will turn to a consideration of those styles.

---

[8]The nominal maturity date is the maturity date stated in the contract. The nominal maturity date of a traditional contract is also its actual maturity date, since the issuer must pay out all principal and interest on that date. The actual maturity date of an extendable contract will be later than its nominal maturity date if the contract is paid out in installments beginning on its nominal maturity date.

EXPERIENCE RATING AND INVESTMENT PARTICIPATION

We have spoken generally thus far about the assumption of risk in a stable-value portfolio and the mechanisms that can be used to allocate risk between the issuer and the contractholder. There are two different types of risk assumption that can occur. The first is experience rating; the second is investment participation.

Experience rating refers to the practice of allocating investment gains or losses back to the contract that generated them. For example, if benefit payments in any period exceed the amount expected in pricing the contract, the issuer will have to sell assets to raise the cash needed to service the benefits. If spot rates are higher than the coupon of the assets sold, the sale will result in an investment loss. In a traditional investment contract, the loss is borne by the issuer. In an experience-rated contract, the loss is amortized against the contract's yield over the remaining life of the contract, thereby reducing its yield.

Investment participation refers to a pass-through of investment experience to the contractholder. Some contracts are invested in mortgage pass-through securities, which are discussed in further detail below. The pass-through securities carry a significant risk of prepayment. If prepayment occurs, the expected investment return of the contract assets will decline, since the prepaid amounts would normally be reinvested at a lower rate. In a nonparticipating contract, the issuer bears this prepayment risk. If reinvestments drive the investment return on contract assets below the guaranteed rate, the issuer bears the loss on the difference between the guaranteed return and the realized return. In a participating contract, the issuer typically will not guarantee a rate of return. Instead, it will pass through the actual returns earned on the underlying assets. If the rate on the underlying investments declines due to prepayments, then the rate credited to the contract declines correspondingly.

Traditional investment contracts are nonparticipating and nonexperience–rated. The insurance carrier assumes all investment risk and cash flow risk associated with the contract. Several of the SDP contracts now available (primarily participating contracts and modified IPGs—see Chapter 1 for a discussion of IPG contracts) are either experience-rated or participating, or both. These features have a direct impact on the nature and extent of the risk assumed by the holder of an SDP contract.

The buyer should carefully evaluate the terms of any experience rating or investment participation offered in an SDP contract. For example, a general rise in interest rates can generate unrealized losses in the assets that back a participating contract. Most participating contracts do not amortize these losses against income.[9] However, at least one contract would amortize such losses, largely negating the benefits of book value accounting.

The nature of the assets backing any contract with investment participation is of critical importance. The underlying assets can range from U.S. Treasury bonds, to privately placed mortgages or promissory notes, to GNMA pools, to credit card or auto loan receivables. In a nonparticipating contract, the nature of the underlying investments is secondary to the overall credit quality of the issuer. In a participating contract, the nature of the investments becomes of primary importance. The plan sponsor should consider the extent of due diligence required and the advisability of retaining outside experts to assist in evaluating any participating product and documenting the due diligence effort.

INDEX MANAGEMENT

As noted previously, the two major styles of stable-value management differ mainly in their posture toward the various elements of risk in a portfolio. The index manager seeks to

---

[9]Most participating contracts amortize only realized losses against income. A loss would normally be realized only if it became necessary to sell assets in order to raise cash to service benefit payments.

minimize the various elements of risk and to optimize portfolio yields within those risk constraints, while the active manager seeks to generate incremental returns for the portfolio by assuming a prudent, controllable degree of investment risk.

The primary investment objective of an index manager is to minimize the risks inherent in the portfolio. Credit risk is managed through portfolio credit standards and diversification among carriers of its approved universe. Benefit liquidity risk is managed by investing only in benefit-responsive contracts, and maturity reinvestment risk is managed through the use of a laddered portfolio.

An index manager adds value through efficient placements. An efficient placement is one that results in:

• An interest rate as favorable as any available in the marketplace at the time the placement is made.

• The ability to negotiate contractual terms required pursuant to the plan design and administrative practices.

• Acceptable credit quality that is within the diversification standards of the plan.

Note that the rate negotiated in an efficient placement will differ between plans. A company in a stable industry would expect to receive a higher rate than a company in a troubled industry, since the latter company presents a somewhat greater risk to the issuer. Placement efficiency assumes only that:

• The manager solicits bids from all qualified issuers.

• The terms specified for the contract are only those that are reasonably required for the plan.

• The manager is skillful at negotiating contracts.

If all three conditions are met, then an index manager would be expected to secure the best rate available in the marketplace with terms acceptable to the plan.

INDEX MANAGEMENT: MARKET-SENSITIVE PORTFOLIOS

An important goal of many index portfolios is rate stability. Since GICs have traditionally enjoyed a two-percentage-point rate advantage over savings accounts, money funds, and other consumer thrift accounts, many index-style managers have strived to provide an interest rate that maintains that advantage but at the same time is level and predictable. These managers feel that a stable rate instills confidence in plan participants and increases their propensity to take a longer-term view of their retirement savings account.

However, some managers and plan sponsors have become increasingly concerned about the ability of a blended-rate GIC portfolio to maintain its rate advantage during periods of rising interest rates. The concern is that during a yield curve inversion or a period of rapidly rising interest rates, the blended rate of a GIC portfolio will fall behind the rates offered on short-term investments such as money market funds and certificates of deposit. Some GIC portfolios experienced this problem in 1989, when interest rates jumped and short-term rates rose above GIC rates. As a result, an increasing amount of attention has been paid to the "tracking efficiency" of a GIC portfolio, that is, how much and how quickly a GIC portfolio's rate will rise during a period of generally rising interest rates.

The tracking efficiency of a GIC portfolio is a function of the amount of money available for reinvestment at any time. The shorter the duration of the portfolio, the more money that will turn over periodically for reinvestment at the new, higher rates. For example, while 20 percent of a five-year portfolio is available for reinvestment each year (assuming no new cash flows into the fund), 33 percent of a three-year portfolio is available for reinvestment each year. Since more money is reinvested each year from the three-year portfolio, it would normally be expected to follow an upward trend of interest rates more closely. Obviously, it would follow a downward trend just as closely.

Some managers have designed portfolios with an eye toward increasing the tracking efficiency of the portfolio. These designs have typically involved shorter-duration contracts and, in some cases, the use of index GICs or cash instruments. The cash component of the portfolio will track rising interest rates very closely and will improve the overall rate earned by the portfolio if short-term rates rise above the portfolio's blended interest rate. If short-term rates fall below the portfolio's blended rate, then the cash component of the portfolio will reduce the overall interest rate of the portfolio. The use of a cash component will improve the tracking efficiency of a GIC portfolio. The cost of the increased tracking efficiency is a lower portfolio rate of return in all environments except one of rapidly rising interest rates.

A simple example will illustrate the point. Assume that a portfolio is fully invested in a single GIC at 8.50 percent that will mature in three years. The rate earned on the portfolio will be fixed at 8.50 percent for the three-year period. Rising or falling interest rates will not affect that return. Now consider the same portfolio, except that one-half the assets are invested in a money market fund paying 6.50 percent. Rising interest rates would affect the two portfolios as shown in Table 11–1.

As can be seen from the table, the GIC portfolio trades part of its spread over cash investments to "buy" tracking efficiency. In other words, the mixed portfolio follows interest rates more closely as they rise, but it tracks them as they fall as well. By adjusting the relative sizes of the GIC and cash components, the

TABLE 11–1
Rates Shown by Percentage

Month	Market Rate	Portfolio A	Portfolio B
1	6.50%	8.50%	7.50%
2	6.75%	8.50%	7.63%
. . .			
8	8.25%	8.50%	8.38%
9	8.50%	8.50%	8.50%
10	8.75%	8.50%	8.63%
11	9.00%	8.50%	8.75%
12	9.25%	8.50%	8.88%
. . .			
25	9.00%	8.50%	8.75%
26	8.75%	8.50%	8.63%
27	8.50%	8.50%	8.50%
28	8.25%	8.50%	8.38%
29	8.00%	8.50%	8.25%
. . .			
35	6.50%	8.50%	7.50%
36	6.25%	8.50%	7.38%

Portfolio A = 36-month GIC at 8.50%.
Portfolio B = 50% 36-month GIC at 8.50%; 50% cash at market rate.

manager can fine-tune the amount of tracking efficiency added to the portfolio and the amount of return given up to do so.

The real world, of course, is not as simple as the example given. Few portfolios are made up of a single GIC. As a result, reinvestment of contract maturities would have to be factored into the design of an actual portfolio. Moreover, the example assumes a 50/50 mix of GICs and cash. In fact, the mix can be varied in order to balance the trade-off between rate and tracking efficiency.

Finally, cash is not generally used for the short-term portion of the portfolio. Index GICs have been popular vehicles for these cash components. They typically offer a higher return than money market funds, often within one-half a percentage point of three-year GICs, a rate generally a percentage point or more higher than money market funds. Rates on these contracts are generally tied to an outside index such as a Lehman Brothers intermediate bond index or a U.S. Treasury bond index, and they are usually reset monthly. Properly employed, these contracts can minimize the rate reduction required to improve the tracking efficiency of a GIC portfolio.

ACTIVE MANAGEMENT

An active manager takes a different approach. Like an index manager, an active manager is expected to produce efficient placements. However, the active managers will not be expected to minimize the various elements of portfolio risk in conducting those placements. Instead, they will be expected to assume various types of risk in a disciplined, prudent, and controllable manner in order to add value to the portfolio in excess of the return that could be generated through index management.

There is no one style of stable-value portfolio management that can be called active management. Instead, active management encompasses any strategy involving the assumption of investment risk in order to enhance portfolio returns. Risk may be assumed in any one of the four areas described above or in other areas not found in traditional investment contracts.

Some have questioned whether any stable-value investment strategy can be fairly described as active management. An investment contract, after all, is a buy-and-hold investment.[10] It is not traded in the open market, and there is no opportunity to realize a capital gain from the investment. An active manager adds value as a portfolio engineer, rather than as a trader of investments. To the extent that the term *active management* implies trading, then it would indeed be a misnomer. The term has been generally accepted within the industry to denote a manager who adds value over and above that which can be added through mere placement efficiency.

Within the context of traditional investment contracts, the opportunities to add value are somewhat limited. In some cases, opportunities have been avoided on the grounds of fiduciary prudence. In other cases, techniques and strategies that have been described as active management are actually methods for increasing placement efficiency and do not involve the assumption of investment risk to enhance returns. A review of the elements of stable-value portfolio risk will illustrate the point.

Credit Risk. Few if any active managers have attempted to enhance returns through the use of marginal or substandard credits.[11] Those who characterize themselves as active managers profess adherence to the same general quality and diversification guidelines as those who follow an index style of management.

Benefit Liquidity Risk. In the mid-to-late-1980s, several managers attempted to add value by assuming benefit liquidity risk. In some cases, the manager built portfolios around nonbenefit-responsive contracts, and the fund self-insured the

---

[10]The SEC has predicated its noninvolvement in GICs on the absence of a secondary market. Rule 151 specifically notes that GICs must generally be held to maturity and that they are not traded on any open exchange. The SEC cites this point as part of its rationale for holding that a GIC is not a security and therefore not subject to the provisions of the Securities Act of 1933. Rule 151 does leave the door open for SEC regulation under the 1933 Act if a secondary market does develop at some point in the future.

[11]During the course of several stable-value manager searches for clients, the author has surveyed major management firms as to their issuer credit-quality criteria. By and large, managers have limited their universe to carriers with medium to high investment-grade ratings. Roughly the same standard appears to prevail among major plan sponsors who manage their portfolios in-house.

benefit liquidity risk. However, concerns about fiduciary prudence and the eligibility of such a portfolio for book value accounting limited the appeal of the strategy, and it never gained broad acceptance within the industry.

As a middle ground, many managers bought "standby" guarantees of benefit liquidity with their contracts. Under a standby guarantee, an issuer agrees to provide benefit liquidity if the portfolio's primary sources of benefit payments (a buffer fund, ongoing contributions, maturing contracts) are exhausted. Given a low probability of actually having to make such payments, an issuer will generally quote a rate on such contracts that is within five basis points or so of its rate on a nonbenefit-responsive contract.

The use of standby contracts is not, in the final analysis, an active management technique. Since the issuer stands as the source of last resort for benefit liquidity, the portfolio really assumes no risk. It is no more than a way to structure a portfolio so as to minimize an issuer's risk charge for benefit responsiveness. In other words, it is simply a technique for achieving placement efficiency.

Another technique that has been used by managers is the "multiple-pay" contract. This type of contract is designed to exploit an inefficiency in the guaranteed market. Two carriers may very well differ in their opinions as to the appropriate risk charge for a given contract. For example, one issuer may reduce its rate by 10 basis points to account for risk, while a second issuer might reduce its rate by only 5 points for risk. The manager can add value if the second issuer will agree to cover not only its own benefits but the benefits payable under another contract as well. This would enable the manager to buy a nonbenefit-responsive contract from the first issuer and cover that contract's share of benefits with a multiple-pay contract from the second issuer.

The multiple-pay contract would be expected to carry a higher risk charge, but the higher charge would be offset by the elimination of risk charges from the nonbenefit-responsive contract. For example, the second issuer above doubles its risk charge to 10 points for the multiple-pay contract. The combined risk charge on both contracts increases by 5 basis points. The elimination of risk charges on the contract purchased from the first issuer reduces combined risk charges by 10 basis points, for a net gain of 5 basis points on the first contract.

Although the multiple-pay technique has been popular with some who describe themselves as active managers, it does not involve the assumption of investment risk in the portfolio. As with a standby contract, the issuer ultimately guarantees benefit liquidity, albeit for some other contract. As such, the multiple-pay technique is another way to increase the placement efficiency of the portfolio and would appear to be appropriate for both index and active managers.[12]

Maturity Reinvestment Risk. This element of stable-value portfolio risk gives an active manager the greatest opportunity to add value within the framework of traditional investment contracts. It has been generally accepted that a laddered portfolio carries the lowest risk of all portfolio structures. Unfortunately, rigorous adherence to a ladder can require a sacrifice of yield, particularly when the yield curve is steeply sloped.

Managers have modified laddered portfolios in a number of ways. A strict ladder would require that the manager place contracts at precise intervals for the same initial term to maturity. For example, a manager following a strict ladder might place a three-year contract at the end of each calendar quarter, so that contracts mature at the end of each quarter starting three years later.

Such a strategy will maximize the effects of dollar cost averaging, but it ignores opportunities that may exist if the yield curve is steeply sloped. For example, many managers follow historical spreads of GICs over U.S. Treasury notes for the spreads between GICs of various lengths. In a steep yield curve, either indicator may signal a favorable buying opportunity at a longer maturity than the ladder's target maturity (i.e., five years versus three). Managers could leave a "hole" in the GIC portfolio by

[12]The future viability of the multiple-pay technique is uncertain at this writing. The staff of the Financial Accounting Standards Board has suggested in informal conferences that FASB's forthcoming Statement of Financial Accounting Standards may deny book value accounting to any GIC that is not fully benefit responsive, even if that contract's share of benefits is covered by another contract with a multiple-pay guarantee.

buying a five-year contract instead of a three-year contract. If the manager allows the hole to remain, the portfolio will have no money to place three years hence, and a potential opportunity may be lost.

Managers that employ this strategy generally try to fill the holes in the portfolio when the yield curve is flat and yields for shorter contracts approach those of longer contracts. The success of the strategy depends on whether the manager has the opportunity to fill the holes in the portfolio before the unfilled maturities come due.

Some managers segment the portfolio into "core" and "tactical" segments. The core segment comprises the greatest part of the portfolio (80 percent is not unusual) and is maintained on a ladder in order to minimize maturity reinvestment risk. The remainder of the portfolio (the tactical segment) departs from the ladder in order to seek out buying opportunities at various points on the yield curve and to utilize alternatives when they are most advantageous for the portfolio.

These strategies are by no means exhaustive and are intended to merely give a flavor of the approaches that are available to a manager willing to assume maturity reinvestment risk in order to enhance portfolio returns. These strategies involve true active management. A manager employing them could not be fairly described as an index manager. The strategies go beyond placement efficiency, since each assumes maximum efficiency in the placement of investments for the portfolio.

These strategies differ from the others considered above in that they involve the assumption of a form of risk in the portfolio. Unlike the assumption of credit risk or benefit liquidity risk, maturity reinvestment risk strategies do not expose the principal amount of participant's accounts to losses. Any losses resulting from the strategy would be limited to income only.

SDPs: GENERAL

The emerging synthetic, derivative, and participating products open new opportunities for active management of stable-value portfolios. Several of the products can be used in index management, but in that role they serve as surrogates for traditional investment contracts. In order to add value to the portfolio in an index management context, the products must carry lower risk than a traditional contract. Within this context, SDPs have found use largely to date as credit enhancements.

SDPs have a potentially greater use in active management. Many SDP products allow an active manager to assume specific risks and to limit those risks to the principal or income components of the portfolio. For example, several participating contracts are backed with GNMA mortgage securities ("Ginnie Maes").[13] Ginnie Maes carry little credit risk, since they are guaranteed by an agency of the federal government. Ginnie Maes are subject to call risk, since the prepayment experience of the underlying mortgages is passed through to the Ginnie Mae security holder. Since they carry this risk, Ginnie Maes pay a higher yield than comparable-duration U.S. Treasuries. A Ginnie Mae-backed participating contract passes the risk and the yield through to the contractholder.

This type of vehicle provides the active manager the opportunity to take on specific risks. The Ginnie Mae-backed contract enables the active manager to isolate call risk from credit risk. The call risk is assumed; the credit risk is not. The instrument also enables the active manager to isolate the risk to the income component of the portfolio, while protecting the principal component from credit risk.

---

[13]A Ginnie Mae is a type of instrument known as a mortgage pass-through security. A pass-through security is structured as a bond and is backed by a pool of homeowner first mortgages. The mortgages are generally guaranteed by a U.S. government agency and consequently have low credit risk. They are called "pass-through" securities because the experience of the mortgage pool (other than defaults) is passed through to the holder of the security. The homeowners in the mortgage pool have the right to prepay their mortgages on a sale or refinancing of their homes. A decline in interest rates will result in significant prepayments as homeowners refinance their mortgages at lower rates. These prepayments will be passed through to security holders and are tantamount to a call provision in the security. For a complete explanation of mortgage-backed securities, see Linda Lowell, "Mortgage Pass-Through Securities" in *The Handbook of Fixed-Income Securities,* 3rd ed. Frank J. Fabozzi, ed. (Homewood, Ill.: Richard D. Irwin, 1991), p. 562.

There are two common elements of any investment suitable for active management:

- Eligibility for book value accounting.
- Participation in the financial experience of the contract.

Participation implies the assumption of a risk normally carried by an insurance company under a traditional investment contract, as in the Ginnie Mae contract example. Is the assumption of such risks appropriate to an employee savings plan? Each plan sponsor must reach its own decision, and the plan's posture toward risk will be the heart of its investment policy.

There is a case to be made against the assumption of risk. A stable-value fund is usually the most conservative investment option available. The assumption of risk in such a fund is inappropriate. Participants who want to assume risk in order to earn a higher return generally have other investments, such as stocks and bonds, available under the particular plan in which to do so. The primary investment objective of a stable-value fund should be minimal risk.

There is also a case to be made for the assumption of a prudent degree of investment risk. The assumption of such risk can enhance returns, and the availability of book value accounting prevents the risk from affecting participant account balances. Most participating contracts protect the principal balances of participant accounts and provide methods for amortizing gains or losses to income over a period of time. Moreover, most participating contracts enable the manager to take on specific risks (such as Ginnie Mae prepayment risk) without taking on risks that may be seen as undesirable, such as credit risk or benefit liquidity risk. Under these circumstances, the assumption of a prudent degree of investment risk in order to enhance the returns earned by participants can be a sound fiduciary strategy.

Although the primary task of an index manager is to minimize risk, the goal can be accomplished in a variety of ways. As one would expect, different managers have different approaches to index management. The dominant approach is the laddered portfolio referred to above, but it is by no means the only approach. Two approaches have attracted considerable interest in the past several years:

- "Tracking efficiency" funds (discussed above).
- "Controlled volatility" funds (discussed below).

Each type of fund is designed to meet a different set of investment objectives that falls within the broad category of *index management*.

Controlled Volatility Funds. These funds arise from a fundamental dissatisfaction with the "one-way" nature of GIC valuation. If a GIC is surrendered prior to maturity, the contractholder receives the lesser of book or market value. If the contract rate is lower than interest rates prevailing at the time of surrender, the contractholder will suffer a loss in the form of a market value adjustment. If, on the other hand, the contract rate is higher than rates prevailing at surrender, the contractholder will receive no gain. In such a case, only the book value of the contract is paid out, and the economic value of the favorable interest rate is lost.

Some plan sponsors have contemplated switching from a GIC fund to a bond fund in order to capture the value of favorable interest rates on their portfolio holdings. However, bond funds must be marked to market each reporting period. In a rising interest rate environment, participant accounts would show losses, even if no bonds were sold by the fund manager. A controlled volatility fund is an attempt to capture the potential investment gains of a bond fund without running the risk of investment losses.

A controlled volatility fund combines GICs (for stability of principal) with bonds (for potential investment gains and additional diversification). GICs make up the bulk of the portfolio, with bonds making up a relatively small portion of the portfolio (generally 10 percent to 33 percent of the portfolio's asset value). The bond component of the portfolio is limited to a size that will provide certainty that bond losses would be covered by the other income of the portfolio. In a "bad" quarter (that is, a quarter of rising interest rates), bond losses might reduce the income of the overall portfolio to near zero, but would not drive the return of the portfolio below zero. In other words, it would not generate an investment loss.

In the following example, a hypothetical portfolio is made up of an even mix of long-term government and corporate bonds. This portfolio has a 95 percent probability of producing a total return between −16.7 percent and 34.4 percent.[14] In order to protect the portfolio from a negative return over a one-year period, bonds should be limited to a portion of the portfolio small enough such that a 16.7 percent loss in the value of the bonds will be offset by the earnings of the portfolio's GICs. Assume that a hypothetical GIC portfolio generates a return (a blended interest rate) of 8.75 percent. A mix of two-thirds GICs and one-third bonds would produce the portfolio returns shown in Table 11–2 at the extremes of the portfolio returns.

In the worst case shown in Table 11–2, the −5.57 percent negative return contributed by the bond portion of the portfolio is almost exactly offset by the 5.83 percent contributed by the GIC component, resulting in a portfolio return of 0.26 percent. There is a 95 percent probability that the mix of one-third bonds and two-thirds GICs will produce a positive return.

The strategy's payoff is on the upside. In the best case, the bond component contributes 11.47 percent to the portfolio's total return of 17.30 percent. The overall return is better than double the return of a pure GIC portfolio. Of course, this result is at the far range of the optimistic scale. Given an expected return from bonds of 8.85 percent,[15] the bond component will contribute three basis points to the overall rate. One would expect the mixed portfolio to behave much like a pure GIC portfolio. But

---

[14]The forecasted returns are based on historical returns between 1973 and 1990. During that period, bonds produced an average annualized compound return of 8.85 percent, with a standard deviation of 12.77 percent. © 1991 *Stocks, Bonds, Bills, and Inflation 1991 Yearbook™*, Ibbotson Associates, Chicago (annually updates work by Roger G. Ibbotson and Rex A. Sinquefield). All right reserved. The forecast assumes that bond returns are normally distributed, a point on which there is not universal agreement. For simplicity, the example calculates returns over a one-year period. In many cases, the performance of a controlled-volatility fund is reported to plan participants quarterly. In that case, the fund must be designed to protect against negative returns each quarter, rather than each year.

[15]See previous footnote.

TABLE 11–2

Worst Case (bonds lose 16.7%)	
GIC returns (8.75% × ⅔)	5.83%
Bond returns (−16.7% × ⅓)	−5.57%
Portfolio return	0.26%
Expected Case (bonds gain 8.85%)	
GIC returns (8.75% × ⅔)	5.83%
Bond returns (8.85% × ⅓)	2.95%
Portfolio return	8.78%
Best Case (bonds gain 34.4%)	
GIC returns (8.75% × ⅔)	5.83%
Bond returns (34.4% × ⅓)	11.47%
Portfolio return	17.30%

in the best case, the mixed portfolio could double returns, and in the worst case the portfolio is virtually guaranteed to have no losses.

Between 1976 and 1990, the hypothetical portfolio would have produced the returns shown in Table 11–2.

For purposes of illustration, Table 11–3 makes the simplifying assumption that the GIC portion of the portfolio earned a constant 8.75 percent over the period. Under those assumptions, the bond component improved the rate of return of the overall portfolio in 7 out of the 15 years. For the 15–year period, the overall portfolio return would have been 9.95 percent, a 120-basis-point improvement over the GIC component of the portfolio.

The static GIC return assumed in the example clarifies the contribution of the bond component. However, the GIC return would actually be expected to change over time as existing contracts mature and new contracts are purchased for the portfolio. These changes would necessitate rebalancing the portfolio in order to minimize the probability of overall negative returns. An increase in the rate of the GIC component would increase the portfolio's tolerance for bond losses. In such a case, the manager

TABLE 11-3

| | Component | | |
Year	Bond	GIC	Total Portfolio
1976	5.90%	5.83%	11.73%
1977	0.17%	5.83%	6.00%
1978	(0.19%)	5.83%	5.65%
1979	(0.90%)	5.83%	4.93%
1980	(1.10%)	5.83%	4.74%
1981	0.15%	5.83%	5.98%
1982	14.03%	5.83%	19.86%
1983	0.89%	5.83%	6.73%
1984	5.31%	5.83%	11.15%
1985	10.31%	5.83%	16.15%
1986	7.40%	5.83%	13.23%
1987	(0.41%)	5.83%	5.43%
1988	3.40%	5.83%	9.23%
1989	5.72%	5.83%	11.56%
1990	2.16%	5.83%	7.99%

could increase the portion of the overall portfolio committed to bonds. Any such increase would have to come from new contributions to the plan, from rollovers, or from single interest payments (if any GICs provided for such).

Any increase in the interest rate of the GIC component would presumably be driven by rising interest rates, which would negatively affect the returns of the bond component. Accordingly, the astute manager would be expected to reduce bond exposure in a rising interest rate environment, in order to minimize bond losses and maximize the return of the GIC component of the portfolio.[16] Then, as interest rates turn and enter the downside of the cycle, the manager will commit available funds to bonds in order to generate capital gains as rates fall.

As market rates fall, the rate on the GIC portion of the portfolio would be expected to fall as well, as older higher-rate

---

[16]If the rise is accompanied by an inverted yield curve, the manager may commit new funds to short-term or cash instruments, in order to track rising interest rates more closely and maintain liquidity to invest in bonds when rates eventually turn.

contracts mature and are replaced by new contracts at lower rates. This decline would reduce the portfolio's tolerance for bond losses, which in turn would require the manager to reduce its bond position (assuming that the manager had invested in bonds to the full extent of the portfolio's tolerance). As a result, the manager would sell into the favorable bond market and reduce its bond commitments before rates turn again to the up side of the cycle.

This particular strategy assumes that a GIC manager can successfully time interest rates. There is ongoing dispute among fixed-income professionals as to whether such market timing can be successfully executed over a market cycle. The less aggressive approach would be to set a relatively fixed size for the bond component, rather than changing the size of the bond position in anticipation of interest rate movements.

The strategies outlined above limit risk exposure to the income component of the portfolio. Successfully implemented, they would be expected to improve the rate of return of the portfolio, at the cost of increased volatility in the portfolio rate of return. The strategy can be implemented in a relatively disciplined manner by maintaining the bond component at a relatively constant portion of the portfolio, as is illustrated by the example that has been shown. More aggressive managers may engage in interest rate anticipation by committing heavily to bonds when they believe that interest rates have reached their peak (and the portfolio's tolerance for bond exposure is at its greatest), then closing out bond positions when they conclude that rates have arrived at a trough. The appropriateness of either strategy will again depend on the investment objectives set for the portfolio.

SDPs: MAJOR TYPES

Currently available SDPs fall into several categories:

- Separate account contracts.
- Modified contracts.
- Modified IPGs.
- Participating contracts.
- Synthetic contracts.

These products differ largely in the allocation of risk between the issuer and the contractholder.

SDPs: Separate Account Contracts

These contracts resemble traditional contracts in most respects. The contract has a fixed maturity date, and principal and interest are fully guaranteed by the issuer. These contracts are fully benefit responsive. They differ from traditional contracts in that they are not issued from an insurance company's general account or as a deposit obligation of a bank. Instead, the contracts are written out of an insurance company's separate account. Separate account contracts are generally invested in government or investment-grade corporate bonds.

Use of a separate account is generally considered to offer two advantages to the contractholder:

• Assets are segregated from the carrier's general account or the bank's deposit obligations, placing them beyond the reach of other policyholders or creditors. This feature increases the security of the plan sponsor's investment.

• The contractholder can identify and monitor specific assets that back the contract, which will facilitate closer monitoring of the investments on an ongoing basis.

The rate paid on a separate account contract will generally be lower than the rate offered on a traditional contract—for several reasons. First, the issuer will normally be expected to use higher-quality investments (which generally have lower coupons) to back a separate account contract. An issuer rated AA can generally issue a traditional contract backed by BBB investments without meeting immediate resistance from the contractholder. The underlying assets are rarely, if ever, disclosed. The purchase of the contract is predicated on the credit quality of the issuer, not the quality of the underlying assets. The issuer of a separate account contract provides more information to the contractholder. The underlying assets are both visible and an integral factor in the purchase of the contract.

Second, the expenses of administering a separate account contract are somewhat higher than the expenses of a traditional contract. Separate account contracts require more monitoring than a traditional contract, and contractholder reporting will normally be more detailed. Third, separate account contracts are not competitively bid to the same degree as traditional contracts. There are fewer issuers of these contracts, and the differences in contract terms make it more difficult to competitively bid.

The major reason for buying separate account contracts has traditionally been for credit enhancement purposes. The general perception is that the separate account vests legal ownership of the underlying assets to the contractholder, effectively immunizing it from an insolvency or default by the issuer.[17]

SDPs: Modified Contracts

Modified investment contracts have been offered since the advent of the GIC contract. They have the primary characteristics of traditional GIC contracts (guaranteed principal and interest, benefit responsiveness); however, they modify one or more elements of the traditional contract in several ways.

The predominant form of modified investment contract is the extendable contract previously discussed. In most respects, it resembles a traditional contract. They differ from an investment contract in that the issuer reserves the right to extend the contract's term on its nominal maturity date. The issuer will normally pay a yield premium for this right. It is not unusual for yields on this type of contract to run 25 basis points over the yield for a straight contract with a maturity equal to the longest term that can be selected by the issuer.

It is possible to modify the contract in other ways (e.g., by experience-rating the benefit responsiveness of the contract). However, such modifications change the basic character of the contract to the extent that it can no longer be fairly characterized as a nonparticipating contract. For this reason, the focus is on the extendable contract as the primary form of modified GIC.

---

[17]See more detailed discussion on separate accounts in Chapter 2, "What Is a GIC?" and Chapter 5, "Quality—Analyzing the Life Insurance Industry."

A modified investment contract can be a useful tool in an active manager's kit, but the suitability of such a contract in an index portfolio is questionable. An extendable contract shifts call risk (more properly, the risk of extension) to the contract-holder, for which the contractholder is paid a risk premium. If spot interest rates at the time of the contract's nominal maturity are lower than the contract's stated rate, then the contract will be called by the issuer and its entire principal and accrued interest will be available for reinvestment. However, if spot interest rates are higher than the contract's stated rate, then the issuer will extend the contract by paying it out in installments over a period of years.

As a result, the index manager has no way of knowing the amount or timing of cash flows from the contract in advance, which limits the ability to structure the portfolio in such a way as to minimize maturity reinvestment risk. The index manager's ability to build a ladder is diminished by the uncertain payout from the extendable contract. The best that the index manager can do is project a payout scenario based on expected spot rates at the time of maturity and attempt to build a ladder around the projected payout. Any subsequent changes in rates will disrupt the strategy. Accordingly, the effectiveness of the strategy will depend on the index manager's ability to forecast interest rates at a point in time several years in the future; this runs directly counter to the mission of an index manager.

An active manager is not faced with the same constraints. Assumption of call risk in order to earn a premium yield is well within the scope of an active manager's mission. The risk assumed in an extendable contract is isolated to the income component of the portfolio, since it relates solely to the amount and timing of contract maturities. Specifically, the portfolio assumes the risk that in a rising interest rate environment, contracts will be extended, reducing the amount available for reinvestment at the higher rates. As a result, the portfolio interest rate will lag the rate of a portfolio using traditional contracts with the same nominal maturities.

The active manager will justify the risk by the higher initial rate paid on each extendable contract purchased. Over time, the skill with which the contracts are selected will cause the active manager to either outperform or underperform an index manager. It may be useful to consider a simple strategy based on the use of extendable contracts. Assume that an active manager purchases a $5 million extendable contract at the end of each quarter. Each contract has a nominal maturity of four years, at which time it will either be paid out in a lump sum or in annual installments over a six-year period.[18] Assume further that the portfolio is structured as a laddered portfolio based on the nominal maturities of the extendable contracts.

The extendable portfolio will initially outperform a laddered portfolio of traditional contracts with the same nominal maturities, due to the risk premium (higher yield) paid on the extendable contract. If interest rates rise consistently as the contracts reach their nominal maturity dates, then one would expect the extendable contracts be paid out on an installment maturity schedule. These extensions will cause reinvestments from the extendable portfolio to lag those of the traditional portfolio, whose maturities are paid out in a lump sum. This lag will erase some of the initial advantage of the extendable portfolio. As additional extendable contracts mature (assuming installment payouts), the aggregate amount of installments will increase (since installments will be received from multiple contracts) and approach the amount of each maturity in the traditional portfolio. In short, the lag effect may be temporary. The active manager will add value if the risk premium earned on the extendables offsets the underperformance due to rate lag on the back end.

---

[18]Most extendable contracts provide that the issuer will make a renewal offer shortly before the contract's nominal maturity date. If the offer is rejected, the terms of payout will depend on whether the renewal offer was higher or lower than the contract's stated rate. If spot interest rates are higher than the contract's stated rate at the time that the renewal offer is made, the renewal offer would be expected to be higher than the contract's stated rate. That doesn't necessarily mean that the renewal offer will be competitive with spot yields, and it has been the author's experience that in many cases the renewal offer is not competitive with yields available on the open market.

SDPs: Modified IPG Contracts

Insurance companies offer products that closely resemble IPG contracts of the 1970s. These contracts contain a nominal guarantee of principal and may have a minimum guaranteed interest rate. They have no fixed maturity date; like traditional IPGs, these contracts continue indefinitely until terminated by the contractholder or the issuer. All cash flows from the contract are adjusted to market value in much the same ways as was done under traditional IPG contracts.

These contracts generally suffer from the same shortcomings as the traditional IPG. These contracts are often written out of an insurance company's general account. As a result, the assets that back the contract are not specifically identified. The contractholder has no assurance as to the investment quality of the assets or the likely default experience. Market value adjustments under these contracts are often calculated according to a formula that is not guaranteed and that is subject to change at any time. The factors used in the market value formula (duration, market yield, coupon rate) may not be derived from the underlying assets, with the result that the market value calculated is less than the true market value of the underlying assets.

Insurance companies offer products designed to address the shortcomings of the traditional IPG. These new-style contracts are designed to provide a level playing field between the contractholder and the issuer. Important factors to look for in a modified IPG would include:

- A clear investment policy that describes eligible investments in detail, or contractholder control (exclusive or shared) over investment policy.
- Specifically identified assets backing the contract or the pool in which the contract participates.
- Guaranteed expense factors, with no issuer overhead allocable to the contract.
- A guaranteed market value adjustment formula keyed to the actual characteristics of the assets backing the contract or the pool in which it participates.

This type of contract has very different implications for the index manager and the active manager.

An IPG of any sort (whether traditional or modified) is inappropriate for an index portfolio. The defining element of an IPG contract is participation in the financial experience of the contract; in other words, the assumption of risk. The assumption of risk runs directly counter to the investment policy of an index portfolio.

A modified portfolio does present intriguing possibilities for an actively managed portfolio. Several insurance companies write modified IPGs as separately managed investment accounts. The assets backing the contract are segregated from all other assets, and the investment policy of the fund is set by the contractholder, subject to the minimum standards of the issuer. This arrangement changes the nature of the relationship between the contractholder and the contract issuer. The contract is no longer a financial commodity resembling a bond; instead, it is more akin to an investment management arrangement.

In fact, the insurance company becomes the active manager of the book value investment portfolio, in much the same manner as it manages its other separate accounts. Instead of periodically buying a new contract from a different issuer, the plan sponsor retains an insurance company to act as an active book value manager of its fund. The plan sponsor or manager no longer acts as the investment manager of the fund; the insurance company assumes that role. It can be argued that the need for an outside intermediary (such as a broker, a consultant, or an outside stable-value manager) to place contracts is eliminated. If the marketplace proceeds along these lines, the roles of all major participants in the marketplace will be redefined.

It is possible to incorporate a modified IPG into a traditional GIC portfolio. Given the indefinite maturity of a modified IPG, it is not practical to work the contract into a laddered portfolio. However, a modified IPG can be placed into a portfolio in tandem with a traditional ladder. For example, a modified IPG with a duration of three years can form the tactical portion of a portfolio whose core position is a traditional ladder with a three-year duration. In this case, the modified IPG is not part of the ladder. Instead, it exists next to the ladder and is duration-matched to the ladder.

The challenge in structuring this type of arrangement is to define the risks that will be assumed by the contractholder. By definition, all investment experience is passed through to the contractholder. If credit quality or benefit liquidity is compromised, then the effects of these decisions will be passed through to the contractholder. Any prepayment risk or maturity reinvestment risk in the assets backing the contract will be similarly passed through. A primary consideration for the plan sponsor will be the extent to which it can exercise control over these risk factors. Some issuers insist on complete control over investment policy. However, an increasing number of issuers will allow the contractholder to set policy, particularly in accounts of roughly $20 million or more.

SDPs: PARTICIPATING CONTRACTS

Participating investment contracts are a hybrid of traditional contracts and modified IPGs. Like the traditional investment contract, they have a guarantee of principal and generally have a fixed maturity date. As with a modified IPG, the interest rate that is paid is not guaranteed. Unlike a traditional investment contract, they pass investment risk through to the contractholder. Unlike a modified IPG, in these contracts the types of investment risk passed through may be specific and unlimited.

Participating contracts are generally experience-rated to some degree and participate in investment experience. It is not unusual for a participating contract to offer a floor guarantee interest rate with the potential for upside participation if contract experience is more favorable. As in the IPG form of contract, the upside potential is limited by the fact that the assets backing the contract are largely invested at the time the contract is entered into. As a result, there is a limited opportunity for the contract rate to rise if general market interest rates rise; in fact, the opposite is quite likely to occur.[19]

A participating investment contract differs from a modified IPG in its fixed maturity. The fixed maturity makes it easier to incorporate a participating contract within the structure of a multiple-issuer, multiple-contract portfolio. This structure gives the active manager the opportunity to determine on a placement-by-placement basis whether to buy a participating or a nonparticipating instrument, depending on investment conditions at the time and the terms offered by issuers.

As is the case with most SDP products, a participating contract is generally not a suitable vehicle for an index manager. The experience rating found in most participating contracts involves the assumption of liquidity risk on the part of the portfolio. And the investment participation found in many participating contracts runs counter to the index manager's policy of reducing investment risk wherever possible.

An experience-rated contract can give the active manager the opportunity to assume benefit liquidity risk in a way that isolates the risk to the portfolio's income component. This strategy would be expected to add value to the portfolio under two circumstances:

- A portfolio with a volatile cash flow history will pay heavy risk charges for a benefit-responsive, nonparticipating contract. If future experience is expected to be favorable, the portfolio can assume the benefit liquidity risk in order to secure a better rate from issuers.
- If interest rates are expected to decline over the life of the contract, then the assets backing the contract will build up unrealized gains. As assets are liquidated to service benefits, these gains will be realized. The gains can be am-

---

[19]A rise in interest rates will result in unrealized losses in the assets backing the contract. Since a modified investment contract, like an IPG contract, qualifies for book value accounting, these unrealized losses are not amortized against the contract's earnings rate. If it becomes necessary to sell assets in order to raise the cash necessary to service benefits, the losses realized on such sales will be amortized against contract earnings. As a result, the contract earnings rate may well decline while other interest rates are rising.

ortized over the remaining life of the contract, thereby increasing its rate as other rates decline. Of course, if the interest rate forecast is incorrect, then withdrawals will cause losses that will be amortized over the life of the contract, lowering its rate.

The second strategy may be limited by the terms of the contract. Nonparticipating contracts almost always limit benefit withdrawals to bona fide benefits provided by the employee benefits plan in question, and to either a pro-rata or LIFO share of those benefits. In other words, the plan sponsor or administrator has no discretion over the amount to be withdrawn from the contract. If a participating contract is experience rated, there would be no reason to limit benefit withdrawals from the contract in such a manner, since the issuer bears no investment risk on the withdrawals. However, some participating contracts may contain such limitation, and the terms of each contract should be reviewed carefully.

There are a number of participating contracts in the marketplace. They are backed with a variety of instruments, ranging from corporate and government bonds, commercial mortgages, Ginnie Maes and other agency securities, and asset-backed securities. These contracts typically pass through some or all of the risks associated with these investments. It is more common for participating contracts to be backed with intermediate-term bonds and mortgages, given the fixed maturity date of most participating investment contracts.

The selection of a participating contract differs in many respects from the selection of a nonparticipating contract. The competitive bidding procedure used on nonparticipating contracts depends on all bidders submitting apples-to-apples quotes. In other words, the contracts bid by all issuers must be the same in all material respects. A non-par contract is a financial commodity, and selection is generally made on the basis of rate and quality.

A participating contract tends not to be a financial commodity. It is certainly conceivable that a number of issuers might offer participating contracts that are backed with the same types of investments, that experience-rate in the same manner, and that pass the same types of investment risk through to the contractholder in the same manner. This certainly has not been the case to date. Participating contracts have common characteristics, but they have significant differences with respect to the factors listed above. The selection of a participating contract bears closer resemblance to the selection of a modified IPG than to the selection of a nonparticipating contract.

SDPs: Synthetic Contracts

A synthetic investment contract is not a GIC. It is not issued by an insurance company or a bank, it is not guaranteed by a general account, and it is not a deposit obligation. A synthetic contract is a product that bears none of those attributes of a traditional investment contract but that nonetheless may qualify for book value accounting. In most cases, synthetic contracts are bond funds that are managed to minimize the spread between book and market value.[20]

Synthetic contracts are typically built around immunization or "horizon management" strategies. *Immunization* is a

---

[20]There is a great deal of uncertainty about the accounting status of synthetic investment contracts. Bond managers that offer their funds as synthetic investment contracts assert that their funds qualify for book value accounting treatment. In support of their position, these managers have offered letters from public accounting firms as to the appropriateness of book value accounting to the fund in question. However, opinion is divided on the issue, and the prudent plan sponsor would be well-advised to secure an opinion from the auditor of its employee benefit plan (or from another leading accounting firm) as to the availability of a synthetic contract for book value accounting.

In at least one case, the manager of a synthetic contract has offered its product with a "wrapper" from an insurance company. The wrapper is a guarantee that the principal and interest will be paid on a timely basis, and it is designed to increase the certainty that the product will qualify for book value accounting. However, as with the separate account contract, there is some uncertainty as to the rights of the insurance company in the synthetic contract by virtue of its guarantee. If the wrapper is written as a simple guarantee of the obligation of the synthetic contract manager, then the creditors and policyholders of the insurance company would seem to gain no rights in the synthetic contract assets. Nonetheless, practice varies widely in this area and the plan sponsor considering the use of this type of product should have its structure reviewed by legal counsel experienced in this area.

technique for matching an asset to a liability.[21] For example, an obligation to pay $1 million plus interest at 8.50 percent in five years can be said to be immunized if the obligation is backed by a creditworthy five-year, zero coupon bond with a coupon rate above 8.50 percent. At the end of five years, when the obligation comes due, the backing asset will mature as well, providing the source of funds for satisfaction of the obligation. Immunization is essentially a passive management strategy; assets and liabilities are matched and held to maturity.

Horizon management is a variant of immunization that is designed to enhance yields through a degree of active management. A horizon manager adheres to the basic principles of bond immunization but may swap sectors, coupons, and quality to increase yields.

From the foregoing discussion it should be clear that synthetic contracts can be structured to mimic traditional nonparticipating contracts (if structured as an immunized portfolio) or participating contracts (if horizon management is implemented). However, both strategies assume that the initial deposit will remain in the fund until its maturity date. In other words, both strategies are essentially nonbenefit responsive.

It is possible in both cases to structure the fund to pay out specific amounts at specific dates. For example, by using semiannual coupon bonds, the fund manager can pay out an amount roughly equal to simple interest at the contract rate. If larger periodic payouts are desired, the maturity of assets backing the fund can be structured to provide the desired amounts at the desired times. However, any withdrawals in excess of the periodic cash flows arranged in advance may result in realized investment losses to the fund (if the manager is required to raise cash to service benefits at a time of high interest rates).

As a result, these types of contracts may not be appropriate to a pure index manager. At the same time, an immunized portfolio may provide limited opportunity for the manager to add

---

[21]For a detailed discussion of bond immunization, see *The Handbook of Fixed-Income Securities*, 3rd ed., ed. Frank J. Fabozzi, (Homewood, Ill.: Richard D. Irwin, 1991), pp. 912–41.

value, since this type of portfolio does not accommodate active management. This type of product provides the same sort of utility as a separate account investment contract—credit enhancement. It permits the plan sponsor to move away from reliance on the credit of an insurance company or bank in favor of a specific portfolio of securities. In return, the plan sponsor can expect to receive a somewhat reduced rate of return (for the reasons discussed above in connection with separate account contracts), and it may pay somewhat higher fees (since these products are often managed on an individual-account basis, rather than as part of a pool).

SUMMARY

During the 1980s, one product dominated the guaranteed market—the nonparticipating GIC. It served one function well: that of providing a minimal risk approach to funding an employee savings plan. The product does pose unique risks to its issuers. These risks have not always been fully reflected in the rates offered by issuers. The mispricing of these contracts is understandable, given the fact that they are largely a competitively bid, low-margin commodity. It is unlikely that this mispricing will continue into the future.

Given these mispricings and the more conservative investment environment that prevails, one would expect to see a decline in the level of investment contract rates (i.e., the spread between the contract and comparable-duration Treasury obligations). A decline in rates would in turn increase the spread between traditional contracts and participating contracts. As that spread increases, more plan sponsors would be expected to assume the risks of participation. In short, there will be room for both types of contracts. The traditional nonparticipating contract will not disappear, but its share of the market may decline along with its rates. And the newer participating contracts are likely to become a permanent fixture in the marketplace.

What are the implications for plan sponsors? Every plan sponsor must develop its posture towards risk. An investment policy must go beyond "safety of principal and a competitive yield." That policy does little to define the types of risk that may be assumed and the reward expected for taking on the risk. As with other fiduciary investment funds, the Statement of Investment Policy serves as the blueprint and marching orders for the fund manager. It should be specific enough to define the style of management to be followed for the fund, while allowing the manager sufficient flexibility to function in a reasonable manner.

Buyers must adopt new methods for evaluating and selecting SDP products. Very few products are apples-to-apples, and they generally cannot be compared simply on the basis of rate and credit. The buyer's analysis should proceed along the following lines:

- What type of product is the contract in question? Is the type of product appropriate to the portfolio under management?

- What types of risk does the product pass through to the contractholder? Do the risks affect income or principal or both?

- What forms the basis for the underlying creditworthiness of the product? The credit quality of the issuer? A third-party guarantee? The credit quality of the investments backing the contract?

- Does the contract provide a sufficient level of accountability on the part of the contract issuer? What constraints are placed on the issuer's ability to invest in undesirable credits? Can income and expenses be verified? Is the market value adjustment keyed to the action investments backing the contract or to a set of criteria (such as a new money rate) under the issuer's control?

- Does the product give the issuer a right to extend the contract under certain circumstances or to otherwise select against the contractholder? If so, does the contract yield adequately compensate the contractholder for that risk?

- Has the product historically provided a yield comparable to other investment products (both book value and nonbook value) with similar types and degrees of risk? Can it be expected to do so in the future?

• Are the management fees and expenses charged in connection with the product fair and reasonable in light of the services provided and are they comparable to other investment products of the same general character?

This type of analysis tends to be much more extensive than the level of analysis of a nonparticipating contract, which has typically centered around whether the offer meets all bid specifications and whether the issuer meets the portfolio's credit quality standards.

Given the additional level of analysis required, why would plan sponsors want participating contracts? Those with an aversion to risk will not. Those plan sponsors willing to assume a prudent degree of investment risk will do so in order to enhance the returns received by their participants.

Some industry observers have suggested that the new generation of products will result in the decline of professional stable-value management firms, or consultants, or both. As noted, a modified IPG puts the contract issuer in the position of investment manager, and an entire portfolio could well be invested in one or two contracts. That type of arrangement would probably displace a manager or a consultant used to negotiate placements.

There are substantial roles for active managers and index managers to play. An active manager would be expected to invest in both participating and nonparticipating contracts, depending on investment conditions. Some managers would certainly be expected to outperform modified IPG contracts. In short, modified IPGs will add to the roster of active managers rather than displace current managers.

Index managers are expected to continue as a force in the 1990s. A large number of plan sponsors remain unwilling to accept any investment risk in an employee savings portfolio and will probably adhere to traditional GIC strategies during the coming decade. While some will continue to manage their funds in-house (with or without the assistance of outside parties), others will turn to outside management firms for the reasons discussed above. As the variety of investment choices increases, the market will most likely continue to segment itself. In the case of a stable-value fund, determining where one wants to go means developing a posture toward investment risk. That posture will determine which roads are appropriate for the plan and how to navigate them.

CHAPTER 12

FIDUCIARY CONSIDERATIONS FOR INVESTMENT CONTRACTS

David M. Walker

Partner

Arthur Andersen & Co.

In recent years, there has been a significant increase in the amount of attention and concern regarding the fiduciary aspects of GIC/BIC and other insurance product transactions. This added attention has occurred as concerns have increased regarding the financial condition of the insurance, banking, and other financial services industries. These matters are of particular concern to many fiduciaries, given the significant increase in the dollar amount of investment contract holdings in retirement plans.[1]

The above factors, when combined with a general increase in the incidence of government ERISA enforcement efforts and participant litigation, have resulted in greater amounts of credit/quality visibility and in the level of litigation risk. In addition, proposed government regulations relating to participant-directed individual account plans have raised other fiduciary issues that are of particular concern to the banking and insurance industries and plan fiduciaries, given the popularity of investment contracts as an investment option in 401 (k) plans.

---

[1]As a result, these and related issues (e.g., annuity purchases relating to pension plans) have been the subject of numerous government hearings and press articles.

GENERAL FIDUCIARY STANDARDS

ERISA imposes certain standards of conduct on fiduciaries of employee benefit plans.[2] Under ERISA, a fiduciary is required to discharge his or her duties solely in the interest of the plan participants and beneficiaries and for the exclusive purpose of providing benefits to participants and their beneficiaries, and defraying reasonable expenses of administering the plan. ERISA fiduciaries are also required to discharge their duties (1) with the care, skill, prudence, and diligence under the circumstances then prevailing that a prudent person acting in a like capacity and familiar with such matters would use in the conduct of a similar enterprise of a like character and with like aims; (2) by diversifying the investments of the plan so as to minimize the risk of large losses, unless it is clearly prudent not to do so; and (3) in accordance with the documents and instruments governing the plan insofar as such documents and instruments are consistent with the provisions of ERISA. In addition, plan fiduciaries are also forbidden from engaging in certain "prohibited transactions."

WHO IS A FIDUCIARY?

Under ERISA, a person is considered to be a plan fiduciary to the extent they (1) exercise any discretionary authority or discretionary control with respect either to the management of the plan or the management or disposition of its assets; (2) render any investment advice for a fee or other compensation, direct or indirect, with respect to any monies or other property of the plan, or have any authority or responsibility to do so; or, (3) have

---

[2]This chapter is designed to provide an overview of selected general and current fiduciary issues relating to investment contracts held by employee benefit plans which are subject to the Employee Income Security Act of 1974 (ERISA). It is not intended to represent a full and complete discussion of ERISA's fiduciary standards, in general, or how these standards apply to investment contracts. Due to the importance and complexity of these matters, interested parties should contact appropriate qualified professionals.

any discretionary authority or discretionary responsibility in the administration of the plan. This functionally based test has been applied broadly and based on the individual facts and circumstances of each case by the courts. In addition to the basic functionally based test, ERISA provides that certain positions, including a "named fiduciary" and an "investment manager" always confer fiduciary status. Other positions such as a trustee or plan administrator by their very nature confer fiduciary status since they routinely require the performance of fiduciary duties.

In general, attorneys, accountants, actuaries, and consultants who render legal, accounting, actuarial, or consulting services to an employee benefit plan are not considered to be fiduciaries solely by rendering such services. They can, however, be deemed to be fiduciaries if they assume de facto fiduciary functions or if they meet one of the functional fiduciary tests.

ERISA expressly permits an official of the plan sponsor to serve as a plan fiduciary. A considerable amount of litigation has occurred in regard to the actions of plan sponsors that impact the plan. Particular care needs to be taken when individuals wear "two hats" so as not to violate ERISA's undivided loyalty standard and other fiduciary provisions. At the same time, the courts have recognized the difference between decisions about plan establishment, design, amendment, or termination (so-called "settlor functions") and plan fiduciary decisions, and have generally not found a violation of ERISA to have occurred merely because the sponsor may have obtained an incidental benefit from a plan-related decision.

ERISA provides that fiduciaries are not liable for breaches that occurred before the fiduciary became, or after they ceased being, a fiduciary. Courts have generally held that fiduciary status does not depend on whether or not a party realizes it is a fiduciary. In general, fiduciary status generally ends on resignation or removal of the fiduciary. Some courts have held that a fiduciary who resigns without assuring that the plan is in good hands, or resigns in an attempt to avoid taking appropriate actions to remedy breach involving another fiduciary, continues to be subject to fiduciary liability.

THE PRUDENCE STANDARD

ERISA's prudence standard imposes a high degree of care. Many courts have held ERISA's standards to be higher than those imposed as a matter of general trust law. Many have referred to ERISA's prudence standard as the "prudent expert rule." In applying ERISA's prudence standard, most courts have looked to such factors as who was acting in the plan's interest, what procedures they employed in investigating the proper course of action for the plan at the time the fiduciary decision was made, and whether and to what extent the fiduciary's actions were properly documented to determine if a fiduciary breach has occurred. Prudence is not limited to plan investment matters. It is also relevant in judging a number of other fiduciary actions, including plan administration.

Given ERISA's prudent expert rule, many plan trustees regularly consult with expert advisers. Courts have frequently held that such consultation with expert advisers is evidence of prudent behavior. At the same time, consultation with outside experts is not per se evidence of prudent behavior and the ultimate responsibility to act prudently remains with the responsible fiduciary.

ERISA does not create a legal list of permissible plan investments. In addition, the prudence of a particular plan investment should be viewed in relation to how that investment fits within the plan's overall portfolio. Most ERISA litigation has focused on individual investments and has viewed prudence primarily in procedural terms. Specifically, in *Donovan* v. *Mazzola* the court stated that the test of prudence is "whether the individual trustees, at the time they engaged in the transactions, employed the appropriate methods to investigate the merits of the investment and the structure of the investment."

Just because a plan investment results in a loss does not mean that a fiduciary has breached its fiduciary duty if it can demonstrate that it followed a prudent course of conduct at the time the investment decision was made. Conversely, the fact that a fiduciary makes a prudent decision does not mean that it followed prudent procedures. In addition, a fiduciary can be held liable for a breach of fiduciary duty even though the plan has not suffered a loss (e.g., sub-optimization of investment performance due to an overly conservative investment policy).

DIVERSIFICATION RULE

ERISA requires plan fiduciaries to diversify the plan's investments so as to minimize the possibility of losses unless it is clearly improvident to do so. ERISA's diversification rule does not, however, apply to "eligible individual account plans" (e.g., certain profit-sharing, stock bonus, and employee-stock ownership plans) to the extent they invest in "qualifying employer real property or qualifying employer securities" (e.g., employer stock and marketable obligations that meet certain requirements). In applying ERISA's diversification rule, plan fiduciaries need to be concerned with diversification both between and within asset classes. Courts have ruled that once a plaintiff proves a failure to diversify, the burden shifts to the fiduciary to justify that both the investment and the failure to diversify is justified. This has proven to be a difficult burden for most fiduciaries to meet.

THE PLAN DOCUMENTS AND INSTRUMENTS RULE

ERISA requires plan fiduciaries to administer the plan and to manage the plan assets in accordance with applicable plan documents and instruments unless they are contrary to the purposes of ERISA. This is one of the simplest of ERISA's fiduciary standards to apply. Plan fiduciaries should generally follow the governing plan documents and instruments. They cannot circumvent ERISA's requirements by incorporating contrary provisions in such documents and instruments. Plan documents and instruments have generally been considered to include the plan document, the plan's investment policy statement, investment manager agreements, and other relevant documents.

PROHIBITED TRANSACTIONS

ERISA fiduciaries are forbidden from causing a plan to engage in a number of transactions between the plan and a party in interest because of their high potential for abuse. Parties in interest include but are not limited to (1) plan fiduciaries; (2) plan service providers; (3) employers, any of whose employees are covered under the plan; (4) employee organizations, any of whose members are covered under the plan; (5) certain significant owners of an entity noted in (3) or (4) above; (6) certain relatives of (1) through (3) and (5) above; (7) entities a majority of which are owned by persons described in (1) through (5) above; and (8) employees, officers, directors, and significant owners, partners and joint-venturers of several of the above.

The precluded or so-called "prohibited transactions" include but are not limited to (1) direct or indirect sales, exchanges, or leasing of property; (2) lending of money or other extension of credit between a plan and a party of interest; (3) furnishing of goods, services, or facilities between a plan and a party in interest; and (4) transfer to, or use by or for the benefit of, a party in interest of any assets or income of the plan. Plan fiduciaries are also precluded from (1) dealing with plan assets in their own interest or for their own account; (2) acting in a transaction involving the plan on behalf of a party with interests adverse to the plan; and (3) receiving any consideration for their own personal account from any party dealing with the plan in connection with a transaction involving the assets of the plan.

Engaging in any of the above prohibited transactions is deemed to represent a per se breach of ERISA's fiduciary responsibility provisions, unless the transaction is otherwise covered by a statutory, class, or individual exemption. All nonexempt prohibited transactions are subject to certain excise taxes in addition to the normal remedies and penalties applicable to fiduciary breaches.

LIABILITY FOR BREACH OF FIDUCIARY DUTY

ERISA provides several remedies against breaching fiduciaries, including (1) requiring fiduciaries to make restitution to the plan of any losses resulting from the breach; (2) disgorgement of any profits obtained by the fiduciary through a breach of fiduciary duty; and (3) other equitable and remedial relief, including removal of the fiduciary. Fiduciaries can be held liable for breaches involving both commissions and omissions.

ERISA's fiduciary standards impose personal liability on the breaching plan fiduciaries for any losses resulting to the plan. The liability to make restitution among breaching fiduciaries is joint and several. ERISA provides that a mandatory 20 percent penalty be imposed on fiduciary breach cases involving the Department of Labor. Fiduciaries can also be prosecuted under certain provisions of the U.S. criminal code for certain types of violations (e.g., embezzlement).

ERISA also imposes co-fiduciary liability on any fiduciary that (1) knowingly participates or knowingly attempts to conceal a breach by another fiduciary; (2) fails to comply with their duties under ERISA and thereby enables another fiduciary to commit a breach; or (3) knows that the breach has occurred and fails to take reasonable efforts to remedy it.

ALLOCATING AND LIMITING FIDUCIARY LIABILITY

Under ERISA, the plan document may expressly provide for procedures for allocating fiduciary responsibilities (other than trustee responsibilities) among named fiduciaries, and for named fiduciaries to name persons other than named fiduciaries to carry out fiduciary responsibilities (other than trustee responsibilities) under the plan. If the plan expressly provides for such a procedure, the named fiduciary will not be held liable for an act or omission of the properly appointed person except to the extent that the named fiduciary violated ERISA's fiduciary responsibility provisions with respect to (1) such allocation or designation, (2) establishment or implementation of the related procedure, or (3) continuing the allocation or designation.

Named fiduciaries, or a fiduciary designated by a named fiduciary pursuant to a procedure provided for in the plan may employ one or more persons to render investment advice with regard to any responsibility that a fiduciary has under the plan. If the appointed person meets certain requirements under ERISA, no trustee will be held liable for the acts or omissions of the investment manager and will not be under an obligation to invest or otherwise manage any asset of the plan that is the responsibility of the investment manager. Plan fiduciaries must, however, be mindful of their fiduciary responsibilities regarding the appointment and retention of the investment manager, including the duty to periodically monitor their performance in order to assure compliance with related guidelines in light of stated objectives.

Under Section 404 (c) of ERISA, certain defined contribution plans that provide for individual accounts (e.g., 401 (k) plans) and permit plan participants or beneficiaries to exercise control over all or a portion of the assets in their account (so-called participant-directed individual account plans) may be eligible for certain fiduciary relief if certain requirements are met. Specifically, if the plan meets the requirements of any related regulations promulgated by the Secretary of Labor (1) the participant or beneficiary will not be deemed to be a fiduciary, and (2) no person who is otherwise a fiduciary will be liable for any loss, or by reason of any breach, which results from the participant's or beneficiary's exercise of control.

404 (C) REGULATIONS

In March of 1991, the Department of Labor published a proposed regulation under ERISA Section 404 (c) which is intended to set out what conditions must be met in order for the special provisions under the statute to be effective. The proposed regulation has been the subject of significant comment, including public hearings conducted by the Department of Labor. The special provisions under section 404 (c) will not become operational until after final regulations have been promulgated.

The proposed regulation includes a number of requirements that must be met in order for a plan to be deemed to be a "404 (c) plan." Participants and beneficiaries must be provided with a broad range of investment options from which to choose. They must have the ability to control their account "in fact" for the relief under 404 (c) to apply. Investment options and activities must be conducted on a nondiscriminatory basis and in accordance with a number of specified requirements.

Under the proposed regulations, participants and beneficiaries must be given at least three investment options, excluding employer securities. Each of the investment options must provide participants with an opportunity to achieve a materially different risk and return profile and the options must meet certain combined tests. Participants and beneficiaries must be allowed to allocate their account balances between the three required investment options at least once in every three-month period. Under the proposed regulations, the frequency with which participants and beneficiaries must be able to direct their account balances to or from any additional investment options will depend on the underlying volatility of the related investment option. Participants with small account balances will have to be offered "look-through investment vehicles" (e.g., pooled or mutual funds) in order to allow them to achieve a reasonable amount of diversification within asset classes. Most plan sponsors will have to retain an independent fiduciary to select or approve any look-through investment options (e.g., pooled funds).

The proposed regulations specifically address GIC and related investment products. This is appropriate, given the popularity of investment contracts as an investment choice in participant-directed individual account plans and due to numerous related comments received as a result of prior proposed regulations (which were published in 1987 and withdrawn on publication of the new regulations in March of 1991). In general, under the new proposed regulations, investment contracts will be able to qualify for one of the three required investment options if they otherwise meet the regulations' requirements (e.g., transfer provisions).

Under the new proposed regulations, the plan sponsor is empowered to decide what options will be offered. Importantly, investments that would be deemed to be competing with GICs and could result in adverse selection or disintermediation are not mandated. Plan sponsor decisions in this regard will have important implications on whether and on what basis banks and insurance companies will issue investment contracts to a particular plan.

Under the new regulations, the Department of Labor has reiterated that plans are not required to be "404 (c) plans." The

DOL noted that failure to comply with the 404 (c) regulations does not mean that the plan is in violation of ERISA. At the same time, under the new proposed regulations if the plan sponsor wants to afford itself of the opportunity to limit its related fiduciary liability for participant investment decisions it must comply with all applicable provisions within any related final regulations.

It is important to understand what Section 404 (c) does and does not do. Section 404 (c) is an optional shield against potential fiduciary liability. If a plan is in compliance with the final 404 (c) regulations, plan fiduciaries will not be liable for the asset allocation and individual investment decisions made by plan participants and beneficiaries. Section 404 (c) does not, however, provide any relief from ERISA's fiduciary responsibility provisions in regard to the selection management or monitoring of individual investment options provided to participants when their choices have been limited (e.g., decision to include a GIC pooled fund option, decisions regarding which contracts should be purchased and retained in the portfolio).

Given the above limitation and the numerous conditions and other limitations contained in the new proposed regulations it is clear that Section 404 (c) is no panacea. As a result, whether or not plan sponsors will decide to adopt it will depend on the individual facts and circumstances of each case. Sponsors are likely to comply with the 404 (c) regulations if doing so involves modest costs and does not conflict with its overall employee benefits philosophy.

Many plan sponsors will want to limit their potential fiduciary liability due to the increasingly litigious society. At the same time, complying with section 404 (c) does not limit a fiduciary's liability in connection with certain actions (e.g., which investment contracts are offered to plan participants and beneficiaries).

ADMINISTRATION AND ENFORCEMENT

The Department of Labor is charged with the responsibility of interpreting and enforcing the fiduciary provisions of ERISA. The DOL has a number of remedies available to remedy fiduciary breaches and achieve other equitable relief. ERISA also provides extensive private rights of action to plan participants, beneficiaries, and fiduciaries through the federal district courts. It allows the federal courts to award reasonable attorney fees and other costs of action to either party. ERISA provides for a six-year statute of limitations for most actions with a three-year statute of limitations applicable to situations where the plaintiff had actual knowledge of the breach or violation.

SELECTED APPLICATIONS OF ERISA'S FIDUCIARY STANDARDS TO INVESTMENT CONTRACT TRANSACTIONS

The decision to purchase or to offer one or more preselected investment contracts as an investment option under an ERISA plan must be made in accordance with ERISA's fiduciary responsibility and prohibited transaction rules. Most aspects of plan administration relating to investment contracts are subject to ERISA's fiduciary responsibility and prohibited transaction provisions and certain requirements under the Internal Revenue Code.

Whether or not a fiduciary violation has occurred in connection with a transaction is based on an analysis of the individual facts and circumstances involved in light of applicable plan documents and instruments and ERISA's fiduciary standards and prohibited transaction requirements. It is important for plan fiduciaries to fully document their related actions. Failure to adequately document important fiduciary actions can make the difference between winning and losing in fiduciary litigation cases.

ERISA's prudence requirement is largely a procedurally based standard and involves consideration of such factors as the players involved, the process employed and the related documentation at the time the investment decision is made. Investment decisions involve a normal risk versus return analysis and the required risk analyses must give appropriate consideration to the creditworthiness of the contract provider, both currently and during the contract's term. In this regard, fiduciaries should consider the ratings attributable to the provider by each of the major rating agencies. In addition to considering the ratings, fiduciaries should conduct where possible appropriate supplemental research and analysis. Such supplemental research and analysis could include such actions as review and analysis of the most recent regulatory filings, recent analyses by investment analysts, and recent press articles.

Supplemental factors for consideration by fiduciaries for insurance companies could include the size of the insurer, current key financial ratios and recent trends, and the nature of the insurer's general account investments (e.g., the relative diversification and liquidity of the insurer's investment portfolio, including the amount of exposure to certain illiquid investments such as "junk bonds" and certain types of real estate and their relative significance as compared to statutory reserve requirements). In addition, it could include current statutory reserve positions and recent trends, current state-imposed investment restrictions on the issuer, whether the contracts are backed by one or more state insurance funds, the status of any applicable state insurance funds and recent trends, any related reinsurance, co-insurance, or participation arrangements by the issuer, and whether and why the provider may have changed independent auditors. For banks, considerations could include the size and strength of the issuing entity, the asset/liability structure, and whether FDIC coverage is afforded.

Fiduciaries must be careful to comply with ERISA's diversification requirements when making plan investments. ERISA generally requires consideration of diversification both between and within asset classes. As a result, investing a significant amount of a plan's assets in investment contracts issued by a single provider can expose the fiduciary to additional risk of litigation. At the same time, ERISA generally allows the fiduciary to consider the underlying assets of the insurance company's general account in meeting ERISA's diversification requirements (e.g., such a provision is included in the new proposed 404 (c) regulations). As a result, plan fiduciaries should give appropriate consideration to analyzing the nature of the provider's underlying assets in assessing the relative risk of the investment.

Diversification among investment contract providers is advisable if a significant percentage of a plan's assets will be invested in such contracts. Offering a portfolio comprised of contracts issued by a number of providers would be required under the new proposed 404 (c) regulations in the case of participants with small account balances in participant-directed individual account plans. Fiduciaries should take extra precautions in avoiding prohibited transactions, since engaging in such transactions represents a per se breach of fiduciary duty and can result in significant damages, excise taxes, and other penalties. Prohibited transactions can occur in the initial investment and in attempting to address any problem investments.[3]

Plan administrators and other fiduciaries must be careful not to violate ERISA's fiduciary requirements and the Internal Revenue Code's discrimination and plan qualification requirements when administering investment contracts. Fiduciaries should take appropriate actions on a timely basis to address any problem contracts in a manner that does not discriminate among participant groups. Care must also be taken not to violate the minimum distribution requirements of the Internal Revenue Code and the benefit distribution provisions of the plan.

COMMUNICATIONS

Plan officials should also be careful as to how they represent GIC investment options to plan participants and what information they provide to participants in participant-directed individual account plans. Consideration should be given to not referring to such contracts as "guaranteed" but rather to refer to them as "fixed-rate contracts" or "stable-value" funds. In addition, participants should be provided information regarding the credit ratings of contract providers for contracts held in participant-directed individual account plans.

---

[3]For example, with the insolvency of several GIC issuers in 1991, a number of plan sponsors voluntarily decided to purchase GICs issued by insolvent providers from their retirement plan at contract value, or to provide interest-free loans to the plan to meet any related distribution requirements and liquidity needs. While it is clear that such actions are designed to benefit the plan, entering into such a transaction without an individual exemption from the DOL would represent a prohibited transaction.

DEFINED BENEFIT VERSUS DEFINED CONTRIBUTION PLAN TRANSACTIONS

While ERISA's basic fiduciary standards apply uniformly to both defined benefit and defined contribution plans, there are differences between the nature and potential for related litigation involving investment contract transactions. In the case of defined benefit plans, participants are promised a stated benefit and the plan sponsor has the obligation to make the contributions necessary to meet the promised benefits. Benefits under most defined benefit plans are guaranteed by the Pension Benefit Guaranty Corporation, subject to stated limits. As a result, in defined benefit plans, plan sponsors, and in certain cases the PBGC, bear the risk of related investment performance.

In defined contribution plans, plan participants and beneficiaries will only receive the balance in their individual account. Individuals' accounts are calculated as the sum of applicable employer contributions, forfeitures, and investment experience less any related administrative expenses assumed by the plan. Benefits under defined contribution plans are not insured by the PBGC. As a result, plan participants and beneficiaries bear the risk of related investment performance in defined contribution plans. Many defined contribution plans allow participants to decide how all or a portion of their account balance will be invested (so-called "participant-directed individual account plans"). Participants and beneficiaries are typically given a choice between various investment vehicles. GICs have historically been one of the most frequent and popular options offered to participants and beneficiaries under these plans. Given the above, the relative risks of fiduciary litigation is greater in defined contribution plans as opposed to defined benefit plans, especially with regard to participant-initiated lawsuits.

SELECTED QUESTIONS

Given the fiduciary responsibilities and related considerations outlined above, the following items represent relevant questions that plan trustees and other fiduciaries should ask themselves regarding any GIC/BIC investments held by ERISA plans:

1. Does the plan sponsor have a written investment policy statement? Does this statement consider all of ERISA's fiduciary requirements and the needs of the plan; for example, diversification, liquidity, current and expected return? Is it being complied with?

2. Does the plan sponsor employ professional investment managers? If so, what process was followed and what criteria were considered regarding the selection of these managers? What documentation exists regarding the basis for their selection?

3. Are all investment managers considered to be "eligible" under ERISA? Have they acknowledged their appointment and acceptance of the related fiduciary responsibility (ERISA Sec. 3(38))? Are they in compliance with ERISA's bonding requirements?

4. Does the plan sponsor have an investment agreement with each investment manager? Does the agreement contain specific investment guidelines for the manager?

5. Are investment managers monitored periodically in order to assure compliance with the investment agreement and investment guidelines? Who performs this monitoring and how is it documented? How frequently and on what basis are investment managers evaluated?

6. Has the plan employed other investment advisers? If so, what process was followed with regard to their selection and how well is it documented? Are these advisers independent of the plan sponsor?

7. How are these investment advisers evaluated? How well are these evaluations documented?

8. Does the adviser render any related advice on a regular basis pursuant to a written agreement, arrangement, or understanding, that such services will serve as a primary basis for investment decisions and that such person will render individualized investment advice to the plan? Does the plan rely on the advice of the investment adviser in making investment decisions?

9. What factors are/were considered in the selection of individual investments; for example, credit risk, diversification, rates of return, benefit responsiveness, term? How well are these considerations documented?

10. Has proper consideration been given to diversification within, as well as between, asset classes?

11. Who was involved, what process was followed, and what factors were considered in evaluating the creditworthiness of any related providers; for example, ratings of several generally recognized rating agencies, size of the issuer, applicable state reserve requirements, applicable state investment restrictions, whether and to what extent the contracts are backed by state insurance funds and/or FDIC, diversification of the provider's assets, including percentage of investments in noninvestment grade and/or illiquid investments such as junk bonds and certain real estate investments? Has the evaluation of the provider's creditworthiness been documented?

12. What, if any, considerations are given to including credit-related provisions in investment contracts; for example, exit clauses due to a decline in the issuer's credit rating?

13. What process is followed and what factors and information are considered in monitoring the creditworthiness of any issuer during its term? Is this monitoring properly documented?

14. Where there any formal or informal agreements in connection with investments that could involve violations of the prohibited transaction provisions or exclusive benefit requirements of ERISA; for example, purchase of investment contracts from one provider in exchange for the provider purchasing certain employer securities or providing financing to the employer or a party-in-interest?

15. Are investments structured and administered in a manner that does not discriminate between participants; for example, blended rate of returns?

16. Are portfolios structured and negotiated in a manner that properly considers and balances the cash flow needs of the plan and rate of return considerations; for example, cash reserves, benefit responsiveness, order of liquidation of contracts?

17. Are participant-directed individual account plans structured in accordance with the applicable regulatory guidance (i.e., 404 (c) regulations)?

18. What information is provided to plan participants regarding the composition of investments, including the creditworthiness of any related providers?

19. How does the plan handle questionable investments; for example, communications, adjustment of related values, effect on distributions and rates of return, minimum distribution requirements? Do the related procedures provide reasonable and timely disclosures to participants and adequate protections regarding the effects between participants (e.g., amounts realized by different participants holding an interest in the same contract)?

20. Are all actions relating to questionable investments consistent with ERISA's fiduciary responsibility and prohibited transaction provisions; for example, prohibited transaction exemptions are necessary for any purchases, sales, or loans between a plan and a party-in-interest irrespective of the merits of the related transaction from the plan's perspective?

CONCLUSIONS

Fiduciary and other related issues regarding investment contracts are matters of growing concern and visibility. Plan fiduciaries must be mindful of their related responsibilities and should take particular care to document any related fiduciary activities and decisions. They should also give appropriate consideration as to whether or not to seek the additional protection afforded by ERISA Section 404 (c) and be careful as to how they characterize these investments to plan participants.

Fiduciaries may wish to seek advice and assistance of qualified professionals with regard to discharging their related fiduciary settlor responsibilities, including related procedural and documentation reviews, creditworthiness reviews, problem contract-related activities and 404 (c)-related considerations. Doing so can serve to reduce the risk of any related exposure to fiduciary suits, while at the same time, increasing real risk-adjusted rates of return and minimizing any related adverse employee relations.

Author's Note

ANNUITY PURCHASES

While a considerable amount of attention has recently been placed on annuity contracts purchased by employee benefit plans, this issue is beyond the scope of this chapter. While the same basic fiduciary principles apply to both GIC and annuity contract investment matters, there are some important differences regarding how these principles are applied. For example, due to the nature and duration of an investment decision regarding an annuity purchase, the Department of Labor (DOL) has stated that plan fiduciaries should place quality and security considerations relating to annuity purchases above all other considerations. Stated differently, the DOL has stated that an annuity purchase decision does not involve a normal risk versus return analysis and that additional credit risk may not be assumed in an effort to obtain such annuities at a lower cost. According to Assistant Secretary of Labor David George Ball, "plan sponsors (fiduciaries) must buy the safest possible annuities . . . from the safest available annuity provider." According to DOL, any actions not in accord with this principle would represent a violation of ERISA's fiduciary responsibility provisions, including the "exclusive purpose" and "solely in interest" requirements.

In 1991, the Department of Labor filed suits against two U.S. corporations alleging multiple fiduciary breaches in their purchase of annuity contracts from an issuer that subsequently became insolvent. The DOL also has a special related enforcement program under way that should result in additional litigation. Both the Department of Labor and the Pension Benefit Guaranty Corporation have announced their intention to propose additional regulations concerning annuity purchases by employee benefit plans. Additional enforcement and regulatory and legislative actions are expected. The final fiduciary standards applicable to these transactions, especially transactions which occurred prior to the DOL's announcements regarding the appreciation of ERISA's fiduciary standards to annuity purchase decisions, will be determined in part through the result of current and prospective litigation.

CHAPTER 13

PERFORMANCE MEASUREMENT OF STABLE-VALUE PORTFOLIOS

Michael L. Hoover
Vice President and Principal
T. Rowe Price Stable Asset Management, Inc.
James C. Templeman II
Assistant Vice President
T. Rowe Price Stable Asset Management, Inc.

As stable-value portfolios have become more actively managed, the desire to quantify the effectiveness of the investment activities has increased. Plan sponsors who manage their portfolios in-house need to evaluate performance for two reasons. First, they want to determine the effectiveness of their individual efforts. Second, they want to be able to justify or refute the added value of external management. Consultants who aid in the selection of external managers seek performance measurement as a way of quantitatively differentiating managers in a competitive search. Investment managers desire a means to compare results between individual portfolio managers, to assess the firm's techniques versus the strategies of other advisers, and to demonstrate superior investment results to clients.

No single performance measurement technique or index has been adopted by the investment and consulting communities as the standard against which all managers, internal or external, can be measured. The primary reason for the lack of an accepted methodology results from the uniqueness of the portfolio management techniques and the decision-making process.

Investment contracts can, if properly negotiated, be carried at cost plus accrued interest. They are not subject to fluctuations in value as a result of changes in market interest rates. Most importantly, these instruments are not marketable. While an equity manager can convert the entire stock position to cash in a matter of minutes, a stable-value manager, by contrast, can change the composition of his portfolio only when an existing asset matures or new flows of investable cash are added to the portfolio (or in certain situations where the contract is terminated prior to its negotiated maturity). As such, stable-value portfolios have very predictable return patterns as a result of "book value accounting" and "buy and hold" investing. The composition of the portfolio does not change rapidly, but rather, evolves over time.

Investment contracts are analogous to private placements. Several key contract features that will influence the portfolio's return must be determined and negotiated for each and every contract. The length of time during which deposits can be made to the contract is one of several key attributes that the purchaser must define when negotiating a contract. The contract may, for example, take a lump-sum deposit for a specific amount to be deposited immediately. On the other hand, the purchaser may arbitrage an expected decline in market rates by negotiating a "window" contract in which funds may be deposited over an extended period of time at today's interest rate levels.

Investment contracts also have repayment features that are tailor-made to the purchaser's requirements. Some contracts have fixed maturity dates with one lump-sum repayment. Others have a series of payouts, occurring on specific dates over several years. Other contracts have "put" features that permit the purchaser to receive the full value of the contract after a relatively short specified notice period. Some of the newer generation of participating contracts have perpetual maturity arrangements where the funds are returned under a predetermined repayment stream after meeting certain minimum requirements.

The purchaser of an investment contract can also negotiate the contract's interest rate sensitivity and interest repayment methodologies in order to satisfy an interest rate outlook or liquidity strategy. The most common type is the fixed-rate, fixed-maturity contract. Interest earnings accrue at a specific rate for the entire term of the contract, and may be paid periodically or at maturity. Earnings paid at maturity permit the contract to reinvest earnings at the contract rate, eliminating reinvestment risk of earnings during the contractual term. Periodic "coupon" payments allow the purchaser to reinvest these flows at prevailing market rates. These fixed-rate, fixed-maturity contracts are effective in capturing high yields in expectation of falling rates. Floating-rate contracts earn interest based on a formula indexed to market yields. The contract's rate changes periodically, usually once a month or once a quarter. Floaters are an excellent means for participating in a rising rate environment. Participating contracts earn interest based on the performance of the underlying investment portfolio. Participating contracts usually offer above spot market rates yet lag market rates as they change.

The final contract decision involves the timing of the placement of funds. The purchaser can negotiate a deposit to be made at a later date but at today's interest rates. This "forward commitment" is a useful way to avoid forecasted market declines or to reduce the reinvestment risk of a large, upcoming maturity. Of course, the vast majority of investment contracts are for the immediate delivery of funds at current rates.

While the purchaser must negotiate the variety of investment characteristics noted above, the measure of a manager's success can only be measured by the portfolio's return over time. Each component of the contract's design ultimately influences the portfolio's return and return sensitivity. These aspects, return and return sensitivity, are the two characteristics that must be compared to a market benchmark in order to evaluate the effectiveness of the manager's activities. Return has historically been the predominant measure of a stable-value manager's ability. However, return sensitivity is also extremely important as it measures how well the portfolio responds to interest rate changes.

A variety of performance measurement methodologies are employed by the groups who evaluate portfolio returns. Each technique has its benefits, drawbacks, and prejudices. In addition, each technique utilizes some definition of the "market" against which all comparisons are made. The ability of each "market" to accurately reflect portfolio behavior solely determines the effectiveness of the technique. Well-constructed market definitions are useful as an objective benchmark, while poorly developed ones create false return images.

MOVING AVERAGE

The most commonly utilized performance measurement technique defines the market in terms of a moving average yield. According to this technique, the market is accurately defined by two elements, the date the portfolio was initiated and the length of the portfolio's investment horizon. The moving average comparison typically assumes that cash flows occur monthly and on a constant dollar basis (e.g., $1 million per month). Some variations of the moving average assume that year over year monthly cash flows grow at a reasonable annual rate.

Portfolio inception has a significant impact on portfolio returns. For example, a portfolio that started investing in 1984 had the ability to initially purchase contracts with rates exceeding 15.0 percent. A portfolio initiated in 1987 began by only choosing contracts in the 8.0 percent range. A performance comparison of each portfolio undertaken on December 31, 1990, would show vastly different blended yields, as shown in Exhibit 13–1. Thus, portfolio inception is a legitimate variable to define when constructing a passive index under this concept.

The second variable that defines the moving average market is the length of the investment horizon. Most stable-value portfolios invest over a predetermined time horizon, usually three, five, or seven years. This choice is discretionary and is usually based on the manager's or the plan sponsor's investment predisposition. Since the moving average method creates individual market benchmarks based on investment horizon, a three-year portfolio is compared against a three-year market, for example. The technique does not attempt to compare a three-year strategy to a seven-year market.

In order to effectively compare the many potential portfolios, the moving average concept typically reports a matrix as

EXHIBIT 13–1
Yields on Two Portfolios with Different Start Dates

	Blended Yield at 12/31/90
Portfolio 1 1/1/84 Inception date	10.31%
Portfolio 2 1/1/87 Inception date	9.42%

These two portfolios are invested in a manner consistent with the market defini-tion. Recurring monthly cash flow was at a fixed dollar amount over the investment horizon. In addition, the portfolios pursued a strategy of, in this case, buying seven-year contracts.

shown in Exhibit 13–2 with various portfolio inception dates and several investment horizons. The inception dates are usu-ally January 1 or July 1 for each of several years. Investment horizons, as previously mentioned, are three, five, or seven years. The moving average concept assumes a contract invest-ment of the designated horizon at inception. The market inter-est rate is usually defined as the average of several, if not all, market quotes for the selected maturity from issuers meeting a particular quality or size criteria. For simplicity, the concept typically assumes all earned interest is reinvested in the con-tract and is paid at maturity. Each succeeding month, an equal

EXHIBIT 13–2
Moving Average Matrix Blended Yield at December 31, 1990

Portfolio Inception	Investment Horizon		
	3 Years	5 Years	7 Years
1/1/88	8.96%	9.25%	9.39%
7/1/88	9.02%	9.26%	9.37%
1/1/89	9.02%	9.25%	9.35%
7/1/89	8.86%	9.12%	9.24%
1/1/90	8.95%	9.23%	9.40%
7/1/90	8.75%	9.08%	9.35%

dollar amount is used to purchase an additional contract with a term equal to the horizon at then current interest rates.

This technique produces, in a general sense, a moving average of monthly rates for the investment horizon chosen. Under some moving average variations, the return is not a pure simple average because interest is reinvested in the contract. As such, the older contracts have a greater proportionate impact on the blended yield since their balance is larger as a result of the accumulated interest. Other variations of the moving average disregard accrued interest. These latter versions produce a simple moving average of the previous 36, 60, or 84 interest rates for the three-, five-, or seven-year horizon, respectively.

The moving average concept is based on a baseline strategy. It assumes the market is totally passive, always purchasing the same type of contract with the same term. The concept, in most applications, is intended to provide a passive benchmark against which active management can be compared. However, active management involves alteration of the portfolio's average maturity to proactively position the portfolio for future interest rate movements. To the extent a portfolio is evaluated against a four-year moving average on one date and then against a five-year moving average one year later, the comparison is not as valid, since both indices evolved over time and not as a result of strategy changes made during the preceding 12 months.

Many of the moving average techniques utilize an average of quotes to determine the "market rate." Since the GIC market is characterized by a significant amount of pricing inefficiency, a wide spread exists between the highest and lowest quotes for any given maturity. The average, thus, is usually 25 to 75 basis points below the best quote on any given day for a particular maturity. The end result is that, since most purchasers buy at the top end of the market, the "market" builds in favorable performance. This built-in advantage, however, can be eliminated if the "market rate" is constructed from the top rate or the average of the top 5 or 10 rates.

The most troublesome aspect of the moving average concept involves the assumption of regular and consistent levels of new cash flow. Now that stable-value portfolios have been around for some time, it can be demonstrated that cash flows are neither regular nor consistent. Cash flows generally increase during times of economic expansion and contract as the economy slows. Also, cash flows are influenced by the level of interest rates and the competitiveness/riskiness of other investment options. For example, participants sought the safety of the GIC options after the shocks against equity-based funds in 1987 and 1989. In practice, a market benchmark that assumes a regular flow of investable contributions may not accurately reflect portfolio behavior or returns.

In summary, the moving average concept is a useful tool in establishing a baseline portfolio benchmark against which yields can be compared. The comparison is most valid for evaluating active versus passive strategies, and in demonstrating value added by an active approach. The measurement of performance under the concept, however, can be distorted by inconsistencies between market and portfolio cash flows. To the extent the actual portfolio does not have cash flow to invest during a period of high interest rates, it would be unfairly penalized. In addition, portfolios that result from large, lump-sum initial funding with little ensuing cash flow cannot be accurately compared against an index based on incremental funding over a period of years.

CUSTOMIZED COMPOSITE

The customized composite technique isolates the individual portfolio cash flows not captured under the moving average concept. However, many of the other rationales that support the moving average concept are present in the customized composite technique.

The composite technique calculates the return of the portfolio, using the returns attributable to only the investments made by the manager under evaluation. Return on assets purchased by parties other than the manager are ignored. This exclusion of assets is based on the premise that the manager had no responsibility for the assets and, thus, should not be included in the performance review.

The portfolio's return is compared against a customized "market" where the asset pool is a mirror image of the actual portfolio in terms of the size, maturity, placement timing, and features of each investment. The only difference between the actual portfolio and the market portfolio, the "composite," is the interest rate assigned to each contract. The composite portfolio and actual portfolio returns are calculated in exactly the same manner and are expressed in terms of yield or period return. Exhibit 13–3 illustrates the performance comparisons made under the composite technique.

Two central elements in the investment process are eliminated by the composite method: timing of placement and alternative investment choices. Timing is not taken into account because the composite is based on the occurrence of actual portfolio investments, ignoring market yields on the date the cash was actually made available. For example, the composite may compare yields on a five-year contract investment actually placed on June 3, 1991. It, however, will ignore the fact that the invested monies came from a contract maturity on April 22, 1991. If market rates had risen, the manager would not get credit for postponing the decision until yields were more advantageous. Conversely, the manager would not be penalized for

EXHIBIT 13–3
Actual Portfolio versus Composite Portfolio

	Purchase Date	Value at 12/31/90	Contract Rate	Maturity Date	Market Rate
Issuer 1	3/23/88	$5,871,009	8.88%	1/27/93	8.35%
Issuer 2	9/01/88	4,563,905	9.45%	9/01/91	8.76%
Issuer 3	9/04/87	6,712,134	9.69%	3/10/92	9.10%
Issuer 4	2/28/90	3,887,790	9.30%	2/28/94	9.12%
Issuer 5	12/27/87	5,561,802	9.45%	8/22/92	8.79%
Issuer 6	11/11/88	4,099,012	9.15%	9/17/93	8.95%
Issuer 7	1/15/90	3,163,543	9.07%	8/24/94	8.83%
Issuer 8	6/20/90	3,740,917	9.30%	3/23/95	9.07%
Weighted Yield of Portfolio					9.31%
Weighted Yield of Composite					8.86%

holding cash if market interest rates had dropped. The composite primarily measures how well the manager did versus an identical investment made on the exact same date.

The composite portfolio also does not assess the performance impact of selecting another maturity structure or contract type. It does not, for example, evaluate whether a fixed rate would have been more opportune as rates declined, or floaters more advantageous as rates rose. The composite implies that the investment selected was the best one suited for the portfolio's circumstance.

In summary, the composite is best suited for assessing "purchasing efficiency." Stated another way, it measures how good a job the manager did in obtaining the best rate available in the marketplace. Arguably, the composite has a built-in advantage for the manager since it compares results versus a market average, not the best rate in the market. Results between managers can be compared since the spread between the actual portfolio and the composite is an absolute measure. If the composites of two managers have a reasonably comparable investment profile, a direct comparison can be made regarding the negotiating skills of one versus the other. Even if the investment profiles are dissimilar, a comparison can be made over time as to the relative magnitude of the spreads. Comparisons in the latter environment are far more subjective than if direct statistical similarities exist. Of course, comparisons can only be made when the market average yields are being determined from an identical universe of issuers.

TOTAL RETURN

Stable-value portfolio returns can be evaluated using a total-return basis comparable to that used for other types of investments. The technique is structured so that it evaluates all of the aforementioned decisions that a portfolio manager makes during the investment process. Another key portfolio characteristic measured is the portfolio's relative earnings trend versus market interest rates, or the "lag effect."

A stable-value portfolio manager is charged with delivering a competitive return throughout all phases of the interest rate cycle. Since the portfolio cannot be traded, a manager can influence a portfolio's underlying return pattern only through the judicious selection of various contract types that will achieve the desired impact on the portfolio's return pattern. In basic terms, the goal is to increase interest rate sensitivity in anticipation of rising interest rates and decrease it for an impending decline in interest rates.

Stable-value portfolio returns will always lag those of the market as shown in Exhibit 13–4. Lag is measured by comparing the rate of change of the portfolio's return versus the rate of change of the market's return. Exhibit 13–5 shows a period to period comparison of the absolute change in terms of basis

EXHIBIT 13–4
Comparison of Return Patterns (Market versus Actual Portfolio)

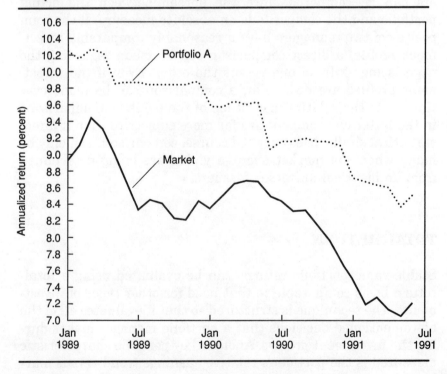

EXHIBIT 13–5
Measuring the Lag Effect

	Portfolio Returns	Market Returns
7/89 through 6/90	8.75%	8.46%
7/90 through 6/91	8.52%	7.71%
Absolute change	−0.23%	−0.75%
Relative change	−2.63%	−8.87%

points as well as the relative change in terms of a percentage of the initial return.

Since a stable-value portfolio's return changes slowly over time, the total-return method will produce the best comparisons over longer periods of time, ideally a minimum of five years. This five-year horizon allows sufficient time for the manager to imprint his style and strategies on the portfolio, and ensures 75 to 100 percent of the portfolio's assets were purchased by the manager. This period most likely will encompass an entire interest rate cycle, allowing the portfolio's absolute returns and lag to be assessed during both rising and falling markets.

Other performance measurement techniques focus on only those investments purchased by the manager. This segregation is based on the premise that the manager should only be evaluated in regard to those assets actually placed. However, the goal of a portfolio manager is to manage the return pattern and lag effect of the entire portfolio. To do so effectively, the maturity structure, cash flow, and estimated return pattern of the existing portfolio must be taken into account. While a manager usually does not have sufficient latitude to change previous investments, these investments must be taken into account when designing and implementing a strategy.

To illustrate this point, consider a portfolio where the new portfolio manager intends to implement a laddered maturity structure over a five-year horizon and the portfolio lacks contract maturities in the two- and three-year maturity range. To accomplish this strategy, the portfolio manager is forced to buy investments with maturities in this range, even though they may yield significantly less than longer-maturity contracts. These actions would produce lower returns in the short term but should produce positive long-term results by diversifying reinvestment risk. A performance calculation such as total return that includes all assets allows the assessment of long-term strategies.

Total return is also important in assessing a portfolio manager's short-term strategy. When a maturity is soon to occur or cash flow has accumulated, the portfolio manager evaluates market conditions and decides either to make a forward commitment, to place the funds on date of availability, or to hold funds in short-term instruments for placement at a later date. Each of these strategies has a different impact on the portfolio's return and this is captured by including contracts and short-term vehicles in the total-return calculation.

The total-return methodology utilizes a market benchmark that encompasses the entire range of investments available to a manager and eliminates the subjectivities associated with investment contracts. Since most stable-value portfolios select investments ranging from cash to long-maturity contracts, the market under the total-return method uses the yield on 91-day U.S. Treasury bills to define cash and the yield of the highest quoted five-year investment contract to describe long maturity contracts. The five-year contract is the highest yielding contract available without regard to issuer quality or contract features. This objectivity eliminates the biases created by credit rating methodologies and portfolio underwriting constraints. This basis also eliminates pricing variances among issuers, enabling different portfolios to be compared on a consistent basis.

The market composite is constructed by determining the weekly total return of each of the two investments and averaging them to create a market proxy with an average maturity of 2.6 years, similar to most stable-value portfolios. The 91-day U.S. Treasury bill and the five-year contract encompass two different points on the yield curve, allowing the market proxy to respond to changes in the shape of the yield curve.

The evaluation of portfolio performance begins by calculating the total return for the portfolio and for the market for two equal consecutive periods. Each period must equal, at a minimum, 12 months. For purposes of discussion, the two periods are referred to as the "most recent" period and the "previous" period. An actual analysis would, for example, use the period July 1990 through June 1991 as the most recent, and July 1989 through June 1990 as the previous.

Two key comparisons, one absolute and one relative, are made using the total returns for the two periods. The absolute measure compares the portfolio's total return to the market's total return for the most recent period. Referring to Exhibit 13–5, this comparison would evaluate 8.52 percent versus 7.71 percent.

The relative comparison measures the rate of change in market and portfolio returns over the two consecutive periods. The same calculation is performed for both returns by dividing the most recent period return by the previous period return. This determines the relative direction and magnitude of return changes over time. The resultant data allows an assessment of whether the strategies employed by a manager enabled a portfolio to respond positively to changes in market rates, or if they negatively impacted a portfolio.

In a rising rate environment, it is doubtful the portfolio's return will keep pace with the market. However, the faster the portfolio's return rate of change, the more effective the strategy. To illustrate, assume the market's relative return increased 1.0 percent on a period over period basis. Therefore, a portfolio return that increased 0.9 percent did better than one which increased by 0.7 percent.

Falling market interest rates create a natural lag effect. Since the market makes it easy, a manager must be evaluated on how much slower the portfolio's return declined versus the market's. A portfolio decline of −.1 percent is much better than a −.5 percent decline. In both rising and falling rate environments, a more favorable rate of change is characterized by a larger number.

The results generated by the total-return methodology are most easily reported within the context of an XY quadrant graph. The X axis displays the results produced by the relative, or lag effect, calculation. The Y axis shows the absolute return for the most recent period. In both instances, market results are shown as the midpoint of the axes with the individual portfolio results plotted accordingly. The resulting graph produces quadrants familiar to most investment management portfolios. As expected, the portfolios producing the best relative and absolute returns would be found in the upper left, or northwest, quadrant. Exhibit 13–6 illustrates sample individual account and market results. The table following the graph details the actual plot points and the respective calculations.

EXHIBIT 13–6

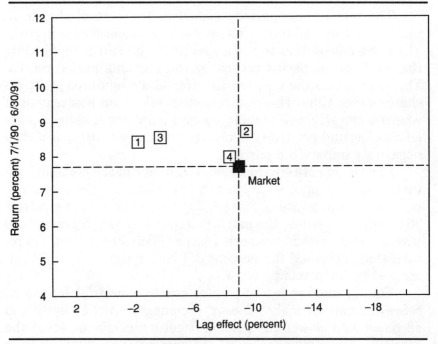

	Most Recent Return (1)	Previous Return	Lag Effect (2)
Market	7.71%	8.46%	−8.87%
Account 1	8.42%	8.61%	−2.21%
Account 2	8.74%	9.63%	−9.24%
Account 3	8.59%	8.91%	−3.59%
Account 4	7.83%	8.56%	−8.53%

The total-return method is a comprehensive performance measurement tool for stable-value portfolios that encompasses both absolute and relative returns and evaluates the effectiveness of investment strategies implemented. Furthermore, the total-return method utilizes an unbiased definition of the market that closely resembles the returns plan participants analyze in making their investment choices. Lastly, given an adequate observation period, the total-return method may be used to evaluate any portfolio without bias to cash flow patterns, inception date, underwriting requirements, or investment strategy.

SUMMARY

The development of performance measurement for stable-value portfolios will continue to progress as do the techniques for managing the portfolios themselves. Each of the methods discussed produces a meaningful result within the framework utilized. Only the performance measurement methods that treat these portfolios as investment portfolios give creditability to the underlying investment techniques and strategies.

CHAPTER 14

THE NONQUALIFIED
MARKETPLACE

David L. Renz, FSA, CFA
Vice President and Director of Alternative Markets
Prudential Asset Management Company

Prior to this chapter, all references to investment contracts have been in context to contracts issued to tax qualified 401(a) retirement plans. Nonqualified investment contracts are issued to the nonpension market. Such contracts are also known as *funding agreements* or *investment agreements*.

The first, and still the most important, purchasers of funding agreements were municipal issuers of tax-exempt bonds. In the early 1980s the spread between the yields on tax-exempt bonds and GICs grew quite large. Tax-exempt issuers discovered they could arbitrage these yield differentials by issuing bonds and investing the proceeds at higher rates until the funds were needed. Since the entities were themselves tax-exempt, the otherwise taxable nature of interest payments was irrelevant. The large number of municipalities involved in this market led to the name of *Muni-GICs*.

This funding source became feasible only after insurance companies sought and obtained ratings on their "claims-paying ability" from the major rating services. Once begun, billions of dollars in nonqualified GICs were issued. The arbitrage earned by municipalities reduced collections by the IRS, leading to federal legislation in 1986 that severely limited the ability to earn and retain arbitrage proceeds from the issuance of tax-exempt bonds. Today, funding agreements are still in common use but for different reasons.

RATIONALE FOR FUNDING AGREEMENTS

Nonqualified investment contracts have several features that make them a viable investment alternative:

Yields are usually attractive, often providing returns higher than U.S. Treasury instruments of similar maturity. Providers typically invest in a diversified portfolio of private placements, mortgages, asset-backed securities, etc. The portfolio is actively managed to produce a positive spread to U.S. Treasuries on a net basis.

Liquidity and the assumption of the "interest rate risk" by the issuer can be a major advantage. Funding agreements normally allow for withdrawal at par or book value for specified reasons, but are nonassignable to allow a secondary transaction. In contrast, a portfolio of fixed-income instruments is marketable but could produce a loss if sold to provide liquidity.

Safety is a major concern of contractholders. The rating agencies and municipal bond insurers usually require the GIC provider to be rated at least as high as the bond issue. Currently the marketplace typically requires that funding agreement providers be limited to those entities with the highest investment grades. As with qualified investment contracts, the provider assumes all investment risk and pays all transaction costs.

PURCHASERS

1. *Municipalities and other issuers of tax-exempt bonds* are the most frequent users of funding agreements. Generally the bond indenture trustee deposits the proceeds of the issue with the funding agreement provider. Funding agreements can be

an alternative to other fixed-income instruments in a number
of ways:

Acquisition funds are used as a depository while loans are
being issued or otherwise acquired. Examples would include student loans acquired by state-sponsored educa-
tional associations or subsidized mortgage loans made
under the auspices of state housing authorities. Under current regulations, if the loans are originated within 18
months, the authority is not restricted in the yield it may
earn on the funding agreement.

Construction funds are similar, except that the ultimate use
of the funds is for construction of highways, hospitals, etc.
These agreements may be "fully flexible," allowing amounts
to be withdrawn without limit to pay for construction, or
may contain restrictions (e.g., "no sooner, no greater" schedules) that place limitations on the timing of permitted withdrawals. Such limitations reduce risk to the issuer and are
intended to produce a higher rate of interest.

Debt service reserves are amounts set aside to be invested
until the bonds mature. If the bond issuer is unable to meet
interest or principal payments as they become due, withdrawals may be made from the reserve. The purpose is to
enhance the rating of the bonds, thus lowering the resulting bond interest rate. Typically 10 percent of the total bond
proceeds may be held in reserve.

Float funds are used to accumulate funds between bond
coupon dates. For example, with housing bonds, mortgagees
typically remit to the lender monthly; interest is paid semi-
annually. A float fund provides a vehicle for investing such
funds. Unlike a money market account, the interest rate is
determined at issue and remains constant over the duration of the agreement. Eliminating the potential variability
of interest earnings enhances the payment certainty of the
bonds.

Black box deals are bonds issued with no real public purpose other than to earn arbitrage. They were effectively
eliminated by changes in the 1986 tax laws and may no
longer be issued.

2. *Corporations* may also wish to use funding agreements as an investment vehicle. Some possible uses include:

Defeasance is a process whereby a borrower purchases an asset, such as a funding agreement or a portfolio of U.S. Treasury strips that exactly meet payments due under outstanding bonds, loans, or other corporate obligations. In essence, the corporation is substituting the credit of the insurance company (or of the federal government if strips are used) for its own. The procedure may be useful in situations where loan covenants make prepayment unattractive. It is often used with refinancings.

Settlements of lawsuits or other liabilities that are due to be paid over several years may use a funding agreement to allow the purchaser to transfer the liability to the funding agreement provider. In some instances, a court may insist that such an agreement be purchased, adopting the view that transferring the obligation to a highly rated insurer may enhance the certainty of receipt to the payees.

Nonqualified deferred compensation plans and other non–ERISA pension plans may use funding agreements within a "Rabbi Trust" to provide an additional layer of protection to participants. Earnings on such "top-hat" or excess plans are not tax deferred as they would be in a qualified plan.

3. *Welfare plans* may use funding agreements to fund retiree health liabilities, unemployment funds, Voluntary Employee Benefit Association Trusts, etc. The tax status of such plans varies according to the type of plan and the parties involved. Collectively bargained plans normally escape tax on the trust earnings.

4. *Insurers* may use claim-responsive funding agreements for liability settlements or as a fixed-income alternative in their general account portfolio. To date, such usage has been limited to smaller property and casualty and captive insurers.

5. *Foundations and endowments* use grant-responsive funding agreements as an alternative to other fixed-income investment alternatives.

6. *Lotteries* use funding agreements to guarantee payouts over a long, fixed period. Normally, there are few or no mortality guarantees issued with such contracts.

PROVIDERS

Funding agreements are issued by either insurance companies or banks. Unless the agreements are collateralized, the rating agencies and bond insurers normally require the agreement provider to have a rating at least as high as that of the bond. This effectively limits the market to investment-grade companies and often to only AAA-rated providers.

UNDERWRITING

Funding agreements may be true GIC "bullets," under which there is no possible variability from the deposit and withdrawal schedule. Under prespecified conditions, some flexibility may be permitted. The issuer is exposed to potential loss (1) if withdrawals are made sooner than anticipated while interest rates have risen (since the assets underlying the agreement have a market value below "book" or "par" and a capital loss will occur if the provider sells such assets while paying out at "books") or (2) if deposits are delayed in a falling interest rate environment (since maturing assets must be reinvested at rates below those guaranteed in the contract).

The underwriting process analyzes the proposed transaction to determine the most likely schedule of cash flows and to estimate the degree of uncertainty contained in such projections. From the issuers' standpoint, this uncertainty risk must be priced into the rate. It is important that such charges be sufficient to compensate for the losses that will invariably occur on some contracts. It is also important that the charge not be excessive, or the resulting rate will be unattractive to potential clients.

The underwriting process also seeks to determine whether there are regulatory or legal issues that need to be addressed. Common sources of information used by the underwriter include the Preliminary Official Statement for the sale of the bonds and discussions with the financial adviser, investment banker, or bond counsel.

THE BIDDING PROCESS

Potential purchasers usually request bids from several prospective providers. Bids will often be requested through one or more financial advisers or brokers, although some agencies will deal directly with providers. Bond counsel will often insist on at least three bidders to verify that the winning provider was at a "market rate." The request will describe the expected cash flows, the time and form of bidding, specifications for the agreement (covenants, options, etc.), the criteria under which awards will be decided, and information to be used in underwriting.

Bidders will provide a proposal with a rate that is normally available only at most for a few hours. This allows for the most competitive rates by limiting the issuer's exposure to market movements after the bid has been made. Under these circumstances, bidding is handled by telephone. To a large extent, the process relies on good faith by all parties concerned since the issuer will typically hedge a winning bid before having a signed contract.

ACCOUNTING

Municipal funding agreements are usually accounted on a book value basis. As noted in Chapter 4, the Financial Accounting Standards Board has begun to question such treatment for qualified investment contracts and may require alternative treatment in the future. The scope of the FASB project may also extend to funding agreements. It is too soon to say whether the Government Accounting Standards Board will follow suit.

CAPITAL REQUIREMENTS

When an insurance company issues a GIC, the liability held on its balance sheet is determined by methods mandated by state insurance commissioners. The conservative nature of such statutory accounting often requires holding a reserve higher than the amount deposited. Capital is required to finance this initial "surplus strain." Also, since brokers' commissions are often paid in advance, capital must be available for contract acquisition.

Higher levels of capital and surplus enhance the provider's guarantees. Ratings agencies have targeted minimum capital/surplus-to-liability ratios required for such rating level.

CREDIT CONCERNS

The creditworthiness of providers has always been a major concern in the nonqualified market. As a rule, purchasers will deal only with companies rated at the highest investment grades. Such caution is important due to the lack of outside guarantees. FDIC insurance is limited on bank agreements. As noted in Chapter 3, some states do not provide coverage for investment contracts issued by insurance companies under their state guaranty funds.

Issuers with lower ratings are occasionally required to provide collateral in the form of Treasury bonds or other government guaranteed debt. The assets are usually held in trust and the issuer is required to "mark-to-market" and deposit additional securities if the market value held in trust falls below a threshold. An alternative used by issuers is to issue contracts in the form of a repurchase agreement.

TAXATION

Purchasers of GICs are taxed as with any other fixed-income investment. To the extent that purchasers are tax-exempt, this tends to make the issue moot, as long as the anti-arbitrage rules are satisfied. No special tax advantages accrue to the issuers.

Section 148 of the Internal Revenue Code requires issuers of tax-exempt bonds to rebate arbitrage profits to the U.S. Treasury (with a few narrow exceptions) in order to maintain the bond's tax-exempt status.

REGULATION

Guaranteed investment contracts and funding agreements may be considered securities under the Securities Act of 1933. However, there are exemptions from the provisions of the act that may be available for GICs. Under Section 3(a) an exemption is provided for:

> Any insurance or . . . annuity contract, issued by a corporation subject to the supervision of the insurance commissioner, bank commissioner . . . of any State or Territory.

The 1970 amendments extended this exemption to separate accounts issued to qualified pension plans, and the 1980 amendments further included qualified GICs in the exemption.

After issuing a series of "no-action" letters on the subject of nonqualified funding agreements in the 1980s, the SEC issued Rule 151 in 1986. (Rule 151 can be found in Appendix 2 on page 304.) This rule provides that a guaranteed investment contract issued by an insurance company would not be considered a security if:

1. The issuer is regulated by a state insurance commission.
2. The issuer must assume the investment risk under the contract.
3. The contract is not marketed primarily as an investment.

In the case of financings of municipalities or other governmental units, another exemption may be available in SEC Rule 131 if the obligation:

1. Is payable from general revenues of a governmental unit . . . having other resources that may be used for payment of the obligation or
2. Relates to a public project owned and operated by or on behalf of and under the control of a governmental unit or
3. Relates to a facility leased to . . . a commercial enterprise but is part of a public project that is, itself, owned by and under control of a governmental unit.

Finally, the so-called "private placement" exemption under Section 4(2) of the 1933 Act may be available for transactions by an issuer not involving any public offering. The SEC has provided a "safe harbor" for meeting the requirements of this section in Rule D.

In addition to federal regulation, investment contracts issued by insurance companies are subject to regulation by the insurance commissioners of each state in which they are licensed. This includes filing and obtaining approval of the contract in every jurisdiction. This can be time-consuming to the point that some companies now issue funding agreements through non-insurance company subsidiaries.

SUMMARY

Nonqualified GICs have the potential to add diversification to an issuer's liabilities. However, the requirements for capital, an investment-grade rating, and the underwriting resources have acted to limit the growth of this market. Whether this continues to be the case remains to be seen.

CHAPTER 15

STRUCTURED GIC-LIKE ARRANGEMENTS: SOME DUE DILIGENCE ISSUES

Hugh Forcier
Partner
Faegre & Benson

INTRODUCTION

A rapidly evolving development in the GIC market is the emergence of several types of structured GIC-like arrangements. The general objective of these arrangements is to significantly reduce the single issuer credit risk associated with traditional "general account" GICs and other types of "general asset" investment contracts.[1]

Structured GIC-like arrangements seek to reduce single issuer credit risk by providing the plan with an "ownership" interest, "security" interest, or similar type of interest in a diversified portfolio of debt instruments. A few such arrangements are designed so that the portfolio of debt instruments will have a fair market value equal to book value on each business day. However, most arrangements are designed so that the portfolio of debt instruments will necessarily equal book value only at the inception of the arrangement and, thereafter, will have a fair market value that can be either greater or less than book value. To the extent the plan has claims above the value of the

---

[1]See discussion at pages 25, 26 and 68 through 134.

portfolio, those claims have only a general creditor priority (or, in the case of an insurance company, perhaps a "policyholder" priority).

Among the most important questions that a plan fiduciary must ask if it is going to consider acquiring a structured GIC-like arrangement for a plan are the following:

1. What due diligence should be performed on the very basic issue of whether the arrangement really provides a significant reduction in the single issuer credit risk?

2. Is book value accounting available with respect to the arrangement? (Book value accounting issues have been discussed in other chapters in this book.)

ARRANGEMENTS OFFERED BY BANKS AND SECURITIES DEALERS

There are several different types of structured GIC-like arrangements offered by banks and securities dealers. Most formats do not closely resemble typical securitized arrangements; but, rather, are hybrid arrangements having some characteristics of repurchase arrangements, some characteristics of interest rate swaps, and some characteristics of guaranty arrangements. A full description of each format is beyond the scope of this chapter.

Background

Under most formats, a diversified portfolio of debt instruments is "sold" to the plan by the bank or securities dealer. The debt instruments are usually high quality. Frequently, the debt instruments are issued, or guaranteed, by the U.S. government or its agencies. However, corporate debt instruments or credit card receivables may be used to obtain a higher yield. To date, most portfolios are "unmanaged." This means that the debt instruments generally have a stated maturity date coincident with the duration of the arrangement as a whole and the arrangement generally requires that the debt instruments be held until they mature.

Note: Recently, a few banks and securities dealers have announced actively managed products. Because the majority of current arrangements are unmanaged, the following discussion will focus only on such arrangements.

Benefit Responsiveness. To accommodate benefit responsive-plan distributions, the arrangement will provide for the disposition of specific debt instruments held in the portfolio prior to their maturity. In some cases, the debt instruments must be sold back to the bank or securities dealer at their book value whether book value is above or below fair market value. In other cases, the debt instruments can be sold in the open market. If gain is realized by the plan in an open market sale (i.e., if the sale price is in excess of book value), the gain must be paid over by the plan to the bank or the securities dealer. If a loss is suffered in an open market sale, the plan is reimbursed for that loss by the bank or securities dealer. In almost all cases, if a sale occurs (to the bank, securities dealer, or in the open market) to accommodate benefit responsive cash flow needs, the debt instruments with the shortest maturities are sold first.

Maintenance of Fair Market Value at Book Value. These arrangements differ considerably with respect to whether a mechanism is provided for the maintenance of debt instruments having a fair market value equal to book value. A few arrangements (particularly those that take the express form of repurchase agreements) will provide that periodically (sometimes on each business day) debt instruments having a fair market value at least equal to book value will be held for the plan's account. (Note: In some cases there is a mechanism to maintain debt instruments having a fair market value greater than book value—for example, 103 percent to 110 percent of book value). However, most arrangements provide no mechanism to maintain fair market value at any particular level.

If the arrangement does not provide for the maintenance of fair market value at book value, the buyer should assess the ability of the bank or securities dealer to honor its benefit-responsive obligation to repurchase the debt instruments at book value (or otherwise hold the plan harmless from a loss when liquidating debt obligations below book value). That is, will the bank or securities dealer be able to "make good" on any losses the plan will incur in connection with benefit-responsive distributions? The measure of the exposure to the bank or securities dealer should be the value of the implicit "put" (not the value of the entire structured arrangement). It should be further discounted for the fact that the "put" can be exercised only to accommodate the benefit-responsive cash flow needs of the plan.

Who Holds the Assets "Sold" to the Plan? These arrangements differ considerably with respect to who is to hold the debt instruments. Some arrangements are structured to discourage the use of third-party custodians and do not permit the plan trustee to hold its debt instruments directly. Others are structured to use a third-party custodian (chosen by the bank or securities dealer) in all cases. Still others permit the plan trustee to hold the debt instruments directly.

Credit and Other Risks Associated with the Debt Instruments "Sold" to the Plan. These arrangements differ considerably with respect to whether they provide protection from default by the issuers of the debt instruments held in the portfolio. A few arrangements provide that the bank or securities dealer will guarantee the plan against credit losses. However, under most arrangements, the bank or securities dealer disclaims any obligation to repurchase defaulted debt obligations at book value (or otherwise make good any loss suffered on the sale or other disposition of a defaulted debt instrument). Obviously these latter arrangements expose the plan to greater risk.

Other risks are also allocated between the plan and the bank or securities dealer. For example, risks associated with substituted debt instruments will usually be disclaimed by the bank or securities dealer. And, in the case of collateralized mortgage obligations, the risk of prepayment will usually be shared between the plan and the bank or securities dealer.

The "True Sale" Issue

The analysis generally applied to arrangements that provide for the securitization of financial assets starts with the following question: *Does the arrangement result in a "true sale" of the fi-*

nancial assets (in this case, debt instruments) to the plan or does the arrangement constitute only an extension of credit by the plan to the bank or securities dealer which is secured by the debt instruments transferred to the plan? In general, if the arrangement involves a "true sale," the plan is exposed to less risk of loss and delay in case the bank or securities dealer is placed in receivership or bankruptcy proceedings.[2] The financial assets will not be the property of the bank or securities dealer if the transaction constitutes a true sale and, therefore, will not be subject to the automatic stay of receivership or bankruptcy. However, whether the transaction constitutes a true sale or not, the plan may face other restrictions in a receivership or bankruptcy if the bank or securities dealer elects to assume (rather than reject) the contract arrangement.[3]

> Note: If the arrangement takes the form of a repurchase agreement that meets the requirements of Section 101(47) of the U.S. Bankruptcy Code, the plan fiduciary might not particularly care whether the arrangement is, or is not, characterized as a true sale. This is because the automatic stay provision of the U.S. Bankruptcy Code[4] and the discretionary stay provision of FIRREA[5] do not apply to an arrangement if it meets the statutory definition of a "repurchase agreement" under Section 101(47).[6]

It is rare that counsel to the plan can give an unqualified opinion on the true sale issue. This is even more likely to be the situation in the case of a GIC-like arrangement than in the case of a more typical securitization arrangement. In a recently

---

[2]See T. Kiriakos, D. de Hoyos and R. Rosenberg, "Bankruptcy," in *Securitization of Financial Assets,* ed. J. Kravitt (1991), pp. 5–11.

[3]11 U.S.C. § 365.

[4]11 U.S.C. § 362(a).

[5]12 U.S.C. § 1821(d)(12).

[6]See 11 U.S.C. § 362(b)(7) and 12 U.S.C. § 1821(e)(8).

Among other requirements, to meet the definition of a "repurchase agreement" under § 101(47) of the U.S. Bankruptcy Code, the agreement must (1) relate to debt instruments issued, or guaranteed, by the U.S. government or its agencies, certificates of deposit or bank acceptances and (2) be either a demand obligation or have a duration not longer than one year.

Most plans look for synthetic GIC-like arrangements structured with durations in excess of one year. In that case, the arrangement might not be exempt from the stay provisions.

published treatise dealing with securitization arrangements in
general, the following advice was given:[7]

> The first advice to the [purchaser] to be given when commenc-
> ing a discussion of how to determine whether a transfer of fi-
> nancial assets constitutes a true sale under applicable state law,
> is to temper one's expectations for guidance. While certain cases
> act as lighthouses illuminating some rocky coasts, the waters are
> intermittently, and on occasion inconsistently, charted. In par-
> ticular, as of [mid-1991], there is no definitive judicial authority
> analyzing the issue of true sale in relation to the sort of so-
> phisticated transfer transactions which commonly characterize
> securitizations.
>
> Sales of financial assets are frequently "hybrids," that is, bear-
> ing attributes of sales, as well as of secured loans. . . . As a result,
> a lawyer's assurances to a client which is a prospective purchaser
> seeking to minimize the risk that transferred financial assets will
> be part of the seller's estate if the seller were to become bankrupt
> will almost certainly be based on that particular lawyer's weigh-
> ing of the attributes of the transaction.

There are two lines of analysis that are applied by legal
counsel in giving "true sale" opinions. One line of analysis focuses on the intent of the parties. The other focuses on the economic characteristics of the arrangement; that is, does the
substance of the arrangement more closely resemble a "sale" or
a "secured loan?" (Under this second line of analysis, a court
would examine the recourse to the bank or securities dealer,
irrevocability of the transaction, administration of financial
assets, notice to third parties, tax and financial accounting

---

Two theories have been advanced as to how a repo GIC with an effective duration in
excess of one year can nevertheless qualify as a "repurchase agreement" under § 101(47):
First, some arrangements that are designed to have the practical effect of a multiyear
duration are actually structured as having a nominal duration of only one year, subject
to mandatory renewals every twelve months. Sponsors of these arrangements contend
that at no time does the arrangement have a duration in excess of one year. Second,
some arrangements have market value withdrawal features. The sponsors of these arrangements take the position that they are "demand" obligations, and, therefore, meet
the statutory definition.

[7]Kiriakos *et al, supra* Note 3, at pages 5–37 to 5–38.

treatment, and relationship to a loan transaction.) Legal counsel differ on which line of analysis should be given principal emphasis.

Because unqualified assurance cannot be provided by counsel to the plan in most cases, from the plan's point of view it is usually important that the terms of the arrangement with the bank or securities dealer expressly state the parties' intent that the arrangement constitute a true sale but that if, in subsequent litigation, the arrangement is held not to have constituted a true sale, it is the parties' intention that the plan have a security interest in the underlying debt instruments thought to be "owned" by the plan. In addition, the plan needs to ensure that in such event the security interest be perfected and prior to any other claims.

The "Transfer" Issue

In order for a transaction to either constitute a true sale or create a secured transaction, a "transfer" must take place. In the absence of a "transfer," the plan will be viewed as only a general unsecured creditor of the bank or securities dealer, even if the transaction would otherwise constitute a true sale. The same rules will govern transfers for the purposes of constituting a true sale or creating a secured transaction; however, the method for effecting a transfer depends upon the type of debt instrument that is the subject of the arrangement.

The method for effecting a transfer of debt instruments is generally governed by applicable state law, which in most states means Section 8-313 of the Uniform Commercial Code. If the debt instrument is a certificated security (i.e., a "physical"), the plan, or its agent as custodian, should take possession of the certificates to effect a transfer. If the debt instrument is an uncertificated security, the plan should have the transfer noted by appropriate book entry. (In some cases, the plan may need to obtain the acknowledgment of the entity, on whose books and records the plan's interest appears, that such entity is acting on behalf of the plan.) Transfers of Treasury securities and certain government agency certificates are not governed by applicable state law, but are instead governed by federal regulations.

Some arrangements presently being used provide that the bank or securities dealer will act as agent or custodian for the plan for the purpose of effecting the transfer by marking its books and records. While this may in some cases work to effect a transfer, the plan will be subject to the risk that the bank or securities dealer may "undo" the transfer since the bank or securities dealer will have the ability to alter the book entry or the designation in its books and records. In this case, bonding of the bank or securities dealer's performance might be considered.

Other Due Diligence Questions

An important question (whether the arrangement is held to be a true sale or only the creation of a security interest) is whether the plan retains the right to pursue additional claims in a receivership or bankruptcy. For example, if the plan suffers a reinvestment loss, the plan fiduciary would want to pursue a claim for that loss.

ARRANGEMENTS OFFERED BY INSURANCE COMPANIES

A number of insurance companies have recently begun to offer structured arrangements to the GIC market. These arrangements almost always take the form of "separate accounts" and are referred to in this chapter as "separate account GICs."

Background

A separate account is a portfolio of assets (assumed in this chapter to be debt instruments) identified on the books and records of the insurance company as intended to be used primarily to satisfy its liabilities to one (or more) specifically identified contractholders. As will be seen, one of the principal questions is whether this segregation of debt instruments on the books and records of the insurance company will be given effect if the insurance company were liquidated and other contractholders and policyholders would receive a smaller recovery (expressed in terms of a percentage of the total amount owed to them).

At this time, separate account GICs are usually issued in a "participating" format. By "participating" is meant that the plan assumes a significant portion of the credit risk and some of the interest rate risk with respect to the assets held in the separate account.

> Note: A number of consultants and managers have negotiated nonparticipating arrangements with insurance companies. Because the majority of current separate account GICs are participating arrangements, the following discussion will focus only on such arrangements.

The extent to which the insurance company provides a general account guarantee against credit losses or interest rate losses under a participating arrangement varies considerably from product to product. It is important for the plan fiduciary to consider the nature of the guarantee provided by the insurance company. In addition to understanding the economics of the guarantee, the plan fiduciary should focus on the impact of the guarantee on the book value accounting issue and on the issue of whether the separate account will be given effect in a rehabilitation or liquidation of the insurance company.

For purposes of the following discussion, a fairly typical type of participating separate account with the following principal features will be assumed:

• The debt instruments held in the "Separate Account" are valued at fair market value periodically throughout the duration of the arrangement.

• The portfolio of debt instruments is actively managed by the insurance company. However, the investment class and risk characteristics of the debt instruments that can be held in the Separate Account are specifically described. The debt instruments are frequently limited to obligations issued, or guaranteed, by the U.S. government or its agencies. The description of the portfolio also includes a target maturity for the portfolio.

• Deposits made by the plan under the contract are used to purchase debt instruments that are to be held in the Separate

Account. Debt instruments held in the Separate Account are liquidated to raise funds to pay expenses charged by the insurance company and to make payments to the plan under the terms of the contract.

• A separate "Book Value Account" is maintained under the GIC contract. This is not an asset account, but rather a bookkeeping account. In specified circumstances, the insurance company will continue to make payments to the plan (up to the amount shown in the Book Value Account) even if the Separate Account has been reduced to $0. Plan deposits, insurance company expenses, and payments to the plan are credited or debited to the Book Value Account in the same way that those items are credited or debited to the Separate Account. However, rather than adjusting the Book Value Account "to market", that Account is credited with interest at a rate established for each year. The rate for a particular year is the greater of 0 percent or the rate that will produce the future expected cash flows from the assets held in the Separate Account given the book value of the assets on the first day of the year for which the rate is being established.

• Benefit-responsive payments are made by the insurance company from the general assets based on the Book Value Account in the unlikely event that the amount in the Separate Account has been reduced to $0.

> Note: If the insurance company has imposed normal underwriting standards limiting its exposure to benefit-responsive payments, there is very little chance that the insurance company will ever become obligated to make payments to the plan because the Book Value Account still has a positive value after the Separate Account has been reduced to $0.

• Most contracts provide for no stated maturity date. However, the plan normally can terminate the arrangement upon giving written notice of 30 to 90 days to the insurance company. Upon such termination, the plan is typically paid the fair market value of the assets held in the Separate Account—whether that amount is above or below the Book Value Account.

> Note: Some accounting firms require a nominal maturity date as a condition to giving a favorable book value accounting opinion.

The net effect of the typical formula used to establish the interest rate for each year is that all credit losses and interest rate losses suffered by the separate account in a prior year are amortized over the remaining period to maturity of the debt instruments held in the separate account—unless the rate necessary to fully amortize the losses is less than 0 percent. Thus, the insurance company will, in fact, be obligated to make good (out of its general account assets) on a guarantee of principal or interest only to the extent that the plan is entitled to a payment that is measured by the Book Value Account prior to the full amortization of all losses. As noted above, if normal underwriting has been used, it is very unlikely that the insurance company will not be able to fully amortize all credit and interest rate losses.

Will the "not chargeable" provision (assuming one exists) be given effect in liquidation proceedings?

The first and most fundamental question presented is the following: *Would a court that is supervising the liquidation of an insurance company give effect to the separate account if the result is that the plan receives a greater percent recovery than other contractholders who must look solely to the insurance company's general account assets?* "Giving effect to the separate account" means that the court would apply the assets identified on the books and records of the insurance company as having been held for the separate account first to satisfy the contract to which the separate account relates.

To state that the question is to be resolved by the court supervising the liquidation is to make two assumptions: First, it is assumed that the assets held in the separate account are part of the assets under the court's supervision. This would be the case in most states. It is typical for the state statute authorizing the establishment of a separate account to provide explicitly that the assets held in a separate account are owned by the insurance company. Also, the chapter of state statutes that governs insurance company liquidations typically provides that all assets owned by the insurance company are seized upon the commencement of liquidation proceedings and that all assets owned by the insurance company are subject to those proceedings.

The second assumption is that it will be the court (not the insurance commissioner) that will decide whether the separate account will be given effect in liquidation proceedings. This is an important point to understand. A number of insurance companies that issue separate account GICs have obtained letters from the insurance commissioners in their state of domicile expressing the view that the separate account would be given effect in a liquidation. As of the date this chapter is written, insurance commissioners in the states of Connecticut, Kentucky, New Jersey, and New York have issued such interpretations. It is certainly helpful to have a favorable interpretation from the insurance commissioner if the issue will have to be litigated. However, the court will not be bound by the interpretation of the insurance commissioner.

The specific analysis of the question usually begins with the so-called "not chargeable" provision found in most state insurance laws. The following is a typical provision:

> If and to the extent so provided in the applicable agreement, the assets in the separate account shall not be chargeable with liabilities arising out of any other business of the insurer.

The not chargeable provision (if one exists in the state law) is found in the statute that authorizes the establishment of the separate account for the GIC arrangement. This statute is invariably located in a different chapter of state law than the chapter that deals with the liquidation of the insurance company.

In a few states, the chapter of state law that deals with liquidation of insurance companies contains a specific provision that gives effect to the not chargeable provision for liquidation purposes. New York is an example of such a state. Immediately following the priority provision of the New York liquidation law, the following provision appears:[8]

> Every claim under a separate account agreement providing, in effect, that the assets in the separate account shall not be chargeable with liabilities arising out of any other business of the

---

[8]New York Insurance Code § 7435(b).

insurer shall be satisfied out of the assets in the separate account equal to the reserves maintained in such account for such agreement and, to the extent, if any, not fully discharged thereby, shall be treated as a class four claim against the estate of the life insurance company.

When dealing with an insurance company domiciled in a state such as New York, a plan fiduciary presumably could obtain an unqualified opinion of its counsel that the not chargeable provision would be given effect in liquidation proceedings.

In contrast to New York, most state liquidation laws do not contain a specific provision giving effect under the liquidation chapter to the not chargeable provision. When dealing with an insurance company domiciled in this more typical type of state, counsel to the plan will have to evaluate the various theories that have been advanced to support a contention that the court will give effect to the not chargeable provision.[9] A plan fiduciary may well have difficulty obtaining an unqualified opinion from its counsel.[10] Distinctions may be drawn between registered products and unregistered products; between classic variable products and products with guarantees of principal and interest; and between participating and nonparticipating products.[11] In any event, many plan fiduciaries will require a

---

[9]Frankel, "Variable Annuities, Variable Insurance and Separate Accounts," *BU Law Review* 177 (1971).

[10]In *Robin & Hass Company* v. *Continental Assurance Company*, 58 Ill. App. 3d 378, 374 N.E. 2d 727 (Appellate Court of Illinois, First District, Third Division, 1978), cert. denied, 412 N.E. 2d 614 (1978), the court assumed that the "not chargeable" provision would be given effect under the Illinois insurance liquidation statute.

However, it appears the point was not contested by the opposing party, the Illinois insurance commissioner. The court noted as follows (374 N.E. 2d at page 730):

> [The Insurance Commissioner] claims he has never admitted to any definitive meaning of [the not-chargeable provision]; he neither endorses nor opposes the plaintiff's interpretation that in the event of insolvency separate account assets are not reachable by a liquidator for the benefit of general creditors.

Note also: The appellate court decision did not disclose what type of separate account contract had been purchased.

[11]In recent liquidations of insurance companies that have sponsored registered, classic variable separate accounts, the not-chargeable provisions have been recognized. For example, in the Mutual Benefit Life rehabilitation, policyholders of classic, registered variable annuities were excepted from the moratorium on withdrawals. *See,* Order

virtually unqualified opinion of counsel before purchasing a separate account GIC.

If the not chargeable provision is given effect, how long will it take for the plan to be paid?

Assuming that the not chargeable provision is given effect, the next most important question that needs to be considered is the following: *How quickly will the assets in the separate account be liquidated and paid to the plan?* Obviously, plan fiduciaries want to be able to have the assets in the separate account quickly applied to the amount owed to the plan. Because these arrangements typically have some general account guarantees of principal and interest, it seems likely that the plan would have to wait for the final resolution of the liquidation proceedings.

Other Due Diligence Questions

Another important question (assuming the not chargeable provision is given effect) is whether the plan retains the right to pursue additional claims in the liquidation. For example, if the plan suffers a reinvestment loss, the plan fiduciary would want to pursue a claim for that loss.

In analyzing a separate account GIC, a plan fiduciary should examine the risk that the separate account will not be administered in accordance with the contract provisions. This might be addressed by bonding.

Frequently, a separate account is established to fund contracts issued to a number of unrelated contractholders. The types of contracts covered may be quite different. These differences can be related to the guarantees made by the insurance company that are supported by its general account. Such differences might result in differences in reserve values which, in turn, could disproportionately affect the share of each contractholder in the assets held in the separate account.

---

continuing Rehabilitators appointment, continuing restraints, and granting the relief (filed August 7, 1991); In the Matter of Rehabilitation of Mutual Benefit Life Insurance Company, a Mutual Insurance Company of New Jersey; Superior Court of New Jersey, Chancery Division—Mercer County, General Equity Part, Docket No. C-91-00109.

On occasion, a separate account GIC will be offered to a plan as an alternative to an existing traditional GIC. For example, the plan fiduciary might be considering withdrawing from a traditional GIC because of credit concerns. In that case, the insurance company may offer a separate account GIC as a structure to address the credit concern. This type of transaction creates the need to analyze whether the transfer to the separate account is a voidable preference under the state's liquidation law.

CONCLUSION

The foregoing discussion shows that the different types of structured GIC-like arrangements vary considerably with respect to issues that will affect the ability of legal counsel to provide substantially unqualified assurance to a plan fiduciary that the arrangement protects the plan from single issuer credit risk. Of course, ultimately the consultant/manager or plan sponsor has to determine the degree of assurance it must receive from legal counsel.

When determining the degree of assurance it must receive, the plan fiduciary will have to consider the investment objectives of the fixed-interest investment option under the plan in which the GIC-like arrangement will be held. Attention will probably also have to be given to past and future employee communications that describe the risk of that option.

Presumably, a plan fiduciary will be hesitant to accept significantly greater exposure to single issuer credit risk than would be accepted by a manager of a trust quality bond fund. Frequently managers of trust quality bond funds will invest in securitized arrangements wrapped around a portfolio of similar debt instruments. In the case of at least some types of structured GIC-like arrangements, it would appear that significantly greater single issuer credit risk is being accepted by plan fiduciaries than would be accepted by managers of trust quality bond funds.

If a plan that invests in a structured GIC-like arrangement suffers a significant actual loss due to the failure of a bank, securities dealer, or insurance company, the plan fiduciary responsible for the purchase decision will wish to point to a clear record that shows that prior to purchasing the arrangement, the additional risk had been clearly identified and considered.

At the present time, it frequently is not clear which plan fiduciary is responsible for the risk evaluation presented by structured GIC-like arrangements. Many consultants and managers believe it is the plan sponsor's responsibility to evaluate that type of risk as part of the plan sponsor's identification of the general categories of investments that are appropriate for the fixed-income investment option under the plan. In contrast, many plan sponsors believe that since there is so much variation between the different types of structured GIC-like arrangements, it is the duty of the consultant or manager to evaluate the exposure to single issuer credit risk that is presented by each specific arrangement. In all events, presumably the funding policy adopted by the plan sponsor (or the contract under which the consultant or manager is engaged) should clearly identify which party has the responsibility to evaluate single issuer credit risk.

If a large number of plan sponsors, consultants, and managers generally cannot agree on the appropriate method to analyze single issuer credit risk, then it may be that third parties will fill the void. Both credit rating agencies and financial guarantee insurers are generally comfortable with securitized arrangements wrapped around portfolios of financial assets. A credit rating for a specific structured GIC-like arrangement could provide the basis for the consultant, manager, and plan sponsor to place the risk/reward analysis in a meaningful context. A policy of financial insurance would provide even greater assurance.

APPENDIX 1

HISTORICAL GIC RATES AND YIELD SPREADS

HIGHEST RATE GICs - 1982
$1 MILLION SIMPLE INTEREST

WEEK ENDING	\multicolumn{7}{c}{MATURITY}						
	1	2	3	4	5	7	10
3.05	15.88	--	16.31	15.10	16.51	--	16.47
3.12	--	15.50	16.21	16.19	16.32	16.53	17.02
3.19	--	15.41	16.41	16.43	16.54	16.18	17.02
3.26	--	--	16.33	16.32	16.33	16.30	17.02
4.02	--	15.85	16.02	16.25	16.27	15.73	16.86
4.09	15.51	16.11	16.22	16.35	16.48	16.13	16.75
4.16	--	15.75	16.22	16.33	16.48	16.18	16.78
4.23	--	15.65	15.92	16.05	16.13	15.28	16.72
4.30	14.99	15.54	15.92	16.03	16.19	15.61	16.65
5.07	--	15.60	15.83	15.82	16.14	16.16	16.40
5.14	15.70	15.60	16.16	16.03	16.18	15.80	16.40
5.21	14.88	15.95	16.26	16.18	16.28	15.61	15.90
5.28	14.25	15.49	16.16	16.15	16.14	16.12	14.38
6.04	14.21	15.75	16.08	16.09	16.20	16.38	16.65
6.11	14.67	15.85	16.21	16.20	16.30	16.48	16.65
6.18	--	15.74	16.15	16.22	17.04	16.51	17.27
6.25	--	15.94	17.06	17.15	17.32	16.88	17.40
7.02	15.31	16.36	16.67	16.60	16.99	16.63	17.14
7.09	--	16.75	16.51	16.76	17.01	16.63	16.65
7.16	14.47	16.10	16.08	16.29	16.49	16.38	15.95
7.23	14.36	15.80	15.89	15.80	16.29	15.93	16.11
7.30	14.56	16.00	16.01	15.81	16.08	16.10	15.63
8.06	14.51	15.23	15.47	15.87	15.73	15.84	15.43
8.13	--	14.97	15.67	15.78	15.88	15.57	15.65
8.20	11.10	14.35	14.62	14.15	15.02	15.07	15.08
8.27	13.37	13.43	14.52	13.98	15.04	15.02	15.03
9.03	--	13.40	14.37	14.43	14.82	14.87	14.88
9.10	12.41	13.44	14.12	14.33	14.33	14.17	13.96
9.17	12.61	13.83	14.37	14.40	14.53	13.92	14.05
9.24	12.36	13.39	13.82	13.51	13.97	14.02	14.30
10.01	12.36	13.39	13.82	13.96	14.08	13.86	13.85
10.08	12.25	12.74	13.15	13.24	13.77	13.26	13.29
10.15	11.55	12.04	12.45	12.08	12.52	12.56	12.59
10.22	10.51	11.27	12.47	12.76	12.88	12.87	12.05
10.29	11.23	11.71	13.06	12.73	12.88	12.53	12.66
11.05	11.43	11.84	13.06	12.20	12.78	12.26	12.40
11.12	11.43	11.84	12.56	12.40	12.72	12.45	12.55
11.19	10.14	11.59	12.22	12.43	12.78	12.77	13.00
11.26	10.36	11.10	11.66	12.10	12.44	12.45	12.30
12.03	11.28	11.69	12.16	12.20	12.79	12.48	12.67
12.10	10.14	11.59	12.16	12.20	12.79	12.57	12.66
12.17	10.78	11.35	12.16	12.20	12.79	12.38	12.69
12.24	10.78	11.99	12.16	12.20	12.48	12.37	12.69
12.31	10.78	11.71	12.16	12.20	12.22	12.28	12.43
ABS HI	15.88	16.75	17.06	17.15	17.32	16.88	17.40
AVG	13.93	14.65	15.17	15.17	15.40	15.23	15.49

MARKET AVG RATE GICs - 1982
$1 MILLION SIMPLE INTEREST

WEEK ENDING	\multicolumn{7}{c}{MATURITY}						
	1	2	3	4	5	7	10
3.05	15.88	--	15.54	15.05	15.78	--	16.47
3.12	--	15.50	15.65	15.83	16.10	16.28	16.57
3.19	--	15.41	15.23	15.87	15.82	16.16	16.12
3.26	--	--	15.34	15.71	15.85	15.85	16.57
4.02	--	15.85	15.80	16.05	16.00	15.73	16.86
4.09	15.51	15.76	15.54	15.93	15.89	15.97	16.07
4.16	--	15.52	15.60	15.97	15.86	16.17	15.94
4.23	--	15.65	15.22	15.85	15.68	14.96	15.79
4.30	14.99	15.13	14.83	15.54	15.64	15.47	15.83
5.07	--	15.60	14.66	15.79	15.77	15.98	16.19
5.14	15.70	15.60	15.38	15.80	15.65	15.54	15.88
5.21	14.88	15.78	15.48	15.97	15.64	15.51	15.90
5.28	14.25	15.37	15.18	15.56	15.64	15.88	14.38
6.04	14.21	15.60	15.50	15.86	15.57	15.79	15.88
6.11	14.67	15.68	15.44	15.96	15.67	15.92	16.44
6.18	--	15.72	15.77	15.95	16.11	16.23	16.63
6.25	--	15.94	16.25	16.53	16.46	16.57	16.90
7.02	15.31	16.26	16.04	16.37	16.47	16.63	17.14
7.09	--	16.40	15.82	16.21	16.18	16.17	16.65
7.16	14.47	15.93	15.64	15.84	15.77	16.14	15.95
7.23	14.36	15.42	15.24	15.50	15.63	15.86	15.73
7.30	14.54	15.58	15.48	15.54	15.65	15.87	15.44
8.06	14.46	14.99	15.12	15.45	15.23	15.47	15.27
8.13	--	14.94	14.71	15.17	15.21	15.18	15.32
8.20	11.10	13.33	13.57	13.54	13.60	13.87	13.93
8.27	12.17	13.15	13.51	13.65	13.79	13.90	14.16
9.03	--	13.34	13.23	13.76	13.89	14.06	14.46
9.10	12.41	13.37	13.15	13.51	13.67	13.73	13.91
9.17	12.25	13.64	13.68	13.88	13.89	13.76	13.96
9.24	12.36	13.27	13.05	13.15	13.34	13.66	13.96
10.01	11.92	13.11	13.00	13.39	13.51	13.49	13.85
10.08	11.48	12.51	12.52	12.79	13.17	12.98	13.22
10.15	11.13	11.73	11.29	11.70	11.69	12.09	12.11
10.22	10.51	11.09	11.33	11.98	12.17	12.14	12.05
10.29	11.02	11.48	12.03	12.15	12.39	12.35	12.45
11.05	11.43	11.34	11.27	11.74	11.88	11.97	12.24
11.12	11.02	11.38	11.68	11.91	12.15	12.16	12.29
11.19	10.14	11.18	11.55	11.88	12.02	11.91	12.10
11.26	10.36	11.05	11.18	11.60	11.75	11.91	12.27
12.03	10.87	11.22	11.43	11.82	12.00	12.04	12.36
12.10	10.13	10.97	11.31	11.65	11.89	11.99	12.44
12.17	10.11	10.99	11.33	11.66	11.91	11.93	12.30
12.24	10.19	11.12	11.31	11.61	11.81	11.88	12.48
12.31	10.12	10.67	11.17	11.52	11.63	11.89	12.18
ABS HI	15.88	16.40	16.25	16.53	16.47	16.63	17.14
AVG	13.23	14.00	13.97	14.31	14.38	14.47	14.68

Source: Rates for the period March 1982, through September 30, 1988, provided courtesy of The Laughlin Group. Rates from October 1, 1988, through December 31, 1991, obtained courtesy of T. Rowe Price Associates.

1982 SPREADS - HIGH RATE GICs vs TREASURIES

WEEK ENDING	MATURITY 1	2	3	4	5	7	10
3.05	2.17	--	2.35	1.24	2.75	--	2.77
3.12	--	1.46	2.27	2.31	2.50	2.73	3.22
3.19	--	1.11	2.22	2.31	2.50	2.22	3.12
3.26	--	--	2.15	2.21	2.30	2.34	3.16
4.02	--	1.34	1.55	1.84	1.93	1.43	2.71
4.09	1.31	1.71	1.86	2.04	2.23	1.92	2.62
4.16	--	1.48	2.01	2.22	2.48	2.28	2.93
4.23	--	1.56	1.83	2.08	2.28	1.52	3.03
4.30	1.24	1.55	1.90	2.08	2.32	1.79	2.87
5.07	--	1.64	1.88	1.91	2.27	2.33	2.67
5.14	2.21	1.79	2.43	2.32	2.49	2.13	2.87
5.21	1.70	2.24	2.55	2.46	2.56	1.92	2.33
5.28	1.25	1.86	2.45	2.42	2.40	2.34	0.72
6.04	0.75	1.80	2.09	2.10	2.22	2.31	2.73
6.11	1.08	1.79	2.13	2.14	2.26	2.37	2.68
6.18	--	1.14	1.58	1.69	2.56	2.00	2.91
6.25	--	1.00	2.11	2.22	2.42	1.98	2.70
7.02	0.90	1.61	1.86	1.83	2.26	1.90	2.60
7.09	--	2.32	2.02	2.27	2.53	2.16	2.35
7.16	1.01	2.10	2.00	2.20	2.39	2.32	2.02
7.23	1.86	2.60	2.36	2.20	2.63	2.26	2.53
7.30	1.83	2.66	2.29	2.00	2.19	2.17	1.78
8.06	2.19	2.24	2.21	2.43	2.11	2.15	1.80
8.13	--	0.96	2.43	2.36	2.29	1.91	2.08
8.20	0.47	2.60	2.55	1.85	2.49	2.39	2.48
8.27	2.74	1.76	2.52	1.79	2.66	2.40	2.52
9.03	--	1.47	2.12	2.03	2.28	2.10	2.19
9.10	1.36	1.54	1.96	2.03	1.90	1.54	1.38
9.17	1.51	1.82	2.14	2.05	2.06	1.32	1.47
9.24	1.69	1.71	1.86	1.47	1.86	1.89	2.16
10.01	2.02	2.02	2.22	2.29	2.34	2.09	2.07
10.08	2.20	1.79	1.96	2.00	2.48	1.94	1.96
10.15	2.73	2.24	2.18	1.71	2.06	2.01	2.02
10.22	1.62	1.47	2.19	2.37	2.38	2.24	1.38
10.29	1.97	1.78	2.54	2.10	2.15	1.69	1.79
11.05	2.40	2.16	3.10	2.05	2.44	1.78	1.92
11.12	2.24	2.04	2.60	2.20	2.28	1.91	2.02
11.19	0.91	1.73	2.21	2.17	2.27	2.21	2.44
11.26	1.29	1.34	1.74	2.03	2.23	1.99	1.78
12.03	2.02	1.80	2.12	2.02	2.48	1.90	1.98
12.10	1.08	1.79	2.21	2.09	2.53	2.09	2.10
12.17	1.95	1.73	2.32	2.16	2.56	1.88	2.13
12.24	1.98	2.42	2.28	2.15	2.26	1.82	2.13
12.31	2.03	2.19	2.37	2.23	2.07	1.88	2.00
ABS HI	2.74	2.66	3.10	2.46	2.75	2.73	3.22
AVG	2.02	2.11	2.41	2.28	2.54	2.30	2.60

1982 SPREADS - MKT AVG RATE GICs vs TREASURIES

WEEK ENDING	MATURITY 1	2	3	4	5	7	10
3.05	2.17	--	1.58	1.19	2.02	--	2.77
3.12	--	1.46	1.71	1.95	2.28	2.48	2.77
3.19	--	1.11	1.04	1.75	1.78	2.20	2.22
3.26	--	--	1.16	1.60	1.82	1.89	2.71
4.02	--	1.34	1.33	1.64	1.66	1.43	2.71
4.09	1.31	1.36	1.18	1.62	1.64	1.76	1.94
4.16	--	1.25	1.39	1.86	1.86	2.27	2.09
4.23	--	1.56	1.13	1.88	1.83	1.20	2.10
4.30	1.24	1.14	0.81	1.59	1.77	1.65	2.05
5.07	--	1.64	0.71	1.88	1.90	2.15	2.46
5.14	2.21	1.79	1.65	2.09	1.96	1.87	2.35
5.21	1.70	2.07	1.77	2.25	1.92	1.82	2.33
5.28	1.25	1.74	1.47	1.83	1.90	2.10	0.72
6.04	0.75	1.65	1.51	1.87	1.59	1.72	1.96
6.11	1.08	1.62	1.36	1.90	1.63	1.81	2.47
6.18	--	1.12	1.20	1.42	1.63	1.72	2.27
6.25	--	1.00	1.30	1.60	1.56	1.67	2.20
7.02	0.90	1.51	1.23	1.60	1.74	1.90	2.60
7.09	--	1.97	1.33	1.72	1.70	1.70	2.35
7.16	1.01	1.93	1.56	1.75	1.67	2.08	2.02
7.23	1.86	2.22	1.71	1.90	1.97	2.19	2.15
7.30	1.81	2.24	1.76	1.73	1.76	1.94	1.59
8.06	2.14	2.00	1.86	2.01	1.61	1.78	1.64
8.13	--	0.93	1.47	1.75	1.62	1.52	1.75
8.20	0.47	1.58	1.50	1.24	1.07	1.19	1.33
8.27	1.54	1.48	1.51	1.46	1.41	1.28	1.65
9.03	--	1.41	0.98	1.36	1.35	1.29	1.77
9.10	1.36	1.47	0.99	1.21	1.24	1.10	1.33
9.17	1.15	1.63	1.45	1.53	1.42	1.16	1.38
9.24	1.69	1.59	1.09	1.11	1.23	1.53	1.80
10.01	1.58	1.74	1.40	1.72	1.77	1.72	2.07
10.08	1.43	1.56	1.33	1.55	1.88	1.66	1.89
10.15	2.31	1.93	1.02	1.33	1.23	1.54	1.54
10.22	1.62	1.29	1.05	1.59	1.67	1.51	1.38
10.29	1.76	1.55	1.51	1.52	1.66	1.51	1.58
11.05	2.40	1.66	1.31	1.59	1.54	1.49	1.76
11.12	1.83	1.58	1.72	1.71	1.71	1.62	1.76
11.19	0.91	1.32	1.54	1.62	1.51	1.35	1.54
11.26	1.29	1.29	1.26	1.53	1.54	1.45	1.75
12.03	1.61	1.33	1.39	1.64	1.69	1.46	1.67
12.10	1.07	1.17	1.36	1.54	1.63	1.51	1.88
12.17	1.28	1.37	1.49	1.62	1.68	1.43	1.74
12.24	1.39	1.55	1.43	1.56	1.59	1.33	1.92
12.31	1.37	1.15	1.38	1.55	1.48	1.49	1.75
ABS HI	2.40	2.24	1.86	2.25	2.28	2.48	2.77
AVG	1.49	1.51	1.37	1.64	1.66	1.67	1.95

WEEK ENDING	HIGHEST RATE GICs - 1983 $1 MILLION SIMPLE INTEREST MATURITY							WEEK ENDING	MARKET AVG RATE GICs - 1983 $1 MILLION SIMPLE INTEREST MATURITY						
	1	2	3	4	5	7	10		1	2	3	4	5	7	10
1.07	10.53	11.71	12.16	12.33	12.83	12.97	12.31	1.07	9.69	10.61	11.38	11.64	11.83	11.92	12.05
1.14	10.53	11.27	12.16	12.20	12.84	12.23	12.27	1.14	9.89	10.39	10.95	11.41	11.77	11.67	11.85
1.21	10.70	11.77	12.16	12.20	12.53	12.67	12.53	1.21	9.87	10.45	11.14	11.38	11.60	11.75	12.13
1.28	10.70	11.96	12.16	12.20	12.63	12.47	12.77	1.28	9.66	10.53	11.27	11.62	11.95	12.08	12.35
2.04	10.80	11.95	12.16	12.20	12.63	12.56	12.86	2.04	9.66	10.56	11.31	11.60	11.90	11.95	12.16
2.11	10.80	11.95	12.16	12.20	12.66	12.47	12.86	2.11	9.66	10.67	11.37	11.61	11.95	11.98	12.18
2.18	9.09	11.10	12.20	12.30	12.74	12.63	12.66	2.18	9.08	10.61	11.40	11.73	12.08	12.26	12.23
2.25	10.80	11.67	12.16	12.30	12.54	12.53	12.47	2.25	9.87	10.81	11.23	11.45	11.83	11.99	12.18
3.04	10.60	11.54	12.16	12.30	12.54	12.23	12.40	3.04	9.72	10.73	11.26	11.49	11.81	11.93	12.22
3.11	10.95	11.64	12.16	12.30	12.66	12.33	12.40	3.11	10.02	10.65	11.27	11.46	11.75	11.94	12.09
3.18	10.95	11.65	12.16	12.30	12.66	12.33	12.27	3.18	9.93	10.76	11.32	11.55	11.86	11.82	11.68
3.25	10.95	11.76	12.16	12.30	12.54	12.43	12.39	3.25	9.96	10.61	11.29	11.49	11.79	11.78	12.02
4.01	10.95	11.22	11.92	12.30	12.54	12.12	12.15	4.01	10.05	10.70	11.30	11.51	11.72	11.81	11.96
4.08	10.70	11.10	11.56	12.05	12.36	11.92	12.22	4.08	9.80	10.53	10.98	11.27	11.63	11.58	11.89
4.15	9.80	10.96	11.70	11.85	12.34	12.32	12.31	4.15	9.69	10.43	11.08	11.25	11.53	11.60	11.78
4.22	9.75	11.30	11.66	11.70	11.86	12.02	12.26	4.22	9.40	10.35	10.99	11.06	11.30	11.57	11.72
4.29	9.75	10.64	11.33	11.67	12.04	12.13	12.00	4.29	9.43	10.21	10.87	11.05	11.39	11.46	11.58
5.06	9.85	10.62	11.33	11.58	12.04	11.92	11.99	5.06	9.18	10.02	10.57	10.83	11.21	11.12	11.45
5.13	9.60	10.54	11.18	11.30	11.74	11.67	11.90	5.13	9.17	9.95	10.62	10.85	11.14	11.22	11.74
5.20	9.80	11.46	11.07	11.32	11.78	11.87	12.06	5.20	9.10	10.31	10.63	10.90	11.20	11.42	11.52
5.27	9.80	10.83	11.67	11.55	12.17	11.91	12.10	5.27	9.53	10.23	10.83	10.92	11.46	11.36	11.57
6.03	10.00	11.43	11.80	11.67	12.30	12.21	12.41	6.03	9.52	10.53	10.93	11.12	11.52	11.62	11.70
6.10	10.17	11.05	11.56	11.80	12.29	12.22	12.45	6.10	9.87	10.44	10.95	11.17	11.65	11.58	11.76
6.17	10.20	11.18	11.56	11.80	12.29	12.43	12.45	6.17	9.54	10.42	10.97	11.26	11.72	11.77	11.88
6.24	9.69	10.32	11.77	11.67	12.21	12.37	12.72	6.24	9.17	10.05	10.84	11.15	11.68	11.76	12.18
7.01	10.30	11.45	12.16	12.02	12.49	12.42	12.52	7.01	9.71	10.71	11.32	11.55	11.84	11.88	12.09
7.08	10.53	11.74	12.17	12.02	12.49	12.47	12.66	7.08	9.92	10.81	11.50	11.62	11.83	11.92	12.11
7.15	10.60	11.73	12.21	12.38	12.58	12.72	12.92	7.15	10.05	11.01	11.50	11.78	12.15	12.18	12.36
7.22	10.96	11.58	12.37	12.42	12.85	13.34	12.98	7.22	10.04	10.95	11.55	11.86	12.22	12.24	12.38
7.29	11.15	12.19	12.25	12.56	12.98	12.97	13.18	7.29	10.30	11.24	11.80	11.97	12.28	12.44	12.61
8.05	11.35	12.58	12.97	13.13	13.28	13.17	13.16	8.05	10.42	11.47	12.09	12.31	12.59	12.65	12.74
8.12	11.25	12.48	12.97	13.13	13.28	13.18	12.78	8.12	10.98	11.86	12.14	12.32	12.62	12.68	12.53
8.19	11.00	12.12	12.55	12.91	13.26	13.27	13.42	8.19	10.29	11.36	11.94	12.17	12.36	12.51	12.55
8.26	10.57	11.85	12.91	12.91	13.29	13.34	13.42	8.26	10.09	10.95	11.99	12.25	12.53	12.52	12.60
9.02	11.00	12.13	12.82	12.98	13.28	13.07	12.79	9.02	10.87	11.71	12.07	12.31	12.54	12.50	12.49
9.09	11.01	12.13	12.82	12.98	13.28	13.46	12.67	9.09	10.90	11.56	12.05	12.37	12.50	12.68	12.56
9.16	10.90	12.10	12.93	12.96	13.34	13.12	13.27	9.16	10.18	11.39	11.89	12.23	12.47	12.40	12.58
9.23	11.20	12.10	12.93	12.96	13.18	13.27	13.42	9.23	10.22	11.33	12.06	12.21	12.47	12.36	12.35
9.30	11.20	11.95	12.36	12.55	13.34	13.02	13.17	9.30	10.17	11.06	11.80	12.19	12.48	12.44	12.42
10.07	11.20	11.97	12.76	12.55	12.94	13.02	13.17	10.07	10.16	11.26	11.79	11.97	12.33	12.35	12.47
10.14	11.21	12.05	12.82	12.98	13.08	12.75	12.67	10.14	10.61	11.25	11.79	12.09	12.37	12.29	12.32
10.21	10.71	11.74	12.47	12.63	12.93	13.02	13.17	10.21	9.94	11.00	11.61	11.98	12.26	12.36	12.40
10.28	10.88	11.76	12.53	12.44	12.79	12.86	12.67	10.28	10.34	11.08	11.61	11.85	12.15	12.32	12.36
11.04	11.20	11.61	12.56	12.73	13.04	12.92	13.07	11.04	10.26	11.10	11.82	12.02	12.33	12.32	12.53
11.11	10.88	11.62	12.42	12.73	12.98	12.96	13.07	11.11	10.05	10.90	11.68	12.00	12.30	12.39	12.55
11.18	10.90	11.60	12.37	12.63	12.88	12.96	12.52	11.18	10.58	11.09	11.66	11.92	12.27	12.31	12.29
11.25	10.90	11.52	12.43	12.54	12.89	12.74	13.12	11.25	10.49	11.24	11.73	11.92	12.30	12.30	12.46
12.02	11.00	11.52	12.43	12.53	12.73	12.60	12.67	12.02	10.52	11.06	11.63	11.86	12.13	12.17	12.33
12.09	11.00	11.59	12.50	12.73	12.93	12.97	13.12	12.09	10.61	11.37	11.80	12.05	12.29	12.44	12.56
12.16	11.05	11.59	12.58	12.73	13.23	13.47	13.12	12.16	10.67	11.46	11.79	12.13	12.40	12.50	12.63
12.23	11.03	11.60	12.58	12.55	13.23	13.47	13.12	12.23	10.51	11.27	11.91	12.18	12.47	12.61	12.66
12.30	11.10	11.60	12.58	12.99	13.23	13.47	13.12	12.30	10.63	11.16	11.90	12.13	12.37	12.56	12.58
ABS HI	11.35	12.58	12.97	13.13	13.34	13.47	13.42	ABS HI	10.98	11.86	12.14	12.37	12.62	12.68	12.74
AVG	10.65	11.58	12.22	12.34	12.72	12.67	12.69	AVG	10.00	10.85	11.45	11.69	12.00	12.06	12.20

1983 SPREADS - HIGH RATE GICs vs TREASURIES

WEEK ENDING	MATURITY						
	1	2	3	4	5	7	10
1.07	1.91	2.36	2.51	2.48	2.79	2.68	1.95
1.14	2.12	2.10	2.71	2.53	2.96	2.01	1.95
1.21	2.14	2.52	2.61	2.46	2.61	2.39	2.12
1.28	1.87	2.47	2.29	2.15	2.41	1.89	2.09
2.04	1.82	2.27	2.16	2.01	2.25	1.82	1.98
2.11	1.74	2.16	2.10	1.94	2.21	1.69	1.94
2.18	0.11	1.41	2.25	2.18	2.46	2.04	1.91
2.25	2.13	2.29	2.50	2.49	2.59	2.36	2.07
3.04	2.01	2.27	2.68	2.68	2.78	2.26	2.15
3.11	2.02	2.03	2.38	2.39	2.63	2.09	1.89
3.18	1.90	1.99	2.33	2.34	2.58	2.03	1.75
3.25	1.67	1.93	2.13	2.15	2.28	1.92	1.79
4.01	1.61	1.33	1.86	2.13	2.26	1.59	1.53
4.08	1.53	1.38	1.66	2.03	2.23	1.52	1.70
4.15	0.86	1.42	1.99	2.00	2.36	2.06	1.94
4.22	0.77	1.73	1.89	1.80	1.84	1.74	1.88
4.29	0.92	1.20	1.65	1.85	2.09	1.93	1.67
5.06	1.21	1.39	1.90	1.98	2.27	1.85	1.80
5.13	0.90	1.27	1.73	1.65	1.90	1.55	1.69
5.20	0.87	1.92	1.38	1.42	1.68	1.49	1.61
5.27	0.57	1.02	1.72	1.41	1.85	1.36	1.51
6.03	0.57	1.44	1.63	1.33	1.79	1.45	1.62
6.10	0.53	0.89	1.27	1.35	1.68	1.37	1.58
6.17	0.66	1.10	1.36	1.45	1.80	1.73	1.74
6.24	-0.13	0.00	1.32	1.09	1.50	1.53	1.85
7.01	0.52	1.16	1.69	1.38	1.69	1.46	1.51
7.08	0.41	1.17	1.40	1.10	1.42	1.23	1.41
7.15	0.33	1.02	1.29	1.31	1.36	1.35	1.52
7.22	0.78	0.88	1.44	1.34	1.63	2.02	1.62
7.29	0.84	1.36	1.19	1.33	1.59	1.44	1.61
8.05	0.72	1.40	1.59	1.57	1.54	1.29	1.21
8.12	0.48	1.14	1.39	1.39	1.39	1.12	0.68
8.19	0.57	1.19	1.38	1.58	1.77	1.66	1.71
8.26	0.30	1.05	1.88	1.72	1.95	1.87	1.84
9.02	0.43	0.99	1.41	1.41	1.55	1.19	0.85
9.09	0.63	1.18	1.59	1.58	1.72	1.73	0.91
9.16	0.69	1.27	1.79	1.66	1.88	1.48	1.58
9.23	1.19	1.40	1.94	1.78	1.81	1.73	1.83
9.30	1.31	1.39	1.54	1.53	2.12	1.60	1.71
10.07	1.43	1.48	2.02	1.60	1.79	1.68	1.79
10.14	1.29	1.38	1.87	1.82	1.72	1.20	1.07
10.21	1.02	1.23	1.68	1.63	1.73	1.62	1.70
10.28	1.02	1.13	1.55	1.25	1.40	1.28	0.99
11.04	1.28	0.96	1.55	1.51	1.62	1.28	1.32
11.11	0.93	0.90	1.38	1.46	1.48	1.26	1.27
11.18	0.98	0.94	1.41	1.44	1.46	1.34	0.82
11.25	1.00	0.89	1.55	1.42	1.54	1.22	1.53
12.02	0.99	0.83	1.45	1.35	1.35	1.01	1.03
12.09	0.90	0.80	1.40	1.42	1.41	1.21	1.30
12.16	0.90	0.70	1.37	1.31	1.61	1.59	1.19
12.23	0.90	0.74	1.45	1.21	1.68	1.70	1.30
12.30	1.01	0.75	1.48	1.67	1.69	1.73	1.33
ABS HI	2.14	2.52	2.71	2.68	2.96	2.68	2.15
AVG	1.06	1.37	1.77	1.71	1.91	1.64	1.58

1983 SPREADS - MKT AVG RATE GICs vs TREASURIES

WEEK ENDING	MATURITY						
	1	2	3	4	5	7	10
1.07	1.07	1.26	1.73	1.79	1.79	1.63	1.69
1.14	1.48	1.22	1.50	1.74	1.89	1.45	1.53
1.21	1.31	1.20	1.59	1.64	1.68	1.47	1.72
1.28	0.83	1.04	1.40	1.57	1.73	1.50	1.67
2.04	0.68	0.88	1.31	1.41	1.52	1.21	1.28
2.11	0.60	0.88	1.31	1.35	1.50	1.20	1.26
2.18	0.10	0.92	1.45	1.61	1.80	1.67	1.48
2.25	1.20	1.43	1.57	1.64	1.88	1.82	1.78
3.04	1.13	1.46	1.78	1.87	2.05	1.96	1.97
3.11	1.09	1.04	1.49	1.55	1.72	1.70	1.58
3.18	0.88	1.10	1.49	1.59	1.78	1.52	1.16
3.25	0.68	0.78	1.26	1.34	1.53	1.27	1.42
4.01	0.71	0.81	1.24	1.34	1.44	1.28	1.34
4.08	0.63	0.81	1.08	1.25	1.50	1.18	1.37
4.15	0.75	0.89	1.37	1.40	1.55	1.34	1.41
4.22	0.42	0.78	1.22	1.16	1.28	1.29	1.34
4.29	0.60	0.77	1.19	1.23	1.44	1.26	1.25
5.06	0.54	0.79	1.14	1.23	1.44	1.05	1.26
5.13	0.47	0.68	1.17	1.20	1.30	1.10	1.53
5.20	0.17	0.77	0.94	1.00	1.10	1.04	1.07
5.27	0.30	0.42	0.88	0.78	1.14	0.81	0.98
6.03	0.09	0.54	0.76	0.78	1.01	0.86	0.91
6.10	0.23	0.28	0.66	0.72	1.04	0.73	0.89
6.17	0.00	0.34	0.77	0.91	1.23	1.07	1.17
6.24	-0.65	-0.27	0.39	0.57	0.97	0.92	1.31
7.01	-0.07	0.42	0.85	0.91	1.04	0.92	1.08
7.08	-0.20	0.24	0.73	0.70	0.76	0.68	0.86
7.15	-0.22	0.30	0.58	0.71	0.93	0.81	0.96
7.22	-0.14	0.25	0.62	0.78	1.00	0.92	1.02
7.29	-0.01	0.41	0.74	0.74	0.89	0.91	1.04
8.05	-0.21	0.29	0.71	0.75	0.85	0.77	0.79
8.12	0.21	0.52	0.56	0.58	0.73	0.62	0.43
8.19	-0.14	0.43	0.77	0.84	0.87	0.90	0.84
8.26	-0.18	0.15	0.96	1.06	1.19	1.05	1.02
9.02	0.30	0.57	0.66	0.74	0.81	0.62	0.55
9.09	0.52	0.61	0.82	0.97	0.94	0.95	0.80
9.16	-0.03	0.56	0.75	0.93	1.01	0.76	0.89
9.23	0.21	0.63	1.07	1.03	1.10	0.82	0.76
9.30	0.28	0.50	0.98	1.17	1.26	1.02	0.96
10.07	0.39	0.77	1.05	1.02	1.18	1.01	1.09
10.14	0.69	0.58	0.84	0.93	1.01	0.74	0.72
10.21	0.25	0.49	0.82	0.98	1.06	0.96	0.93
10.28	0.48	0.45	0.63	0.66	0.76	0.74	0.68
11.04	0.34	0.45	0.81	0.80	0.91	0.68	0.78
11.11	0.10	0.18	0.64	0.73	0.80	0.69	0.75
11.18	0.66	0.43	0.70	0.73	0.85	0.69	0.59
11.25	0.59	0.61	0.85	0.80	0.95	0.78	0.87
12.02	0.51	0.37	0.65	0.68	0.75	0.58	0.69
12.09	0.51	0.58	0.70	0.74	0.77	0.68	0.74
12.16	0.52	0.57	0.58	0.71	0.78	0.62	0.70
12.23	0.38	0.41	0.78	0.84	0.92	0.84	0.84
12.30	0.54	0.31	0.80	0.81	0.83	0.82	0.79
ABS HI	1.48	1.46	1.78	1.87	2.05	1.96	1.97
AVG	0.42	0.63	0.99	1.06	1.19	1.03	1.09

HIGHEST RATE GICs - 1984
$1 MILLION SIMPLE INTEREST

WEEK ENDING	\multicolumn{7}{c}{MATURITY}						
	1	2	3	4	5	7	10
1.07	10.93	11.60	12.51,	12.74	12.98	13.23	12.91
1.13	10.88	11.60	12.38	12.61	12.90	13.23	12.91
1.20	10.75	11.60	12.37	12.55	12.86	13.23	12.91
1.27	10.75	11.60	12.37	12.55	12.81	13.23	12.91
2.03	10.75	11.60	12.37	12.55	12.79	13.23	12.81
2.10	10.70	11.60	12.38	12.61	12.85	13.16	12.71
2.17	10.70	11.60	12.50	12.45	12.97	13.16	12.71
2.24	10.80	11.60	12.55	12.78	12.98	13.16	12.76
3.02	10.80	11.60	12.42	12.67	12.92	13.16	12.76
3.09	10.98	11.81	12.57	12.83	13.14	13.16	12.86
3.16	11.03	11.91	12.57	12.83	13.14	13.16	12.92
3.23	11.13	12.11	12.58	12.98	13.23	13.27	13.11
3.30	11.30	12.24	12.73	13.13	13.38	13.41	13.11
4.06	11.30	12.24	12.73	13.13	13.38	13.66	13.22
4.13	11.31	12.05	12.81	13.13	13.38	13.66	13.41
4.20	11.38	12.29	12.93	13.28	13.53	13.66	13.41
4.27	11.43	12.38	13.08	13.43	13.68	13.66	13.51
5.04	11.53	12.52	13.17	13.43	13.69	13.67	13.71
5.11	11.95	12.68	13.31	13.56	13.81	13.90	14.02
5.18	12.40	13.05	13.72	13.96	14.21	14.41	14.37
5.25	12.50	13.36	13.72	13.96	14.38	14.41	14.46
6.01	12.75	13.52	13.94	14.28	14.53	14.68	14.44
6.08	12.70	13.24	13.72	14.03	14.05	14.31	14.06
6.15	12.70	13.23	13.78	14.18	14.43	14.31	14.06
6.22	12.70	13.57	13.94	14.18	14.44	14.41	14.10
6.29	12.95	13.66	13.98	14.38	14.69	14.57	14.31
7.06	12.95	13.65	14.06	14.31	14.56	14.68	14.31
7.13	12.95	13.57	14.05	14.30	14.55	14.55	14.31
7.20	12.85	13.44	14.12	14.18	14.43	14.42	14.31
7.27	12.85	13.35	13.82	14.29	14.34	14.24	14.16
8.03	12.70	13.20	13.65	13.84	14.16	13.87	13.50
8.10	12.70	13.04	13.37	13.62	13.89	13.87	13.71
8.17	12.70	12.89	13.42	13.67	13.92	13.92	13.46
8.24	12.51	12.85	13.42	13.67	13.92	13.92	13.36
8.31	12.50	13.08	13.52	13.77	14.02	14.02	13.82
9.07	12.56	13.14	13.42	13.67	13.92	13.98	13.40
9.14	12.36	12.81	13.23	13.23	13.48	13.56	13.36
9.21	11.99	12.55	13.08	13.21	13.57	13.68	13.36
9.28	12.10	12.58	12.97	13.21	13.54	13.48	13.36
10.05	12.19	12.56	12.87	13.18	13.54	13.43	13.26
10.12	12.08	12.48	12.88	13.13	13.54	13.30	13.26
10.19	12.04	12.42	12.71	12.93	13.26	13.24	13.26
10.26	11.42	12.14	12.55	13.08	13.09	13.05	13.01
11.02	11.30	11.64	12.45	12.62	12.89	12.92	12.81
11.09	11.30	11.61	12.17	12.58	12.83	12.83	12.56
11.16	11.35	11.61	12.04	12.58	12.83	12.83	12.41
11.23	11.25	11.47	12.20	12.27	12.54	12.39	12.41
12.07	10.42	11.02	11.53	11.82	12.29	12.29	11.91
12.14	10.38	10.91	11.68	11.93	12.23	12.41	11.92
12.21	9.85	10.65	11.48	11.73	12.04	11.95	12.21
12.28	9.80	10.75	11.37	11.58	12.04	12.09	12.21
ABS HI	12.95	13.66	14.12	14.38	14.69	14.68	14.46
AVG	11.69	12.35	12.93	13.19	13.46	13.53	13.30

MARKET AVG RATE GICs - 1984
$1 MILLION SIMPLE INTEREST

WEEK ENDING	\multicolumn{7}{c}{MATURITY}						
	1	2	3	4	5	7	10
1.06	10.51	11.30	11.86	12.07	12.34	12.41	12.36
1.13	10.51	11.27	11.78	12.05	12.26	12.39	12.35
1.20	10.26	11.06	11.60	11.92	12.15	12.28	12.40
1.27	10.42	11.24	11.65	11.97	12.16	12.31	12.37
2.03	10.38	11.20	11.65	11.95	12.12	12.31	12.31
2.10	10.42	11.27	11.69	11.97	12.16	12.35	12.33
2.17	10.44	11.31	11.76	11.95	12.22	12.38	12.45
2.24	10.55	11.37	11.81	12.09	12.26	12.44	12.42
3.02	10.56	11.42	11.84	12.16	12.30	12.48	12.46
3.09	10.60	11.48	11.86	12.20	12.33	12.55	12.56
3.16	10.66	11.58	11.97	12.29	12.44	12.62	12.62
3.23	10.81	11.72	12.10	12.42	12.59	12.85	12.85
3.30	10.90	11.85	12.16	12.45	12.64	12.93	12.84
4.06	10.91	11.86	12.23	12.52	12.72	12.99	12.92
4.13	10.94	11.84	12.20	12.51	13.11	12.96	12.92
4.20	11.01	11.94	12.32	12.62	13.23	13.06	13.08
4.27	11.09	12.07	12.41	12.66	13.28	13.16	13.13
5.04	11.14	12.28	12.52	12.79	13.01	13.25	13.22
5.11	11.37	12.43	12.74	12.97	13.18	13.47	13.55
5.18	11.64	12.80	13.03	13.33	13.49	13.74	13.64
5.25	11.83	12.92	13.13	13.38	13.57	13.80	13.67
6.01	12.03	13.11	13.35	13.65	13.75	14.05	13.94
6.08	12.02	12.90	13.29	13.54	13.55	13.87	13.65
6.15	12.05	12.86	13.24	13.52	13.72	13.84	13.64
6.22	12.18	13.12	13.38	13.58	13.77	13.93	13.71
6.29	12.33	13.21	13.52	13.80	13.93	14.05	13.83
7.06	12.22	13.23	13.56	13.87	13.99	14.14	13.86
7.13	12.16	13.04	13.45	13.71	13.91	13.96	13.69
7.20	12.14	13.01	13.35	13.60	13.75	13.82	13.60
7.27	12.09	12.89	13.21	13.46	13.65	13.67	13.48
8.03	12.02	12.74	13.01	13.18	13.43	13.46	13.27
8.10	11.92	12.50	12.81	12.98	13.22	13.28	13.23
8.17	11.91	12.51	12.82	12.99	13.19	13.33	13.19
8.24	11.69	12.44	12.77	12.93	13.16	13.28	13.15
8.31	11.70	12.57	12.88	13.01	13.22	13.33	13.22
9.07	11.78	12.59	12.88	13.06	13.25	13.38	13.27
9.14	11.48	12.27	12.66	12.80	13.02	13.07	13.00
9.21	11.32	12.07	12.48	12.66	12.88	12.96	12.86
9.28	11.36	12.13	12.49	12.67	12.91	12.98	12.90
10.05	11.48	12.13	12.48	12.68	12.88	12.96	12.86
10.12	11.38	12.00	12.43	12.60	12.83	12.91	12.78
10.19	11.03	11.73	12.19	12.25	12.55	12.57	12.40
10.26	10.63	11.52	11.88	12.05	12.32	12.29	12.24
11.02	10.56	11.28	11.74	11.86	12.12	12.13	12.01
11.09	10.50	11.14	11.52	11.71	11.91	12.04	11.99
11.16	10.42	11.06	11.48	11.68	11.93	12.05	12.03
11.23	10.28	10.88	11.39	11.58	11.85	11.94	11.98
12.07	9.72	10.61	10.99	11.27	11.54	11.74	11.66
12.14	9.79	10.59	11.04	11.30	11.61	11.79	11.73
12.21	9.51	10.30	10.79	11.09	11.44	11.61	11.77
12.28	9.46	10.26	10.75	11.10	11.46	11.63	11.76
ABS HI	12.33	13.23	13.56	13.87	13.99	14.14	13.94
AVG	11.10	11.94	12.32	12.56	12.79	12.92	12.85

1984 SPREADS - HIGH RATE GICs vs TREASURIES
$1 MILLION SIMPLE INTEREST

WEEK ENDING	MATURITY						
	1	2	3	4	5	7	10
1.06	0.91	0.83	1.47	1.47	1.48	1.52	1.12
1.13	0.97	0.94	1.40	1.41	1.48	1.60	1.20
1.20	0.89	1.04	1.51	1.48	1.57	1.73	1.32
1.27	0.88	0.97	1.48	1.45	1.50	1.71	1.28
2.03	0.94	1.04	1.50	1.46	1.48	1.70	1.18
2.10	0.76	0.93	1.42	1.42	1.42	1.51	0.97
2.17	0.65	0.82	1.46	1.16	1.42	1.41	0.86
2.24	0.59	0.66	1.38	1.36	1.31	1.29	0.79
3.02	0.56	0.60	1.18	1.17	1.17	1.19	0.71
3.09	0.65	0.72	1.19	1.21	1.29	1.07	0.68
3.16	0.50	0.67	1.04	1.07	1.16	0.94	0.63
3.23	0.28	0.59	0.81	1.01	1.06	0.87	0.65
3.30	0.51	0.70	0.93	1.13	1.18	1.02	0.65
4.06	0.39	0.57	0.77	0.97	1.02	1.12	0.61
4.13	0.55	0.50	0.97	1.09	1.14	1.25	0.92
4.20	0.44	0.60	0.94	1.10	1.15	1.08	0.75
4.27	0.45	0.59	1.00	1.16	1.21	1.00	0.77
5.04	0.34	0.56	0.91	0.98	1.04	0.85	0.82
5.11	0.43	0.35	0.72	0.77	0.82	0.73	0.79
5.18	0.72	0.55	0.94	0.95	0.97	1.00	0.88
5.25	0.66	0.71	0.79	0.82	1.03	0.91	0.87
6.01	0.65	0.58	0.69	0.81	0.84	0.86	0.58
6.08	0.78	0.53	0.73	0.86	0.71	0.86	0.59
6.15	0.68	0.40	0.70	0.96	1.07	0.85	0.63
6.22	0.55	0.59	0.70	0.82	0.95	0.86	0.55
6.29	0.67	0.51	0.52	0.79	0.97	0.80	0.52
7.06	0.78	0.53	0.68	0.78	0.89	0.91	0.51
7.13	0.85	0.60	0.86	1.01	1.16	1.09	0.85
7.20	0.82	0.56	1.06	1.03	1.20	1.11	0.99
7.27	0.95	0.65	0.96	1.35	1.31	1.14	1.05
8.03	0.86	0.70	1.02	1.14	1.39	1.04	0.68
8.10	0.90	0.66	0.93	1.09	1.26	1.18	1.04
8.17	0.97	0.49	0.97	1.11	1.25	1.18	0.75
8.24	0.71	0.42	0.96	1.11	1.26	1.22	0.70
8.31	0.53	0.53	0.92	1.08	1.23	1.16	1.00
9.07	0.61	0.59	0.79	0.93	1.08	1.07	0.57
9.14	0.75	0.57	0.89	0.78	0.93	0.96	0.85
9.21	0.58	0.51	0.89	0.94	1.23	1.26	1.01
9.28	0.68	0.52	0.70	0.85	1.08	0.95	0.90
10.05	0.80	0.53	0.61	0.82	1.08	0.87	0.75
10.12	0.92	0.66	0.82	0.97	1.28	0.91	0.93
10.19	1.11	0.79	0.83	0.94	1.16	1.05	1.07
10.26	0.96	0.92	1.07	1.49	1.40	1.25	1.16
11.02	0.99	0.56	1.12	1.17	1.31	1.23	1.05
11.09	1.32	0.77	1.11	1.31	1.36	1.20	0.85
11.16	1.36	0.79	0.99	1.29	1.30	1.17	0.66
11.23	1.61	0.98	1.45	1.29	1.33	1.03	0.97
12.07	0.79	0.55	0.73	0.81	1.08	0.77	0.33
12.14	0.89	0.55	0.97	0.98	1.04	0.85	0.31
12.21	0.76	0.71	1.16	1.12	1.14	0.64	0.84
12.28	0.70	0.81	0.98	0.90	1.08	0.70	0.79
ABS HI	1.61	1.04	1.51	1.49	1.57	1.73	1.32
AVG	0.76	0.66	0.99	1.08	1.18	1.09	0.82

1984 SPREADS - MARKET AVG RATE GICs vs TREASURIES
$1 MILLION SIMPLE INTEREST

WEEK ENDING	MATURITY						
	1	2	3	4	5	7	10
1.06	0.49	0.53	0.82	0.80	0.84	0.70	0.57
1.13	0.60	0.61	0.80	0.85	0.84	0.76	0.64
1.20	0.40	0.50	0.74	0.85	0.86	0.78	0.81
1.27	0.55	0.61	0.76	0.87	0.85	0.79	0.74
2.03	0.57	0.64	0.78	0.86	0.81	0.78	0.68
2.10	0.48	0.60	0.73	0.77	0.73	0.70	0.59
2.17	0.39	0.53	0.72	0.66	0.67	0.63	0.60
2.24	0.34	0.43	0.64	0.67	0.59	0.57	0.45
3.02	0.32	0.42	0.60	0.66	0.55	0.51	0.41
3.09	0.27	0.39	0.48	0.59	0.48	0.46	0.38
3.16	0.13	0.34	0.44	0.53	0.46	0.40	0.33
3.23	-0.04	0.20	0.33	0.45	0.42	0.45	0.39
3.30	0.11	0.31	0.36	0.45	0.44	0.54	0.38
4.06	0.00	0.19	0.27	0.36	0.36	0.45	0.31
4.13	0.18	0.29	0.36	0.47	0.87	0.55	0.43
4.20	0.07	0.25	0.33	0.43	0.85	0.48	0.42
4.27	0.11	0.28	0.33	0.38	0.81	0.50	0.39
5.04	-0.05	0.32	0.26	0.34	0.36	0.43	0.33
5.11	-0.15	0.10	0.15	0.18	0.19	0.30	0.32
5.18	-0.04	0.30	0.25	0.32	0.25	0.33	0.15
5.25	-0.01	0.27	0.20	0.24	0.22	0.30	0.08
6.01	-0.07	0.17	0.10	0.18	0.06	0.23	0.08
6.08	0.10	0.19	0.30	0.37	0.21	0.42	0.18
6.15	0.03	0.03	0.16	0.30	0.36	0.38	0.21
6.22	0.03	0.14	0.14	0.21	0.28	0.38	0.16
6.29	0.05	0.06	0.06	0.21	0.21	0.28	0.04
7.06	0.05	0.11	0.18	0.34	0.32	0.37	0.06
7.13	0.06	0.07	0.26	0.42	0.52	0.50	0.23
7.20	0.11	0.13	0.29	0.45	0.52	0.51	0.28
7.27	0.19	0.19	0.35	0.51	0.62	0.57	0.37
8.03	0.18	0.24	0.38	0.48	0.66	0.63	0.45
8.10	0.12	0.12	0.37	0.44	0.59	0.59	0.56
8.17	0.18	0.11	0.37	0.43	0.52	0.59	0.48
8.24	-0.11	0.01	0.31	0.37	0.50	0.58	0.49
8.31	-0.27	0.02	0.28	0.32	0.43	0.47	0.40
9.07	-0.17	0.04	0.25	0.32	0.41	0.47	0.44
9.14	-0.13	0.03	0.32	0.35	0.47	0.47	0.49
9.21	-0.09	0.03	0.29	0.39	0.54	0.54	0.51
9.28	-0.06	0.07	0.22	0.30	0.45	0.45	0.44
10.05	0.09	0.10	0.22	0.32	0.42	0.40	0.35
10.12	0.22	0.18	0.37	0.44	0.57	0.52	0.45
10.19	0.10	0.10	0.31	0.26	0.45	0.38	0.21
10.26	0.17	0.30	0.40	0.46	0.63	0.49	0.39
11.02	0.25	0.20	0.41	0.41	0.54	0.44	0.25
11.09	0.52	0.30	0.46	0.44	0.44	0.41	0.28
11.16	0.43	0.24	0.43	0.39	0.40	0.39	0.28
11.23	0.64	0.39	0.64	0.60	0.64	0.58	0.54
12.07	0.09	0.14	0.19	0.26	0.33	0.22	0.08
12.14	0.30	0.23	0.33	0.35	0.42	0.23	0.12
12.21	0.42	0.36	0.47	0.48	0.54	0.30	0.40
12.28	0.36	0.32	0.36	0.43	0.50	0.24	0.34
ABS HI	0.64	0.64	0.82	0.87	0.87	0.79	0.81
AVG	0.17	0.25	0.38	0.45	0.51	0.48	0.37

HIGHEST RATE GICs - 1985
$1 MILLION SIMPLE INTEREST

WEEK ENDING	1	2	3	4	5	7	10
1.04	9.95	10.91	11.63	11.88	12.08	12.13	12.60
1.11	9.90	10.82	11.38	11.68	12.04	12.13	12.41
1.18	9.97	10.74	11.47	11.71	12.08	12.13	12.60
1.25	9.72	10.46	11.28	11.58	12.14	11.99	12.41
2.01	9.72	10.56	11.28	11.58	11.94	11.89	12.31
2.08	9.98	10.82	11.35	11.63	11.94	12.08	12.46
2.15	9.72	10.72	11.27	11.53	12.04	12.08	12.46
2.22	9.77	10.84	11.43	11.83	12.12	12.27	12.46
3.01	10.20	11.14	11.73	11.98	12.43	12.48	12.61
3.08	10.32	11.28	11.87	12.18	12.38	12.73	12.61
3.15	10.43	11.25	11.84	12.04	12.38	12.73	12.64
3.22	10.43	11.25	11.93	12.33	12.64	13.03	12.76
3.29	10.40	11.41	11.84	12.18	12.64	13.03	12.76
4.05	10.23	11.25	11.82	12.15	12.64	12.67	12.76
4.12	10.07	10.86	11.66	11.87	12.34	12.52	12.76
4.19	9.80	10.82	11.61	11.63	12.39	12.46	12.51
4.26	9.80	10.75	11.34	11.63	12.39	12.29	12.36
5.03	9.70	10.60	11.43	11.67	12.14	12.29	12.36
5.10	9.60	10.58	11.37	11.62	12.02	12.25	12.36
5.17	9.27	10.40	11.03	11.42	11.89	12.03	11.98
5.24	9.08	10.27	10.63	10.99	11.42	11.56	11.80
5.31	8.93	9.79	10.44	10.86	11.19	11.27	11.61
6.07	8.43	9.23	10.07	10.49	11.14	10.88	11.13
6.14	8.55	9.71	10.13	10.49	11.04	11.20	11.23
6.21	8.43	9.34	10.13	10.53	10.98	11.17	11.31
6.28	8.80	9.57	10.29	10.68	11.19	11.49	11.65
7.05	8.55	9.41	10.19	10.64	10.99	11.29	11.01
7.12	8.68	9.35	10.13	10.64	10.97	11.18	11.01
7.19	8.55	9.27	10.13	10.64	10.97	11.18	11.19
7.26	8.80	9.62	10.48	10.86	11.03	11.53	11.59
8.02	9.09	10.04	10.64	11.00	11.18	11.37	11.20
8.09	9.25	10.04	10.63	10.96	11.36	11.37	11.52
8.16	8.93	9.82	10.55	10.96	11.28	11.63	11.54
8.23	8.79	9.69	10.44	11.00	11.29	11.47	11.52
8.30	8.84	9.84	10.44	10.96	11.24	11.37	11.52
9.06	8.99	9.89	10.39	10.86	11.18	11.47	11.41
9.13	8.95	9.82	10.57	11.01	11.30	11.52	11.47
9.20	8.85	9.72	10.53	11.01	11.30	11.42	11.47
9.27	8.95	9.85	10.55	11.01	11.30	11.48	11.47
10.04	8.95	9.85	10.53	11.01	11.36	11.48	11.47
10.11	9.00	9.85	10.55	11.03	11.36	11.48	11.47
10.18	8.85	9.62	10.52	11.01	11.32	11.45	11.47
10.25	8.94	9.48	10.52	11.01	11.32	11.45	11.46
11.01	8.73	9.33	10.41	10.93	11.24	11.26	11.18
11.08	8.63	9.20	10.17	10.60	11.24	11.21	10.93
11.15	8.58	9.10	10.19	10.53	10.99	11.21	10.93
11.22	8.55	9.02	10.15	10.45	10.69	11.08	10.68
11.29	8.55	9.13	10.15	10.40	10.64	11.08	10.68
12.06	8.54	8.88	10.09	10.25	10.54	10.98	10.42
12.13	8.49	8.64	9.76	10.10	10.29	10.58	10.58
12.20	8.59	8.53	9.52	9.80	10.04	10.43	9.97
12.27	7.98	8.41	9.52	9.75	9.99	10.33	9.82
ABS HI	10.43	11.41	11.93	12.33	12.64	13.03	12.76
AVG	9.21	10.01	10.77	11.13	11.50	11.67	11.69

MARKET AVG RATE GICs - 1985
$1 MILLION SIMPLE INTEREST

WEEK ENDING	1	2	3	4	5	7	10
1.04	9.58	10.40	10.89	11.20	11.57	11.80	12.00
1.11	9.34	10.38	10.85	11.14	11.55	11.80	11.99
1.18	9.41	10.36	10.83	11.14	11.55	11.77	11.95
1.25	9.09	10.10	10.53	10.84	11.29	11.50	11.69
2.01	9.05	10.14	10.52	10.84	11.25	11.48	11.62
2.08	9.25	10.25	10.72	11.05	11.43	11.67	11.84
2.15	9.20	10.30	10.70	11.04	11.45	11.66	11.84
2.22	9.54	10.47	10.85	11.29	11.59	11.89	12.10
3.01	9.61	10.75	11.14	11.46	11.81	12.09	12.27
3.08	9.96	10.89	11.31	11.62	11.99	12.22	12.31
3.15	9.99	10.90	11.38	11.74	12.04	12.33	12.37
3.22	10.10	11.02	11.46	11.80	12.13	12.36	12.42
3.29	9.82	10.92	11.37	11.67	12.01	12.28	12.31
4.05	9.62	10.77	11.22	11.55	11.89	12.16	12.22
4.12	9.60	10.49	11.03	11.34	11.73	11.97	12.07
4.19	9.19	10.21	10.72	11.13	11.50	11.66	11.76
4.26	9.15	10.23	10.64	11.08	11.38	11.63	11.80
5.03	9.28	10.24	10.78	11.13	11.46	11.68	11.81
5.10	9.20	10.15	10.62	11.02	11.34	11.54	11.72
5.17	8.90	9.86	10.35	10.69	11.06	11.26	11.42
5.24	8.61	9.53	9.91	10.31	10.62	10.90	11.09
5.31	8.56	9.42	9.83	10.13	10.51	10.77	10.98
6.07	8.07	8.86	9.34	9.68	10.10	10.30	10.43
6.14	8.11	9.05	9.46	9.79	10.24	10.47	10.56
6.21	8.03	8.95	9.34	9.69	10.10	10.54	10.53
6.28	8.11	9.15	9.59	9.92	10.38	10.72	10.78
7.05	8.11	9.05	9.57	9.86	10.29	10.60	10.63
7.12	7.94	8.93	9.45	9.78	10.17	10.54	10.64
7.19	7.88	8.91	9.53	9.82	10.24	10.58	10.69
7.26	8.21	9.23	9.77	10.12	10.49	10.86	10.92
8.02	8.51	9.44	9.92	10.26	10.63	10.96	10.99
8.09	8.60	9.45	10.01	10.28	10.74	11.00	11.11
8.16	8.47	9.30	9.91	10.17	10.62	10.92	10.96
8.23	8.26	9.15	9.76	10.07	10.49	10.74	10.77
8.30	8.25	9.18	9.78	10.06	10.43	10.71	10.72
9.06	8.44	9.32	9.83	10.14	10.54	10.82	10.84
9.13	8.55	9.47	10.00	10.25	10.63	10.95	10.90
9.20	8.40	9.32	9.93	10.14	10.56	10.84	10.88
9.27	8.46	9.19	9.81	10.08	10.48	10.78	10.79
10.04	8.38	9.23	9.83	10.06	10.49	10.82	10.81
10.11	8.52	9.33	9.87	10.16	10.55	10.84	10.87
10.18	8.43	9.23	9.81	10.13	10.48	10.73	10.77
10.25	8.42	9.19	9.78	10.11	10.48	10.72	10.82
11.01	8.24	8.99	9.63	9.95	10.31	10.52	10.58
11.08	8.17	8.89	9.55	9.85	10.21	10.42	10.39
11.15	8.15	8.87	9.48	9.71	10.10	10.35	10.33
11.22	8.09	8.72	9.26	9.58	9.91	10.15	10.16
11.29	8.13	8.75	9.28	9.55	9.87	10.12	10.17
12.06	8.04	8.67	9.20	9.49	9.78	10.04	10.08
12.13	7.91	8.27	8.89	9.17	9.52	9.76	9.78
12.20	7.80	8.12	8.70	8.95	9.26	9.53	9.48
12.27	7.60	8.01	8.57	8.84	9.12	9.40	9.41
ABS HI	10.10	11.02	11.46	11.80	12.13	12.36	12.42
AVG	8.70	9.58	10.09	10.40	10.78	11.04	11.12

1985 SPREADS - HIGH RATE GICs vs TREASURIES

WEEK ENDING	MATURITY 1	2	3	4	5	7	10
1.04	0.76	0.86	1.06	1.02	0.93	0.54	0.97
1.11	0.86	0.81	0.87	0.89	0.97	0.74	0.91
1.18	0.92	0.75	0.98	0.96	1.07	0.78	1.11
1.25	0.82	0.67	1.04	1.11	1.44	0.97	1.25
2.01	0.69	0.70	0.94	1.03	1.18	0.85	1.16
2.08	0.80	0.79	0.93	0.93	0.95	0.80	1.09
2.15	0.53	0.70	0.87	0.84	1.05	0.78	1.09
2.22	0.47	0.65	0.88	0.97	0.95	0.77	0.89
3.01	0.59	0.61	0.82	0.79	0.96	0.70	0.78
3.08	0.43	0.55	0.80	0.89	0.87	0.90	0.74
3.15	0.52	0.52	0.76	0.73	0.84	0.89	0.79
3.22	0.46	0.44	0.80	0.96	1.04	1.13	0.84
3.29	0.72	0.82	0.91	1.00	1.21	1.30	0.99
4.05	0.70	0.76	0.99	1.07	1.32	1.03	1.05
4.12	0.75	0.57	1.00	0.94	1.15	1.03	1.19
4.19	0.85	0.94	1.33	1.09	1.58	1.31	1.27
4.26	0.91	0.91	1.05	1.09	1.60	1.13	1.09
5.03	0.78	0.75	1.11	1.08	1.29	1.08	1.03
5.10	0.87	0.90	1.31	1.25	1.34	1.19	1.19
5.17	0.75	0.96	1.28	1.35	1.50	1.25	1.09
5.24	0.86	1.14	1.20	1.24	1.36	1.11	1.20
5.31	0.84	0.78	1.08	1.26	1.35	1.02	1.22
6.07	0.63	0.60	1.10	1.28	1.69	0.95	1.13
6.14	0.70	0.99	1.07	1.16	1.44	1.14	1.11
6.21	0.77	0.79	1.23	1.33	1.48	1.16	1.23
6.28	0.89	0.72	1.02	1.12	1.34	1.17	1.22
7.05	0.89	0.83	1.21	1.38	1.46	1.31	0.87
7.12	0.95	0.73	1.17	1.41	1.47	1.21	0.89
7.19	0.73	0.54	1.00	1.25	1.33	1.10	0.96
7.26	0.77	0.65	1.07	1.20	1.12	1.17	1.08
8.02	0.95	0.99	1.13	1.24	1.17	0.92	0.59
8.09	1.10	0.98	1.17	1.24	1.38	0.99	0.99
8.16	0.86	0.87	1.27	1.40	1.44	1.39	1.17
8.23	0.84	0.84	1.26	1.57	1.62	1.43	1.36
8.30	0.87	0.98	1.22	1.52	1.58	1.32	1.35
9.06	0.95	0.92	1.03	1.30	1.42	1.29	1.12
9.13	0.75	0.71	1.06	1.28	1.35	1.16	0.99
9.20	0.74	0.67	1.10	1.37	1.45	1.15	1.07
9.27	1.07	1.07	1.38	1.60	1.64	1.35	1.17
10.04	0.99	1.00	1.28	1.53	1.65	1.32	1.15
10.11	0.94	0.89	1.20	1.44	1.54	1.22	1.10
10.18	0.84	0.75	1.27	1.54	1.62	1.34	1.24
10.25	0.91	0.63	1.31	1.59	1.69	1.43	1.30
11.01	0.76	0.57	1.28	1.59	1.69	1.35	1.11
11.08	0.72	0.54	1.17	1.41	1.86	1.47	1.01
11.15	0.70	0.50	1.25	1.41	1.69	1.58	1.11
11.22	0.70	0.50	1.37	1.45	1.48	1.55	1.00
11.29	0.68	0.62	1.41	1.45	1.48	1.56	1.03
12.06	0.64	0.38	1.34	1.31	1.42	1.46	0.77
12.13	0.84	0.52	1.35	1.52	1.53	1.43	1.27
12.20	1.02	0.53	1.29	1.41	1.49	1.49	0.88
12.27	0.39	0.41	1.28	1.36	1.46	1.43	0.78
ABS HI	1.10	1.14	1.41	1.60	1.86	1.58	1.36
AVG	0.78	0.74	1.12	1.23	1.36	1.16	1.06

1985 SPREADS - MARKET AVG RATE GICs vs TREASURIES

WEEK ENDING	MATURITY 1	2	3	4	5	7	10
1.04	0.39	0.35	0.32	0.34	0.42	0.21	0.37
1.11	0.30	0.37	0.34	0.35	0.48	0.41	0.49
1.18	0.36	0.37	0.34	0.39	0.54	0.42	0.46
1.25	0.19	0.31	0.29	0.37	0.59	0.48	0.53
2.01	0.02	0.28	0.18	0.29	0.49	0.44	0.47
2.08	0.07	0.22	0.30	0.34	0.44	0.39	0.47
2.15	0.01	0.28	0.30	0.34	0.46	0.36	0.47
2.22	0.24	0.28	0.30	0.43	0.42	0.39	0.53
3.01	0.00	0.22	0.23	0.27	0.34	0.31	0.44
3.08	0.07	0.16	0.24	0.33	0.48	0.39	0.44
3.15	0.08	0.26	0.30	0.43	0.50	0.49	0.52
3.22	0.13	0.21	0.33	0.43	0.53	0.46	0.50
3.29	0.14	0.33	0.44	0.49	0.58	0.55	0.54
4.05	0.09	0.28	0.39	0.47	0.57	0.52	0.51
4.12	0.28	0.20	0.37	0.41	0.54	0.48	0.50
4.19	0.24	0.33	0.44	0.59	0.69	0.51	0.52
4.26	0.26	0.39	0.35	0.54	0.59	0.47	0.53
5.03	0.36	0.39	0.46	0.54	0.61	0.47	0.48
5.10	0.47	0.47	0.56	0.65	0.66	0.48	0.55
5.17	0.38	0.42	0.60	0.62	0.67	0.48	0.53
5.24	0.39	0.40	0.48	0.56	0.56	0.45	0.49
5.31	0.47	0.41	0.47	0.53	0.67	0.52	0.59
6.07	0.27	0.23	0.37	0.47	0.65	0.37	0.43
6.14	0.26	0.33	0.40	0.46	0.64	0.41	0.44
6.21	0.37	0.40	0.44	0.49	0.60	0.53	0.45
6.28	0.20	0.30	0.32	0.36	0.53	0.40	0.35
7.05	0.45	0.47	0.59	0.60	0.76	0.62	0.49
7.12	0.21	0.31	0.49	0.55	0.67	0.57	0.52
7.19	0.06	0.18	0.40	0.43	0.60	0.50	0.46
7.26	0.18	0.26	0.36	0.46	0.58	0.50	0.41
8.02	0.37	0.39	0.41	0.50	0.62	0.51	0.38
8.09	0.45	0.39	0.55	0.56	0.76	0.62	0.58
8.16	0.40	0.35	0.63	0.61	0.78	0.68	0.59
8.23	0.31	0.30	0.58	0.64	0.82	0.70	0.61
8.30	0.28	0.32	0.56	0.62	0.77	0.66	0.55
9.06	0.40	0.35	0.47	0.58	0.78	0.64	0.55
9.13	0.35	0.36	0.49	0.52	0.68	0.59	0.42
9.20	0.29	0.27	0.50	0.50	0.71	0.57	0.48
9.27	0.58	0.41	0.64	0.66	0.82	0.65	0.49
10.04	0.42	0.38	0.58	0.58	0.78	0.66	0.49
10.11	0.46	0.37	0.52	0.57	0.73	0.58	0.50
10.18	0.42	0.36	0.56	0.66	0.78	0.62	0.54
10.25	0.39	0.34	0.57	0.69	0.85	0.70	0.66
11.01	0.27	0.23	0.50	0.61	0.76	0.61	0.51
11.08	0.26	0.23	0.55	0.66	0.83	0.68	0.47
11.15	0.27	0.27	0.54	0.59	0.80	0.72	0.51
11.22	0.24	0.20	0.48	0.58	0.70	0.62	0.48
11.29	0.26	0.24	0.54	0.60	0.71	0.60	0.52
12.06	0.14	0.17	0.45	0.55	0.66	0.52	0.43
12.13	0.26	0.15	0.48	0.58	0.76	0.61	0.47
12.20	0.23	0.12	0.47	0.56	0.71	0.59	0.39
12.27	0.01	0.01	0.33	0.45	0.59	0.50	0.37
ABS HI	0.58	0.47	0.64	0.69	0.85	0.72	0.66
AVG	0.27	0.30	0.44	0.51	0.64	0.52	0.49

HIGHEST RATE GICs - 1986
$1 MILLION SIMPLE INTEREST

WEEK ENDING	1	2	3	4	5	7	10
1.03	8.54	8.36	9.41	9.73	9.94	10.33	9.82
1.10	8.31	8.60	9.51	9.75	9.99	10.43	10.12
1.17	8.39	8.72	9.71	9.85	10.09	10.38	10.07
1.24	8.49	8.66	9.56	9.75	10.19	10.43	10.13
1.31	8.34	8.51	9.56	9.85	10.09	10.43	9.93
2.07	8.54	8.68	9.51	9.80	10.09	10.38	9.92
2.14	8.25	8.41	9.41	9.65	9.99	10.23	10.03
2.21	8.15	8.36	9.36	9.55	9.89	10.13	9.82
2.28	8.05	8.19	9.01	9.20	9.44	9.63	9.50
3.07	7.74	8.11	8.76	9.00	9.29	9.43	8.95
3.14	7.47	7.63	8.56	8.70	8.94	9.13	8.82
3.21	7.57	7.66	8.56	8.70	8.89	9.08	8.72
3.28	7.75	7.72	8.41	8.60	8.94	9.03	8.42
4.04	7.54	7.63	8.36	8.50	8.74	8.98	8.40
4.11	7.20	7.29	8.12	8.35	8.54	8.83	8.33
4.18	7.10	7.17	7.91	8.20	8.46	8.58	8.16
4.25	7.30	7.46	8.26	8.60	8.79	8.98	8.48
5.02	7.22	7.56	8.26	8.55	8.74	8.93	8.52
5.09	7.22	7.56	8.41	8.70	8.89	9.53	8.52
5.16	7.64	7.98	8.61	8.85	9.14	9.33	8.74
5.23	7.59	8.12	8.76	9.00	9.29	9.48	8.79
5.30	7.74	8.12	8.81	9.10	9.39	9.58	8.98
6.06	8.00	8.26	9.26	9.55	9.69	9.83	9.29
6.13	7.65	8.31	9.16	9.45	9.59	9.73	9.40
6.20	7.73	8.30	8.76	9.05	9.19	9.49	9.13
6.27	7.58	8.06	8.64	8.85	9.11	9.31	9.13
7.03	7.48	7.91	8.65	8.81	8.96	9.09	8.85
7.11	7.40	7.91	8.65	8.81	8.96	9.09	8.85
7.18	7.35	7.78	8.87	8.81	9.18	9.09	8.85
7.25	7.93	7.96	8.51	8.85	9.03	9.23	8.85
8.01	7.45	7.81	8.55	8.81	9.05	9.12	8.85
8.08	7.25	7.68	8.38	8.81	8.90	9.09	8.85
8.15	7.13	7.68	8.38	8.81	8.96	8.94	8.85
8.22	6.87	7.23	8.08	8.29	8.96	8.75	8.44
8.29	6.57	7.10	8.08	8.29	8.91	8.75	8.44
9.05	6.84	7.61	8.00	8.29	8.64	8.97	8.63
9.12	6.84	7.46	8.20	8.59	8.83	8.97	9.22
9.19	6.99	7.50	8.21	8.58	8.94	9.27	9.08
9.26	6.93	7.55	8.22	8.58	8.94	9.15	9.06
10.03	6.74	7.48	8.25	8.56	8.89	9.09	9.09
10.10	6.74	7.60	8.23	8.56	8.83	9.09	8.95
10.17	6.77	7.50	8.15	8.54	8.83	9.18	8.98
10.24	6.85	7.50	8.23	8.51	8.85	9.23	9.07
10.31	6.70	7.48	8.08	8.39	8.68	8.93	8.97
11.07	6.69	7.48	8.13	8.46	8.73	8.93	8.97
11.14	6.69	7.48	8.13	8.46	8.73	8.98	9.52
11.21	6.61	7.48	8.03	8.36	8.43	8.89	8.87
12.05	6.58	7.30	8.03	8.11	8.43	8.73	8.72
12.12	6.65	7.26	8.00	8.14	8.43	8.77	8.72
12.19	6.79	7.45	7.91	8.19	8.48	8.82	8.72
12.26	6.42	--	7.81	8.11	8.43	8.73	8.72
ABS HI	8.54	8.72	9.71	9.85	10.19	10.43	10.13
AVG	7.38	7.81	8.56	8.81	9.09	9.30	9.02

MARKET AVG RATE GICs - 1986
$1 MILLION SIMPLE INTEREST

WEEK ENDING	1	2	3	4	5	7	10
1.03	7.70	8.03	8.56	8.84	9.12	9.42	9.49
1.10	7.82	8.23	8.69	8.98	9.23	9.57	9.68
1.17	8.07	8.43	8.84	9.11	9.41	9.67	9.68
1.24	8.04	8.39	8.84	9.11	9.42	9.66	9.70
1.31	7.86	8.22	8.65	8.97	9.24	9.48	9.58
2.07	7.91	8.24	8.69	8.94	9.22	9.52	9.58
2.14	7.87	8.15	8.60	8.83	9.19	9.41	9.45
2.21	7.79	8.08	8.51	8.70	8.96	9.13	9.18
2.28	7.65	7.86	8.21	8.42	8.66	8.78	8.79
3.07	7.38	7.59	7.94	8.11	8.38	8.54	8.45
3.14	7.20	7.33	7.70	7.91	8.19	8.35	8.34
3.21	7.22	7.32	7.76	7.94	8.21	8.40	8.30
3.28	7.16	7.27	7.70	7.83	8.12	8.22	8.10
4.04	6.95	7.12	7.54	7.75	7.98	8.12	8.03
4.11	6.69	6.87	7.40	7.57	7.83	7.99	7.88
4.18	6.50	6.68	7.19	7.39	7.65	7.80	7.81
4.25	6.72	7.05	7.54	7.74	7.99	8.18	8.18
5.02	6.79	7.14	7.62	7.75	8.02	8.18	8.09
5.09	6.75	7.14	7.66	7.80	8.06	8.26	8.23
5.16	6.94	7.36	7.83	8.07	8.06	8.54	8.46
5.23	7.15	7.63	8.03	8.23	8.51	8.70	8.65
5.30	7.22	7.72	8.13	8.36	8.60	8.79	8.75
6.06	7.43	7.93	8.33	8.58	8.82	8.99	8.99
6.13	7.20	7.77	8.20	8.40	8.67	8.82	8.67
6.20	7.15	7.71	8.04	8.28	8.53	8.71	8.58
6.27	7.03	7.51	7.90	8.15	8.40	8.50	8.36
7.03	6.93	7.43	7.84	8.09	8.34	8.42	8.36
7.11	6.58	7.25	7.71	7.95	8.21	8.33	8.33
7.18	6.70	7.21	7.47	7.90	8.19	8.30	8.29
7.25	7.38	7.22	7.67	7.91	8.23	8.34	8.36
8.01	6.56	7.22	7.70	7.93	8.21	8.37	8.39
8.08	6.53	7.23	7.66	7.94	8.23	8.41	8.50
8.15	6.36	7.08	7.53	7.81	8.13	8.26	8.35
8.22	6.40	6.89	7.31	7.63	7.97	8.10	8.19
8.29	6.20	6.75	7.23	7.56	7.90	8.09	8.14
9.05	6.20	6.92	7.37	7.69	8.00	8.20	8.27
9.12	6.23	7.08	7.51	7.87	8.19	8.39	8.60
9.19	6.33	6.72	7.67	7.98	8.32	8.56	8.77
9.26	6.34	7.02	7.60	7.90	8.25	8.50	8.65
10.03	6.22	6.83	7.46	7.77	8.15	8.40	8.57
10.10	6.15	6.82	7.39	7.74	8.06	8.35	8.54
10.17	6.21	6.10	7.45	7.82	8.12	8.44	8.61
10.24	6.30	6.96	7.47	7.76	8.14	8.45	8.62
10.31	6.22	6.85	7.35	7.68	8.02	8.32	8.53
11.07	6.21	6.86	7.36	7.73	8.05	8.34	8.60
11.14	6.31	6.91	7.39	7.74	8.06	8.35	8.71
11.21	6.24	6.83	7.33	7.66	7.99	8.26	8.53
12.05	6.19	6.69	7.25	7.53	7.86	8.10	8.43
12.12	6.21	6.72	7.24	7.51	7.84	8.07	8.39
12.19	6.27	6.79	7.16	7.53	7.84	8.06	8.36
12.26	6.21	--	7.14	7.52	7.88	8.12	8.30
ABS HI	8.07	8.43	8.84	9.11	9.42	9.67	9.70
AVG	6.86	7.30	7.77	8.03	8.32	8.53	8.59

1986 SPREADS - HIGH RATE GICs vs TREASURIES

WEEK ENDING	MATURITY						
	1	2	3	4	5	7	10
1.03	0.91	0.35	1.16	1.35	1.44	1.43	0.79
1.10	0.57	0.45	1.12	1.23	1.34	1.42	0.96
1.17	0.53	0.45	1.14	1.13	1.23	1.20	0.72
1.24	0.76	0.49	1.10	1.14	1.44	1.36	0.89
1.31	0.72	0.48	1.27	1.42	1.53	1.53	0.84
2.07	0.91	0.67	1.30	1.43	1.57	1.53	0.90
2.14	0.56	0.36	1.24	1.34	1.55	1.50	1.16
2.21	0.53	0.36	1.26	1.34	1.57	1.61	1.20
2.28	0.53	0.38	1.10	1.21	1.38	1.43	1.21
3.07	0.52	0.68	1.25	1.41	1.63	1.53	0.94
3.14	0.44	0.46	1.30	1.37	1.54	1.52	1.10
3.21	0.56	0.46	1.27	1.32	1.43	1.37	0.92
3.28	0.86	0.62	1.22	1.32	1.58	1.51	0.79
4.04	0.87	0.73	1.33	1.37	1.52	1.71	1.01
4.11	0.79	0.62	1.30	1.42	1.50	1.68	1.02
4.18	0.89	0.70	1.32	1.50	1.66	1.66	1.06
4.25	0.84	0.76	1.32	1.58	1.69	1.74	1.13
5.02	0.66	0.71	1.19	1.41	1.53	1.62	1.08
5.09	0.73	0.74	1.43	1.61	1.70	2.19	1.08
5.16	0.99	0.89	1.33	1.42	1.56	1.62	0.99
5.23	0.85	0.90	1.31	1.38	1.51	1.61	0.89
5.30	0.95	0.86	1.34	1.51	1.69	1.72	1.10
6.06	1.00	0.77	1.52	1.67	1.67	1.67	1.06
6.13	0.80	0.99	1.59	1.75	1.76	1.80	1.42
6.20	1.12	1.23	1.51	1.70	1.74	1.90	1.51
6.27	1.04	1.13	1.50	1.61	1.78	1.89	1.68
7.03	1.12	1.13	1.66	1.71	1.75	1.80	1.50
7.11	1.11	1.19	1.73	1.78	1.83	1.82	1.52
7.18	1.17	1.20	2.14	1.99	2.27	1.98	1.66
7.25	1.68	1.33	1.69	1.93	2.02	2.06	1.59
8.01	1.18	1.16	1.66	1.81	1.95	1.83	1.44
8.08	1.09	1.10	1.63	1.90	1.84	1.83	1.46
8.15	1.12	1.26	1.83	2.10	2.09	1.88	1.66
8.22	1.02	1.02	1.73	1.76	2.26	1.87	1.40
8.29	0.90	1.05	1.83	1.89	2.36	1.94	1.42
9.05	1.18	1.49	1.65	1.80	2.01	1.98	1.45
9.12	1.05	1.11	1.56	1.79	1.87	1.67	1.76
9.19	1.18	1.07	1.50	1.72	1.93	1.89	1.52
9.26	1.13	1.13	1.51	1.73	1.95	1.80	1.54
10.03	0.95	1.13	1.60	1.77	1.96	1.91	1.64
10.10	1.17	1.46	1.80	1.98	2.11	1.96	1.64
10.17	1.04	1.20	1.56	1.80	1.95	1.85	1.45
10.24	1.03	1.13	1.57	1.72	1.93	1.88	1.55
10.31	0.96	1.18	1.51	1.70	1.88	1.76	1.58
11.07	0.93	1.21	1.65	1.84	1.97	1.81	1.66
11.14	0.80	1.11	1.58	1.76	1.88	1.80	2.18
11.21	0.82	1.22	1.59	1.76	1.88	1.85	1.66
12.05	0.80	1.09	1.66	1.62	1.82	1.80	1.63
12.12	0.82	1.04	1.62	1.64	1.81	1.84	1.63
12.19	0:89	1.15	1.46	1.62	1.80	1.84	1.60
12.26	0.50	--	1.35	1.53	1.74	1.77	1.64
ABS HI	1.68	1.49	2.14	2.10	2.36	2.19	2.18
AVG	0.89	0.90	1.47	1.60	1.75	1.73	1.32

1986 SPREADS - MKT AVG RATE GICs vs TREASURIES

WEEK ENDING	MATURITY						
	1	2	3	4	5	7	10
1.03	0.07	0.02	0.31	0.46	0.62	0.52	0.46
1.10	0.08	0.08	0.30	0.46	0.58	0.56	0.52
1.17	0.21	0.16	0.27	0.39	0.55	0.49	0.33
1.24	0.31	0.22	0.38	0.50	0.67	0.59	0.46
1.31	0.24	0.19	0.36	0.54	0.68	0.58	0.49
2.07	0.28	0.23	0.48	0.57	0.70	0.67	0.56
2.14	0.18	0.10	0.43	0.52	0.75	0.68	0.58
2.21	0.17	0.08	0.41	0.49	0.64	0.61	0.56
2.28	0.13	0.05	0.30	0.43	0.60	0.58	0.50
3.07	0.16	0.16	0.43	0.52	0.72	0.64	0.44
3.14	0.17	0.16	0.44	0.58	0.79	0.74	0.62
3.21	0.21	0.12	0.47	0.56	0.75	0.69	0.50
3.28	0.27	0.17	0.51	0.55	0.76	0.70	0.47
4.04	0.28	0.22	0.51	0.62	0.76	0.85	0.64
4.11	0.28	0.20	0.58	0.64	0.79	0.84	0.57
4.18	0.29	0.21	0.60	0.69	0.85	0.88	0.71
4.25	0.26	0.35	0.60	0.72	0.89	0.94	0.83
5.02	0.23	0.29	0.55	0.61	0.81	0.87	0.65
5.09	0.26	0.32	0.68	0.71	0.87	0.92	0.79
5.16	0.29	0.27	0.55	0.64	0.48	0.83	0.71
5.23	0.41	0.41	0.58	0.61	0.73	0.83	0.75
5.30	0.43	0.46	0.66	0.77	0.90	0.93	0.87
6.06	0.43	0.44	0.59	0.70	0.80	0.83	0.76
6.13	0.35	0.45	0.63	0.70	0.84	0.89	0.69
6.20	0.54	0.64	0.79	0.93	1.08	1.12	0.96
6.27	0.49	0.58	0.76	0.91	1.07	1.08	0.91
7.03	0.57	0.65	0.85	0.99	1.13	1.13	1.01
7.11	0.29	0.53	0.79	0.92	1.08	1.06	1.00
7.18	0.52	0.63	0.74	1.08	1.28	1.19	1.10
7.25	1.13	0.59	0.85	0.99	1.22	1.17	1.10
8.01	0.29	0.57	0.81	0.93	1.11	1.08	0.98
8.08	0.37	0.65	0.91	1.03	1.17	1.15	1.11
8.15	0.35	0.66	0.98	1.10	1.26	1.20	1.16
8.22	0.55	0.68	0.96	1.10	1.27	1.22	1.15
8.29	0.53	0.70	0.98	1.16	1.35	1.28	1.12
9.05	0.54	0.80	1.02	1.20	1.37	1.21	1.09
9.12	0.44	0.73	0.87	1.07	1.23	1.09	1.14
9.19	0.52	0.29	0.96	1.12	1.31	1.18	1.21
9.26	0.54	0.60	0.89	1.05	1.26	1.15	1.13
10.03	0.43	0.48	0.81	0.98	1.22	1.12	1.14
10.10	0.58	0.68	0.86	1.16	1.34	1.22	1.23
10.17	0.48	-0.20	0.86	1.08	1.24	1.11	1.08
10.24	0.48	0.59	0.81	0.97	1.22	1.10	1.10
10.31	0.48	0.55	0.78	0.99	1.22	1.15	1.14
11.07	0.45	0.59	0.88	1.11	1.29	1.22	1.29
11.14	0.42	0.54	0.84	1.04	1.21	1.17	1.37
11.21	0.45	0.57	0.89	1.06	1.24	1.22	1.32
12.05	0.41	0.48	0.88	1.04	1.25	1.17	1.34
12.12	0.38	0.50	0.86	1.01	1.22	1.14	1.30
12.19	0.37	0.49	0.71	0.96	1.16	1.08	1.24
12.26	0.29	--	0.68	0.94	1.19	1.16	1.22
ABS HI	1.13	0.80	1.02	1.20	1.37	1.28	1.37
AVG	0.37	0.39	0.68	0.82	0.99	0.95	0.89

HIGHEST RATE GICs - 1987
$1 MILLION SIMPLE INTEREST

WEEK ENDING	MATURITY 1	2	3	4	5	7	10
1.02	6.58	7.18	7.89	8.11	8.43	8.73	8.72
1.09	6.70	7.38	7.75	8.19	8.43	8.77	8.58
1.16	6.66	7.36	7.75	8.19	8.43	8.77	8.58
1.23	6.60	7.36	7.70	8.14	8.38	8.75	8.72
1.30	6.55	7.36	7.75	8.24	8.38	8.75	8.97
2.06	6.60	7.13	7.60	8.09	8.28	8.67	8.73
2.13	6.60	7.13	7.75	8.19	8.42	8.67	8.73
2.20	6.57	7.12	7.70	8.14	8.38	8.62	8.58
2.27	6.62	7.17	7.75	8.19	8.33	8.62	8.57
3.06	6.64	7.09	7.67	8.08	8.26	8.59	8.50
3.13	6.50	7.11	7.74	8.12	8.29	8.59	8.52
3.20	6.45	7.13	7.74	8.14	8.33	8.61	8.50
3.27	6.46	7.09	7.71	8.12	8.29	8.64	8.52
4.03	6.85	7.29	7.91	8.31	8.48	8.78	8.77
4.10	6.76	7.29	8.15	8.39	8.56	8.88	8.94
4.16	7.41	7.80	8.23	8.50	8.76	8.98	9.17
4.24	7.41	7.89	8.30	9.05	9.11	9.31	9.53
5.01	7.40	7.95	8.44	9.05	9.17	9.34	9.45
5.08	7.51	8.01	8.45	8.93	9.19	9.59	9.55
5.15	7.60	8.21	8.66	9.00	9.37	9.57	9.73
5.22	7.85	8.46	8.98	9.25	9.56	9.83	9.87
5.29	7.59	8.31	8.88	9.14	9.46	9.58	9.75
6.05	7.65	8.25	8.78	9.14	9.46	9.66	9.65
6.12	7.52	8.18	8.78	9.14	9.46	9.63	10.17
6.19	7.42	8.01	8.65	8.84	9.39	9.43	9.35
6.26	7.45	8.02	8.60	8.74	9.39	9.38	9.25
7.02	7.25	8.01	8.53	8.74	9.31	9.38	9.41
7.10	7.15	8.01	8.48	8.70	9.13	9.34	9.30
7.17	7.15	8.01	8.49	8.70	9.13	9.41	9.30
7.24	7.25	8.01	8.62	8.82	9.14	9.52	9.50
7.31	7.35	8.13	8.53	8.82	9.26	9.58	9.50
8.07	7.50	8.23	8.68	9.05	9.36	9.66	9.65
8.14	7.45	8.05	8.68	9.01	9.35	9.64	9.60
8.21	7.50	8.07	8.91	9.10	9.39	9.68	9.65
8.28	7.81	8.34	8.91	9.15	9.50	9.85	9.91
9.04	8.08	8.48	9.13	9.31	9.80	10.19	10.00
9.11	8.19	8.82	9.24	9.48	9.86	10.20	10.40
9.18	8.10	9.10	9.46	9.54	9.95	10.27	10.30
9.25	8.05	9.00	9.28	9.47	10.00	10.33	10.30
10.02	8.31	9.20	9.51	9.75	10.31	10.67	10.45
10.09	8.65	9.20	9.66	9.93	10.42	10.79	10.56
10.16	8.98	9.60	9.96	10.25	10.65	11.03	11.03
10.23	7.83	8.60	9.75	9.82	9.97	10.62	9.45
10.30	7.55	8.50	8.96	9.25	9.54	10.02	9.57
11.06	7.75	8.50	9.06	9.31	9.50	9.79	9.50
11.13	7.85	8.21	8.77	9.14	9.51	9.86	9.81
11.20	7.57	8.45	8.91	9.05	9.54	9.93	9.56
11.25	7.55	8.45	8.91	8.95	9.23	9.59	9.65
12.04	7.65	8.55	9.01	9.15	9.76	10.04	9.70
12.11	8.20	8.75	9.21	9.45	9.80	10.19	9.74
12.18	7.69	8.65	9.11	9.30	9.73	10.00	9.87
12.23	7.70	8.65	9.11	9.30	9.68	9.93	9.71
12.30	7.65	8.70	9.06	9.35	9.53	9.80	9.71
ABS HI	8.98	9.60	9.96	10.25	10.65	11.03	11.03
AVG	7.41	8.08	8.61	8.90	9.23	9.52	9.46

MARKET AVG RATE GICs - 1987
$1 MILLION SIMPLE INTEREST

WEEK ENDING	MATURITY 1	2	3	4	5	7	10
1.02	6.29	6.70	7.24	7.54	7.83	8.12	8.38
1.09	6.19	6.68	7.06	7.40	7.73	8.01	8.29
1.16	6.15	6.66	7.03	7.37	7.71	7.98	8.28
1.23	6.09	6.65	6.99	7.35	7.64	7.90	8.26
1.30	6.13	6.66	7.03	7.36	7.68	7.97	8.31
2.06	6.18	6.66	7.05	7.37	7.68	7.96	8.25
2.13	6.21	6.69	7.09	7.42	7.74	8.02	8.14
2.20	6.14	6.63	7.09	7.41	7.75	7.97	8.14
2.27	6.15	6.64	7.09	7.37	7.70	7.93	8.17
3.06	6.11	6.60	7.08	7.37	7.71	7.92	8.22
3.13	6.09	6.60	7.05	7.37	7.66	7.91	8.23
3.20	6.06	6.58	7.05	7.36	7.67	7.91	8.20
3.27	6.09	6.61	7.07	7.40	7.67	7.94	8.15
4.03	6.28	6.82	7.26	7.58	7.88	8.18	8.36
4.10	6.38	6.91	7.32	7.70	7.98	8.30	8.38
4.16	6.69	7.08	7.56	7.94	8.25	8.54	8.72
4.24	6.87	7.42	7.85	8.23	8.48	8.81	9.03
5.01	6.89	7.52	7.95	8.32	8.58	8.87	9.12
5.08	7.06	7.6.	8.13	8.45	8.72	9.03	9.23
5.15	7.23	7.79	8.29	8.60	8.90	9.18	9.34
5.22	7.46	8.11	8.56	8.88	9.13	9.40	9.58
5.29	7.29	7.89	8.39	8.67	8.94	9.19	9.37
6.05	7.30	7.95	8.38	8.67	8.93	9.20	9.37
6.12	7.19	7.79	8.27	8.57	8.84	9.11	9.38
6.19	7.06	7.61	8.11	8.38	8.69	8.95	9.04
6.26	7.08	7.63	8.07	8.38	8.67	8.90	8.99
7.02	6.95	7.56	8.05	8.37	8.64	8.91	9.03
7.10	6.92	7.51	7.99	8.31	8.58	8.87	8.99
7.17	6.83	7.46	8.01	8.33	8.62	8.88	8.97
7.24	6.92	7.59	8.11	8.46	8.70	8.99	9.07
7.31	7.03	7.69	8.17	8.51	8.78	9.04	9.12
8.07	7.11	7.81	8.27	8.58	8.87	9.14	9.28
8.14	7.10	7.70	8.27	8.58	8.89	9.15	9.27
8.21	7.17	7.76	8.30	8.65	8.90	9.17	9.33
8.28	7.30	7.92	8.42	8.75	9.01	9.29	9.42
9.04	7.48	8.13	8.68	8.96	9.24	9.53	9.59
9.11	7.67	8.37	8.90	9.18	9.47	9.78	9.90
9.18	7.70	8.36	8.86	9.16	9.45	9.71	9.86
9.25	7.72	8.39	8.87	9.19	9.46	9.75	9.86
10.02	8.00	8.60	9.12	9.42	9.70	9.98	10.15
10.09	8.22	8.83	9.24	9.58	9.80	10.07	10.18
10.16	8.50	9.17	9.52	9.87	10.08	10.34	10.41
10.23	7.15	7.83	8.41	8.80	9.05	9.28	9.19
10.30	7.05	7.72	8.23	8.62	8.92	9.18	9.29
11.06	7.16	7.79	8.26	8.61	8.83	9.10	9.21
11.13	7.25	7.82	8.23	8.61	8.79	9.08	9.47
11.20	7.07	7.78	8.21	8.56	8.80	9.06	9.25
11.25	7.17	7.78	8.23	8.55	8.79	9.06	9.19
12.04	7.28	7.83	8.29	8.64	8.89	9.15	9.30
12.11	7.49	8.01	8.40	8.79	8.99	9.28	9.42
12.18	7.38	7.94	8.39	8.72	8.95	9.12	9.32
12.23	7.36	7.91	8.36	8.67	8.87	9.12	9.27
12.30	7.29	7.86	8.31	8.66	8.84	9.09	9.25
ABS HI	8.50	9.17	9.52	9.87	10.08	10.34	10.41
AVG	6.97	7.55	8.02	8.34	8.62	8.88	9.06

1987 SPREADS - HIGH RATE GICs vs TREASURIES

WEEK ENDING	MATURITY 1	2	3	4	5	7	10
1.02	0.61	0.82	1.35	1.44	1.64	1.66	1.52
1.09	0.90	1.16	1.37	1.68	1.80	1.86	1.53
1.16	0.90	1.14	1.36	1.68	1.80	1.85	1.51
1.23	0.91	1.18	1.33	1.66	1.80	1.89	1.69
1.30	0.73	1.10	1.29	1.68	1.72	1.79	1.82
2.06	0.68	0.76	1.07	1.45	1.54	1.64	1.51
2.13	0.55	0.65	1.10	1.42	1.54	1.54	1.42
2.20	0.59	0.73	1.13	1.45	1.57	1.53	1.30
2.27	0.72	0.82	1.23	1.56	1.59	1.61	1.37
3.06	0.70	0.73	1.15	1.46	1.55	1.60	1.32
3.13	0.44	0.68	1.18	1.45	1.52	1.55	1.30
3.20	0.46	0.73	1.21	1.49	1.57	1.58	1.29
3.27	0.39	0.64	1.08	1.39	1.46	1.56	1.25
4.03	0.67	0.68	1.05	1.33	1.39	1.42	1.21
4.10	0.50	0.60	1.17	1.28	1.32	1.37	1.23
4.16	0.81	0.75	0.83	0.96	1.08	1.06	1.05
4.24	0.74	0.65	0.73	1.35	1.28	1.21	1.23
5.01	0.64	0.51	0.73	1.23	1.25	1.18	1.13
5.08	0.63	0.41	0.58	0.95	1.10	1.26	1.06
5.15	0.57	0.48	0.66	0.88	1.13	1.10	1.12
5.22	0.65	0.46	0.71	0.85	1.04	1.12	1.03
5.29	0.64	0.53	0.87	1.02	1.23	1.16	1.20
6.05	0.74	0.51	0.78	1.04	1.27	1.22	1.07
6.12	0.72	0.53	0.89	1.14	1.36	1.25	1.67
6.19	0.69	0.56	0.97	1.06	1.52	1.29	1.08
6.26	0.68	0.53	0.88	0.92	1.48	1.24	0.97
7.02	0.54	0.56	0.81	0.90	1.35	1.18	1.06
7.10	0.54	0.65	0.83	0.92	1.22	1.20	0.98
7.17	0.62	0.66	0.84	0.91	1.20	1.22	0.92
7.24	0.54	0.55	0.85	0.91	1.09	1.19	0.98
7.31	0.47	0.51	0.62	0.77	1.08	1.13	0.88
8.07	0.54	0.54	0.66	0.89	1.06	1.10	0.90
8.14	0.52	0.38	0.75	0.92	1.11	1.13	0.92
8.21	0.49	0.34	0.93	0.96	1.09	1.13	0.94
8.28	0.65	0.45	0.78	0.88	1.09	1.18	1.06
9.04	0.67	0.37	0.72	0.76	1.11	1.19	0.82
9.11	0.47	0.43	0.54	0.65	0.90	0.91	0.97
9.18	0.45	0.79	0.82	0.75	1.01	1.00	0.87
9.25	0.35	0.63	0.57	0.63	1.03	1.04	0.85
10.02	0.43	0.62	0.62	0.72	1.14	1.19	0.84
10.09	0.55	0.37	0.56	0.68	1.03	1.14	0.78
10.16	0.65	0.47	0.53	0.67	0.92	1.06	0.92
10.23	0.61	0.51	1.21	1.10	1.07	1.39	0.09
10.30	0.82	0.90	0.95	1.05	1.16	1.31	0.67
11.06	0.88	0.88	1.10	1.17	1.18	1.13	0.66
11.13	0.89	0.54	0.81	1.01	1.21	1.22	1.01
11.20	0.56	0.73	0.93	0.88	1.19	1.27	0.73
11.25	0.53	0.69	0.86	0.72	0.82	0.82	0.70
12.04	0.63	0.80	0.97	0.93	1.36	1.24	0.58
12.11	0.96	0.82	1.00	1.07	1.26	1.23	0.43
12.18	0.46	0.74	0.94	0.96	1.23	1.12	0.69
12.23	0.51	0.80	0.99	1.03	1.27	1.21	0.74
12.30	0.50	0.88	0.98	1.12	1.15	1.11	0.76
ABS HI	0.96	1.18	1.37	1.68	1.80	1.89	1.82
AVG	0.62	0.65	0.92	1.08	1.27	1.28	1.04

1987 SPREADS - MKT AVG RATE GICs vs TREASURIES

WEEK ENDING	MATURITY 1	2	3	4	5	7	10
1.02	0.32	0.34	0.70	0.87	1.04	1.05	1.18
1.09	0.39	0.46	0.68	0.89	1.10	1.10	1.24
1.16	0.39	0.44	0.64	0.86	1.08	1.06	1.21
1.23	0.40	0.47	0.62	0.87	1.06	1.04	1.23
1.30	0.31	0.40	0.57	0.80	1.02	1.01	1.16
2.06	0.26	0.29	0.52	0.73	0.94	0.93	1.03
2.13	0.16	0.21	0.44	0.65	0.86	0.89	0.83
2.20	0.16	0.24	0.52	0.72	0.94	0.88	0.86
2.27	0.25	0.29	0.57	0.74	0.96	0.92	0.97
3.06	0.17	0.24	0.56	0.75	1.00	0.93	1.04
3.13	0.03	0.17	0.49	0.70	0.89	0.87	1.01
3.20	0.07	0.18	0.52	0.71	0.91	0.88	0.99
3.27	0.02	0.16	0.44	0.67	0.84	0.86	0.88
4.03	0.10	0.21	0.40	0.60	0.79	0.82	0.80
4.10	0.12	0.22	0.34	0.59	0.74	0.79	0.67
4.16	0.09	0.03	0.16	0.40	0.57	0.62	0.60
4.24	0.20	0.18	0.28	0.53	0.65	0.71	0.73
5.01	0.13	0.08	0.24	0.50	0.66	0.71	0.80
5.08	0.18	0.08	0.26	0.47	0.63	0.70	0.74
5.15	0.20	0.06	0.29	0.48	0.66	0.71	0.73
5.22	0.26	0.11	0.29	0.48	0.61	0.69	0.74
5.29	0.34	0.11	0.38	0.55	0.71	0.77	0.82
6.05	0.39	0.21	0.38	0.57	0.74	0.76	0.79
6.12	0.39	0.14	0.38	0.57	0.74	0.73	0.88
6.19	0.33	0.16	0.43	0.60	0.82	0.81	0.77
6.26	0.31	0.14	0.35	0.56	0.76	0.76	0.71
7.02	0.24	0.11	0.33	0.53	0.68	0.71	0.68
7.10	0.31	0.15	0.34	0.53	0.67	0.73	0.67
7.17	0.30	0.11	0.36	0.54	0.69	0.69	0.59
7.24	0.21	0.13	0.34	0.55	0.65	0.66	0.55
7.31	0.15	0.07	0.26	0.46	0.60	0.59	0.50
8.07	0.15	0.12	0.25	0.42	0.57	0.58	0.53
8.14	0.17	0.03	0.34	0.49	0.65	0.64	0.59
8.21	0.16	0.03	0.32	0.51	0.60	0.62	0.62
8.28	0.14	0.03	0.29	0.48	0.60	0.62	0.57
9.04	0.07	0.02	0.27	0.41	0.55	0.53	0.41
9.11	-0.05	-0.02	0.20	0.35	0.51	0.49	0.47
9.18	0.05	0.05	0.22	0.37	0.51	0.44	0.43
9.25	0.02	0.02	0.16	0.35	0.49	0.46	0.41
10.02	0.12	0.02	0.23	0.39	0.53	0.50	0.54
10.09	0.12	0.00	0.14	0.33	0.41	0.42	0.40
10.16	0.17	0.04	0.09	0.29	0.35	0.37	0.30
10.23	-0.07	-0.26	-0.13	0.08	0.15	0.05	-0.17
10.30	0.32	0.12	0.22	0.42	0.54	0.47	0.39
11.06	0.29	0.17	0.30	0.47	0.51	0.44	0.37
11.13	0.29	0.15	0.27	0.48	0.49	0.44	0.67
11.20	0.06	0.06	0.23	0.39	0.45	0.40	0.42
11.25	0.15	0.02	0.18	0.32	0.38	0.29	0.24
12.04	0.26	0.08	0.25	0.42	0.49	0.35	0.18
12.11	0.25	0.08	0.19	0.41	0.45	0.32	0.11
12.18	0.15	0.03	0.22	0.38	0.45	0.24	0.14
12.23	0.17	0.06	0.24	0.40	0.46	0.40	0.30
12.30	0.14	0.04	0.23	0.43	0.46	0.40	0.30
ABS HI	0.40	0.47	0.68	0.89	1.10	1.10	1.24
AVG	0.19	0.13	0.33	0.52	0.66	0.65	0.64

HIGHEST RATE GICs - 1988
$1 MILLION SIMPLE INTEREST

WEEK ENDING	MATURITY 1	2	3	4	5	7	10
1.08	7.75	8.60	9.06	9.15	9.49	9.80	9.65
1.15	7.60	8.55	8.96	8.97	9.48	9.81	9.65
1.22	7.39	8.30	8.74	8.98	9.20	9.48	9.28
1.29	7.18	8.00	8.51	8.70	9.17	9.31	9.02
2.05	7.00	7.85	8.13	8.37	8.89	9.19	9.28
2.12	7.08	7.85	8.11	8.35	8.39	9.02	8.76
2.19	7.23	8.00	8.21	8.45	8.84	9.15	8.86
2.26	7.10	7.90	8.13	8.36	8.95	9.21	8.81
3.04	7.15	7.91	8.16	8.40	8.57	8.92	8.82
3.11	7.20	7.95	8.18	8.45	8.82	9.10	8.82
3.18	7.10	7.92	8.17	8.46	8.72	9.06	8.98
3.25	7.25	7.99	8.21	8.56	8.96	9.30	9.21
4.01	7.50	8.10	8.31	8.65	8.94	9.31	9.27
4.08	7.70	8.30	8.54	8.83	9.03	9.23	9.28
4.15	7.24	8.21	8.42	8.75	8.96	9.32	9.32
4.22	7.28	8.24	8.84	8.80	9.04	9.33	9.44
4.29	7.36	8.24	8.55	8.81	9.15	9.28	9.47
5.06	7.53	8.30	8.63	8.83	9.20	9.33	9.52
5.13	7.52	8.39	8.68	9.01	9.26	9.49	9.53
5.20	7.69	8.50	8.76	9.35	9.44	9.69	9.74
5.27	7.96	8.65	8.96	9.25	9.57	9.74	9.90
6.03	7.86	8.60	8.81	9.10	9.49	9.70	10.13
6.10	7.76	8.40	8.75	8.95	9.24	9.55	9.87
6.17	7.79	8.43	8.62	8.98	9.21	9.46	9.82
6.24	8.02	8.63	8.83	9.08	9.19	9.55	9.92
7.01	7.97	8.50	8.73	8.91	9.17	9.45	9.82
7.08	8.29	8.59	8.75	8.93	9.24	9.47	9.77
7.15	8.54	8.83	8.98	9.18	9.59	9.83	9.97
7.22	8.55	8.93	9.05	9.21	9.59	9.83	9.97
7.29	8.54	8.95	9.06	9.22	9.51	9.77	9.92
8.05	8.41	8.99	9.15	9.22	9.44	9.62	9.68
8.12	8.65	9.16	9.21	9.41	9.68	9.88	10.02
8.19	8.90	9.31	9.45	9.53	9.81	9.97	10.12
8.26	8.90	9.41	9.47	9.68	9.81	9.91	10.07
9.02	8.93	9.43	9.51	9.61	9.65	9.70	9.81
9.09	8.70	9.04	9.15	9.22	9.44	9.51	9.81
9.16	8.45	9.36	9.63	9.20	9.29	9.46	9.81
9.23	8.45	8.91	9.04	9.18	9.36	9.51	9.81
9.30	8.45	8.97	9.12	9.23	9.36	9.56	9.81
10.07	8.19	8.47	8.78	9.05	9.14	9.28	9.81
10.14	8.19	8.64	8.84	8.90	9.21	9.41	9.81
10.21	8.28	8.62	8.71	9.05	9.08	9.23	9.81
10.28	8.19	8.52	8.78	8.88	9.11	9.16	9.81
11.04	8.39	8.67	8.71	8.81	9.01	9.26	9.81
11.11	8.46	8.68	8.85	9.03	9.21	9.36	9.81
11.18	8.63	8.87	9.01	9.21	9.37	9.45	9.81
11.25	8.81	8.97	9.09	9.23	9.49	9.46	9.81
12.02	9.35	9.16	9.29	9.43	9.56	9.58	9.63
12.09	9.35	9.26	9.33	9.45	9.52	9.58	9.81
12.16	9.55	9.37	9.57	9.56	9.66	9.68	9.67
12.23	9.17	9.47	9.53	9.62	9.73	9.70	9.81
12.30	9.13	9.34	9.53	9.62	9.73	9.68	9.81
ABS HI	9.55	9.47	9.63	9.68	9.81	9.97	10.13
AVG	8.07	8.62	8.84	9.02	9.27	9.47	9.61

MARKET AVG RATE GICs - 1988
$1 MILLION SIMPLE INTEREST

WEEK ENDING	MATURITY 1	2	3	4	5	7	10
1.08	7.32	7.88	8.29	8.60	8.86	9.13	9.30
1.15	7.10	7.69	8.14	8.48	8.74	9.04	9.24
1.22	6.94	7.52	7.99	8.31	8.56	8.83	9.00
1.29	6.77	7.29	7.77	8.08	8.34	8.61	8.74
2.05	6.67	7.15	7.54	7.87	8.16	8.46	8.72
2.12	6.64	7.07	7.54	7.84	8.08	8.40	8.60
2.19	6.77	7.15	7.61	7.92	8.19	8.49	8.68
2.26	6.69	7.15	7.55	7.86	8.14	8.43	8.63
3.04	6.61	7.13	7.56	7.85	8.12	8.42	8.66
3.11	6.67	7.17	7.62	7.95	8.25	8.52	8.72
3.18	6.61	7.13	7.60	7.94	8.24	8.53	8.76
3.25	6.75	7.33	7.76	8.11	8.41	8.72	8.99
4.01	6.88	7.43	7.83	8.18	8.46	8.78	9.00
4.08	6.96	7.48	7.91	8.28	8.55	8.85	9.09
4.15	6.92	7.48	7.92	8.28	8.58	8.88	9.15
4.22	6.96	7.57	8.21	8.38	8.67	8.98	9.23
4.29	7.07	7.68	8.08	8.46	8.72	9.01	9.27
5.06	7.13	7.73	8.20	8.52	8.80	9.10	9.38
5.13	7.18	7.81	8.26	8.60	8.88	9.18	9.43
5.20	7.29	7.91	8.30	8.72	8.98	9.28	9.57
5.27	7.43	8.03	8.49	8.83	9.09	9.36	9.63
6.03	7.41	8.00	8.44	8.76	9.03	9.31	9.61
6.10	7.28	7.87	8.31	8.63	8.92	9.20	9.48
6.17	7.22	7.80	8.25	8.54	8.82	9.11	9.37
6.24	7.28	7.88	8.29	8.58	8.84	9.12	9.43
7.01	7.22	7.86	8.23	8.48	8.74	9.01	9.36
7.08	7.43	7.96	8.33	8.63	8.87	9.13	9.46
7.15	7.50	8.12	8.46	8.75	8.99	9.24	9.56
7.22	7.55	7.81	8.52	8.78	9.04	9.29	9.59
7.29	7.61	8.21	8.55	8.79	9.04	9.24	9.58
8.05	7.63	8.23	8.54	8.78	9.02	9.26	9.56
8.12	7.94	8.60	8.80	9.03	9.25	9.46	9.71
8.19	8.08	8.60	8.93	9.14	9.37	9.54	9.79
8.26	8.13	8.61	8.96	9.18	9.39	9.57	9.79
9.02	7.97	8.48	8.76	8.97	9.17	9.36	9.60
9.09	7.88	8.28	8.60	8.82	9.00	9.18	9.43
9.16	7.79	8.29	8.57	8.77	8.93	9.13	9.40
9.23	7.87	8.23	8.57	8.78	8.95	9.13	9.42
9.30	7.93	8.30	8.62	8.81	8.97	9.14	9.39
10.07	7.82	8.10	8.42	8.59	8.78	8.96	9.26
10.14	7.84	8.11	8.43	8.58	8.77	8.97	9.29
10.21	7.90	8.15	8.42	8.59	8.77	8.95	9.18
10.28	7.83	8.10	8.38	8.53	8.71	8.90	9.14
11.04	7.86	8.13	8.43	8.56	8.74	8.92	9.18
11.11	8.03	8.28	8.58	8.73	8.90	9.06	9.26
11.18	8.24	8.43	8.71	8.85	9.02	9.14	9.32
11.25	8.31	8.51	8.81	8.95	9.09	9.20	9.37
12.02	8.40	8.67	8.94	9.08	9.20	9.29	9.39
12.09	8.43	8.67	8.95	9.10	9.21	9.27	9.38
12.16	8.64	8.81	9.10	9.24	9.33	9.37	9.45
12.23	8.61	8.88	9.10	9.26	9.34	9.39	9.49
12.30	8.62	8.87	9.12	9.28	9.35	9.41	9.50
ABS HI	8.64	8.88	9.12	9.28	9.39	9.57	9.79
AVG	7.49	7.95	8.34	8.59	8.81	9.04	9.28

1988 SPREADS - HIGH RATE GICs vs TREASURIES

WEEK ENDING	MATURITY 1	2	3	4	5	7	10
1.08	0.60	0.79	1.01	0.94	1.12	1.11	0.81
1.15	0.48	0.80	0.97	0.81	1.15	1.16	0.81
1.22	0.49	0.73	0.94	1.04	1.12	1.11	0.71
1.29	0.41	0.61	0.88	0.93	1.26	1.12	0.63
2.05	0.30	0.78	0.80	0.85	1.31	1.22	1.01
2.12	0.29	0.62	0.71	0.77	0.69	0.93	0.37
2.19	0.49	0.84	0.85	0.92	1.16	1.07	0.46
2.26	0.43	0.78	0.81	0.90	1.36	1.25	0.56
3.04	0.32	0.71	0.73	0.80	0.87	0.84	0.42
3.11	0.40	0.77	0.77	0.81	1.09	0.98	0.42
3.18	0.29	0.65	0.67	0.73	0.89	0.81	0.47
3.25	0.34	0.67	0.63	0.75	1.06	1.02	0.62
4.01	0.63	0.74	0.67	0.79	0.96	0.92	0.58
4.08	0.65	0.85	0.84	0.89	0.97	0.88	0.66
4.15	0.22	0.65	0.59	0.64	0.72	0.80	0.46
4.22	0.23	0.62	0.97	0.67	0.78	0.79	0.51
4.29	0.29	0.57	0.63	0.71	0.88	0.68	0.65
5.06	0.30	0.50	0.57	0.60	0.81	0.62	0.59
5.13	0.19	0.44	0.49	0.65	0.73	0.65	0.49
5.20	0.29	0.48	0.50	0.90	0.80	0.74	0.60
5.27	0.38	0.47	0.56	0.68	0.84	0.70	0.68
6.03	0.27	0.48	0.47	0.62	0.88	0.79	1.06
6.10	0.30	0.40	0.55	0.60	0.74	0.75	0.91
6.17	0.39	0.49	0.49	0.71	0.80	0.76	0.98
6.24	0.49	0.55	0.57	0.69	0.67	0.75	0.98
7.01	0.45	0.46	0.52	0.57	0.71	0.72	0.96
7.08	0.67	0.47	0.48	0.55	0.73	0.67	0.84
7.15	0.75	0.54	0.53	0.69	0.92	0.89	0.84
7.22	0.76	0.59	0.54	0.59	0.87	0.86	0.84
7.29	0.69	0.56	0.50	0.57	0.77	0.80	0.80
8.05	0.52	0.63	0.63	0.62	0.77	0.72	0.64
8.12	0.48	0.55	0.45	0.56	0.74	0.75	0.75
8.19	0.63	0.58	0.60	0.58	0.76	0.75	0.76
8.26	0.62	0.66	0.58	0.70	0.75	0.67	0.71
9.02	0.69	0.77	0.72	0.75	0.73	0.60	0.60
9.09	0.61	0.59	0.59	0.60	0.76	0.65	0.83
9.16	0.44	0.96	1.11	0.62	0.65	0.65	0.88
9.23	0.38	0.47	0.50	0.57	0.69	0.66	0.85
9.30	0.27	0.45	0.50	0.55	0.63	0.66	0.82
10.07	0.06	0.08	0.30	0.52	0.57	0.53	0.98
10.14	0.12	0.31	0.40	0.41	0.68	0.70	1.00
10.21	0.16	0.26	0.28	0.57	0.56	0.54	1.01
10.28	0.06	0.18	0.36	0.43	0.64	0.50	1.04
11.04	0.29	0.38	0.33	0.40	0.57	0.67	1.09
11.11	0.11	0.13	0.24	0.38	0.52	0.55	0.90
11.18	0.08	0.15	0.24	0.40	0.53	0.53	0.82
11.25	0.10	0.08	0.15	0.26	0.50	0.41	0.71
12.02	0.60	0.20	0.31	0.44	0.56	0.50	0.52
12.09	0.46	0.27	0.32	0.45	0.53	0.54	0.78
12.16	0.45	0.21	0.40	0.39	0.50	0.49	0.51
12.23	0.17	0.38	0.41	0.51	0.63	0.58	0.73
12.30	0.06	0.16	0.33	0.43	0.55	0.46	0.64
ABS HI	0.76	0.96	1.11	1.04	1.36	1.25	1.09
AVG	0.39	0.52	0.58	0.64	0.79	0.76	0.73

1988 SPREADS - MKT AVG RATE GICs vs TREASURIES

WEEK ENDING	MATURITY 1	2	3	4	5	7	10
1.08	0.17	0.07	0.24	0.39	0.49	0.44	0.46
1.15	-0.02	-0.06	0.15	0.32	0.41	0.39	0.40
1.22	0.04	-0.05	0.19	0.37	0.48	0.46	0.43
1.29	0.00	-0.10	0.14	0.31	0.43	0.42	0.35
2.05	0.02	-0.05	0.12	0.29	0.43	0.44	0.52
2.12	0.05	-0.07	0.20	0.33	0.41	0.41	0.42
2.19	0.07	-0.09	0.19	0.31	0.40	0.39	0.39
2.26	0.06	-0.02	0.20	0.34	0.44	0.43	0.43
3.04	-0.02	0.01	0.23	0.37	0.49	0.46	0.49
3.11	-0.05	-0.06	0.17	0.33	0.47	0.41	0.40
3.18	-0.02	-0.08	0.16	0.33	0.46	0.38	0.43
3.25	-0.02	-0.05	0.16	0.33	0.46	0.41	0.51
4.01	0.10	0.01	0.17	0.33	0.43	0.38	0.43
4.08	-0.09	0.03	0.21	0.34	0.49	0.50	0.47
4.15	-0.10	-0.08	0.09	0.17	0.34	0.36	0.29
4.22	-0.09	-0.05	0.34	0.25	0.41	0.44	0.30
4.29	0.00	0.01	0.16	0.36	0.45	0.41	0.45
5.06	-0.10	-0.07	0.14	0.29	0.41	0.39	0.45
5.13	-0.15	-0.14	0.07	0.24	0.35	0.34	0.39
5.20	-0.11	-0.11	0.04	0.27	0.34	0.33	0.43
5.27	-0.15	-0.15	0.09	0.26	0.36	0.32	0.41
6.03	-0.18	-0.12	0.10	0.28	0.42	0.40	0.54
6.10	-0.18	-0.13	0.11	0.28	0.42	0.40	0.52
6.17	-0.18	-0.14	0.12	0.27	0.41	0.41	0.53
6.24	-0.25	-0.20	0.03	0.19	0.32	0.32	0.49
7.01	-0.30	-0.18	0.02	0.14	0.28	0.28	0.50
7.08	-0.19	-0.16	0.06	0.25	0.36	0.33	0.53
7.15	-0.29	-0.17	0.01	0.26	0.32	0.30	0.43
7.22	-0.24	-0.53	0.01	0.16	0.32	0.32	0.46
7.29	-0.24	-0.18	-0.01	0.14	0.30	0.27	0.46
8.05	-0.26	-0.13	0.02	0.18	0.35	0.36	0.52
8.12	-0.23	-0.01	0.04	0.18	0.31	0.33	0.44
8.19	-0.19	-0.13	0.08	0.19	0.32	0.32	0.43
8.26	-0.15	-0.14	0.07	0.20	0.33	0.33	0.43
9.02	-0.27	-0.18	-0.03	0.11	0.25	0.26	0.39
9.09	-0.21	-0.17	0.04	0.20	0.32	0.32	0.45
9.16	-0.22	-0.11	0.05	0.19	0.29	0.32	0.47
9.23	-0.20	-0.21	0.03	0.17	0.28	0.28	0.46
9.30	-0.25	-0.22	0.00	0.13	0.24	0.24	0.40
10.07	-0.31	-0.29	-0.06	0.06	0.21	0.21	0.43
10.14	-0.23	-0.22	-0.01	0.09	0.24	0.26	0.48
10.21	-0.22	-0.21	-0.01	0.11	0.25	0.26	0.38
10.28	-0.30	-0.24	-0.04	0.08	0.24	0.24	0.37
11.04	-0.24	-0.16	0.05	0.15	0.30	0.33	0.46
11.11	-0.32	-0.27	-0.03	0.08	0.21	0.25	0.35
11.18	-0.31	-0.29	-0.06	0.04	0.18	0.22	0.33
11.25	-0.40	-0.38	-0.13	-0.02	0.10	0.15	0.27
12.02	-0.35	-0.29	-0.04	0.09	0.20	0.21	0.28
12.09	-0.46	-0.32	-0.06	0.10	0.22	0.23	0.35
12.16	-0.46	-0.35	-0.07	0.07	0.17	0.18	0.29
12.23	-0.39	-0.21	-0.02	0.15	0.24	0.27	0.41
12.30	-0.45	-0.31	-0.08	0.09	0.17	0.19	0.33
ABS HI	0.17	0.07	0.34	0.39	0.49	0.50	0.54
AVG	-0.17	-0.15	0.07	0.21	0.33	0.33	0.42

HIGHEST RATE GICs - 1989
$1 MILLION SIMPLE INTEREST

WEEK ENDING	1	2	3	4	5	7	10
1.06	9.27	9.52	9.58	9.64	9.67	9.85	10.04
1.13	9.13	9.28	9.42	9.50	9.60	9.75	9.94
1.20	9.02	9.20	9.37	9.42	9.46	9.54	9.54
1.27	9.03	9.21	9.33	9.41	9.46	9.46	9.49
2.03	9.28	9.33	9.40	9.43	9.46	9.54	9.49
2.10	9.33	9.49	9.59	9.61	9.65	9.66	9.66
2.17	9.43	9.69	9.79	9.77	9.76	9.72	9.75
2.24	9.62	9.84	9.87	9.87	9.95	9.94	9.95
3.03	9.76	9.75	9.87	9.93	9.97	9.97	9.94
3.10	9.92	9.83	9.91	9.84	9.95	9.89	9.92
3.17	9.87	10.03	10.02	10.04	10.10	10.01	10.01
3.24	10.09	10.09	10.01	10.11	10.13	10.06	10.06
3.31	10.13	10.11	10.09	10.08	10.11	10.06	10.15
4.07	9.94	9.91	9.93	9.94	9.95	9.94	9.92
4.14	9.98	9.92	10.02	9.95	9.91	9.87	9.93
4.21	9.71	9.84	9.86	9.88	9.86	9.83	9.80
4.28	9.44	9.60	9.79	9.87	9.82	9.75	9.80
5.05	9.50	9.48	9.70	9.62	9.85	9.75	9.80
5.12	9.24	9.30	9.60	9.65	9.61	9.65	9.64
5.19	9.31	9.33	9.40	9.43	9.50	9.55	9.55
5.26	9.38	9.34	9.36	9.40	9.45	9.50	9.41
6.02	9.11	9.05	9.24	9.25	9.28	9.31	9.41
6.09	8.75	8.84	8.85	8.90	8.99	8.92	8.95
6.16	8.66	8.79	8.85	8.88	9.03	9.00	9.10
6.23	8.70	8.94	8.89	8.99	9.09	9.05	9.04
6.30	8.48	8.65	8.70	8.77	8.84	8.82	8.80
7.07	8.48	8.38	8.70	8.70	8.77	8.75	8.80
7.14	8.05	8.14	8.33	8.55	8.75	8.90	8.69
7.21	8.33	8.25	8.46	8.80	8.90	9.00	8.81
7.28	8.20	8.15	8.36	8.54	8.62	8.75	8.60
8.04	8.35	8.27	8.36	8.75	8.85	8.64	8.79
8.11	8.35	8.31	8.47	8.70	8.85	8.60	8.60
8.18	8.72	8.79	8.84	9.15	9.25	9.11	8.99
8.25	8.60	8.73	8.78	8.92	9.03	9.71	8.96
9.01	8.63	8.78	8.88	9.01	9.09	9.20	9.07
9.08	8.52	8.69	8.85	9.00	9.05	9.10	9.00
9.15	8.35	8.65	8.71	8.80	8.96	9.05	9.00
9.22	8.58	8.84	8.79	8.95	9.09	9.15	9.00
9.29	8.99	9.09	9.05	9.15	9.34	9.25	9.35
10.06	8.52	8.78	8.94	8.98	9.08	9.25	9.35
10.13	8.18	8.46	8.69	8.88	8.94	9.00	8.92
10.20	8.28	8.23	8.53	8.65	8.80	8.95	8.72
10.27	8.23	8.23	8.52	8.65	8.75	8.85	8.75
11.03	8.36	8.50	8.69	8.68	8.84	8.91	8.94
11.10	8.28	8.30	8.55	8.65	8.75	8.85	8.80
11.17	8.18	8.25	8.47	8.59	8.72	8.73	8.71
11.22	8.13	8.28	8.47	8.59	8.74	8.76	8.70
12.01	8.13	8.21	8.44	8.60	8.74	8.80	8.81
12.08	8.16	8.50	8.60	8.65	8.76	8.81	8.80
12.15	8.08	8.50	8.60	8.67	8.81	8.75	8.79
12.22	8.22	8.32	8.41	8.54	8.73	8.73	8.73
12.29	8.18	8.36	8.55	8.67	8.80	8.90	8.81
ABS HI	10.13	10.11	10.09	10.11	10.13	10.06	10.15
AVG	8.87	8.97	9.09	9.17	9.26	9.29	9.26

MARKET AVG RATE GICs - 1989
$1 MILLION SIMPLE INTEREST

WEEK ENDING	1	2	3	4	5	7	10
1.06	9.01	9.17	9.36	9.45	9.53	9.56	9.71
1.13	8.87	9.04	9.25	9.32	9.43	9.46	9.60
1.20	8.75	8.97	9.18	9.26	9.32	9.36	9.45
1.27	8.76	8.95	9.16	9.22	9.27	9.30	9.41
2.03	8.89	9.05	9.22	9.28	9.33	9.36	9.41
2.10	9.00	9.22	9.36	9.42	9.48	9.49	9.54
2.17	9.10	9.27	9.45	9.51	9.57	9.56	9.63
2.24	9.37	9.49	9.57	9.65	9.71	9.72	9.78
3.03	9.31	9.43	9.55	9.64	9.71	9.69	9.76
3.10	9.43	9.50	9.61	9.66	9.73	9.71	9.76
3.17	9.57	9.66	9.77	9.83	9.87	9.84	9.86
3.24	9.64	9.73	9.84	9.88	9.83	9.88	9.90
3.31	9.71	9.72	9.85	9.86	9.91	9.85	9.91
4.07	9.49	9.52	9.66	9.70	9.72	9.68	9.74
4.14	9.46	9.51	9.64	9.68	9.69	9.66	9.77
4.21	9.35	9.44	9.54	9.59	9.61	9.58	9.65
4.28	9.15	9.22	9.38	9.42	9.46	9.46	9.58
5.05	9.10	9.19	9.31	9.34	9.39	9.40	9.51
5.12	8.91	8.99	9.12	9.21	9.25	9.31	9.41
5.19	8.83	9.04	9.14	9.21	9.25	9.25	9.30
5.26	8.84	9.03	9.11	9.15	9.18	9.19	9.20
6.02	8.56	8.73	8.84	8.91	8.95	8.95	9.04
6.09	8.32	8.42	8.55	8.62	8.67	8.68	8.72
6.16	8.31	8.49	8.61	8.67	8.70	8.72	8.76
6.23	8.35	8.53	8.65	8.72	8.76	8.77	8.80
6.30	8.13	8.26	8.41	8.48	8.52	8.54	8.62
7.07	7.93	7.98	8.22	8.32	8.37	8.47	8.57
7.14	7.72	7.80	8.02	8.19	8.26	8.37	8.46
7.21	7.90	7.97	8.17	8.31	8.38	8.45	8.56
7.28	7.68	7.73	8.01	8.13	8.23	8.31	8.44
8.04	7.77	7.86	8.07	8.20	8.29	8.32	8.42
8.11	7.80	7.98	8.12	8.25	8.33	8.33	8.46
8.18	8.24	8.42	8.54	8.66	8.75	8.74	8.76
8.25	8.12	8.39	8.52	8.63	8.69	8.80	8.72
9.01	8.38	8.57	8.66	8.77	8.82	8.88	8.88
9.08	8.30	8.46	8.62	8.69	8.73	8.79	8.77
9.15	7.98	8.25	8.41	8.54	8.62	8.70	8.71
9.22	8.18	8.43	8.53	8.66	8.73	8.76	8.77
9.29	8.54	8.64	8.79	8.88	8.95	8.97	8.96
10.06	8.15	8.29	8.49	8.58	8.65	8.73	8.75
10.13	7.98	8.14	8.41	8.48	8.56	8.66	8.69
10.20	7.90	8.01	8.28	8.34	8.45	8.59	8.55
10.27	7.92	7.95	8.26	8.31	8.41	8.53	8.53
11.03	7.94	8.09	8.38	8.44	8.53	8.63	8.64
11.10	7.89	7.97	8.32	8.37	8.47	8.55	8.54
11.17	7.77	7.95	8.22	8.32	8.43	8.50	8.53
11.22	7.85	7.98	8.26	8.36	8.47	8.52	8.53
12.01	7.81	7.99	8.30	8.43	8.52	8.63	8.61
12.08	7.82	8.03	8.27	8.40	8.47	8.55	8.61
12.15	7.80	8.01	8.25	8.35	8.44	8.54	8.59
12.22	7.92	7.98	8.23	8.33	8.44	8.54	8.54
12.29	7.86	8.15	8.40	8.48	8.59	8.67	8.70
ABS HI	9.71	9.73	9.85	9.88	9.91	9.88	9.91
AVG	8.49	8.63	8.81	8.89	8.95	8.99	9.04

1989 SPREADS - HIGH RATE GICs vs TREASURIES

WEEK ENDING	MATURITY 1	2	3	4	5	7	10
1.06	0.10	0.24	0.28	0.35	0.39	0.54	0.80
1.13	0.02	0.05	0.15	0.25	0.37	0.50	0.76
1.20	0.06	0.07	0.23	0.30	0.37	0.47	0.52
1.27	0.06	0.11	0.22	0.33	0.42	0.44	0.52
2.03	0.23	0.19	0.26	0.32	0.39	0.50	0.49
2.10	0.18	0.23	0.35	0.42	0.51	0.55	0.61
2.17	0.16	0.30	0.43	0.43	0.44	0.44	0.54
2.24	0.21	0.30	0.45	0.44	0.52	0.56	0.64
3.03	0.36	0.20	0.44	0.50	0.55	0.58	0.61
3.10	0.53	0.32	0.49	0.44	0.58	0.57	0.65
3.17	0.31	0.36	0.41	0.49	0.61	0.59	0.66
3.24	0.31	0.23	0.19	0.35	0.44	0.48	0.57
3.31	0.42	0.30	0.35	0.40	0.50	0.59	0.78
4.07	0.47	0.39	0.46	0.51	0.59	0.65	0.72
4.14	0.50	0.36	0.49	0.47	0.49	0.51	0.66
4.21	0.43	0.45	0.51	0.58	0.61	0.64	0.66
4.28	0.22	0.27	0.53	0.66	0.66	0.62	0.71
5.05	0.34	0.26	0.52	0.48	0.76	0.68	0.73
5.12	0.19	0.19	0.52	0.58	0.55	0.59	0.59
5.19	0.42	0.38	0.50	0.55	0.64	0.74	0.76
5.26	0.52	0.48	0.54	0.62	0.72	0.83	0.78
6.02	0.31	0.29	0.53	0.59	0.68	0.70	0.84
6.09	0.35	0.46	0.52	0.59	0.71	0.61	0.67
6.16	0.21	0.38	0.47	0.54	0.73	0.70	0.84
6.23	0.17	0.44	0.44	0.58	0.72	0.67	0.70
6.30	0.20	0.42	0.50	0.60	0.71	0.66	0.66
7.07	0.51	0.43	0.76	0.76	0.84	0.68	0.72
7.14	0.20	0.35	0.53	0.74	0.94	0.98	0.68
7.21	0.37	0.37	0.58	0.91	1.02	1.02	0.74
7.28	0.34	0.40	0.59	0.78	0.87	0.89	0.63
8.04	0.62	0.66	0.70	1.10	1.21	0.92	0.97
8.11	0.23	0.30	0.46	0.70	0.86	0.60	0.56
8.18	0.42	0.53	0.63	0.96	1.07	0.94	0.84
8.25	0.24	0.37	0.45	0.62	0.77	1.44	0.73
9.01	0.31	0.37	0.51	0.69	0.83	0.91	0.82
9.08	0.25	0.35	0.56	0.76	0.87	0.89	0.83
9.15	0.28	0.50	0.60	0.71	0.89	0.91	0.87
9.22	0.40	0.60	0.60	0.79	0.97	0.97	0.85
9.29	0.77	0.81	0.79	0.93	1.17	1.02	1.16
10.06	0.46	0.68	0.86	0.93	1.06	1.19	1.31
10.13	0.62	0.85	0.93	1.16	1.20	1.19	1.08
10.20	0.43	0.37	0.59	0.72	0.88	0.97	0.73
10.27	0.42	0.42	0.66	0.80	0.92	0.95	0.86
11.03	0.47	0.62	0.77	0.79	0.98	1.00	1.02
11.10	0.41	0.44	0.66	0.77	0.88	0.96	0.88
11.17	0.47	0.50	0.73	0.82	0.93	0.89	0.85
11.22	0.53	0.62	0.82	0.93	1.02	0.99	0.89
12.01	0.40	0.45	0.68	0.84	0.97	0.97	0.96
12.08	0.43	0.73	0.83	0.90	1.02	0.98	0.96
12.15	0.35	0.72	0.86	0.94	1.09	0.92	0.97
12.22	0.56	0.61	0.69	0.83	1.04	0.92	0.95
12.29	0.38	0.47	0.65	0.78	0.92	0.91	0.88
ABS HI	0.77	0.85	0.93	1.16	1.21	1.44	1.31
AVG	0.35	0.41	0.54	0.65	0.77	0.78	0.77

1989 SPREADS - MKT AVG RATE GICs vs TREASURIES

WEEK ENDING	MATURITY 1	2	3	4	5	7	10
1.06	-0.16	-0.11	0.06	0.16	0.25	0.25	0.47
1.13	-0.24	-0.19	-0.02	0.07	0.20	0.21	0.42
1.20	-0.21	-0.16	0.04	0.14	0.23	0.29	0.43
1.27	-0.21	-0.15	0.05	0.14	0.23	0.28	0.44
2.03	-0.16	-0.09	0.08	0.17	0.26	0.32	0.41
2.10	-0.15	-0.04	0.12	0.23	0.34	0.38	0.49
2.17	-0.17	-0.12	0.09	0.17	0.25	0.28	0.42
2.24	-0.04	-0.05	0.15	0.22	0.28	0.34	0.47
3.03	-0.09	-0.12	0.12	0.21	0.29	0.30	0.43
3.10	0.04	-0.01	0.19	0.26	0.36	0.39	0.49
3.17	0.01	-0.01	0.16	0.28	0.38	0.42	0.51
3.24	-0.14	-0.13	0.02	0.12	0.14	0.30	0.41
3.31	0.00	-0.09	0.11	0.18	0.30	0.38	0.54
4.07	0.02	0.00	0.19	0.27	0.36	0.39	0.54
4.14	-0.02	-0.05	0.11	0.20	0.27	0.30	0.50
4.21	0.07	0.05	0.19	0.29	0.36	0.39	0.51
4.28	-0.07	-0.11	0.12	0.21	0.30	0.33	0.49
5.05	-0.06	-0.03	0.13	0.20	0.30	0.33	0.44
5.12	-0.14	-0.12	0.04	0.14	0.19	0.25	0.36
5.19	-0.06	0.09	0.24	0.33	0.39	0.44	0.51
5.26	-0.02	0.17	0.29	0.37	0.45	0.52	0.57
6.02	-0.24	-0.03	0.13	0.25	0.35	0.34	0.47
6.09	-0.08	0.04	0.22	0.31	0.39	0.37	0.44
6.16	-0.14	0.08	0.23	0.33	0.40	0.42	0.50
6.23	-0.18	0.03	0.20	0.31	0.39	0.39	0.46
6.30	-0.15	0.03	0.21	0.31	0.39	0.38	0.48
7.07	-0.04	0.03	0.28	0.38	0.44	0.40	0.49
7.14	-0.13	0.01	0.22	0.38	0.45	0.45	0.45
7.21	-0.06	0.09	0.29	0.42	0.50	0.47	0.49
7.28	-0.18	-0.02	0.24	0.37	0.48	0.45	0.47
8.04	0.04	0.25	0.41	0.55	0.65	0.60	0.60
8.11	-0.32	-0.03	0.11	0.25	0.34	0.33	0.42
8.18	-0.06	0.16	0.33	0.47	0.57	0.57	0.61
8.25	-0.24	0.03	0.19	0.33	0.43	0.53	0.49
9.01	0.06	0.16	0.29	0.45	0.56	0.59	0.63
9.08	0.03	0.12	0.33	0.45	0.55	0.58	0.60
9.15	-0.09	0.10	0.30	0.45	0.55	0.56	0.58
9.22	0.00	0.19	0.34	0.50	0.61	0.58	0.62
9.29	0.32	0.36	0.53	0.66	0.78	0.74	0.77
10.06	0.10	0.19	0.41	0.53	0.63	0.67	0.72
10.13	0.42	0.53	0.65	0.76	0.82	0.85	0.85
10.20	0.05	0.15	0.34	0.41	0.53	0.61	0.56
10.27	0.11	0.14	0.40	0.46	0.58	0.63	0.64
11.03	0.05	0.21	0.46	0.55	0.67	0.72	0.72
11.10	0.02	0.11	0.43	0.49	0.60	0.66	0.62
11.17	0.06	0.20	0.48	0.55	0.64	0.66	0.67
11.22	0.25	0.32	0.61	0.70	0.75	0.75	0.72
12.01	0.08	0.23	0.54	0.67	0.75	0.80	0.76
12.08	0.09	0.26	0.50	0.65	0.73	0.72	0.77
12.15	0.07	0.23	0.51	0.62	0.72	0.71	0.77
12.22	0.26	0.27	0.51	0.63	0.75	0.73	0.76
12.29	0.06	0.26	0.50	0.59	0.71	0.68	0.77
ABS HI	0.42	0.53	0.65	0.76	0.82	0.85	0.85
AVG	-0.03	0.07	0.26	0.37	0.46	0.48	0.55

HIGHEST RATE GICs - 1990
$1 MILLION SIMPLE INTEREST

WEEK ENDING	MATURITY						
	1	2	.3	4	5	7	10
1.05	8.23	8.40	8.67	8.79	8.96	8.95	8.95
1.12	8.18	8.43	8.67	8.79	8.94	9.00	9.09
1.19	8.48	8.68	8.93	9.05	9.15	9.12	9.25
1.26	8.53	8.83	9.06	9.10	9.22	9.29	9.40
2.02	8.58	8.88	9.05	9.17	9.34	9.31	9.42
2.09	8.48	8.85	9.02	9.15	9.23	9.33	9.43
2.16	8.43	8.85	9.15	9.20	9.25	9.32	9.37
2.23	8.49	8.90	9.17	9.25	9.30	9.38	9.58
3.02	8.57	9.01	9.16	9.32	9.38	9.44	9.58
3.09	8.72	9.30	9.36	9.38	9.48	9.51	9.58
3.16	8.78	9.15	9.34	9.49	9.47	9.53	9.72
3.23	8.68	9.11	9.25	9.39	9.47	9.46	9.53
3.30	8.71	9.15	9.30	9.41	9.47	9.53	9.64
4.06	8.61	8.96	9.20	9.31	9.40	9.41	9.56
4.12	8.62	9.01	9.25	9.35	9.46	9.52	9.68
4.20	8.83	9.25	9.50	9.62	9.69	9.72	9.78
4.27	9.01	9.55	9.77	9.87	9.94	9.90	9.92
5.04	8.97	9.38	9.65	9.77	9.80	9.84	9.81
5.11	8.69	9.08	9.34	9.52	9.60	9.66	9.64
5.18	8.58	9.07	9.28	9.41	9.50	9.60	9.57
5.25	8.52	9.05	9.27	9.40	9.44	9.48	9.51
6.01	8.57	8.90	9.15	9.30	9.34	9.42	9.55
6.08	8.42	8.78	9.04	9.17	9.25	9.37	9.54
6.15	8.34	8.80	9.07	9.25	9.29	9.30	9.47
6.22	8.47	8.88	9.11	9.25	9.36	9.41	9.37
6.29	8.38	8.78	9.03	9.13	9.28	9.49	9.61
7.06	8.41	8.80	9.08	9.18	9.32	9.52	9.64
7.13	8.32	8.65	8.97	9.15	9.24	9.31	9.32
7.20	8.20	8.60	9.02	9.15	9.24	9.35	9.54
7.27	8.20	8.50	8.83	9.05	9.15	9.30	9.51
8.03	8.04	8.29	8.62	8.80	8.90	9.13	9.40
8.10	8.03	8.47	8.75	8.97	9.10	9.41	9.68
8.17	8.18	8.55	8.89	9.11	9.29	9.53	9.81
8.24	8.31	8.70	9.02	9.33	9.49	9.70	9.83
8.31	8.13	8.65	9.02	9.25	9.34	9.61	9.91
9.07	8.07	8.65	9.02	9.25	9.34	9.61	9.87
9.14	8.02	8.45	8.81	9.17	9.28	9.66	9.98
9.21	8.12	8.60	8.92	9.20	9.34	9.58	9.71
9.28	8.05	8.63	8.89	9.25	9.30	9.73	10.04
10.05	7.86	8.40	8.74	9.05	9.19	9.50	9.84
10.12	7.92	8.57	8.85	9.10	9.24	9.68	10.02
10.19	7.91	8.36	8.65	8.94	9.09	9.47	9.79
10.26	7.97	8.45	8.67	8.90	9.09	9.48	9.83
11.02	7.80	8.35	8.57	8.85	9.04	9.40	9.75
11.09	7.81	8.25	8.54	8.85	8.99	9.36	9.65
11.16	7.81	8.31	8.51	8.80	8.87	9.22	9.48
11.22	7.81	8.30	8.51	8.70	8.82	9.12	9.38
11.30	7.84	8.40	8.52	8.71	8.88	9.17	9.42
12.07	7.65	8.17	8.48	8.70	8.70	8.96	9.19
12.14	7.57	8.13	8.28	8.50	8.67	8.89	9.12
12.21	7.38	8.04	8.26	8.45	8.60	8.91	9.16
12.28	7.25	7.76	8.11	8.41	8.58	8.83	9.02
ABS HI	9.01	9.55	9.77	9.87	9.94	9.90	10.04
AVG	8.26	8.69	8.95	9.13	9.23	9.40	9.57

MARKET AVG RATE GICs - 1990
$1 MILLION SIMPLE INTEREST

WEEK ENDING	MATURITY						
	1	2	3	4	5	7	10
1.05	7.87	8.12	8.39	8.49	8.60	8.71	8.75
1.12	7.85	8.18	8.47	8.57	8.67	8.78	8.84
1.19	8.05	8.36	8.66	8.79	8.88	8.93	9.03
1.26	8.20	8.50	8.79	8.90	9.00	9.07	9.14
2.02	8.34	8.58	8.87	8.99	9.08	9.13	9.24
2.09	8.20	8.53	8.79	8.93	9.03	9.08	9.17
2.16	8.18	8.54	8.80	8.91	9.03	9.08	9.22
2.23	8.21	8.61	8.93	9.06	9.13	9.19	9.31
3.02	8.29	8.74	8.99	9.12	9.20	9.28	9.38
3.09	8.46	8.88	9.12	9.23	9.29	9.32	9.39
3.16	8.47	8.87	9.14	9.22	9.28	9.34	9.44
3.23	8.36	8.84	9.07	9.13	9.19	9.22	9.31
3.30	8.38	8.85	9.10	9.16	9.24	9.28	9.37
4.06	8.30	8.74	9.00	9.09	9.15	9.20	9.30
4.12	8.38	8.79	9.70	9.16	9.25	9.30	9.42
4.20	8.53	9.02	9.26	9.34	9.42	9.49	9.58
4.27	8.71	9.26	9.52	9.61	9.67	9.66	9.75
5.04	8.58	9.05	9.30	9.41	9.48	9.53	9.63
5.11	8.30	8.79	9.08	9.20	9.28	9.35	9.50
5.18	8.36	8.84	9.10	9.21	9.30	9.38	9.43
5.25	8.28	8.78	9.05	9.15	9.23	9.30	9.41
6.01	8.16	8.62	8.88	9.01	9.09	9.19	9.26
6.08	8.17	8.61	8.84	8.97	9.06	9.17	9.22
6.15	8.09	8.52	8.79	8.93	9.02	9.10	9.21
6.22	8.20	8.65	8.90	9.03	9.11	9.21	9.26
6.29	8.15	8.51	8.80	8.92	9.02	9.18	9.27
7.06	8.20	8.53	8.85	8.97	9.07	9.19	9.28
7.13	8.02	8.37	8.70	8.84	8.95	9.10	9.19
7.20	7.95	8.32	8.68	8.83	8.94	9.10	9.23
7.27	7.86	8.22	8.58	8.74	8.87	9.04	9.19
8.03	7.68	7.97	8.35	8.49	8.66	8.90	9.13
8.10	7.80	8.17	8.50	8.74	8.91	9.18	9.41
8.17	7.91	8.31	8.64	8.87	9.06	9.26	9.51
8.24	8.00	8.46	8.79	9.03	9.19	9.40	9.62
8.31	7.83	8.28	8.68	8.92	9.09	9.34	9.55
9.07	7.82	8.27	8.64	8.90	9.09	9.34	9.55
9.14	7.77	8.21	8.55	8.84	9.02	9.29	9.53
9.21	7.74	8.31	8.62	8.93	9.11	9.33	9.55
9.28	7.77	8.30	8.64	8.91	9.09	9.31	9.56
10.05	7.61	8.14	8.48	8.74	8.93	9.16	9.38
10.12	7.67	8.28	8.57	8.86	9.04	9.27	9.51
10.19	7.65	8.15	8.42	8.68	8.82	9.09	9.29
10.26	7.65	8.14	8.41	8.67	8.83	9.11	9.32
11.02	7.51	8.03	8.30	8.58	8.76	9.03	9.24
11.09	7.48	8.03	8.31	8.60	8.79	9.03	9.25
11.16	7.44	7.96	8.21	8.45	8.62	8.87	9.06
11.22	7.48	7.96	8.21	8.44	8.62	8.86	9.04
11.30	7.49	7.96	8.22	8.46	8.63	8.88	9.06
12.07	7.32	7.79	8.06	8.31	8.46	8.69	8.88
12.14	7.28	7.74	7.98	8.23	8.40	8.61	8.77
12.21	7.04	7.64	7.90	8.12	8.31	8.62	8.83
12.28	7.08	7.57	7.87	8.17	8.36	8.67	8.84
ABS HI	8.71	9.26	9.70	9.61	9.67	9.66	9.75
AVG	7.96	8.40	8.70	8.86	8.99	9.14	9.28

1990 SPREADS - HIGH RATE GICs vs TREASURIES

WEEK ENDING	MATURITY 1	2	3	4	5	7	10
1.05	0.41	0.49	0.74	0.87	1.05	0.93	0.97
1.12	0.40	0.52	0.72	0.84	1.00	0.96	1.05
1.19	0.51	0.52	0.74	0.87	0.98	0.89	1.01
1.26	0.50	0.58	0.72	0.75	0.87	0.87	0.95
2.02	0.49	0.57	0.67	0.79	0.95	0.88	0.95
2.09	0.35	0.48	0.64	0.74	0.79	0.86	0.95
2.16	0.38	0.55	0.85	0.87	0.89	0.92	0.98
2.23	0.30	0.42	0.68	0.74	0.77	0.78	1.00
3.02	0.43	0.58	0.72	0.88	0.94	0.91	1.08
3.09	0.38	0.71	0.76	0.79	0.89	0.85	0.97
3.16	0.36	0.45	0.64	0.80	0.79	0.82	1.07
3.23	0.33	0.45	0.62	0.78	0.87	0.84	0.98
3.30	0.37	0.53	0.67	0.81	0.90	0.91	1.08
4.06	0.32	0.39	0.58	0.74	0.81	0.76	0.97
4.12	0.33	0.46	0.64	0.74	0.86	0.87	1.06
4.20	0.42	0.50	0.70	0.82	0.90	0.88	0.95
4.27	0.44	0.60	0.75	0.85	0.93	0.86	0.90
5.04	0.41	0.44	0.64	0.76	0.79	0.81	0.79
5.11	0.33	0.40	0.61	0.76	0.81	0.83	0.83
5.18	0.34	0.51	0.68	0.78	0.83	0.89	0.89
5.25	0.30	0.53	0.70	0.78	0.85	0.78	0.83
6.01	0.39	0.44	0.65	0.79	0.82	0.81	0.97
6.08	0.34	0.45	0.66	0.77	0.84	0.87	1.08
6.15	0.29	0.49	0.71	0.88	0.90	0.82	1.03
6.22	0.33	0.47	0.67	0.80	0.89	0.85	0.85
6.29	0.25	0.42	0.61	0.70	0.83	0.94	1.10
7.06	0.35	0.55	0.86	0.83	0.96	1.04	1.20
7.13	0.43	0.54	0.76	0.87	0.94	0.89	0.89
7.20	0.33	0.48	0.79	0.88	0.93	0.91	1.07
7.27	0.35	0.43	0.62	0.80	0.85	0.87	1.03
8.03	0.37	0.41	0.61	0.74	0.78	0.85	1.03
8.10	0.33	0.49	0.60	0.72	0.74	0.81	0.96
8.17	0.45	0.55	0.74	0.84	0.90	0.93	1.10
8.24	0.38	0.47	0.64	0.83	0.87	0.89	0.91
8.31	0.35	0.60	0.80	0.92	0.90	0.97	1.16
9.07	0.33	0.59	0.78	0.89	0.86	0.85	1.02
9.14	0.27	0.39	0.57	0.81	0.81	0.93	1.14
9.21	0.35	0.52	0.67	0.81	0.82	0.78	0.79
9.28	0.26	0.51	0.56	0.80	0.72	0.88	1.08
10.05	0.28	0.52	0.67	0.85	0.86	0.91	1.15
10.12	0.30	0.60	0.67	0.77	0.77	0.93	1.15
10.19	0.33	0.46	0.55	0.72	0.75	0.86	1.05
10.26	0.47	0.62	0.68	0.79	0.85	0.98	1.19
11.02	0.39	0.60	0.62	0.76	0.82	0.91	1.11
11.09	0.46	0.60	0.73	0.88	0.86	0.97	1.12
11.16	0.51	0.72	0.81	0.95	0.87	0.98	1.13
11.22	0.52	0.72	0.82	0.87	0.86	0.93	1.08
11.30	0.54	0.86	0.84	0.91	0.95	0.97	1.13
12.07	0.41	0.72	0.91	1.01	0.90	0.88	1.03
12.14	0.49	0.85	0.88	0.97	1.02	0.99	1.15
12.21	0.42	0.77	0.84	0.89	0.91	0.95	1.13
12.28	0.30	0.48	0.62	0.77	0.79	0.75	0.87
ABS HI	0.54	0.86	0.91	1.01	1.05	1.04	1.20
AVG	0.38	0.54	0.70	0.82	0.87	0.88	1.02

1990 SPREADS - MKT AVG RATE GICs vs TREASURIES

WEEK ENDING	MATURITY 1	2	3	4	5	7	10
1.05	0.05	0.21	0.46	0.57	0.69	0.69	0.78
1.12	0.07	0.27	0.52	0.63	0.73	0.74	0.80
1.19	0.08	0.20	0.47	0.61	0.71	0.70	0.79
1.26	0.17	0.25	0.45	0.55	0.65	0.65	0.69
2.02	0.25	0.27	0.49	0.61	0.69	0.70	0.77
2.09	0.07	0.16	0.41	0.52	0.59	0.61	0.69
2.16	0.13	0.24	0.50	0.58	0.67	0.68	0.83
2.23	0.02	0.13	0.44	0.55	0.60	0.59	0.73
3.02	0.15	0.31	0.55	0.68	0.76	0.75	0.88
3.09	0.12	0.29	0.52	0.63	0.70	0.66	0.78
3.16	0.05	0.17	0.44	0.53	0.60	0.63	0.79
3.23	0.01	0.18	0.44	0.52	0.59	0.60	0.76
3.30	0.04	0.24	0.47	0.56	0.67	0.66	0.81
4.06	0.01	0.17	0.38	0.52	0.56	0.55	0.71
4.12	0.09	0.24	1.09	0.55	0.65	0.65	0.80
4.20	0.12	0.27	0.46	0.55	0.63	0.65	0.75
4.27	0.14	0.31	0.50	0.59	0.66	0.62	0.73
5.04	0.02	0.11	0.29	0.40	0.47	0.50	0.61
5.11	-0.06	0.11	0.35	0.44	0.49	0.52	0.69
5.18	0.12	0.28	0.50	0.58	0.63	0.67	0.75
5.25	0.06	0.26	0.48	0.53	0.64	0.60	0.73
6.01	-0.02	0.16	0.38	0.50	0.57	0.58	0.68
6.08	0.09	0.28	0.46	0.57	0.65	0.67	0.76
6.15	0.04	0.21	0.43	0.55	0.63	0.62	0.77
6.22	0.06	0.24	0.46	0.57	0.64	0.65	0.74
6.29	0.02	0.15	0.38	0.48	0.57	0.63	0.76
7.06	0.14	0.28	0.63	0.63	0.71	0.71	0.84
7.13	0.13	0.26	0.49	0.56	0.65	0.68	0.76
7.20	0.08	0.20	0.45	0.56	0.63	0.66	0.76
7.27	0.01	0.15	0.37	0.48	0.57	0.61	0.71
8.03	0.01	0.09	0.34	0.43	0.54	0.62	0.76
8.10	0.10	0.19	0.35	0.48	0.55	0.58	0.69
8.17	0.18	0.31	0.49	0.60	0.67	0.66	0.80
8.24	0.07	0.23	0.41	0.53	0.57	0.59	0.70
8.31	0.05	0.22	0.46	0.59	0.65	0.70	0.80
9.07	0.08	0.21	0.40	0.54	0.61	0.58	0.70
9.14	0.02	0.15	0.31	0.48	0.55	0.56	0.69
9.21	-0.03	0.23	0.37	0.55	0.59	0.53	0.63
9.28	-0.02	0.18	0.31	0.46	0.51	0.46	0.60
10.05	0.03	0.26	0.41	0.54	0.60	0.57	0.69
10.12	0.05	0.31	0.39	0.53	0.57	0.52	0.64
10.19	0.07	0.25	0.32	0.46	0.48	0.48	0.55
10.26	0.15	0.31	0.42	0.55	0.59	0.61	0.68
11.02	0.10	0.28	0.35	0.49	0.54	0.54	0.60
11.09	0.13	0.38	0.50	0.63	0.66	0.64	0.72
11.16	0.14	0.37	0.51	0.60	0.62	0.63	0.71
11.22	0.19	0.38	0.52	0.61	0.66	0.67	0.74
11.30	0.19	0.42	0.54	0.66	0.70	0.68	0.77
12.07	0.08	0.34	0.49	0.63	0.66	0.61	0.72
12.14	0.20	0.46	0.58	0.71	0.75	0.71	0.80
12.21	0.08	0.37	0.48	0.56	0.62	0.66	0.80
12.28	0.13	0.29	0.38	0.53	0.57	0.59	0.69
ABS HI	0.25	0.46	1.09	0.71	0.76	0.75	0.88
AVG	0.08	0.25	0.45	0.55	0.62	0.62	0.73

HIGHEST RATE GICs - 1991
$1 MILLION SIMPLE INTEREST

WEEK ENDING	1	2	3	4	5	7	10
1.04	7.30	7.80	8.32	8.50	8.69	8.95	9.14
1.11	7.36	7.94	8.32	8.53	8.74	8.97	9.00
1.18	7.14	7.87	8.23	8.48	8.69	8.96	9.18
1.25	7.10	7.77	8.14	8.41	8.63	8.90	9.12
2.01	6.80	7.52	8.00	8.30	8.39	8.72	8.98
2.08	6.71	7.52	7.92	8.15	8.40	8.71	8.94
2.15	6.76	7.50	7.88	8.13	8.35	8.66	8.89
2.22	6.82	7.67	8.07	8.27	8.52	8.79	8.99
3.01	6.94	7.82	8.22	8.46	8.68	8.95	9.17
3.08	6.87	7.79	8.23	8.45	8.69	8.92	9.14
3.15	6.76	7.75	8.22	8.45	8.69	8.92	9.14
3.22	6.86	7.88	8.18	8.50	8.77	9.04	9.27
3.29	6.66	7.64	8.18	8.40	8.65	8.84	8.94
4.05	7.00	7.65	8.08	8.35	8.57	8.84	9.07
4.12	6.63	7.61	7.87	8.17	8.61	8.90	9.12
4.19	7.00	7.76	8.26	8.47	8.75	8.94	9.15
4.26	7.00	7.70	8.15	8.40	8.68	8.98	9.23
5.03	6.70	7.56	8.03	8.30	8.64	8.91	9.14
5.10	6.67	7.57	7.91	8.20	8.61	8.89	9.11
5.17	6.72	7.67	7.98	8.25	8.77	9.04	9.28
5.24	6.66	7.45	7.88	8.20	8.59	8.81	8.98
5.31	6.66	7.43	7.88	8.15	8.61	8.89	9.14
6.07	7.02	7.77	8.25	8.43	8.87	9.18	9.08
6.14	7.01	7.77	8.25	8.44	8.89	9.02	9.18
6.21	6.90	7.56	8.14	8.45	8.89	9.07	9.16
6.28	6.93	7.70	8.17	8.50	8.94	9.06	9.16
7.05	6.96	7.78	8.21	8.55	8.94	9.05	9.13
7.12	6.82	7.55	8.20	8.45	8.84	9.02	9.10
7.19	6.78	7.59	8.11	8.35	8.80	8.93	9.07
7.26	6.72	7.59	8.12	8.37	8.74	8.88	9.02
8.02	6.55	7.44	7.98	8.37	8.55	8.89	9.12
8.09	6.19	7.00	7.87	8.05	8.40	8.71	8.95
8.16	6.14	7.05	7.87	8.05	8.30	8.56	8.80
8.23	6.32	7.20	7.57	7.79	8.24	8.51	8.70
8.30	6.19	7.06	7.48	7.85	8.24	8.50	8.76
9.06	6.15	7.02	7.48	7.75	8.24	8.45	8.66
9.13	5.99	6.88	7.27	7.65	8.14	8.27	8.49
9.20	6.04	6.90	7.23	7.60	7.91	8.27	8.42
9.27	5.94	6.77	7.18	7.50	7.81	8.12	8.33
10.04	5.83	6.67	7.08	7.40	7.79	8.07	8.27
10.11	5.81	6.65	7.03	7.40	7.74	8.17	8.37
10.18	5.90	6.70	6.97	7.40	7.72	8.12	8.37
10.25	5.83	6.71	7.02	7.45	7.94	8.27	8.52
11.01	5.74	6.49	7.00	7.42	7.75	8.08	8.47
11.08	5.26	6.20	6.82	7.25	7.74	8.07	8.42
11.15	5.28	6.25	6.83	7.25	7.69	7.97	8.35
11.22	5.24	6.15	6.88	7.30	7.59	7.87	8.28
11.29	5.08	6.11	6.88	7.30	7.53	7.94	8.46
12.06	4.85	5.71	6.88	7.30	7.30	7.72	8.29
12.13	4.85	5.70	6.78	7.15	7.24	7.62	8.16
12.20	4.85	5.40	6.58	6.95	7.24	7.54	8.15
12.27	4.41	5.40	5.96	6.47	6.94	7.44	7.88
ABS HI	7.36	7.94	8.32	8.55	8.94	9.18	9.28
AVG	6.36	7.19	7.69	7.99	8.32	8.59	8.83

MARKET AVG RATE GICs - 1991
$1 MILLION SIMPLE INTEREST

WEEK ENDING	1	2	3	4	5	7	10
1.04	6.93	7.51	7.88	8.15	8.36	8.62	8.79
1.11	6.86	7.51	7.90	8.24	8.46	8.70	8.90
1.18	6.78	7.51	7.90	8.19	8.40	8.64	8.89
1.25	6.68	7.43	7.83	8.14	8.36	8.60	8.83
2.01	6.45	7.25	7.63	7.96	8.20	8.45	8.71
2.08	6.34	7.20	7.57	7.90	8.13	8.42	8.64
2.15	6.33	7.14	7.53	7.82	8.07	8.35	8.55
2.22	6.40	7.30	7.68	7.96	8.21	8.45	8.63
3.01	6.57	7.47	7.88	8.18	8.40	8.63	8.82
3.08	6.54	7.45	7.86	8.16	8.41	8.64	8.82
3.15	6.37	7.33	7.78	8.11	8.37	8.61	8.82
3.22	6.46	7.46	7.89	8.21	8.47	8.73	8.95
3.29	6.37	7.37	7.84	8.16	8.43	8.66	8.83
4.05	6.39	7.26	7.71	8.03	8.34	8.58	8.77
4.12	6.23	7.18	7.62	7.95	8.30	8.58	8.79
4.19	6.46	7.34	7.73	8.05	8.40	8.61	8.81
4.26	6.35	7.27	7.70	8.04	8.38	8.66	8.88
5.03	6.17	7.14	7.63	7.97	8.30	8.57	8.79
5.10	6.17	7.15	7.61	7.94	8.31	8.57	8.80
5.17	6.23	7.18	7.65	7.98	8.40	8.69	8.93
5.24	6.11	7.02	7.57	7.90	8.31	8.58	8.83
5.31	6.18	7.00	7.53	7.88	8.29	8.56	8.84
6.07	6.44	7.31	7.83	8.14	8.54	8.80	8.99
6.14	6.44	7.37	7.88	8.18	8.57	8.83	9.05
6.21	6.33	7.19	7.79	8.12	8.51	8.79	9.01
6.28	6.42	7.27	7.83	8.14	8.55	8.82	9.04
7.05	6.47	7.30	7.84	8.15	8.54	8.78	8.99
7.12	6.25	7.13	7.77	8.09	8.48	8.74	8.97
7.19	6.43	7.20	7.75	8.08	8.48	8.71	8.98
7.26	6.25	7.13	7.68	7.99	8.38	8.65	8.91
8.02	6.10	6.96	7.47	7.81	8.23	8.52	8.84
8.09	5.78	6.64	7.32	7.63	8.06	8.37	8.66
8.16	5.71	6.54	7.17	7.48	7.92	8.24	8.56
8.23	5.73	6.62	7.17	7.47	7.90	8.26	8.53
8.30	5.68	6.54	7.09	7.42	7.86	8.21	8.49
9.06	5.66	6.52	7.10	7.43	7.87	8.21	8.49
9.13	5.51	6.38	6.91	7.25	7.67	8.01	8.29
9.20	5.57	6.37	6.86	7.21	7.62	7.97	8.25
9.27	5.45	6.25	6.74	7.10	7.53	7.88	8.19
10.04	5.37	6.17	6.65	7.01	7.42	7.78	8.09
10.11	5.34	6.15	6.65	7.02	7.42	7.82	8.21
10.18	5.38	6.16	6.64	7.01	7.44	7.82	8.24
10.25	5.36	6.18	6.67	7.06	7.54	7.94	8.35
11.01	5.05	5.87	6.45	6.87	7.35	7.75	8.23
11.08	4.91	5.83	6.40	6.79	7.26	7.69	8.16
11.15	4.90	5.77	6.36	6.75	7.19	7.60	8.08
11.22	4.78	5.69	6.29	6.68	7.13	7.56	8.09
11.29	4.75	5.68	6.27	6.69	7.13	7.59	8.12
12.06	4.45	5.35	5.98	6.41	6.84	7.27	7.81
12.13	4.42	5.28	5.91	6.35	6.81	7.27	7.87
12.20	4.21	5.11	5.75	6.21	6.72	7.20	7.78
12.27	4.06	5.04	5.58	6.05	6.59	7.06	7.59
ABS HI	6.93	7.51	7.90	8.24	8.57	8.83	9.05
AVG	5.90	6.76	7.26	7.61	7.98	8.29	8.59

1991 SPREADS - HIGH RATE GICs vs TREASURIES

WEEK ENDING	1	2	MATURITY 3	4	5	7	10
1.04	0.52	0.68	0.98	1.02	1.07	1.02	1.14
1.11	0.65	0.78	0.91	0.94	0.97	0.91	0.82
1.18	0.52	0.69	0.80	0.88	0.92	0.94	1.03
1.25	0.52	0.68	0.79	0.91	0.97	0.98	1.08
2.01	0.29	0.49	0.71	0.86	0.79	0.85	0.96
2.08	0.48	0.71	0.91	0.94	0.99	1.02	1.12
2.15	0.56	0.71	0.90	0.95	0.96	1.00	1.11
2.22	0.52	0.76	0.95	0.95	1.01	1.03	1.13
3.01	0.54	0.77	0.95	1.00	1.03	1.07	1.17
3.08	0.39	0.66	0.87	0.89	0.94	0.92	1.04
3.15	0.44	0.73	0.96	0.97	0.99	0.98	1.08
3.22	0.45	0.73	0.76	0.87	0.92	0.97	1.09
3.29	0.32	0.54	0.82	0.83	0.86	0.83	0.84
4.05	0.74	0.68	0.83	0.88	0.88	0.92	1.04
4.12	0.41	0.67	0.63	0.70	0.92	0.98	1.08
4.19	0.74	0.81	1.05	1.02	1.05	1.05	1.15
4.26	0.75	0.72	0.90	0.91	0.94	1.02	1.14
5.03	0.59	0.75	0.87	0.90	1.00	1.02	1.12
5.10	0.54	0.73	0.78	0.79	0.92	0.96	1.05
5.17	0.59	0.82	0.85	0.80	1.01	1.05	1.17
5.24	0.51	0.67	0.76	0.77	0.86	0.85	0.90
5.31	0.53	0.79	0.81	0.66	0.95	0.97	1.08
6.07	0.72	0.92	0.96	0.85	1.01	1.10	0.88
6.14	0.61	0.73	0.81	0.73	0.92	0.81	0.87
6.21	0.53	0.60	0.73	0.77	0.94	0.88	0.85
6.28	0.57	0.72	0.75	0.81	0.98	0.86	0.85
7.05	0.56	0.78	0.79	0.87	0.99	0.87	0.85
7.12	0.52	0.60	0.76	0.74	0.87	0.81	0.78
7.19	0.46	0.69	0.73	0.70	0.88	0.78	0.79
7.26	0.50	0.75	0.91	1.03	0.93	0.83	0.83
8.02	0.37	0.64	0.77	0.88	0.79	0.87	0.95
8.09	0.31	0.44	0.95	0.82	0.86	0.88	0.97
8.16	0.42	0.65	1.10	0.97	0.90	0.85	0.93
8.23	0.70	0.92	0.91	0.81	0.95	0.87	0.88
8.30	0.45	0.70	0.78	0.82	0.89	0.82	0.92
9.06	0.45	0.72	0.82	0.77	0.94	0.80	0.86
9.13	0.41	0.67	0.71	0.78	0.96	0.74	0.78
9.20	0.48	0.72	0.75	0.81	0.81	0.84	0.81
9.27	0.44	0.68	0.80	0.79	0.77	0.75	0.78
10.04	0.43	0.70	0.82	0.83	0.91	0.81	0.82
10.11	0.45	0.72	0.80	0.86	0.89	0.95	0.89
10.18	0.57	0.80	0.76	0.87	0.87	0.93	0.87
10.25	0.44	0.73	0.72	0.82	0.98	0.93	0.86
11.01	0.59	0.74	0.88	0.97	0.96	0.88	0.95
11.08	0.26	0.45	0.83	0.90	1.03	0.93	0.94
11.15	0.32	0.64	0.88	0.96	1.05	0.93	0.98
11.22	0.42	0.64	1.04	1.10	1.03	0.87	0.90
11.29	0.34	0.57	1.07	1.13	0.99	0.91	1.04
12.06	0.24	0.46	1.25	1.31	0.96	0.90	1.04
12.13	0.41	0.63	1.32	1.30	0.99	0.86	0.95
12.20	0.50	0.39	1.20	1.16	1.03	0.81	1.02
12.27	0.24	0.57	0.79	0.88	0.94	0.93	1.02
ABS HI	0.75	0.92	1.32	1.31	1.07	1.10	1.17
AVG	0.49	0.68	0.87	0.89	0.94	0.91	0.97

1991 SPREADS - MKT AVG RATE GICs vs TREASURIES

WEEK ENDING	1	2	MATURITY 3	4	5	7	10
1.04	0.15	0.39	0.54	0.67	0.74	0.69	0.79
1.11	0.15	0.35	0.49	0.65	0.69	0.64	0.72
1.18	0.16	0.33	0.47	0.59	0.63	0.62	0.74
1.25	0.10	0.34	0.48	0.64	0.70	0.68	0.79
2.01	-0.06	0.22	0.34	0.51	0.60	0.58	0.69
2.08	0.11	0.39	0.56	0.69	0.72	0.73	0.82
2.15	0.13	0.35	0.55	0.63	0.68	0.69	0.77
2.22	0.10	0.39	0.56	0.64	0.70	0.69	0.77
3.01	0.17	0.42	0.61	0.72	0.75	0.75	0.82
3.08	0.06	0.32	0.50	0.60	0.66	0.66	0.75
3.15	0.05	0.31	0.52	0.63	0.67	0.67	0.76
3.22	0.05	0.31	0.47	0.58	0.62	0.66	0.77
3.29	0.03	0.27	0.48	0.59	0.64	0.65	0.73
4.05	0.13	0.29	0.46	0.56	0.65	0.66	0.74
4.12	0.01	0.24	0.38	0.48	0.61	0.66	0.75
4.19	0.20	0.39	0.52	0.60	0.70	0.72	0.81
4.26	0.10	0.29	0.45	0.54	0.64	0.70	0.79
5.03	0.06	0.33	0.47	0.57	0.66	0.68	0.77
5.10	0.04	0.31	0.48	0.53	0.62	0.64	0.74
5.17	0.10	0.33	0.52	0.54	0.64	0.70	0.82
5.24	-0.04	0.24	0.45	0.47	0.58	0.62	0.75
5.31	0.05	0.36	0.46	0.38	0.63	0.64	0.78
6.07	0.14	0.46	0.54	0.57	0.68	0.72	0.79
6.14	0.04	0.33	0.44	0.47	0.60	0.62	0.74
6.21	-0.04	0.23	0.38	0.44	0.56	0.60	0.70
6.28	0.06	0.29	0.41	0.45	0.59	0.62	0.73
7.05	0.07	0.30	0.42	0.46	0.59	0.60	0.71
7.12	-0.05	0.18	0.33	0.38	0.51	0.53	0.65
7.19	0.11	0.30	0.37	0.43	0.56	0.56	0.70
7.26	0.03	0.29	0.47	0.65	0.57	0.60	0.72
8.02	-0.08	0.16	0.28	0.32	0.47	0.50	0.67
8.09	-0.10	0.08	0.40	0.40	0.52	0.54	0.68
8.16	-0.01	0.14	0.40	0.40	0.52	0.53	0.69
8.23	0.11	0.34	0.51	0.49	0.61	0.62	0.71
8.30	-0.06	0.18	0.39	0.39	0.51	0.53	0.65
9.06	-0.04	0.22	0.44	0.45	0.57	0.56	0.69
9.13	-0.07	0.17	0.35	0.38	0.49	0.48	0.58
9.20	0.01	0.19	0.38	0.42	0.52	0.54	0.64
9.27	-0.05	0.16	0.36	0.39	0.49	0.51	0.64
10.04	-0.03	0.20	0.39	0.44	0.54	0.52	0.64
10.11	-0.02	0.22	0.42	0.48	0.57	0.60	0.73
10.18	0.05	0.26	0.43	0.48	0.59	0.63	0.74
10.25	-0.03	0.20	0.37	0.43	0.58	0.60	0.69
11.01	-0.10	0.12	0.33	0.42	0.56	0.55	0.71
11.08	-0.09	0.08	0.41	0.44	0.55	0.55	0.68
11.15	-0.06	0.16	0.41	0.46	0.55	0.56	0.71
11.22	-0.04	0.18	0.45	0.48	0.57	0.56	0.71
11.29	0.01	0.14	0.46	0.52	0.59	0.56	0.70
12.06	-0.16	0.10	0.35	0.42	0.50	0.45	0.56
12.13	-0.02	0.21	0.45	0.49	0.56	0.51	0.66
12.20	-0.14	0.10	0.37	0.42	0.51	0.47	0.65
12.27	-0.11	0.21	0.41	0.46	0.59	0.55	0.73
ABS HI	0.20	0.46	0.61	0.72	0.75	0.75	0.82
AVG	0.02	0.26	0.44	0.51	0.60	0.61	0.72

APPENDIX 2

RULE 151

[1941] Rule 151. Safe harbor definition of certain "annuity contracts or optional annuity contracts" within the meaning of Section 3(a)(8).—(a) Any annuity contract or optional annuity contract (a "contract") shall be deemed to be within the provisions of section 3(a)(8) of the Securities Act of 1933 [15 U.S.C. 77c(a)(8)], *Provided,* That

(1) The annuity or optional annuity contract is issued by a corporation (the "insurer") subject to the supervision of the insurance commissioner, bank commissioner, or as an issuer of insurance any agency or officer performing like functions, of any State or Territory of the United States or the District of Columbia.

(2) The insurer assumes the investment risk under the contract as prescribed in paragraph (b) of this rule; and

(3) The contract is not marketed primarily as an investment.

(b) The insurer shall be deemed to assume the investment risk under the contract if:

(1) The value of the contract does not vary according to the investment experience of a separate account;

(2) The insurer for the life of the contract;

(i) Guarantees the principal amount of purchase payments and interest credited thereto, less any deduction (without regard to its timing) for sales, administrative or other expenses or charges; and

(ii) Credits a specified rate of interest as defined in paragraph (c) of this rule to net purchase payments and interest credited thereto; and

(3) The insurer guarantees that the rate of any interest to be credited in excess of that described in paragraph (b)(2)(ii) will not be modified more frequently than once per year.

(c) The term "specified rate of interest," as used in paragraph (b)(2)(ii) of this rule, means a rate of interest under the contract that is at least equal to the minimum rate required to be credited by the relevant nonforfeiture law in the jurisdiction in which the contract is issued. If that jurisdiction does not have an applicable nonforfeiture law at the time the contract is no longer mandated in that jurisdiction, the specified rate under the contract must at least be equal to the minimum rate then required for individual annuity contracts by the NAIC Standard Nonforfeiture Law. (*Adopted by Sec Act Rel No 6645, eff 6/4/86.*)

APPENDIX 3

NEW YORK REGULATION 126, SECTION 95.9

§ 95.9 Details to be considered for actuarial memorandum
　(a) Identification of liabilities and assets.
　(1) Identification of liabilities.
　(i) In examining the contractual obligations under the contracts and single premium policies represented by the reserves being tested, the actuary shall review and describe the source of the inforce data on the valuation date. This may take the form of an actual inventory of the inforce business on the valuation date, a projection of the inforce business from an earlier inventory, or another approach. Whichever approach is taken should be described in the memorandum.
　(ii) The tests should reflect contracts and single premium policies in force on the valuation date, but not contracts and single premium policies sold or entered into after the valuation date. However, considerations for new contracts may be reflected indirectly, for example, in the unit expense assumptions. If a binding commitment has been made by the valuation date to enter into a contract or single premium policy with an effective date after the valuation date, or if the contract is already in effect but no actual considerations have been received as of the valuation date, the inclusion or exclusion of such commitment or contract or single premium policy should be disclosed.
　(iii) The reserves being tested should be the reserves held in the company's annual statement, whether in the general account or a separate account. Subject to subdivision (d) of this Section, the reserve value for guaranteed benefits where assets are either held in the general account or in the separate account but valued as though they were general account assets, may be the reserves based on statutory

---

Revised 1990-1. © 1990, NILS Publishing Company.

formulae and rules in this Part, except that such reserves may be reduced to the extent they are offset by excess statutory reserves in other blocks of business. If an aggregate test is used to comply with statutory minimum reserve requirements or to support the cash flow analysis required to submit an actuarial opinion, details of the valuation basis of the reserves being tested and the allocation of the assets to the various classes of contract or single premium policy reserves should be included in the memorandum. Above all, it should be clear that all reserves and supporting assets that entered into the aggregate test and all the actuarial obligations represented by such reserves are included in the actuarial opinion.

(2) Identification of assets.

The actuary should identify which assets on the valuation date are deemed to support the statutory reserve being tested for each class of contract or single premium policy business. This determination should consider the investment allocation method used by the company (e.g., segmentation, dedicated or allocated assets and/or a proration of segmented, dedicated or allocated assets in the general account). In allocating or assigning assets to the blocks being tested, the qualified actuary should ascertain that such selection is such that the adequacy of assets for blocks not being tested is not prejudiced or endangered. The actuary should disclose the inclusion or exclusion of investment commitments where the monies have not been disbursed as of the valuation date. If the statement value of the assets is less than the statement value of the reserves being tested, the difference should be explained. Subject to subdivision (d) of this Section, the memorandum must disclose the company's allocation of assets for each class of contract or single premium policy business and demonstrate that the assets are appropriate and that there is consistency from year to year in asset allocation. It is unacceptable to begin the analysis with assets having a statement value greater than the statement value of the reserves being tested since this implies a commitment of surplus.

(3) Market-value adjusted products subject to Section 4221 or Section 4223 of the Insurance Law.

In assessing the adequacy of reserves of deferred annuities subject to Section 4223 of the Insurance Law, and of reserves for single premium policies subject to Section 4221(n-2) of the Insurance Law, the qualified actuary should consider the effect of any market-value adjustment formula. If the formula does not closely approximate the gain or loss with respect to actual assets, additional fund reserves may be necessary. Reserves for such annuities must comply with Part 44 of this Title.

(b) Projection of cash flows.

(1) Projection of insurance cash flows.

In projecting insurance cash flows, the actuary should pay particular attention to those contractual provisions that can affect future cash flows, such as:

(i) the duration of the current interest rate guarantee and the levels of interest rates guaranteed, using lapse and persistency factors in accordance with subdivision (d) of this Section;

(ii) whether future considerations are permitted under the current interest rate guarantee and any limitation on the amounts and incidence of such considerations, including the effect of market interest rates on such considerations;

(iii) the amounts and incidence of the guaranteed benefit payments and, for structured settlements, the amounts and incidence of any large irregular or discontinuous payouts and, for flexible contracts, any guarantees on additional payments;

(iv) the amounts and incidence of nonguaranteed obligations to contractholders or single premium policyholders as defined by a company's experience rating plan or dividend distribution policies which the actuary's analysis indicates would be distributed to contractholders or single premium policyholders in accordance with current practices;

(v) any mortality risk such as death benefits or survivor income benefits associated with the annuities and single premium life insurance, including the risk that the actual future mortality rate will be higher or lower than current or expected experience;

(vi) the effect on lapses or policy loans of any changes in the mortality charges on single premium policies;

(vii) any rights to commute the value of the benefit payments (for example, deferred cash surrender benefits) or to otherwise modify the amounts and incidence of the payments;

(viii) whether the group or individual contractholders or, where the group contractholder does not control the surrender or transfer of funds, group certificate holders or individual participants under group contracts, are permitted to withdraw or transfer funds before the date of expiry of the interest rate guarantee and on what terms (e.g., surrender charge or market-value adjustment, if any);

(ix) the terms of surrender provisions and any bail-out provisions in the contracts or single premium policies;

(x) any rights to negotiate the terms of the interest rate guarantee before the date of expiry of the guarantee;

(xi) the effect of policy loans on single premium policies, especially loans which have little or no net cost to the single premium policyholder;

(xii) expenses and taxes as applicable;

(xiii) life contingencies, where applicable; and

(xiv) the amounts and incidence of dividends to stockholders which the actuary's analysis indicates would be payable in years where surplus is shown under a given scenario.

(2) Projection of investment cash flows.

Projections of investment cash flows should commence with scheduled interest payments and principal repayments and any other cash flows from the assets backing the liabilities. In projecting investment cash flows, the actuary should pay particular attention to those characteristics of the invested assets that can affect future investment cash flows, such as:

(i) the types of investments and whether future investment cash flows are fixed or variable (e.g., due to equity features in the investment);

(ii) the amounts and incidence of scheduled (or expected) investment earnings;

(iii) the amounts and incidence of scheduled repayments of principal;

(iv) early repayment provisions (e.g., call provisions);

(v) the expected marketability of the investments (e.g., privately placed bonds and mortgages vs. public issues);

(vi) the impact of hedging, options or similar investment strategies;

(vii) investment related expenses and taxes as applicable;

(viii) the quality of assets;

(ix) bond put provisions; and

(x) the risk of default.

(3) Future cash flows dependent upon interest rates.

(i) Each factor should be examined to determine the extent to which future cash flows may vary due to changes in interest rate scenarios. For example, with insurance cash flows, as interest rates rise, future considerations under fixed interest rate guarantee contracts may be expected to decline and future withdrawals may be expected to rise; as interest rates fall, considerations may rise and withdrawals decline.

The specific assumptions used in the projections for future considerations and future withdrawals, including the extent to which these assumptions vary with future interest rates, should be covered in the actuarial memorandum.

(ii) Future investment cash flows should be determined by taking account of the investment characteristics and assumptions on recent and future investment portfolios as to prevailing interest rates and the shape of the yield curve. For example, as interest rates fall, non-scheduled repayments may be expected to rise; as interest rates rise, such repayments may decline. Each assumption used should be appropriate to the particular interest rate and yield curve scenario being tested and should reflect any investment actions predicated by the company to respond to such a situation. All assumptions should be described in the actuarial memorandum.

(4) Additional considerations with regard to investment cash flows.

(i) The projections of investment cash flows should include investment earnings and repayments of principal, not only from the invested assets held by the company on the valuation date, but also from assets to be acquired after the valuation date to support the business in force on the valuation date. This requires an explicit assumption in the projections as to how any future net positive cash flows will be invested, with particular emphasis on the maturity structure of such new investments and the extent to which the maturity structure of future investments may vary with the prevailing interest rate scenario at the time of acquisition.

(ii) To handle negative cash flows, assumptions may be made that money will be borrowed, or that assets will be sold. If money will be borrowed, assumptions as to interest rates and durations of borrowed money shall be made. To the extent assets are assumed to be sold, either to cover future negative cash flows at any time during the projection period or for other reasons, an explicit assumption with respect to the determination of the assets' market value at the time of the sale needs to be made.

(iii) In expressing an opinion, the actuary should describe the specific investment assumptions that were used in the projection of asset cash flows. Subject to Section 95.7(b)(3) of this Part, the actuary may rely on other responsible company persons for the current investment policy of the company.

(5) Quality of assets.

The actuary should take account of the quality of assets in the projection of investment cash flows. Assumptions as to the quality of assets should be consistent with the actual investment portfolio and investment policy. The actuary may rely on others in the company to determine the quality of assets. Adjustments shall be made to the cash flow projections for obligations that are not investment grade.

(6) Risk of default.

In determining the sufficiency of assets to cover liabilities, the actuary shall take into account the risk of default on obligations, mortgage notes and preferred stocks in one of the following ways:

(i) By making annual expense charges or reductions in annual investment income based on 75% of the appropriate annual reserve factors (that is, the factors based on an annual accumulation factor of 1.00 and exclusive of capital gains and losses) for the Bond and Preferred Stock Reserve Component of the MSVR (interest and dividends earned on assets assigned to the MSVR are recognized approximately by the 25% reduction in the normal factor) and by making an appropriate expense charge for other assets such as mortgage notes. Under this method the charges are accumulated to provide for current and future defaults in payment and no explicit testing for actual defaults need be done; or

(ii) By explicitly recognizing defaults in scenario testing. In determining the assets available to support liabilities under this method, the actuary may include assets supporting the Bond and Preferred Stock Reserve Component of the MSVR and other similar voluntary statement reserves, provided the contract reserves determined using this method are not less than what the amount of assets supporting contract liabilities would be under subparagraph (i) of this paragraph, unless the actuary can demonstrate to the satisfaction of the Superintendent that using default rates not less than 100% of the appropriate annual reserve factors for the MSVR that assets from the MSVR are not used for risks other than for default; (an acceptable demonstration would be to run the scenarios twice, each without any MSVR assets, one run without any default, the other run with default and then to utilize MSVR assets as limited by the extent of the difference in the present values at the statement date of the accumulated surpluses); or

(iii) By using any other method approved by the Department for recognizing default risk.

(7) Call Options.

The valuation actuary must consider call options, the right of the borrower to prepay the bond.

(i) The following are examples of acceptable procedures for coupon bonds without a call premium:

(a) Assume no calls until the current rate is two percent less than the coupon rate, and then assume 100 percent call;

(b) Assume calls begin when the coupon rate exceeds the current rate and calls increase to 100 percent when the spread reaches three percent.

(ii) The following are examples of acceptable procedures for coupon bonds with a call premium of five percent:

(a) Assume no calls until the current rate is three percent less than the coupon rate and then assume 100 percent call;

(b) Assume calls begin when the coupon rate exceeds the current rate by one percent and calls increase to 100 percent when the spread reaches four percent.

(iii) In the case of GNMA's, some prepayment can be assumed such as, for example, five percent when the current rate equals or exceeds the coupon rate, with prepayments increasing to 50 percent when the coupon rate exceeds the current rate by four percent.

(iv) Other procedures may be used, including a comparison of discounted values based on the current rate with the amount payable on call. Other procedures may be used for other types of obligations and other call premiums.

(v) Any comparison of coupon rate and current rates and any comparison of present values with amount payable on call should be for like type and quality of assets and remaining duration to maturity.

(c) Scenarios to be tested.

(1) The scenarios used in the tests should extend far enough into the future to cover the major portion of the future runout of insurance cash flows from the contractual obligations on the valuation date. This period will vary for different blocks of business, as for example, it might be five years for group guaranteed interest contracts with assumption of all surrendering at the end of the guarantee period; it might be ten years for individual deferred annuities and for single premium life insurance assuming persistency for subsequent interest guarantee periods and full surrender at the end of the projection period; it might be twenty years or more for annuities in course of payout. Without the prior approval of the Department, this period may not be greater than ten years for individual deferred annuities and for single premium life insurance. If the Department approves a period of greater than ten years, the book value of projected assets and liabilities, as well as the market value of the projected assets and the aggregate liability assuming full surrender, at the end of ten years must be reported and the reasonableness of the persistency and other related assumptions from the tenth year to the end of the projection period must be justified. In each case sufficiency should be indicated by the end of the projection period. Provision should be made to discount any remaining cash flows beyond the end of the projection period, preferably by assuming the interest rate assumed at the end of the projection period for the interest path tested will remain level thereafter.

(2) The scenarios to be tested should include at least one which reflects higher interest rates than those prevailing on the valuation date, and at least one with lower future interest rates. It is desirable to test both interest rate scenarios which change gradually over a number of years and interest rate scenarios which increase or decrease quickly in one year and remain level thereafter. Testing of cyclical interest rate scenarios may also be helpful. One scenario assuming a continuation of current interest rates would be desirable as a reference.

(3) Tests should cover as many alternative interest rate scenarios as the actuary deems necessary to generate an understanding of the dynamics relating the insurance and investment cash flows. Variations by yield curve slope should also be examined if the product or products or the assets tested are sensitive to such variations. The range of paths tested should be broad enough to enable the actuary to form an opinion that the investment cash flows make appropriate provision for the contractual obligations under reasonable sets of assumptions. Also, it may be useful as a bench mark to present tests using the level interest rates shown in earlier reports. While for some particular classes of liabilities and supporting assets, one path and range of variation may be justified, and for other classes of liabilities and assets, many paths and ranges should be tested, it is recommended that the qualified actuary consider testing at least the following interest rate scenarios with a zero-percent deviation for (i), three percent deviation for (iv) and (vii) and five percent deviation for the others, subject to an overall maximum rate of 25% and overall minimum interest rate of four percent per year:

(i) level;

(ii) uniformly increasing over 10 years and then level;

(iii) uniformly increasing over five years and then uniformly decreasing to the original level at the end of 10 years and then level;

(iv) a pop-up and then level;

(v) uniformly decreasing over 10 years and then level;

(vi) uniformly decreasing over five years and then uniformly increasing to the original level at the end of 10 years and then level; and

(vii) a pop-down and then level.

(4) The Department will review the interest scenarios and may request additional analysis as to the length of the projection period, path of interest rate change, or magnitude of interest rate change for the products included in the opinion.

(5) A description of the interest crediting philosophy should be provided. In addition, a table should be provided which shows the crediting rates under each of the interest rate scenarios.

(6) The actuarial memorandum should state what assumption was used to determine the beginning interest rate among the proposed interest rate scenarios. The beginning interest rate may be based on the rates for new investments as of the valuation date similar to recent investments allocated to support the product or be based on any outside index, such as U.S. Treasury yields, of assets of the appropriate length on a date close to the valuation date. The beginning interest rate used in the projection should be appropriate for the class of business being examined. For example, a company which sells only single premium immediate annuities and single premium deferred annuities and invests separately for each product may have different beginning rates for each. This is because the funds backing the deferred annuities may be invested in short-term assets that may have different expected earning rates because of the yield curve than longer-term assets used to back immediate annuities. The beginning interest rate should be consistent for all interest rate scenarios. Any pop-up or pop-down scenario should be so identified.

(d) Additional considerations with regard to lapse rates.

(1) In the case of group contracts involving guaranteed interest rates where the transfer or surrender of the fund is under the control of the group contractholder, all contracts shall be assumed to surrender or terminate at the end of the interest guarantee maturity date. Prior to such date, if permitted by the terms of the contract, some surrender and termination may be assumed. Recognition must be given to all relevant items such as:

(i) The difference between the actual interest crediting rate and the interest rate to be earned on new monies under the various scenarios;

(ii) any fixed-value adjustments;

(iii) any market-value adjustments; and

(iv) any installment payout provisions including the length thereof and the crediting rate during the installment payout period.

(2) In the case of group contracts where the transfer or surrender of the funds is not under the control of the group contractholder but under the control of the individual certificate holders, and in the case of individual contracts where the individuals have control over the transfer or surrender of funds, if the contract permits, lapse rates may be considered prior to the interest guarantee maturity date, but assumptions should be made that many individuals will renew for a new interest guarantee period such that lapse may occur prior to, at, or after the interest guarantee maturity date. Recognition must be given to all relevant items such as:

(i) the difference between the new money rate and the assumed interest crediting rate under various interest rate scenarios;

(ii) any fixed-value adjustments such as surrender charges;

(iii) any market-value adjustments;

(iv) any installment payout provision including the length thereof and the interest crediting rate during the installment payout period;

(v) loyalty of the business (e.g., single premium annuities sold through stockbrokers may have higher lapse rates than those sold by career agents);

(vi) any incentives for persistency (e.g., a higher interest crediting rate for persisting contractholders);

(vii) contract loans;

(viii) any free withdrawals which may occur (e.g., the effect of bailouts or free withdrawal provisions); and

(ix) taxation of contract benefits.

(3) In the case of contracts under paragraph (1) of this subdivision, there may be some control of surrender or transfer of the funds under the control of individual certificate holders. In such situations, appropriate lapse assumptions may be assumed prior to the interest guarantee maturity date, using factors such as in paragraph (2) of this subdivision.

(4) In case of single premium policies where the individuals have control over surrender of the policies, the relevant factors may include any or all of those under paragraph (2) of this subdivision.

(5) The lapse rates used in the testing under paragraphs (2), (3), and (4) of this subdivision may be stated in the form of a dynamic function which takes appropriate account of the credited rate versus the market rate and surrender charges, and may be subject to a minimum and maximum limit. Other considerations are the duration of the contract and duration of surrender charges. If the lapse factors used in the testing are not based on such a dynamic function, the lapse rates used in the testing shall be justified in the memorandum. An example of such a formula is as follows:

Base $+ A(MR - CR)^B - C(SC)$

(NOTE: $MR - CR$ is equal to or greater than 0)

with a minimum lapse rate equal to the base and a maximum equal to a number such as 50% where Base = those who surrender independent of changes in interest rates, grading up in later years to reflect maturities, expressed as a percent.

MR = market rate, expressed as a percent.

CR is the credited rate, expressed as a percent.

SC = surrender charge

A, B and C are constants designed to produce conservative results, and where company experience is available, such may be considered.

A numerical example of the above, assuming the market rate is 10%, the credited rate is 8%, the surrender charge is 4%, and the minimum lapse rate is 10% is as follows:

$[10 + 2(10 - 8)^2 - .5(4)]\%$ lapse rate.

Other formulas may be acceptable.

(6) At the end of the projection period, all contracts and policies having surrender privileges shall be assumed to surrender at that time, or on the earliest date thereafter.

(e) Methodology.

(1) Initially, the annual statement value of the assets deemed to support the reserves being tested should be set equal to or less than the annual statement amount of such reserves on the valuation date. It should be noted whether the assets and liabilities tested are market value or book value. The values of assets and liabilities should be on the same basis.

(2) The memorandum should include a description of the method used to project insurance and investment cash flows under the various paths of future interest rates and to relate the result to a common date of reference. Grouping, approximations, modeling and other acceptable actuarial techniques may be employed in determining asset and liability cash flows. If the common reference date is the valuation date, the discount rates used should reflect the interest rates and reinvestment assumptions used in each scenario. If aggregate testing is done in accordance with Section 95.8(d) of this Part for blocks of business with different projection periods, the common reference date must be the valuation date.

(3) One approach would be to project the total cash flow, including insurance and investment cash flows. This would include the reinvestment of net positive cash flows, and borrowing or selling of assets to cover net negative cash flows. The market value of any remaining assets and/or borrowed funds at the end of the projection period can be determined. Such market value would be based on the assumption that interest rates after such date would be frozen at the prevailing rate as of that date. The market value of the remaining liabilities is the cash values where the assumption of 100% lapse is used; otherwise it is the present value of future liability payments and expenses discounted at the prevailing scenario interest rate. If the market value of remaining assets and borrowed funds minus the value of remaining liabilities is positive, the investment cash flows would be deemed to be sufficient to meet the contractual obligations for that path.

(f) Reinsurance.

The actuary of the ceding company must elevate the risks retained and the actuary of the assuming company must evaluate the risks assumed. There are many forms of reinsurance. Reinsurance agreements need careful review to ascertain whether or not the investment risk which is affected by changes in interest rates has been transferred to the reinsurer. Normally under coinsurance agreements wherein the funds are transferred to the reinsurance for investing, the investment risk is transferred. However, in case of coinsurance with funds withheld or in case of modified coinsurance, the investment risk might not be transferred in full. In case of some agreements, the reinsurer does guarantee the sufficiency of a segregated asset portfolio held by the ceding insurer for a portion of the risks. Coordination may be required between the ceding insurer and the assuming insurer to demonstrate the sufficiency of assets.

(g) Numerical summary.

The numerical summary should show the excess (or deficiency) of the reserves held over those needed at a common reference date for each interest rate path.

Stat. Authority.—Insurance Law, §§ 107, 201, 301, 1301, 1303, 1304, 4217, 4232 and 4240.

History.—Sec. filed Dec. 17, 1986; repealed new filed Nov. 22, 1988 eff. Dec. 13, 1988; amd. filed Dec. 1, 1989 eff. Dec 20, 1989.

Parallel Citation.—Regulation 126.

APPENDIX 4

NEW YORK REGULATION 130

Part 176
Investments in "High Yield-High Risk Obligations" by
Domestic Life Insurers

(Regulation 130)

§ 176.1 Purposes

The purposes of this Part are:

(a) To protect the interests of the life insurance-buying public by establishing limitations on the concentration of high yield-high risk obligations in which a domestic life insurer can invest;

(b) To implement the Insurance Law of New York by regulating the acts and practices of domestic life insurers with respect to the concentration of investments in high yield-high risk obligations.

Stat. Authority.—Insurance Law, §§ 201, 301(c) and 1405(c).

History.—Sec. filed June 3, 1987 eff. June 24, 1987.

Parallel Citation.—Regulation 130.

§ 176.2 Preamble

(a) High yield-high risk obligations constitute a category of investment in which there has been significant innovation in recent

---

Added, 1990-1. © 1990, NILS Publishing Company.

years. There is not an adequate historical record with which to project the behavior of such obligations through all types of economic cycles. The Insurance Department is concerned, therefore, that changes in economic conditions and other market variables could adversely affect domestic life insurers having a high concentration of these investments. Accordingly, the department has concluded that a limitation on the percentage of total admitted assets that a domestic life insurer may prudently invest in such obligations, without the prior approval of the superintendent, is reasonable, necessary and required in order to carry out the department's responsibilities under relevant statutory law.

(b) Only one licensed life insurer in New York (out of the 146 currently licensed) clearly exceeds the limitation set forth in this Part. One other life insurer marginally exceeds the limit. None of the remaining 144 life insurers even remotely approaches a 20 percent concentration in high yield-high risk investments.

(c) This Part is consistent with the "prudent individual" rule as set forth in section 1405(c) of the Insurance Law. The department is providing a standard which is a reasonable interpretation of the statute and which is necessary for the public's protection. The standard is supported by the actual investment practices within the life insurance industry and by the clear inability to predict the behavior of these investments in all types of economic circumstances. The actual investment practices of nearly 99 percent of New York's licensed life insurers demonstrate that this Part is a reasonable construction of the quoted statutory language pursuant to section 301(c)—empowering the superintendent to prescribe regulations interpreting provisions of the Insurance Law, and is, in all respects, appropriate.

(d) The relevant language of section 1405(c) of the Insurance Law provides:

> "In addition to other requirements of law (statutory or otherwise) that affect the standard of care of directors and officers of corporations, in making investments under this section, directors and officers shall perform their duties in good faith and with that degree of care that an ordinarily prudent individual in a like position would use under similar circumstances."

(e) With the enactment of chapter 567 of the Laws of 1983, the Legislature took specific action to insert a "prudent individual" rule in the Insurance Law, rather than rely merely on other requirements of law, statutory or otherwise. By such action, the Legislature made such provision subject to the superintendent's interpretative authority under section 301(c) of the Insurance Law. The legislative history of chapter 567 demonstrates that the "prudent individual" provision was added to the Insurance Law at the insistence of the Insurance Department, and that the Legislature expected that the investment operations of life insurers would be monitored closely by the Insurance Department in order to ensure that the boards of directors are appropriately discharging their responsibilities.

(f) The department understands that high yield-high risk obligations can have a place in a well-diversified portfolio. However, it is also understood that the special risks associated with these investments require a high degree of management even when they are held within an aggregate limit. While this Part will leave all domestic life insurers with authority to invest a substantial portion of their assets in high yield-high risk obligations, the prudent management of the attendant risks will remain an essential element of such investment.

Stat. Authority.—Insurance Law, §§ 201, 301(c) and 1405(c).

History.—Sec. filed June 3, 1987 eff. June 24, 1987.

Parallel Citation.—Regulation 130.

§ 176.3 Definitions

For purposes of this Part:

(a) *High yield-high risk obligations* means obligations which, at the time of acquisition, (1) are not investment grade and (2) are publicly traded obligations, or obligations issued in a transaction involving the acquisition of substantially all the stock or assets of a corporation or substantially all the assets of a division thereof, or substantial directly negotiated obligations.

(b) *Investment grade* means that the obligation has been determined to be in one of the top four generic-lettered rating classifications by a securities rating agency acceptable to the superintendent, or that the obligation has been identified in writing by such a rating agency to be of investment grade quality, or that the obligation has been determined to be investment grade (as indicated by a "yes" rating) by the Securities Valuation Office of the National Association of Insurance Commissioners.

(c) *Publicly traded obligations* means obligations which are not acquired by the domestic life insurer from an issuer, underwriter or dealer, or which are qualified for public sale at the time of acquisition by the domestic life insurer.

(d) *Substantial directly negotiated obligations* means obligations which the domestic life insurer and its subsidiaries and affiliates that are insurers acquire at an aggregate cost of not less than $50 million in a single transaction directly from the issuer thereof or from an underwriter or dealer that acquired such obligations directly from the issuer.

(e) *Not acquired by the domestic life insurer from an issuer, underwriter or dealer* means acquired by the domestic life insurer in an exempt transaction described in section 4(1) or 4(3) of the Federal Securities Act of 1933, 15 U.S.C. 77(d)(1) or 77(d)(3), as from time to time amended.

(f) *Qualified for public sale* means registered under the Federal Securities Act of 1933.

(g) *Admitted assets* means the amount thereof as of the last day of the most recently concluded annual statement year, computed in the same manner as "admitted assets" in section 1405 of the Insurance Law.

(h) *Aggregate amount of high yield-high risk obligations* means the aggregate cost thereof.

(i) *Institution* means a corporation, a joint-stock company, an association, a trust, a business partnership, a business joint venture or similar entity.

Stat. Authority.—Insurance Law, §§ 201, 301(c) and 1405(c).

History.—Sec. filed June 3, 1987 eff. June 24, 1987.

Parallel Citation.—Regulation 130.

§ 176.4 Provisions

(a) Without the prior approval of the superintendent, no domestic life insurer shall acquire, directly or indirectly, any high yield-high risk obligation of any institution, if, after giving effect to any such acquisition, the aggregate amount of all high yield-high risk obligations then held by the domestic life insurer would exceed 20 percent of its admitted assets. In determining approval, the superintendent, in addition to other requirements of law relating to such acquisitions or investments, statutory or otherwise, shall review the standard of care of the directors and officers of the domestic life insurer in making such investments or acquisitions. Directors and officers of domestic life insurers shall perform their duties, in making investments, in good faith and with the degree of care that an ordinarily prudent individual in a like position would use under similar circumstances.

(b) The board of directors of any domestic life insurance company which acquires or invests in, directly or indirectly, high yield-high risk obligations of any institution, shall adopt a written plan for the making of such investments. Such plan, in addition to guidelines with respect to the quality of the issues invested in, shall contain diversification standards, including but not limited to standards for issuer, industry, duration, liquidity and geographic location.

(c) Except as provided in section 4240(a)(2)(A) of the Insurance Law, this part shall not apply to investments made for separate accounts.

Stat. Authority.—Insurance Law, §§ 201, 301(c) and 1405(c).

History.—Sec. filed June 3, 1987 eff. June 24, 1987.

Parallel Citation.—Regulation 130.

INDEX